The Colorado Book

Second Edition

The Colorado Book

Second Edition

Edited by

Sandra Dallas, Thomas J. Noel, and Pam Sandlian Smith

IM Education
Lakewood, Colorado

Fulcrum Publishing
Lakewood, Colorado

Library of Congress Cataloging-in-Publication Data
On file with the Library of Congress

Cover illustration and design by
Kateri Kramer-Dominic

Printed in the United States of America
0 9 8 7 6 5 4 3 2 1

IM Education and Fulcrum Publishing
7333 W. Jefferson Ave., Suite 225
Lakewood, CO 80235
(800) 992-2908 • (303) 277-1623
www.fulcrumbooks.com

Contents

The Shape of Time
A Foreword to the Second Edition

ONLY 180 YEARS AGO, much of what we now call Colorado was still part of Mexico.

And before statehood, borders, railroads, and commercial mining, this land was home to the Ute, Apache, Arapaho, Cheyenne, and many others—each with their own rhythms, stories, and relationships to place.

Before them, the Ancestral Puebloans carved stone dwellings into the cliffs of Mesa Verde. They hunted and hauled game from the rich valleys below into suspended shelters where the earth itself became part of the architecture of belonging.

Go back even further, and you'll find an inland sea, tropical islands, and massive dinosaurs. At one point—over 270 million years ago—the tallest peaks in the ancestral Rockies were estimated to tower 20,000 feet above sea level.

No matter what it's looked like or who's called it home, *this* has always been one the most geologically and culturally complex slices of earth. It's been shaped by erosion and upheaval. By migration and extraction. By ceremony and conquest. Colorado holds multitudes—from the beauty of the Spanish Peaks to the horror of the Sand Creek Massacre; from the triumphs of civil rights to the scars of racism.

This book is an attempt to honor that complexity.

The Colorado Book was originally published by Fulcrum in 1993 and returns in this second edition with new entries and updated imagery that reflect the evolving story of the Centennial State. But it also preserves many original texts, including first-hand accounts from the 19th and early 20th centuries. Some of these texts contain language and perspectives that are racist, sexist, or otherwise offensive by today's standards. We include them not to endorse their views but to document the realities of the time. History is not always comfortable. But it must be confronted.

Additionally, some figures and accounts in this book may reflect outdated data or statistical inaccuracies—products of their time, shaped by the limits of recordkeeping or the passage of years.

We also acknowledge that no single volume can capture the full sweep of Colorado's history. There are stories we couldn't fit, voices we couldn't include, and places we couldn't map. This book is not comprehensive. But it is sincere. It is an invitation to engage with Colorado's past—its beauty and brutality; its contradictions and continuities—with honesty, curiosity, and care.

Because to understand this land is to understand change. And to understand change is to understand ourselves.

—*Anthony Dominic, contributing editor*

Introduction

COLORADO HAS ALWAYS INSPIRED writers. Native Americans expressed themselves through petroglyphs. Early Spanish explorers and fur trappers recorded their journeys in letters and documents. Gold Rush pioneers kept journals. And contemporary authors wrote in notebooks and on iPads—and in the case of one author (Jack Kerouac) a roll of teletype paper. Everyone who lived or passed through Colorado, it seems, wrote about the Centennial State.

From the pens and typewriters and computers of these authors has come a wealth of literature. In both fiction and nonfiction, writers recorded the state's landscape, the snow-clad mountains and vast high plains. They wrote of major events and the diverse people who made Colorado home.

More than thirty years ago, four Coloradans—Eleanor M. Gehres, Maxine Benson, Stanley Cuba, and Sandra Dallas—put together *The Colorado Book.* It was made up of some 150 excerpts on the state, from a variety of sources. Published by Fulcrum Publishing, *The Colorado Book* became a classic.

The volume has long been out of print. So some three decades later, Fulcrum decided to publish an updated version of *The Colorado Book,* to be issued in connection with Colorado's 150th anniversary as a state. Since the original publication, Colorado has experienced vast changes in culture, population, attitudes, and communities. This edition contains a significant number of the original writings as well as recent works from a new generation of authors and their perspectives. Fulcrum Publisher Robert Baron asked three of us—Sandra Dallas, Tom Noel, and Pam Smith--to cull the previous edition and replace the deleted excerpts with the work of contemporary writers as well as early Colorado writings that were overlooked the first time around.

This edition of *The Colorado Book* is no more a complete anthology of Colorado writing than the earlier work. It is a sample of what we believe to be the best and most interesting writing about the state. We hope these excerpts will lead readers to further explore the authors selected. One thing remains constant, the love and awe of the majesty of this land and the Colorado lifestyle. The character of this state and those who are inspired by its endless sense of optimism continues to grow. We invite you to sample these nuggets of inspired Colorado writing. We started with a total of 210 excerpts, which we reluctantly whittled down to 155. If your favorite isn't included, stick around. There will be another edition thirty years from now.

—Sandra Dallas, Thomas J. Noel, and Pam Sandlian Smith

SECTION I

The Centennial State

The Land Where the Columbines Grow

Arthur J. Fynn

(Adopted by the State Legislature as State Song, 1915)

Where the snowy peaks gleam in the moonlight,
    Above the dark forests of pine,
And the wild foaming waters dash onward
    Toward lands where the tropic stars shine;
Where the scream of the bold mountain eagle
    Responds to the notes of the dove,
Is the purple-robed West, the land that is best,
    The pioneer land that we love.

CHORUS
'Tis the land where the columbines grow,
Overlooking the plains far below,
While the cool summer breeze
In the evergreen trees
Softly sings where the columbines grow.

The bison is gone from the upland,
    The deer from the canyon has fled,
The home of the wolf is deserted,
    The antelope mourns for his dead,
The war-whoop re-echoes no longer,
    The Indian's only a name,
And the nymphs of the grove in their loneliness rove,
    But the columbine blooms just the same.

Let the violets brighten the brookside,
    In the sunlight of earlier spring,
Let the clover bedeck the green meadow,
    In days when the orioles sing,
Let the goldenrod herald the autumn,
    But, under the midsummer sky,
In its fair western home, may the columbine bloom
    Till our great mountain rivers run dry.

Where the West Begins

Arthur J. Chapman

Out where the handclasp's a little stronger,
Out where a smile dwells a little longer,
  That's where the West begins;
Out where the sun is a little brighter,
Where the snows that fall are a trifle whiter,
Where the bonds of home are a wee bit tighter—
  That's where the West begins.

Out where the skies are a trifle bluer,
Out where friendship's a little truer,
  That's where the West begins;
Out where a fresher breeze is blowing,
Where there's laughter in every streamlet flowing,
Where there's more of reaping and less of sowing—
  That's where the West begins.

Out where the world is in the making,
Where fewer hearts with despair are aching-
  That's where the West begins;
Where there's more of singing and less of sighing,
Where there's more of giving and less of buying,
And a man makes friends without half trying—
  That's where the West begins.

Dedication to Thomas Hornsby Ferril

Robert Frost

"A man is as tall as his height
Plus the height of his home town.
I know a Denverite
Who measured from sea to crown,
Is one mile five feet ten.
And he swings a commensurate pen."

(Robert Frost to Thomas Ferril in Thomas Ferril's copy of *Collected Poems of Robert Frost*)

Centennial

James A. Michener

IT IS NOT HOSPITABLE LAND, like that farther east in Kansas or back near the Appalachians. It is mean and gravelly and hard to work. It lacks adequate topsoil for plowing. It is devoid of trees or easy shelter. A family could wander this land for weeks and never find enough wood to build a house.

It lacks water—my God, how it lacks water. Rainfall at Centennial is only 13 inches a year, when any farmer knows that to produce even a miserable corn or wheat crop requires 21. The extremes of temperature can be unbearable, from 109 in August to 38 below in February.

It is a land subject to wild whims of nature. Sometimes a score of years will pass without rain, so that crops perish and organized society stands in peril. Sometimes winds whip over the land for three months on end, exhausting the land and everything that grows upon it. Dust storms can sweep the region with a fury greater than hurricanes and more persistent than storms at sea, filling all the air and darkening the sky for days running. Locusts can suddenly emerge from the west at unexpected times, more extensive than storms, and capriciously they alight, eating every green thing that stands in their path. Then they rise and fly mysteriously on, landing and eating a few more times, then vanishing as inexplicably as they appeared.

But there is one thing about this land. Theoretically, it can be farmed. It is rich in minerals. It is the inheritor of two great mountain ranges; over several hundred million years it conserved deposits sent down by the mountains and is entitled to the richness it possesses. The growing season is adequate for most crops: last frost on May 10, and first frost on September 27, with an average 139 frost-free days in between for the prudent farmer. The governing rule is simple:

"If you can lead water onto this land, you can grow anything."

"Well, you wouldn't try apples or oranges, would you?"

"No, but only because they can be grown better somewhere else."

"Corn and wheat? Magnificent. Sorghum? The best. Garden vegetables? None better."

"Like I said, you can grow anything. But two things grow better here than anywhere else on earth."

"Such as?"

"Melons of any kind. You name it. And great big juicy sugar beets."

The land cries for water. The bleakest desert, even the forbidding land about the two pillars, will flourish like a garden if only water can be got to it. Consequently, the crucial problem of this area will be the attempt of man to lead water onto his intractable land. If he can do that, if only he can do that, he will have at his disposal a paradise.

And finally there is the river—a sad, bewildered nothing of a river. It carries no great amount of water; and when it has some, it is uncertain where it wants to take it. No ship can navigate it, nor even a canoe, with reasonable assurance. It is the butt of more jokes than any other river on earth, and the greatest joke is to call it a river at all. It's a sand bottom. A wandering afterthought. A useless irritation. A frustration. And when you've said all that, it suddenly rises up, spreads out to a mile wide, engulfs your crops, and lays waste your farms.

Its name is as flat as its appearance, the South Platte, yet for a while it was the highway of empire. It was the course of stir, adventure, and the means whereby the adventurers lived. Once mighty enough to help build a continent, it is now a mean, pestiferous bother.

"I swear to God, sometimes you can tell where that damned river is only by spotting cottonwoods that line its bank."

"You're right, and those useless trees drink far more of the water than they're entitled to."

The Colorado

Frank Waters

MOST RIVERS ARE CONFINED to the needs and the histories of men. Like roads, they seem inconsequential without their travelers. The Colorado is an outlaw. It belongs only to the ancient, eternal earth. As no other, it is savage and unpredictable of mood, peculiarly American in character. It has for its background the haunting sweep of illimitable horizons, the immensities of unbroken wilderness. From perpetually snow-capped peaks to stifling deserts below sea level, it cuts the deepest and truest cross section through the continent.

As the Rocky Mountains are the backbone of physical North America, the Colorado is the vertebral tube carrying the spinal fluid of the continent. From this viscous, reddish flow, the river derives its name. Despite a score of other names, it has become known at last simply by its one unchanging color—in Spanish, the *Rio Colorado*, the great Red River of the West.

Its landscapes are never anywhere urban or commercial—not even pastoral. They are purely mystical in tone. There are the wind-swept rocky wastes high

The Colorado River is 1,450 miles long and flows through seven US states and two Mexican states—from the Rocky Mountains to the Gulf of California. Photo by Luca Galuzzi—www.galuzzi.it.

above timberline and the sunless gloom of deep gorges. When the river does rise to the surface again, it is upon the face of an earth whose expressions are never twice the same.

The black volcanic picachos creep closer in the moonlight, baring their saw-tooth fangs. By day, the crinkled desert hills diminish and recede, or merely float, bottomless, upon the horizon. More often than not, the mountains are mirages. Glistening salt beds and alkali flats turn into seas; uncovered veins of legendary native gold into mere banks of micaceous gravel.

In this shifting realm of the fantastic unreal, only the river is permanent. It is the one enduring mesmer from whose spectral spell no man who has once seen it is ever quite freed.

Those who love it best are those who fear it most. For like all things touched with the sublime, it carries a lurking horror, and its mysteries wear the mask of the commonplace. To allude to it as something more than a river would sound like a literary affectation only to the literary. The illiterate might well comprehend most fully all that it expresses. As from a Navajo sand painting or ceremonial blanket, he would read the river's cryptic meaning in the earth it threads.

The dreamlike vacuousness, wild beauty, and barbaric boldness of design form but the pattern of the warp which underlies the subtle, inimical resistance of the woof. Old, ancient America! With its own great spirit of place; with the shadows of aboriginal ghosts still gliding across it; and with its own demons not yet appeased—the haunting promise of the far-off. Its tormenting unrest.

It is still a wilderness. To understand it, you must think in new dimensions. You must feel in terms of depth, as well as space of eternity and not of time.

Inside U.S.A.

John Gunther

COLORADO, THE MOST SPECTACULAR of the mountain states, lives on many things: scenery, beet sugar, gold, molybdenum, livestock, tourists, and tuberculosis. As to this last, I heard an ungentle and tasteless Coloradan complain, "Some fiend in human form discovered that rest, not altitude, was the best cure for T.B., and so the tuberculosis cases don't come to Colorado so much anymore, and the economy of suffered terribly as a result, so I suppose you could say that T.B. is killing us, not the patients."

Very little in the world can compare to the scenery of Colorado. The vistas here stretch the eyes, enlighten the heart, and make the spirit humble. Colorado has more than 1,500 peaks—literally—more than 10,000 feet high, and of the 65 in the United States higher than 14,000 feet, it has not less than 51. This is indeed the top of the nation. Colorado has the highest automobile road in the country, the highest automobile races, the highest ski courses, the highest astronomical laboratory, the highest railway tunnel, the highest lake, the highest yacht anchorage, and the highest suspension bridge. It has two national parks and six national monuments, 14 million acres of national forest, and more than 7,000 miles of fishing streams. And no matter where you turn, up and down or left and right, the overwhelming variety and magnitude of the views makes you blink. But—the state has had to learn these past years that scenery alone, no matter how stupefyingly dramatic, does not pay the bills. Scenery alone is not enough.

Colorado, like Oregon among the western states, is distinctly on the conservative side. It is conservative politically, economically, financially. I do not mean reactionary. Just conservative—with the kind of conservativeness that does not budge an inch for anybody or anything unless pinched and pushed. For instance, one point among several, Colorado is the 39th state in amount of state aid to education. Or consider reconversion. Washington and California, as we know, worked hard and concretely on postwar planning, to ease the gap toward peace. Colorado did almost nothing—and was proud of it. It has ridden for year after year on its prestige and its reputation. Nothing better illustrates this than affairs in Denver.

But to return to scenery and tourist traffic for a moment. In a normal year, tourists bring into the state something like 65 million dollars. This sum is not to be sneezed at, but it could be greater. I heard complaints generally that Colorado "has missed the boat on tourism." Scenery is to Colorado what sunshine is to California, but it makes nothing like California's effort to capitalize on this asset and dramatize and buttress it. There will be many, I grant, who will congratulate Colorado for its lack of organized booster spirit. But progressive Coloradans themselves worry about how the state is becoming a backwater. Until quite recently, for instance, it employed no director of public relations, and the governor had no press advisor. This was mostly the result of negative influence by the *Denver Post*, which held that it, exclusively, provided enough publicity for Colorado; it vehemently opposed creation of any other agency. As a consequence, the state paid comparatively small attention to roads, country hotels, and the like; it built no enterprises like Sun Valley, and the general mood was to give the visitor a quick glimpse of Pike's Peak, and then let him get out.

Colorado is divided down the middle by the sharp and impenetrable spine of the Continental Divide; its western and eastern sections differ considerably, though the cleavage is not so sharp as in Washington. The Western Slope faces Salt Lake City, the eastern Denver. The west, behind the divide, is mostly mining and livestock country; the east is irrigated and merges into the Great Plains. The Western Slope is dominated by two or three land-owning families; the eastern—including Denver—has one overriding magnate, Claude K. Boettcher. I use this somewhat old-fashioned word, "magnate," because Mr. Boettcher so precisely evokes its spirit. The word "tycoon" connotes a touch of the parvenu or the adventurous. Boettcher is no parvenu. He is solidlike a plinth, adhesive, and pachydermatous. If I were a casting director in Hollywood and wanted a type to play one of the railroad barons of the last century, I would hire Mr. Boettcher at once. This margrave of the sugar beets, this padishah of cement, potash, mining, and what not—one of the richest men in America and one of the least known—is a magnate like the antique Astors and Vanderbilts.

But the chief element of difference between eastern and western Colorado is water. Touch water, and you touch everything; about water, the state is as sensitive as a carbuncle. Water—as is true all over the West—is everybody's chief preoccupation. In the briefest kind of summary, the situation is that western Colorado has more water than it can use, while eastern Colorado has less than it needs. Hence, the east must have irrigation, and the problem—this is reminiscent of California—is to get the water over. This, the west resents. It thinks it is being milked of water for the benefit of capitalists in Denver, which, in many respects, is almost as foreign a city as Wilmington, Delaware, or Brookline, Massachusetts. The east replies that the water is "spare" water, and that the west wastes it anyway.

* * *

Historically, Colorado is of mixed origin; in whole or in part it has variously belonged to Spain, France, Mexico, and Texas. There is still a strong Spanish underlay in the southern tier of counties; all these bear Spanish names. Its modern annals begin with the discovery of gold in 1858, nine years after the California Gold Rush, and the mines at Leadville and Cripple Creek became a mud-and-canvas Meccas. It is an interesting revelation of the national character—James Truslow Adams makes a point of this—that California and the far West, though farther away, should have been settled *before* the states of the Rockies and Great Plains. It is as if a crazy impetuosity carried the first frontiersmen as far as they could possibly go geographically; they swooped straight across the continent without pause (of course, this generalization is too broad); then, later, a second wave, less volatile, descended on the states between.

Coloradans are proud of being Coloradans, and the state has a large proportion of citizens born within its borders. This is in acute contrast to Oklahoma and Arizona, say. A very real cleavage, especially in Denver, is that between old-timers born locally and those who moved in from outside; I felt this more strongly in Colorado than anywhere else in the country, except possibly New England. This prompts one to a word about the Indians who, after all, were in Colorado even before the first families of Denver got there. Colorado is the only western state where I never once heard the word "Indian" spoken, which is the more interesting in that the Utes were the only Indian tribe in the United States—like the Araucanians in Chile—never conquered. Today, they play no role in state life at all.

The total wealth of Colorado was estimated in 1937 at $3,434,000,000, and the foundation of the state's economy is not, as one would be apt to think, mining, but agriculture. Mining began to decline 30 years ago. The easy gold got scooped out; easy money ended when it became necessary to use complex and expensive metallurgical processes to refine ore. People turned instead to sugar beets and livestock. Today, it is not gold or even comparatively rare metals like uranium and vanadium that are the heart of the mining industry that remains but prosaic coal. Colorado is the first state in the union in coal reserves, with—in theory—enough deposits to last forever.

Colorado has more big game than any other American state, and Denver is the largest manufactory of fishhooks in the world. Colorado Springs is the glisteningly suave "Newport of the West," and the greatest man the state ever produced was Judge Ben Lindsey, who was of course reviled by the city he worked so hard to improve. Once, when he sentenced a utilities executive to jail, the man shouted in the courtroom, "This state has more sunshine and more bastards than any place on earth!"

Rotunda Murals

Thomas Hornsby Ferril

Here is a land where life is written in water
the West is where the water was and is
Father and Son of old Mother and Daughter
Following Rivers up immensities
of Range and Desert thirsting the Sundown ever
Crossing a hill to climb a hill since Drier
Naming tonight a City by some River
a different Name from last night's Camping Fire.

Look to the Green within the Mountain Cup
Look to the Prairie parched for water lack
Look to the Sun that pulls the Ocean up
Look to the Cloud that gives the oceans back
Look to your Heart and may your Wisdom grow
to power of Lightning and peace of Snow.

The Colorado Guide
Landscapes, Cityscapes, Escapes

Bruce Caughey and Dean Winstanley

This Is Colorado

NO ONE SUMMED UP Colorado better than Teddy Roosevelt when he said, "The scenery bankrupts the English language." The Rocky Mountains dominate this striking landscape as they run through the middle of the state, constituting a mountainous area three times as large as the Swiss Alps. Colorado's peaks are legendary: more than 1,100 of them rise to 10,000 feet or higher; 54 mountains top off at over 14,000 feet.

The state's colorful history becomes most apparent at the ancient cliff dwellings of Mesa Verde National Park and in former mining boomtowns such as Leadville and Silverton. Woven into the historical fabric are the unmistakable impacts of Anglo, Hispanic, and Native American culture, all indelibly etched into Colorado's character. Colorado is a rich and varied land; its four million residents appreciate the healthy mix of recreation and culture combined with a dash of the Wild West.

More than 20 million visitors make their way to the state each year, not only for personal adventure and wilderness travel but also to enjoy some of the best powder skiing in the world. As the "Winter Sports Capital of the Country," Colorado offers 25 major ski areas.

Colorado is a place with so much to do that up-to-date, accurate advice is a precious commodity—and that's the main reason for creating this newly revised fifth edition of *The Colorado Guide.* As native Coloradans, we enjoy sharing tips about the state with friends who come to visit. We hope our guidebook accomplishes the same by capturing the essence and spirit of Colorado for you. With an insider's perspective of Colorado cities, small mountain towns, and areas for family utilization, we try to unlock some of the state's best-kept secrets, including popular whitewater rafting. We also offer information about mountain resorts, the arts and museums of Denver, and the region's many hot springs.

When we first set to work on this massive guidebook project in 1987, we had a feeling it would strike a chord with our readers. More than a dozen printings and revisions later, we are still going strong. But when we consider all the revisions to this guide during the past 12 years, it's mind-boggling. Along with continually updating the 1,600 or so business descriptions in the book, we've encountered a host of changes in the life of our state.

Geography and Geology

Some residents say if Colorado were to be ironed out flat, its area would be larger than Texas. This may be an exaggeration, but it does draw attention to Colorado's most distinctive feature—the Rocky Mountains. The Rockies slice north-south through the state with more than 54 peaks rising higher than 14,000 feet, including the highest "14er," Mount Elbert, at 14,433 feet. Covering the eastern third of Colorado, the Great Plains extend east to Kansas and Nebraska and north into Wyoming. On the western side of the Rockies, the Colorado Plateau is characterized by beautiful canyons and valleys.

Along the spine of the Rockies lies the Continental Divide, which acts as a watershed for North America. All waters on the Western Slope drain into the Pacific, while Eastern Slope waters eventually drain into the Atlantic. Colorado encompasses the headwaters for more than 10 major rivers, including Western giants such as the Colorado, Rio Grande, Arkansas, and Platte. The state has been called the "Father of Rivers," an apt nickname.

Looking at the rugged peaks, deep, beautiful canyons, and windswept plains of Colorado, one doesn't have to be a scientist to guess that the state has had a long, active geologic past. This history began 300 million years ago with the uplift of the Ancestral Rockies. These mountains consisted of two ranges similar to the present-day Rockies, located 100 miles west of today's Front Range. After 20 million years, the uplift ceased and erosion began. A million years of exposure to water, wind, and ice eroded away the Ancestral Rockies to small hills similar to the Appalachian Mountains of the eastern U.S. Remnants of these ancient mountains can be seen in the red formations throughout the mountains of Colorado (Red Rocks, Garden of the Gods, and the area around Vail are good examples).

Flora and Fauna

Colorado's varied terrain (grassland, mountains, arid plateaus) provides habitat for diverse plant and animal life. Throughout the book, we have tried to include relevant information about the predominant flora and fauna in different parts of the state, but you may want more. The state of Colorado maintains more than 220 wildlife areas, which serve as excellent observation locations, especially for birdwatchers. The Colorado Division of Wildlife—at 6060 Broadway, Denver, CO, 80216, (303) 297-1192—has a very friendly staff; they will be happy to answer your questions about Colorado wildlife or to send you brochures and pamphlets.

The Coloradans

Robert G. Athearn

THUS, AS THE STATE PASSED its hundredth birthday, there were disagreements among its people as to the proper course to follow in the days that lay ahead. Schooled in the frontier tradition that the Lord had placed resources on earth to be used by the chosen, yet continuously influenced for decades by the philosophy of eastern nature lovers who long had regarded the place as a national scenic and natural preserve, Coloradans in more recent years had felt an increasing pressure from the latter group. A good many of the new immigrants were refugees from more heavily congested portions of the nation, both East and West, who had become disenchanted with what they regarded as the rat race of their daily lives, of crowded conditions, of polluted air, of a dwindling sense of individuality. It was the growing weight of their numbers, combined with that of residents who long had cherished the "champagne air" of Colorado, that had struck a new balance, the first real fruits of which were seen in the 1974 statewide election. As the implications of that contest began to be understood, it appeared that some kind of a consensus would have to be reached, a "use-but-not-abuse" program, and that it would serve as a working plan for the immediate future.

Aspen trees. Photo by the Bureau of Land Management.

SECTION II

Discovering Colorado

The Domínguez-Escalante Journal

Francisco Silvestre Vélez de Escalante

ON THE 1ST OF SEPTEMBER we set out, headed north from San Ramon, and after three leagues through small narrow valleys of abundant pastures and thick lines of scrub oak, we came upon eighty Yutas, all on good horses and most of them from the encampment to which we were going. They told us that they were going out to hunt, but we figured that they came together like this, either to show off their strength in numbers or to find out if any other Spanish people were coming behind us or if we came alone; for, since they knew from the night before that we were going to their encampment, it was unnatural for almost all of its men to come out at the very time that they knew we were to arrive, unless motivated by what we have just said.

We kept on going with only the Laguna, descended a very steep incline, and came into a very pleasant narrow valley, in which there was a small river and all along its bank a spreading grove of spruces, very tall and straight, among them certain poplars which seem to ape the erectness and height of the pines. Through this narrow valley we traveled eastward for a league and reached the encampment, which had numerous people and must have consisted of thirty tents. We stopped a mile down from it by the edge of the river mentioned, naming the site San Antonio Martir. Today four leagues—199 [in all].

As soon as we halted, Padre Fray Francisco Atanasio went on to the encampment with Andres the interpreter to see the chieftain and the others who had remained. He went into the chieftain's tent and, after greeting and embracing him and his children, asked him to gather there the people who were on hand. He did so, and when those of either sex who could attend had been assembled, he announced the Gospel to them through the interpreter. All listened with pleasure, and especially six Lagunas who were present, among whom our guide and another Laguna stood out. As soon as the padre began instructing them, the new guide mentioned interrupted them so as to predispose the Sabuganas as well as his own fellow tribesmen "to believe whatever the padre was telling them because it all was true." In the same way, the other Laguna relayed the pleasure and eagerness with which he heard the news of his eternal salvation.

Among those listening there was one a bit deaf who, not grasping what was being treated, asked what it was the padre was saying. Then this Laguna said: "The padre says that this which he shows us"—it was the image of Christ crucified—"is the one Lord of all, who dwells in the highest part of the skies, and in order to please Him and go to Him one has to be baptized and must beg His forgiveness." He did his part for his never having seen it made before, either by the padre or by the interpreter. When the padre saw the evident joy with which they heard him, he suggested to the chieftain now in charge of the encampment that if, after he had conferred with his people, they would accept Christianity, we would come to instruct them and set them in a way of living that would lead to baptism. He replied that he would propose it to his people, but he did not return all afternoon to provide further cause whereon to base a likely hope of their accepting the proposal.

Filled with joy by the open declaration of the Lagunas mentioned, the padre asked how the latter one was called (the guide we had already named Silvestre) and on learning that they called him Red Bear, he instructed them all by explaining to them the difference existing between men and brutes, the purpose for which either of them were created, and the wrong thing they did in naming themselves after wild beasts—thus placing themselves on a par with them, and even below them. Promptly he told the Laguna to call himself Francisco from then on. When the rest saw this, they began repeating this name, although with difficulty, the Laguna joyfully pleased for being so named.

It also happened that when the padre addressed as chief the one who, as already said, was in charge of the encampment, he replied that he was not it and that the real chief was a fine-looking youth who was present; and when the padre asked him if he [the youth] was married, he answered that he was and that he had two wives. This embarrassed the said youth (whom the other had done the honor of pointing out for his being the brother of a greatly revered chieftain among the Sabuganas named Yamputzi), and he tried to make out that he had only one wife. From this, it can be inferred that these barbarians are aware or cognizant of the repugnance inherent in having multiple wives at one and the same time. From here, the padre grasped the opportunity to instruct them on this point, and to exhort them not to have more than one.

When this was all over, some jerked bison meat was bought from them, they being paid for it with white beads, and they were asked if they wanted to exchange some horses for other now hoofsore ones that we brought along. They replied that they would exchange them later in the afternoon. This done, the padre came back to the king's camp.

The Journal of Jacob Fowler

Jacob Fowler

13th Novr 1821 Tuesday

WENT TO THE HIGHEST of the mounds near our Camp and took the bareing of the Soposed mountain Which Stud at north 80 West of all So all of the River Which is West. We then proceed on two an a half miles to a Small Creek Crosed it and ascended a gradual Rise for about three miles to the Highest ground in the nibourhood—Wheare We Head a full vew of the mountains this must be the place Whare Pike first discovered a full view of the mountains. Heare I took the bareing of two that Ware the Highest the longest South 71 W—the other Which appeered looking forward we saw a branch pulling from the mountain, which we supposed to be Pike's first fork and make for it from the south side. We camped in a grove of bushes and timber about two miles up it from the river. We made eleven miles west this day. We stopped here about one o'clock. We were not able to keep up. We here found some grapes among the bushes. Some were hunting and others cooking. Some were picking grapes. A gun was fired off and the cry of a white bear was raised. Each man ran his own course to look for the bear and in an instant, we were alarmed. The brush in which we camped contained from 10 to 20 acres. The brush was desperate and the bear had run for shelter, finding himself surrounded on all sides. The bear, with four others, attempted to run but the bear threw the brush undiscovered till they were within a few feet of it. When it sprung up, it caught Lewis Dawson and pulled him down. He would have relieved the man but in an instant, Colonel Glann's gun misfired. The bear, with such fury, left a large slut which belongs to the party. Each time the man got up and ran a few steps but was overtaken by the bear. The Colonel made a second attempt to shoot but his gun misfired again. The bear seemed intent on his destruction. The Colonel again ran close up and the slut made another attack. The Colonel now became alarmed lest the bear would pursue the wounded man and was close up to the tree. The Colonel stepped on that and let the man and bear pass till the bear caught him by the leg before any of the party arrived to relieve him. The bear soon rose again but was shot by several others who had got up to the place of action. It is to be remarked that the other three men with him ran off and the brush was so thick that those on the outside were some time getting through.

I was myself down the creek below the brush and heard the dreadful screams of a man in the clutches of the bear, the yelping of the slut, and the hollering of the men to run in, run in, the man will be killed. Knowing the distance so great that I could not get there in time to save the man, it is much easier to imagine my feelings than describe them. But before I got to the place of action, the bear was killed and I met the wounded man with Robert Fowler and one or two more assisting him to camp where his wounds were examined. It appears his head was in the bear's mouth at least twice and that when the monster gave the crush that was to mash the man's head, it being too large for the span of his mouth, the head slipped out, only the teeth cutting the skin to the bone wherever they touched it. So that the skin of the head was cut from about the ears to the top in several directions, all of which wounds were sewed up as well as could be done by men in our situation, having no surgeon nor surgical instruments. The man still retained his understanding but said, "I am killed, I heard my skull break." But we were willing to believe he was mistaken as he spoke cheerfully on the subject till in the afternoon of the second day when he began to be restless and somewhat delirious. On examining a hole in the upper part of his right temple, which we believed only skin deep, we found the brains working out. We then supposed that he did hear his skull break. He lived till a little before day on the third day after being wounded. All which time we lay at camp and buried him as well as our means would admit. Immediately after the fatal accident and having done all we could for the wounded man, we turned our attention to the bear and found him a large fat animal. We skinned him but found the smell of a polecat so strong that we could not eat the meat. On examining his mouth, we found that three of his teeth were broken off near the gums, which we suppose was the cause of his not killing the man at the first bite, and the one not broken to be the cause of the hole in the right temple which killed the man at last. The hunters killed two deer, cased the skins for bags. We dried out the bear's oil and carried it with us. The skin was also taken care of.

A rough and tumble with a grizzley, sketch circa 1875.

A Report on the Exploration of the Country Lying Between the Missouri River and the Rocky Mountains

John Charles Frémont

JULY 9. [1842]—THIS MORNING we caught the first faint glimpse of the Rocky Mountains, about 60 miles distant. Though a tolerably bright day, there was a slight mist, and we were just able to discern the snowy summit of "Longs peak" ("*les deux oreilles*" of the Canadians), showing like a small cloud near the horizon. I found it easily distinguishable, there being a perceptible difference in its appearance from the white clouds that were floating about the sky. I was pleased to find that among the traders and voyageurs the name of Longs Peak had been adopted and become familiar in the country. In the ravines near this place, a light brown sandstone made its first appearance. About eight, we discerned several persons on horseback a mile or two ahead on the opposite side of the river. They turned in towards the river, and we rode down to meet them. We found them to be two white men and a mulatto named Jim Beckwith, who had left St. Louis when a boy and gone to live with the Crow Indians. He had distinguished himself among them by some acts of daring bravery, and had risen to the rank of a chief, but had now for some years left them. They were in search of a band of horses that had gone off from a camp some miles above, in charge of Mr. Chabonard. Two of them continued down the river, in search of the horses, and the American turned back with us, and we rode on towards the camp. About eight miles from our sleeping place, we reached Bijou's Fork [Bijou Creek], an affluent of the right bank. Where we crossed it, a short distance from the Platte, it has a sandy bed about 400 yards broad; the water in various small streams, a few inches deep. Seven miles further brought us to a camp of some four or five whites, New Englanders, I believe, who had accompanied Captain Wyeth to the Columbia river, and were independent trappers. All had their squaws with them, and I was surprised at the number of little fat buffalo-fed boys that were tumbling about the amp, all apparently of the same age, about three or four years old. They were encamped on a rich bottom, covered with a profusion of fine grass, and had a large number of fine-looking horses and mules. We rested with them a few minutes, and in about two miles arrived at Chabonard's camp, on an island in the Platte. On the heights above, we met the first Spaniard I had seen in the country. Mr.

Longs Peak by Albert Bierstadt, 1876.

Chabonard was in the service of Bent and St. Vrain's company and had left their fort some 40 or 50 miles above, in the spring, with boats laden with the furs of the last year's trade. He had met the same fortune as the voyageurs on the North Fork, and finding it impossible to proceed, had taken up his summer's residence on this island, which he had named St. Helena. The river hills appeared to be composed entirely of sand, and the Platte had lost the muddy character of its waters, and here was tolerably clear. From the mouth of the South fork, I had found it occasionally broken up by small islands, and at the time of our journey, which was at a season of the year when the waters were at a favorable stage, it was not navigable for anything drawing six inches waters. The current was very swift—the bed of the stream a coarse gravel.

From the place at which we had encountered the Arapahos, the Platte had been tolerably well fringed with timber, and the island here had a fine grove of very large cottonwoods, under whose broad shade the tents were pitched. There was a large drove of horses in the opposite prairie bottom; smoke was rising from the scattered fires, and the encampment had quite a patriarchal air. Mr. C. received us hospitably. One of the people was sent to gather mint, with the aid of which he concocted very good julep, and some boiled buffalo tongue, and coffee with the luxury of sugar, were soon set before us. The people in his employ were generally Spaniards, and among them I saw a young Spanish woman from Taos, whom I found to be Beckwith's wife.

July 10.—We parted with our hospitable host after breakfast the next morning, and reached St. Vrain's fort, about 45 miles from St. Helena, late in the evening. The post is situated on the South Fork of the Platte, immediately under the mountains, about 17 miles east of Longs Peak. It is on the right bank, on the verge of the upland prairie, about 40 feet above the river, of which the immediate valley is about 600 yards wide. The stream is divided into various branches by small islands, among which it runs with a swift current. The bed of the river is sand and gravel, the water very clear, and here may be called a mountain stream. This region appears to be entirely free from the limestones and marls which give to the lower Platte its yellow and dirty color. The black hills lie between the stream and the mountains, whose snowy peaks glitter a few miles beyond. At the fort, we found Mr. St. Vrain, who received us with much kindness and hospitality. Maxwell had spent the last two or three years between this post and the village of Taos, and here he was at home and among his friends. Spaniards frequently came over in search of employment, and several came in shortly after our arrival. They usually obtain about six dollars a month, generally paid to them in goods. They are very useful in a camp in taking care of horses and mules, and I engaged one, who proved to be an active, laborious man, and was of very considerable service to me. The elevation of the Platte here is 5,400 feet above the sea. The neighboring mountains did not appear to enter far the region of perpetual snow, which was generally confined to the northern side of the peaks. On the southern, I remarked very little. Here, it appeared, so far as I could judge in the distance, to descend but a few hundred feet below the summits.

I regretted that time did not permit me to visit them; but the proper object of my survey lay among the mountains further north; and I looked forward to an exploration of their snowy recesses with great pleasure.

Down the Santa Fe Trail and Into Mexico

Susan Shelby Magoffin

BENT'S FORT, JULY 27, 1846. Monday noon. I have been rather negligent in my writing. The last I wrote was on Tuesday 21st after our little shipwreck. Afterward, I supposed an Indian fracas would be our next adventure, for the Yumas were over. We passed their sign, such as old *moccasins*, and a post set in the ground, stuck at the other end in which were a sword and bundle of fagots, many in number, representing, as I was told a sign to some other of their tribe passing after them, the army of the whites they were numerous; The sword was painted red, for the use they made with it, and it also had several notches cut in it to represent the number of days since they passed.

We met with no very strange adventure. I was careful enough at every little hill to get out and walk, for the last narrow escape we had is not out of my mind yet.

One evening we had an abundance of mosquitoes and another slight thunderstorm. It was not so fearful tho' as the other in more than one respect. We had the tent secured by ropes fastened to the top of the pole and to the carriage and *la cara* [*carro*-wagon] wheels.

The road has been very sandy and almost on the river bank, which is poorly timbered till some 120 miles from the crossing. It is rather thicker for 10 or 12 miles, and taller the trees with more the appearance of the Mississippi banks. In some places, the country is hilly and covered with large stones; but generally speaking, it is perfectly level plain, destitute of everything, even grass, the great reliever of the eye, and making it painful to the sight.

Saturday morning, we saw in front of us and many miles distant, perhaps 80, a mountain called, I think, James Peak.

In the evening, we came on some five miles ahead of the wagons, to where Messrs Davie, Harmony, and Hickman were encamped till we have permission to take a final start. Here, we pitched our tent for the night and, I believe, for the 45th time.

Sunday morning, after getting the wagons up there and encamped some 15 miles from the fort we came on ourselves.

Some four miles below the Fort we passed the soldiers' encampment, another novel sight to me, perhaps there were 50 or more little tents stretched around in a ring with here and there a wagon and a little shade made of tree limbs. The idle soldiers were stretched under these; others were out watering horses staked about the camp; some were drying clothes in the sun; &c., &c.

At the outer edge of the encampment stood a sentinel, who with all the dignity and pomp, though by no means a Samson in stature, of his office shouldered his musket, marched up, and stopped us with the words, "Where go you?" We gave him our directions, he reported us to the sergeant at arms, and without further ceremony we were permitted to pass on. In a little time, we were in sight of the fort and, soon after, were in it.

And now for something of a description. Well, the outside exactly fills my idea of an ancient castle. It is built of adobes, unburnt brick, and Mexican style so far. The walls are very high and very thick with rounding corners. There is but one entrance; this is to the east rather.

Inside is a large space some 90 or 100 feet square, all around this and next to the wall are rooms, some 25 in number. They have dirt floors which are sprinkled with water several times during the day to prevent dust. Standing in the center of some of them is a large wooden post as a firmer prop to the ceiling which is made of logs. Some of these rooms are occupied by boarders as bed chambers. One is a dining room, another a kitchen, a little store, a blacksmith's shop, a barber's shop, and an ice house, which receives perhaps more customers than any other.

On the south side is an enclosure for stock in dangerous times and often at night. On one side of the top wall are rooms built in the same manner as below. We are occupying one of these, but of that anon.

They have a well inside, and fine water it is, especially with ice. At present, they have quite a number of boarders. The traders and soldiers chiefly, with a few *loafers* from the States, come out because they can't live at home.

There is no place on earth, I believe, where man lives and gambling in some form or other is not carried on. Here in the Fort—and who could have supposed such a thing—they have a *regularly established billiard room*! They have a regular race track. And I hear the cackling of chickens at such a rate sometimes I shall not be surprised to hear of a cockpit.

Now for our room: It is quite roomy. Like the others, it has a dirt floor, which I keep sprinkling constantly during the day; we have two windows, one looking out on the plain, the other is on the *patio* or yard. We have our own furniture, such as a bed, chairs, wash basin, table furniture, and we eat in our own room. It is keeping house regularly, but I beg leave not to be allowed *that* privilege much longer.

They have one large room as a parlor; there are no chairs but a cushion next to the wall on two sides, so the company sits all around in a circle. There is no other furniture than a table on which stands a bucket of water, free to all. Any water that may be left in the cup after drinking is unceremoniously tossed onto the floor.

When we came last evening, while they were fixing our room, I sat in the parlor with *las senoritas* [the ladies], the wife of Mr. George Bent, and some others. One of them sat and combed her hair all the while notwithstanding the presence of Mr. Lightendoffer, whose lady (a Mexican) was present. After the combing, she paid her devoirs to a crock of oil or grease of some kind, and it is not exaggeration to say it almost *dripped* from her hair to the floor. If I had not seen her at it, I never would have believed it grease but that she had been washing her head.

We had Capt. Moore, of the U.S. dragoons, to call this P.M.; he promises me protection, as an American citizen, and as a Kentuckian; he is from that noble state himself, and even claims a kinship! Both yesterday and this evening, we have taken a walk up the river, such as we used to take last winter in N.Y. from Spring to Wall Street.

Tuesday 28th. The Dctr has just left, and I shall endeavor to write a little before dinner. I've been busy all the morning. Wrote a long letter to Mama, which Capt. Moore says I can send by the government express. The army affords me one convenience in this. Though I cannot hear from home, it is a gratification to know that I can send letters to those who will take pleasure in reading them.

Dctr. Mesure brought me more medicine and advises *mi alma* to travel me through Europe. The advice is rather better to take than the medicine—anything though to restore my health. I never should have consented to take the trip on the plains had it not been with the view and a hope that it would prove beneficial; but so far my hopes have been blasted, for I am rather going downhill than up, and it is so bad to be sick and under a physician all the time. But cease my rebellious heart. How prone human nature is to grumble and to think his lot harder than any one of his fellow creatures, many of whom are a hundred times more diseased and poor in earthly assistance and still they endure all—and would endure more.

Had Capt. Waldo, of the Mo. Volunteers, to call this P.M. *Mi alma* is paving his way to "protection" and polite treatment from all the chief men, &c.

Wednesday 29th. The same routine today as yesterday, several gentlemen, among the traders and officers, called and paid their respects to the "Madam." My health, though not good, is drank by them all, and sometimes a complimentary toast is ingeniously slipped in. The Fort is not such a bad place after all. There are some good people in and about it as well as in other places. I am not very much displeased with Col. Kearny for sending us here, but he has arrived himself this P.M. and gives the command to leave in three days. The idea of getting onto those rough, jolting roads, and they say this is rather worse, if anything, than the one we have passed, is truly sickening.

I have concluded that the plains are not very beneficial to my health so far; for I am thinner by a good many lbs. than when I came out. The dear knows what is the cause!

Thursday, July 30th. Well, this is my nineteenth birthday! And what? Why, I feel rather strange, not surprised at its coming, nor to think that I am growing rather older, for that is the way of the human family, but this is it—I am sick! Strange sensations in my head, my back, and hips. I am obliged to lie down most of the time, and when I get up to hold my hand over my eyes.

There is the greatest possible noise in the *patio* [yard]. The shoeing of horses, neighing, and braying of mules, the crying of children, the scolding and fighting of men, are all enough to turn my head. And to add to the scene, like some of our neighbors, we have our own private troubles. The servants are all quarreling and fighting among themselves, running to us to settle their difficulties; they are gambling off their clothes till some of them are next to nudity, and though each of them is in debt to *mi alma* for advancement of their wages, they are coming to him to get them out of their scrapes.

Jose, our principal Mexican about the camp, and my maid Jane, have had a cat and dog difficulty; he says he can't stand it and she puts on airs, does her business when and how she pleases, leaving a part of it for *me* to do, and here we have it. In addition to all this, the doctor comes to tell how his men have treated him, therefore we have our own and our neighbors' trials to encounter.

The Fort is crowded to overflowing. Col. Kearny has arrived and it seems the world is coming with him. Volunteers are under his command now only as he, on his arrival, dispatched them under Capt. Moore ahead, for the purpose

Bent's Fort was a key trading hub along the Santa Fe Trail from 1833–1849.

of repairing 15 miles of the road called the Raton, a bed of rocks impassable for wagons, of which there are a goodly number to pass.

Three Indian warriors came in today; they belong to a large war party of the Arapaho Indians who are, they say, some 60 miles off. They are believed by the company to be spies, though they come rather with the appearance of trading.

With the intention of awing them a little, Mr. Bent and others are about taking them down to the soldiers' encampment. They hesitate rather, saying they have "two hearts on the subject; one of which says go! and the other says don't go!" They are cunning people, and no doubt 'twould be a rich treat to hear, on their returning to their tribe, their graphic account of the American Army as "the white-faced Warriors."

August 1846. Thursday 6. The mysteries of a new world have been shown to me since last Thursday! In a few short months I should have been a happy mother and made the heart of a father glad, but the ruling hand of a mighty Providence has interposed and by an abortion deprived us of the hope, the fond hope of mortals! But with the affliction, he does not leave us comfortless!

We have permission to "come unto him when our burden is grievous and heavy to be borne; we have permission to pray for more submission and reliance on his goodness, and in that petition we have an intercessor with the Father, Jesus Christ, who himself came into the world an infant, after the manner of man.

Friday morning, 31st of July. My pains commenced and continued till 12 o'clock at night, when after much agony and severest of pains, which were relieved a little at times by medicine given by Dctr. Mesure, *all was over.* I sunk off into a kind of lethargy, in *mi alma's* arms. Since that time, I have been in my bed till yesterday, a little while, and a part of today.

My situation was very different from that of an Indian woman in the room below me. She gave birth to a fine healthy baby, about the same time, *and in half an hour after she went to the river and bathed herself and it,* and this she has continued each day since. Never could I have believed such a thing, if I had not been convinced and *mi alma's* own eyes had not seen her coming from the river. And some gentleman here tells him; he has often seen them immediately after the birth of a child go to the water and *break the ice* to bathe themselves!

It is truly astonishing to see what customs will do. No doubt many ladies in civilized life are ruined by too careful treatments during childbirth, for this custom of the heathen is not known to be disadvantageous, but it is a "*heathenish custom.*"

The Oregon Trail

Francis Parkman

MEETING ARAPAHOES HERE on the Arkansas was a very different thing from meeting the same Indians among their native mountains. There was another circumstance in our favor. General Kearney had seen them a few weeks before, as he came up the river with his army, and, renewing his threats of the previous year, he told them that if they ever again touched the hair of a white man's head he would exterminate their nation. This placed them for the time in an admirable frame of mind, and the effect of his menaces had not yet disappeared. I wished to see the village and its inhabitants. I thought it also our best policy to visit them openly, as if unsuspicious of any hostile sign; and Shaw and I, with Henry Chatillon, prepared to cross the river. The rest of the party, meanwhile, moved forward as fast as they could, in order to get as far as possible from our suspicious neighbors before night came on.

The Arkansas, at this point, and for several hundred miles below, is nothing but a broad sand bed, over which glide a few scanty threads of water, now and then expanding into wide shallows. At several places, during the autumn, the water sinks into the sand and disappears altogether. At this season, were it not for the numerous quicksands, the river might be forded almost anywhere without difficulty, though the channel is often a quarter of a mile wide. Our horses jumped down the bank, and wading through the water, or galloping freely over the hard sandbeds, soon reached the other side. Here, as we were pushing through the tall grass, we saw several Indians not far off; one of them waited until we came up, and stood for some moments in perfect silence before us, looking at us askance with his little snake-like eyes. Henry explained by signs what we wanted, and the Indian, gathering his buffalo-robe about his shoulders, led the way towards the village without speaking a word.

The language of the Arapahos is so difficult, and its pronunciation so harsh and guttural, that no white man, it is said, has ever been able to master it. Even Maxwell, the trader who has been most among them, is compelled to resort to the curious sign language common to most of the prairie tribes. With this sign language, Henry Chatillon was perfectly acquainted.

Approaching the village, we found the ground strewn with piles of waste buffalomeat in incredible quantities. The lodges were pitched in a circle. They resembled those of the Dahcotah in everything but cleanliness. Passing between two of them, we entered the great circular area of the camp, and instantly hundreds of Indians, men, women, and children, came flocking out of their habitations to look at us; at the same time, the dogs all around the village set up a discordant baying. Our Indian guide walked towards the lodge of the chief. Here, we dismounted, and loosening the trailropes from our horses' necks, held them fast as we sat down before the entrance, with our rifles laid across our laps. The chief came out and shook us by the hand. He was a mean-looking fellow, very tall, thin-visaged, and sinewy, like the rest of the nation, and with scarcely a vestige of clothing. We had not been seated a moment before a multitude of Indians came crowding around us from every part of the village, and we were shut in by a dense wall of savage faces. Some of our visitors crouched around us on the ground; others sat behind them; others, stooping, looked over their heads; while many more stood behind, peering over each other's shoulders, to get a view of us. I looked in vain among this throng of faces to discover one manly or generous expression; all were wolfish, sinister, and malignant, and their complexions, as well as their features, unlike those of the Dahcotah, were exceedingly bad. The chief, who sat close to the entrance, called to a squaw within the lodge, who soon came out and placed a wooden bowl of meat before us. To our surprise, however, no pipe was offered. Having tasted of the meat as a matter of form, I began to open a bundle of presents—tobacco, knives, vermilion, and other articles which I had brought with me. At this there was a grin on every countenance in the rapacious crowd; their eyes began to glitter, and long thin arms were eagerly stretched towards us on all sides to receive the gifts.

An 1869 oil painting by Albert Bierstadt depicts emigrants on their way to Oregon along the Oregon Trail.

The Arapahos set great value upon their shields, which they transmit carefully from father to son. I wished to get one of them; and displaying a large piece of scarlet cloth, together with some tobacco and a knife, I offered them to anyone who would bring me what I wanted. After some delay, a tolerable shield was produced. They were very anxious to know what we meant to do with it, and Henry told them that we were going to fight their enemies, the Pawnees. This instantly produced a visible impression in our favor, which was increased by the distribution of the presents. Among these was a large paper of awls, a gift appropriate to the women; and as we were anxious to see the beauties of the Arapahoe village, Henry requested that they might be called to receive them. A warrior gave a shout, as if he were calling a pack of dogs together. The squaws, young and old, hags of 80 and girls of 16, came running with screams and laughter out of the lodges; and as the men gave way for them, they gathered round us and stretched out their arms grinning with delight, their native ugliness considerably enhanced by the excitement of the moment.

Mounting our horses, which during the whole interview we had held close to us, we prepared to leave the Arapahos. The crowd fell back on each side and stood looking on. When we were half across the camp, an idea occurred to us. The Pawnees were probably in the neighborhood of the Caches; we might tell the Arapahos of this and instigate them to send down a war-party and cut them off while we ourselves could remain behind for a while and hunt the buffalo. At first thought, this plan of setting our enemies to destroy one another seemed to us a masterpiece of policy; but we immediately recollected that should we meet the Arapahoe warriors on the river below, they might prove quite as dangerous as the Pawnees themselves. So rejecting our plan as soon as it presented itself, we passed out of the village on the farther side. We urged our horses rapidly through the tall grass, which rose to their necks. Several Indians were walking through it at a distance, their heads just visible above its waving surface. It bore a kind of seed, as sweet and nutritious as oats; and our hungry horses, in spite of whip and rein, could not resist the temptation of snatching at this unwonted luxury as we passed along. When about a mile from the village, I turned and looked back over the undulating ocean of grass. The sun was just set; the western sky was all in a glow, and sharply defined against it, on the extreme verge of the plain, stood the clustered lodges of the Arapahoe camp.

Reminiscences of General William Larimer and of his son William H. H. Larimer

William H.H. Larimer

Denver City, Kansas Territory
23rd November, 1858

Dear Wife:

I AM KEEPING CAMP TODAY, and I thought I would commence this letter not to be closed until the last of the month. In the first place, Will and I are in clover. … Will and I have agreed so well we have never had a cross word, and I do say with pleasure that he ever consults my wishes and does all the work for him and me both. In short, he is the finest boy I ever saw in every way. He is noted here and along the road as very promising. Truly, I cannot express my feelings when I think of his feelings towards me, and he so often talks of you and all the family. One Sunday he said to me: "Only think how they are so uneasy until they hear from us." Will and I have had a hard trip, but we stand it so well we do not feel the cold. Still, I may say we are out of doors and in the weather nearly all the time. I may want either John or Mr. Jones to come here; still, I will get along, if possible. We cannot make any rash calculations yet as something might occur to spoil our calculations.

The weather is not favorable for digging, and nearly everyone is fixing for winter; still, some are digging and doing well. There is a man above here a few miles that everybody says is making from $5 to $10 every day. I did not see him myself, but I believe it. I have seen plenty of specimens of gold, one lot about $70. The immigration appears about over for this season; very few have arrived since we came. I guess some have stopped over upon the Arkansas. Captain Humphreys was to leave Leavenworth the Monday after we did, but he had not yet arrived here. A part of the road we came over has now, they say, about two feet of snow. We got here at the nick of time.

I want you to tell all inquirers about roads to be sure to take the Laramie Road to Fort Ramsey, and they will find a good road up the South Platte and save at least 150 miles. Over the route we came, it took us at least two weeks longer than it should have done. St. Matthews, the man that was in the office with the two dogs, has never reached here; neither has Mr. Wade. I think Mr. Wade must have gone back from Topeka.

We made a mistake by coming so many in one wagon. Our load was too heavy; moreover, when we divided, we had small portions. If Will and I had each taken a light wagon with two yoke of oxen, we should have done better. Only Will and I never rode one mile on our wagon, nor did any of us. We had to trudge along day after day on foot, while the Oscaloosa boys could lay all day in the wagon and we, too, had no one driver, but had to drive day about and had to wheel the oxen from morning till night. It surprises me to think we ever got through. Our team was 47 days on the road, only think of it. I am very anxious to hear from home. Our Laramie Express will run once a month. By the 12th of December, I expect to get your letters. It will cost 25 cents for each letter and 50 cents for newspapers. Let all your letters be good, large ones and send me no papers except important ones; but do write me often. I have plenty of money with which to pay postage.

Will and I now cook by ourselves. We have the little stove, and I was so fortunate in drawing it when we divided our baggage. A few little sticks will get a breakfast.

I wish you could look into our quarters; you would go up! I am writing while sitting on my trunk with a little board stuck through the logs with one end to write upon. It works nicely. Mr. Sanders, James Sanders, has just called in to see me. I want you to direct your letters to me in care of Sanders & Co. Express. This will save the trouble of sending an order every time.

25th November: The weather is now mild and beautiful, very much like Pennsylvania weather. Will is out busily engaged chopping logs for our house. We expect to get them all hauled tomorrow. I am keeping camp today again. You would laugh to see Will and me eating breakfast and supper. We eat only two meals a day. Will makes first-rate cakes (biscuits). We have venison nearly all the time; if not, we have plenty of bacon. Will and I both feel rich. We shall have about 500 lots, each, in Denver City. I am selected to donate lots to actual settlers. We shall have at least 50 each in Sacramento City, at least. Everybody here is delighted with the prospects, more so than Will and I. We may open an office here. Everyone has nothing to do so. We haven't the whole matter at present in our own hands, having nothing to do nor can anything be done, until they dig the gold and our regular express starts. But all this is in the future, and I will write you every chance I get fixed up. Will is going to dig. We have our claims staked off about four miles above here. Everybody here is confident of success.

Sunday, 28th: I have just returned from church. A Mr. Fisher, a Methodist minister, came in our party. He preached here last Sunday also. You can imagine my feelings last Sunday when we had Mr. McLane to lead the music. He was not here today; he is stopping four miles below town. Mr. Moyne, a young Omaha deacon, also a lawyer, is here; his cabin and ours are right opposite each other. Mr Moyne is that young man with fair hair that you always saw at our church in Omaha, so you see that we are not out of the world yet. The church was better attended last Sunday than this. Everybody is busy today building and hunting. The weather is now very warm and pleasant. We have got all our logs and hope to get well housed next week. We have plenty of dry wood nearby, so you need not fear for one moment about Will and I being warm and comfortable. Besides, I think the weather here is warmer than with you, certainly warmer than in Nebraska; the mountains protect us. Everything looks cheering. Will and I get along nicely, so think no more about us. We are perhaps more comfortable than you, and we have plenty of people all around us. We shall have a good hotel here by spring. Stephens of Omaha is going to keep it; he is starting early in the spring. Stephens formerly kept the Douglas House and is now keeping the Saratoga Hotel. Old Spooner is here building the hotel in our city. Our town is now the county seat. I believe I wrote you I was appointed Treasurer. I am also Treasurer of Denver City, our town.

30 November: I'll have to close my letter tonight, I guess. I will send it by the hands of Ed. Wynkoop and Dr. A. B. Steinberger of Bellevue. They leave tomorrow. The express also leaves tomorrow.

Say to Mr. Reed that Mr. Lawrence and Dorsett are well. We will stick together. Whitsett and Jewett have gone to Montana, six miles above here; they are also very well. Mr. Whitsett was down today. The news of gold diggings is better and better every day. If things go well here, I may be home by mid-summer, if not before. I have instructed Mr. Wynkoop to leave John a map of Denver City when he gets them lithographed. When you get this map, notice that my lot is on the northwest corner of C and Larimer streets; Will's lot is on the northeast corner of D and Larimer streets. Larimer Street at present is the best; Lawrence and McGaa next.

Yours affectionately,
Wm. Larimer, Jr.

A Hit at the Times

A.O. McGrew

Way out upon the Platte, near Pike's Peak we were told
There by a little digging, we could get a pile of gold,
So we bundled up our duds, resolved at least to try
And tempt old Madam Fortune, root hog, or die.

So we traveled across the country, and we got upon the ground,
But cold weather was ahead, the first thing we found.
We built our shanties on the ground, resolved in spring to try,
To gather up the dust and slugs, root hog, or die.

Speculation is the fashion even at this early stage,
And corner lots and big hotels appear to be the rage,
The emigration's bound to come, and to greet them we will try,
Big pig, little pig, root hog, or die.

Washing and panning gold in 1889

Let shouts resound, the cup pass 'round, we all came for gold,
The politicians are all gas, the speculators sold,
The "scads" are all we want, and to get them we will try,
Big pig, little pig, root hog, or die.

Surveyors now are at their work, laying off the towns,
And some will be of low degree, and some of high renown.
They don't care a jot nor tittle who do buy
The corner lots, or any lots, root hog, or die.

The doctors are among us, you can find them where you will,
They say their trade it is to cure; I say it is to kill,
They'll dose you, and they'll phsyic you, until they make you sigh,
And their powders and their lotions make you root hog, or die.

The next in turn comes Lawyers, a precious set are they;
In the public dairy they drink the milk, their clients drink the whey.
A cunning set these fellows are; they'll sap you 'till you're dry,
And never leave you 'till you have to root hog, or die.

A Preacher, now is all we want, to make us all do good;
But at present, there's no lack of *spiritual* food,
The kind that I refer to, will make you laugh or cry,
And its real name is Taos, root hog, or die.

I have finished now my song, or, if you please, my ditty;
And that it was not shorter, is about the only pity.
And now, that I have had my say, don't say I've told a lie;
For now the subject I've touched, will make us root hog, or die.

An Overland Journey

Horace Greeley

Denver, June 15, 1859

I KNOW FEW GREATER CONTRASTS than that between the region which stretches hundreds of miles eastward from this spot toward the Missouri, and is known as The Plains, and that which overlooks us on the west and, alike by its abrupt and sharp-ridged foothills seeming just at hand, and its glittering peaks of snow in the blue distance, vindicates its current designation, *The Mountains*. Let me elucidate: The Plains are nearly destitute of human inhabitants. Aside from the buffalo range—which has been steadily narrowing ever since Daniel Boone made his home in Kentucky, and is now hardly two hundred miles wide—it affords little sustenance and less shelter to man. The antelope are seldom seen in herds—three is the highest number I observed together, while one, or at most two, is a more common spectacle. One to each mile square would be a large estimate for all that exist on the plains. Elk are scarcely seen at all, even where they have hardly ever been hunted or scared. Of deer, there are none, or next to none. For the Plains are the favorite haunt of beasts and birds of prey—of the ravenous and fearless gray wolf, of the coyote, the raven, and the hawk—the first hanging on the flanks of every great herd of buffalo, ready to waylay any foolish calf or heedless heifer that may chance to stray for water or fresher grass beyond the protection of the hard-headed and chivalrous patriarchs, behind whose vigilant ranks there is comparative safety, and counting as their property any bull, even, whom wounds or disease or decrepitude shall compel to fall behind in the perpetual march. For, while a stray buffalo, or two, or three, may linger in some lonely valley for months—for all winter, perhaps—the great herds which blacken the earth for miles in extent cannot afford to do so—they are so immensely numerous and find their safety in traveling so compactly that they must keep moving or starve. Avoiding, so far as possible, the wooded ravines of the slender watercourses, where experience has taught them to dread the lance-like arrow of the lurking Indian, they keep to the high "divides," or only feed in the valleys while they have these well covered by sentinel bulls to give warning of any foe's approach. Take away the buffalo, and the Plains will be desolate far beyond their present desolation; and I cannot but regard with sadness the inevitable and not distant fate of these noble and harmless brutes, already crowded into a breadth of country too narrow for them, and continually hunted, slaughtered, decimated by the wolf, the Indian, the white man. They could have stood their ground against all in the absence of firearms, but "villainous saltpeter" is too much for them. They are bound to perish; I trust it may be oftener by sudden shot than by slow starvation.

Wood and water—the prime necessities of the traveler as of the settler—are in adequate though not abundant supply for a hundred miles and more on this as they are throughout on the other side of the buffalo range; at length they gradually fail, and we are in a desert indeed. No spring, no brook, for a distance of 30 to 60 miles (which would be stretched to more than a hundred if the few tracks called roads were not all run so as to secure water so far as possible)—rivers which have each had 50 to a 100 miles of its course gradually parched up by force of sun and wind, and its waters lost in their own sands, so that the weary, dusty traveler vainly digs for hours in their dry beds in quest of drink for his thirsty cattle—rivers which dare not rise again till some friendly brook, having its source in some specially favored region, pours in its small but steady tribute, moistens the sands of the river bed, and encourages its waters to rise to the surface again. In one case, an emigrant assures me that he dug down to the bedrock of one of these rivers—yet found all dry sand.

I know not that I can satisfactorily account, even to myself, for the destitution of wood which the Plains everywhere present, especially the western half of them. The poverty of the soil will not suffice, for these lands, when sufficiently moistened by rain or thawing snowdrifts, produce grass, and are not so sterile as the rocky hills, the pebbly knolls, of New England, which, nevertheless, produce wood rapidly and abundantly. On the prairies of Illinois, Missouri, and eastern Kansas, the absence of wood is readily accounted for by the annual fires which, in autumn or spring, sweep over nearly every acre of dead grass, killing every tree sprout that may have started up from scattered seeds or roots running from the timber in the adjacent ravine beneath the matted grass. But here are thousands of acres too poorly grassed to be swept by the annual fires—on which the thinly scattered reed stalks and bunch grass of last year shake dryly in the fierce winds—yet not a tree nor shrub relieves the sameness, the bareness, the desolation of thousands after thousands of acres—not a twig, a scion, gives promise of trees that are to be. For a time, the narrow ravine or lowest intervale of the current streams were fairly timbered with cottonwood, and low, sprawling elm, with a very little oak, or white ash at long intervals intermixed; but these grew gradually thinner and feebler until nothing but a few small cottonwoods remained, these skulking behind bluffs, or in sheltered hollows at intervals of twenty to forty miles. Once in 10 or 20 miles, a bunch of dwarf willows, perhaps two feet high, would be found cowering in some petty basin washed out by a current of water many years ago; but these, like the cottonwoods, are happy if able to hold their own; indeed, I have seen much evidence that wood was more abundant on the plains a hundred years ago than it now is. Dead cottonwoods of generous proportions lie in the channels of dry brooks on which no tree nor shrub now grows; and, at one or more stations of the express company, near the sink of the Republican, they find dead pine eight miles up a creek, where no living pine has been seen for generations. I judged that the desert is steadily enlarging its borders and at the same time intensifying its barrenness.

The fierce drought that usually prevails throughout the summer doubtless contributes to this, but I think the violent and all but constant winds exert a still more disastrous potency. High winds are of frequent, all but daily, occurrence here, within a dozen miles of the great protecting bulwark of the Rocky Mountains; while, from a point fifty miles eastward of this, they sweep over the Plains almost constantly, and at times with resistless fury. A driver stated on our way up, with every appearance of sincerity, that he had known instances of tires being blown off from wagon wheels by the tornadoes of the Plains; and, hard to swallow as that may seem, I have other and reliable assurance that when the Missourians' camp on the express road was swept by a hurricane five or six weeks ago, so that, after the wreck, but three decent wagons could be patched up out of their six, as I have already narrated, one of the wheel tires was not only blown off but nearly straightened out! There is almost always a good breeze at midday and after, on the Plains; but, should none be felt during the day, one is almost certain to spring up at sunset, and blow fiercely through the night. Thus, though hot days, or parts of days, are frequent on the Plains, I have experienced

A tornado on the great plains.

not even a moderately warm night. And thus trees are not; mainly because the winds uproot or dismember them, or so rock and wrench them while young, that their roots cannot suck up even the little nourishment that this soil of baking clay resting on porous sand would fain afford them. Thus the few shoots that cleave the surface of the earth soon wither and die, and the broad landscape remains treeless, cheerless, forbidding.

But the dearth of water and wood on the Plains is paralleled by the poverty of shrubbery and herbage. I have not seen a strawberry leaf—far from me be the presumption of looking for a berry!—since I left the Missouri three weeks ago; and the last blackberry bramble I observed grew on Chapman's Creek—at all events the other side of the buffalo range. A raspberry cane has not blessed my sight these three weary weeks, nor aught else that might be hoped to bear an old-fashioned fruit, save the far-off blackberries aforesaid, and two or three doubtful grapevines on some creek a great way back. The prickly pear, very rare and very green, is the only semblance of fruit I discovered on the Plains; a dwarfish cactus, with its leaves close to the ground; the Spanish nettle—a sort of vegetable porcupine—a profusion of wild sage, wild wormwood, and other such plants, worthless alike to man and beast, relieved by some well-gnawed grass in the richer valleys of winter watercourses (the flora usually very scanty and always coarse and poor)—such are my recollections of the three hundred miles or so that separate the present buffalo range from the creeks that carry snow water to the Platte and the pines that herald our approach to the Rocky Mountains.

The Rocky Mountains

And now all changes, but slowly, gradually. The cactus, the Spanish nettle, the prickly pear continue, even into and upon the mountains; but the pines, though stunted and at first scattered, give variety, softness, and beauty to the landscape, which becomes more rolling, with deeper and more frequent valleys, and water in nearly all of them; the cottonwoods along the streams no longer skulk behind bluffs or hide in casual hollows; you may build an honest campfire without fear of robbing an embryo county of its last stick of wood, and water your mules generously without drying up some long, pretentious river, and condemning those who come after you to weary, thirsty marches through night and day. The cottonwoods, as you near the wind-quelling range of protecting heights, which rise, rank above rank, to the westward (the more distant still white-robed with snow) grow large and stately—some of them sixty to seventy feet high, and at least three feet in diameter; the unwooded soil ceases to be desert and becomes prairie once more; but still this is in the main a sandy, thinly grassed region, which cannot compare with the prairies of Illinois, of Iowa, or eastern Kansas.

There seems to be as rich and deep soil in some of the creek bottoms, especially those of the South Platte, as almost anywhere; and yet I fear the husbandman is doomed to find even this belt of grassed and moderately rolling land, which stretches along the foot of the mountains to a width of perhaps 20 miles, less tractable and productive than fertile. It lies at such an elevation—from 5,000 to 6,000 feet above the ocean level—that, though its winters are said to be moderate, its springs cannot be early. There was a fall of a foot of snow in this region on the 26th of May, when ice formed to a quarter-inch thickness on the Plains; and when summer suddenly sets in, about the 1st of June, there are hot suns by day, and cool, strong winds by night, with a surfeit of petty thunder squalls, but little or no rain. The gentle rain of last Thursday in the mountains fell, for a short time, in sheets just at their feet—say for a breadth of five miles—and there ceased. Hardly a drop fell within five miles west, or any distance east of this place, though the earth was soaked only ten miles further west. Hence, the enterprising few who have commenced farms and gardens near this point tell me that their crops have made no progress for a week or two, and can make none till they have rain. I trust wheat and rye will do well here whenever they shall be allowed a fair chance; barley and oats, if sowed very early on deeply plowed land, may do tolerably; but corn, though it comes up well and looks rank at present, will hardly ripen before frost, even should it escape paralysis by drought; while potatoes, peas, and most vegetables will probably require irrigation, or yield but sparingly. Yet, should the gold mines justify their present promise, farming, in the right localities at the base of these mountains, even by the help of irrigation, will yield—to those who bring to it the requisite sagacity, knowledge, and capital—richer rewards than elsewhere on earth. Everything that can be grown here will command treble or quadruple prices for years; and he who produces anything calculated to diversify and improve the gross, mountainous diet of salt pork, hot bread, beans, and coffee, now necessarily all but universal in this region, will be justly entitled to rank with public benefactors.

And the Rocky Mountains, with their grand, aromatic forests, their grassy glades, their frequent springs, and dancing streams of the brightest, sweetest water, their pure, elastic atmosphere, and their unequalled game and fish, are destined to be a favorite resort and home of civilized man. I never visited a region where physical life could be more surely prolonged or fully enjoyed. Thousands who rush hither for gold will rush away again disappointed and disgusted, as thousands have already done; and yet the gold is in these mountains, and the right men will gradually unearth it. I shall be mistaken if two or three millions are not taken out this year, and some ten millions in 1860; though all the time there will be, as now, a stream of rash adventurers heading away from the diggings, declaring that there is no gold there, or next to none.

So it was in California and in Australia; so it must be here, where the obstacles to be overcome are greater, and the facilities for getting home decidedly better. All men are not fitted by nature for gold-diggers; yet thousands will not realize this until they have been convinced of it by sore experience. Any good phrenologist should have been able to tell half the people who rushed hither so madly during the last two months that, if these mountains had been half made of gold, they never would get any of it except by minding their own proper business, which was quite other than mining. And still the long procession is crossing the Platte and Clear Creek, and pressing up the Hill of Difficulty in mad pursuit of gold, whereof not one-fifth will carry back to the states so much as they brought away. New leads will doubtless be discovered, new veins be opened, new diggings or districts become the rage—for it were absurd to suppose that little ravine known as Gregory's, running to Clear Creek, the sole depository of gold worth working in all this region—and in time the Rocky Mountains will swarm with a hardy, industrious, energetic white population. Not gold alone, but lead, iron, and (I think) silver or cobalt, have already been discovered here, and other valuable minerals, doubtless will be, as the mountains are more thoroughly explored—for, as yet, they have not been even run over. Those who are now intent on the immediate organization and admission of a new state may be too fast, yet I believe the Rocky Mountains, and their immediate vicinity—say between Fort Laramie on the north and Taos on the south—will within three years have a white population of 100,000, one half composed of men in the full vigor of their prime, separated by deserts and waste places from the present states, obliged to rely on their own resources in any emergency, and fully able to protect and govern themselves. Why not let them be a state so soon as reasonably may be.

Mining is a pursuit akin to fishing and hunting, and, like them, enriches the few at the cost of the many. This region is doubtless foreordained to many changes of fortune; today, giddy with the intoxication of success—tomorrow, in the valley of humiliation. One day, report will be made on the Missouri by a party of disappointed gold-seekers, that the "Pike's Peak humbug" has exploded, and that everybody is fleeing to the states who can possibly get away; the next report will represent these diggings as yellow with gold. Neither will be true, yet each in its turn will have a certain thin substratum of fact for its justification. Each season will see its thousands turn away disappointed, only to give place to other thousands, sanguine and eager as if none had ever failed. Yet I feel a strong conviction that each succeeding month's researches will enlarge the field of mining operations, and diminish the difficulties and impediments which now stretch across the gold-seeker's path, and that, 10 years hence, we shall be just beginning.

A Trip to Pikes Peak

C.M. Clark

AFTER LEAVING ST. VRAIN'S, a distance of two miles brought us to the junction of the Denver City road, at which place a shoe maker had erected his tent, and had displayed on a rough board, in one corner, a row of black bottles, containing doubtless, a variety of whisky from *proof to waterproof.* He was evidently on his last pegs, and, with his a(w)ll had located there, having been disappointed in his *findings* at the mountains, to raise the wind to get home, for the want of boots to *sole,* he frequently *tapped* the bottles and *sold* the contents, which was decidedly the most profitable business.

We continued back, following along the road, which no doubt the reader is sufficiently familiar with; and after 35 days of hard travel, over the monotonous prairie, through rain and shine, heat and cold, and many times through the entire night, for the purpose of escaping the torturous fangs of innumerable mosquitoes, and at times when the night was as dark as Erebus, and we could not see the length of our noses, when one of us would start ahead with the lantern, in order that we might keep the track, we finally reached our starting point of the spring previous—having accomplished an over-land travel of some 1,500 miles in six months, behind slow bullocks, that had required about as much effort on our part as on theirs, to keep them moving—feeling rich in experience, if not in money.

A large emigration is expected next spring, by those remaining in the mountains, and doubtless, they will not be disappointed, for the country is fast being developed and settled; and as the mists of uncertainty that have hung over the country for the past two years, are fast dissolving before the warming rays of a progressive and determined spirit, disclosing that substance of things hoped for—"that more than philosopher's stone"—the public confidence is being restored, and thousands will again prepare to try their fortune and their fate.

The country is destined to be more than is "dreamt of in their philosophy," and its mines will yet open richly and reward the persevering industry of the many who have not "fear'd their fate too much," and whose deserts are fully equal to their hopes.

Quartz mining is to be the permanent feature of the region, and it is the only thing that will hold out and pay. The gulches and bars that have been discovered and worked have not generally paid, and they never will, unless means can be adopted to facilitate the working of them, and to save the gold, much of which is very fine, and wastes in the washing.

It is not at all probable that all who again start on the expedition, will realize a tithe of their expectations, and for reasons that have been enumerated in the previous pages, and for reasons that cannot but be apparent to every man who possesses common sense. All men are not successful in their avocations and experiments at home, and the laws that govern their finances and fortunes in the States, will not be suspended in the mountains. If they are not suited for the business, and if they have not the means to carry it forward successfully, they will necessarily fail; and if they have not the courage to face difficulties, the ability for hard labor, and the perseverance and patience that is necessary, the probability is that they will be disappointed; and if any man goes there with the hope of making

A sterioscopic photo of Pikes Peak from 1870 taken near Colorado City. US Geological Service.

a fortune in one season, he will find himself mistaken, unless he is content with a very small one.

A large number went last spring without knowing exactly what they should do upon reaching the mountains; and the majority of them left without finding out, after standing around through the various mines, with the hope of "jumping into somebody's shoes," for which there is seldom a chance. Capitalists can do well there, for they can turn their money in half the time that would be possible elsewhere; but the laboring man, who has but little means, or with scarcely sufficient to furnish a comfortable outfit, and who will be entirely dependent on his wits or muscle, had better remain at home, for he cannot get rich there any sooner than at home, and he will escape much hardship, toil, and privation, which is necessarily entailed on those who sojourn amid the mountains. But it is not my purpose to either encourage or discourage any person. If a man thinks he can do well, and wants to go—let him go—"*chacun son goût!*"

The best route is, I think, the one that I have described; but perhaps the one from Omaha is the most direct and shortest, and it will eventually take precedence over all the others when the railroad is completed to that point. All persons intending to start for that country next spring should be at their starting point as early as the 20th of April, and proceed out as soon as the feed will permit—the grass is generally far enough advanced at that time to afford good forage.

The outfit of companies would be too tedious to mention. Generally, a light wagon—one sufficiently strong to convey 2,000 or 2,500 pounds—is the best vehicle; and, with regard to the team, cattle are the best if you have much load to draw, and they are by far the most sure and safe, and will not occasion one-half the anxiety and trouble that horses or mules do; but then the latter will perform the journey in one-half the time that is required where bullocks are used, as they will not travel to exceed an average of 15 miles per day.

The best method to pursue in the matter of traveling is, to get as early a start in the morning as possible—say four o'clock, and proceed until nine o'clock, and halt until two o'clock P.M.—then resume, and travel until six o'clock, or until such time as may suit convenience. By pursuing this course, you will avoid the heat of the day, your team will travel faster and better, and they, as well as yourself, will reach the end of your trip in better condition than those who follow the old methodic system of reaching certain specified camps each night, where the feed is poor, and perhaps all consumed by those who have preceded.

As regards the many other items that constitute a proper outfit, one will be governed by his own peculiarities, or according to their taste and means. Everyone should be well supplied with waterproof clothing and with a sufficient quantity of blankets and bedding, if they desire to pass the nights comfortably. The items of flour, meal, bacon, potatoes, molasses, sugar, and coffee are the essentials; dried and preserved fruits, the condiments, and a good article of whisky are the (so considered) luxuries.

Every company should make it a point to take a cow, as she will more than pay for herself and the trouble during the trip and can be sold to good advantage after reaching the mountains.

The items of beans and Bologna sausage should be left out. The first can never be properly cooked, especially while traveling, and will ever occasion more or less sickness when they are not properly prepared; and sausage, when eaten, creates great thirst, which cannot always be gratified, and even if it can be, the drinking of large quantities of water should be guarded against, as it weakens the system.

Pleas and Petitions
Competing Claims on the Land

Virginia Sánchez

SPANISH EXPLORERS WERE THE FIRST Europeans to enter the southern portion of what is now the state of Colorado. They found the land already occupied by indigenous peoples, including Utes, Apaches, and Comanches. Colorado, at that time, was part of New Mexico, a province on the far northern frontier of New Spain. With the Louisiana Purchase, acquired from France in 1803, the territorial claims of the United States overlapped with Spanish New Mexico in the region of the Arkansas River drainage, including southeastern Colorado. Those competing claims were settled by treaty in 1819.

On its independence from Spain in 1821, the new republic of Mexico also ratified the 1819 treaty with the United States. However, in the 1830s, Texas declared and asserted its own independence from Mexico and was annexed as a new state by the United States in 1845. Due to encroachment, Spanish and later Mexican military expeditions, with orders from Santa Fe, also traveled north from Taos in search of the French and English. Early settlement into the same area occurred by French and North American fur trappers and later by miners seeking precious ores, mainly gold or silver, in the Rocky Mountains.

On this frontier of different cultures, there was a reliance on warfare, raids, and retaliation to redeem property (stolen sheep, cattle, horses, and even family members). Early Hispano settlers who had migrated farther north maintained close relations with the Utes, and languages and culture were shared. Honest and fair trade enabled permanent settlement. With peace came settlement, and Mexican citizens petitioned for land from the Mexican government. Two land grants are briefly discussed in this chapter: the Guadalupe, later known as the Conejos, and the Sangre de Cristo. The history of these grants is sad to relate as it does not end well for the Hispano settlers.

Charles Beaubien, a Mexican citizen of French-Canadian descent, acquired 600,000 acres of free land from the Mexican government in exchange for his loyalty and defense of the country from encroaching Americans. He became a traitor to his government in 1846 when he assisted U.S. Army Major Stephen W. Kearny in establishing an American system of laws in New Mexico.

The war between the United States and Mexico followed in 1846 with disastrous results for Mexico. Additionally, the Mexican government could not arrest Beaubien as he was on U.S. soil and now a U.S. citizen. In addition to the challenges of frontier life, the Hispanos were now introduced to a new culture and new legal system. Mexican land grants would emerge as a locus of confusion and cultural conflict, to say nothing of outright fraud, under American frontier governance.

In 1860, the U.S. Congress confirmed Beaubien's title to land on the Sangre de Cristo grant. Meanwhile, the Guadalupe grantees would have a much more difficult time proving to the surveyor general that they had in fact tried several times to settle Los Conejos after being forced to return to New Mexico due to incursions by indigenous bands.

The Life and Adventures of James P. Beckwourth

Moutaineer, Scout, and Pioneer, and Chief of the Crow Nation of Indians

T.D. Bonner

BUT IF THE GOVERNMENT IS DETERMINED to make war upon the Western tribes, let it be done intelligently and so effectually that mercy will temper justice. To attempt to chastise Indians with United States troops is simply ridiculous; the expense of such campaigns is only surpassed by their inefficiency. The Indians live on horseback, and they can steal and drive off the government horses faster than it can bring them together. The Indians having no stationary villages; they can travel faster, even with the incumbrance of their lodges, women, and children, subsisting themselves on buffalo slain on the way, than any force, however richly appointed, the country could send against them. An army must tire out in such a chase before summer is gone, while the Indians will constantly harass it with their sharpshooters. And should several powerful tribes unite—not an unusual occurrence—many thousand men would make no impression.

Colorado
A Summer Trip

Bayard Taylor

Denver, Colorado, July 15, 1866

THIS IS MY LAST NIGHT IN DENVER. After a month beside and among the Rocky Mountains, I am going (as the people here say) "to America." My place is taken in the stage which leaves to-morrow morning for the East, by the Platte route.

Had not the commencement of the rainy season and the condition of our animals prevented me from reaching Cañon and Colorado cities, my tour would have embraced all of the mountain regions which are easily accessible, and some that are not so. What I have seen is amply sufficient to convince me how much more there is to see. During a journey on horseback of 400 miles, which led me through two of the three Parks and thrice across the great range, I have obtained a tolerably extensive knowledge of the climate, scenery, and other features of a region which is destined, I think, to become for us what Switzerland is to Europe. Our artists, with true instinct, have first scented this fact, and they are the pioneers who point out to ignorant fashion the way it should go.

Whoever comes to the Rocky Mountains with pictures of the Alps in his memory, expecting to find them repeated on a grander and wilder scale, will certainly be disappointed. He will find no upper world of unbroken snow, as in the Bernese Oberland; no glaciers, thrusting far down between the forests their ever-moving fronts of ice; no contrast of rich and splendid vegetation in the valleys; no flashing waterfalls; no slopes of bright green pasturage; no moss, and but rarely the gleam of lakes and rivers, seen from above. With no less lofty chain can the Rocky Mountains be measured, it is true; but it is merely a general comparison of height, not of resemblance in any important feature.

In the first place, the atmospheric effects are those which result from the intense dryness of the heart of a continent in the temperate zone. The Alps not only touch the Mediterranean at either extremity but are no further from the Atlantic than from here to the Missouri River. Four or five cloudless days in succession are considered a rare good fortune by the tourist; the higher peaks are seldom without their drapery of shifting cloud. Here, a clear sky is the rule. There is seldom vapor enough—except just at present, during the brief rainy season—for the artist's needs. Perspective is only obtained by immense distances. The wonderful, delicate grays of the mountain landscapes demand changes of light and shadow which are often lacking; they lie too barely in the broad, unobstructed sunshine. Yet, an air more delicious to breathe can scarcely be found anywhere. It is neither too sedative nor too exciting but has that pure, sweet, flexible quality which seems to support all one's happiest and healthiest moods. Moreover, it holds in solution an exquisite variety of odors. Whether the resin of the coniferous trees, the balm of the sagebrush, or the breath of the orchis and wild rose, it is equally grateful and life-giving. After a day in this atmosphere, you have the lightest and most restorative slumber you ever knew.

On first entering the Rocky Mountains, you find the scenery rugged, cramped, and somewhat monotonous. Press forward, and they open anon—the higher the summits become the more breadth of base, the clearer outline they demand. They push away the crowd of lower ridges, leaving valleys for the streams, parks with every variety of feature, and finally gather into well-defined ranges, or spurs of ranges, giving you still broader and grander landscapes.

The San Luis Park, from the accounts I have heard, must be equally remarkable. It is on a much grander scale, and has the advantage of a milder climate, from its lesser elevation above the sea level. The North Park is rarely visited except by an occasional prospector or trapper. It has no settlement, as yet, and I have met with no one who has thoroughly explored it. There are a number of smaller parks on both sides of the main chain, and some of them are said to possess great natural beauties. The singular rock formations at the eastern base of the mountains furnish in themselves a rare and most original field for the tourist and the artist. The glimpse I had of those on the south bank of the Platte, on my return from the South Park, satisfy me that they surpass in magnitude and picturesque distortion the celebrated basaltic formations of Saxony.

It was part of my plan to have ascended either Pike's or Longs Peak, but I find that it is too soon in the season to make the attempt. Pike's Peak is comparatively easy of ascent; the summit, 13,200 feet above the level of the sea, has several times been reached by ladies. It is a very laborious but in no sense a dangerous undertaking. On account of its isolated position, the view from the top, in favorable weather, must be one of the finest panoramas in the world. Longs Peak has never yet been ascended. Mr. Byers, two years ago, reached a point about five hundred feet below the summit, and was then compelled to return. He is quite confident, however, that it can be scaled from another side, and if the summer were six weeks further advanced, I should be willing to join him in making the attempt. On the northern side, he says there is a valley or rather gulf, with walls of perpendicular rock between 2,000 and 3,000 feet in height, resembling a section of the Yosemite.

A comparison of this peak with Mont Blanc—the altitude of both being just about the same—may give a clear idea of the differences between the Alps and the Rocky Mountains. When you see Mont Blanc from the western part of Lake Leman, in July or August, he appears to you as a dome of complete snow—the few rocky pinnacles which pierce his mantle being hardly discernible specks. He is a white vision on the horizon. Longs Peak, at the same distance, is of the faint blue or purple which a rocky mass assumes, veined and streaked with white, but showing only one snow field of much apparent extent. His outline is very fine, a little sharper than Mont Blanc, the western side (as seen from Denver) having convex, and the eastern principally concave curves. He rests on a dark, broad base of forest and rock, his snows marking the courses of deep clefts and ravines. At present, the top-most is bare on the southern side. It is rare that one sees Mont Blanc from summit to base: I have not yet seen Longs Peak (except during a passing thundershower) otherwise.

I do not think the parks and the upper valleys of the mountains will produce anything except hardy vegetables and perhaps barley and rye. But they abound with the richest grasses; and "Colorado cheese" may one day be as celebrated as Gruyere or Neufchatel. They offer precisely those things which the summer tourist seeks—pure air, lovely nights, the finest milk, butter, trout, and game, and a variety of mineral springs. The summer climate I know; and I am told that the winter is equally enjoyable. It sounds almost incredible to hear of persons in the latitude of New York, and 8,000 feet above the sea, rarely needing an overcoat during the whole winter season. There is a great depth of snow, and an occasional severe day, but the skies are generally cloudless and the air temperate and bracing. The extremes of heat and cold are greater in Denver than in the mountains. As nearly as I can learn, the coldest weather yet experienced in San Luis Park was seven degrees below zero; in the Middle Park, 15 degrees; and in Denver, 30 degrees below.

The heavy snowfall, while it is a godsend to the agriculture of Colorado, by swelling all the streams at the very season when water is needed for irrigation, nevertheless interferes with the mining interests. There are many rich placers in the mountains where gold-washing can only be carried on for three or four months in the year, and even the stamp and smelting mills are hindered in procuring their supplies. It will also be the principal difficulty which the Pacific Railroad will be obliged to overcome. All other obstacles are much less than I had imagined. Greater achievements have already been done in railroading than the passage of the Rocky Mountains. By the Clear Creek, the South Park, or the Arkansas Valley, the Pacific slope can be reached, with not much more labor than you find on the Baltimore and Ohio road between Piedmont and Grafton. The facilities of construction beyond the range, however, must determine where the range should be crossed. A thorough exploration of the region watered by the Green and Blue Rivers must first be made.

I am, therefore, quite unable to tell you where the road will cross the Rocky Mountains; it is enough that they will be crossed. My conjectures—given for what they may be worth—take this form: that the Central Pacific Railroad, now rapidly advancing up the Platte, will cross in the neighborhood of Bridger's

Pass; that the Eastern Division will follow the Smoky Hill, and make directly for Denver; that a road running northward along the base of the mountains will connect the two; that this road will then be extended to Montana on one side and New Mexico on the other; and that, finally, a second central road will be pushed westward from Denver into and across the Middle Park, and so to Nevada. The business of Colorado alone, with the stimulus which a completed road would give, will keep that road fully employed. By the time the last rail is spiked down on the road connecting New York and San Francisco, we shall want, not one line across the continent, but *five*.

I hazard nothing, at least, in predicting that Colorado will soon be recognized as our Switzerland. The enervated luxury, the ignorant and imitative wealth, and the overtasked business of our cities will come hither, in all future summers, for health and rest, and recreation. Where Kit Carson chased Arapahos, and Fremont's men ate mule-meat, and Jim Beckworth went through apocryphal adventures, there will be drawling dandies, maidens both fast and slow, ungrammatical mammas, and the heaviest of fathers. The better sort of people will come first, nor be scared away afterward by the rush of the unappreciating. We shall, I hope, have Alpine clubs, intelligent guides, good roads, bridges, and access to a thousand wonders yet unknown. It will be a national blessing when this region is opened to general travel. That time is not now distant. Before the close of 1868, Denver will only be four days from New York, and you can go through with one change of cars. Therefore, I am doubly glad that I have come *now*, while there are still buffaloes and danger of Indians on the Plains, campfires to build in the mountains, rivers to swim, and landscapes to enjoy which have never yet been described.

The weather continues intensely hot by day, with cool and perfect nights. Sometimes the edge of the regular afternoon thunderstorm overlaps Denver and lays the hot dust of the streets. These storms are superb aerial pictures. After they pass, their cloudy ruins become the material out of which the setting sun constructs unimaginable splendors. If I were to give the details of them it would seem like color run mad. Such cool rose-gray, such transparent gold, such purple velvet as are worn by the mountains and clouds, are fresh wonders to me every evening. The vault of heaven seems ampler than elsewhere; the lines of cloud cover vaster distances, probably because a hundred miles of mountains give you a more palpable measure of their extent, and your eye recognizes infinite shades, gradations, and transitions either unseen before or unnoticed. This amplification of the sky and sky-effects struck me when I first entered upon the Plains. It is grand, even there; but here, with such accessories, it is truly sublime.

I do not wonder at the attachment of the inhabitants of the territory for their home. These mountains and this atmosphere insensibly become a portion of their lives. I foresee that they will henceforth be among the clearest and most vivid episodes of mine.

The Rocky Mountain West in 1867

Louis L. Simonin

TRAVEL BY TRAIN IS TOO SWIFT when one is crossing picturesque country; then the tourists curses the speed and would willingly prefer the old stagecoach, voyaging comfortably, watching the landscape unroll little by little. But on the prairie, since the landscape is monotonous and always horizontal, train travel is more appropriate. From North Platte to Julesburg, all the natural grasses, families, species, pass in a few hours before one's eyes; also the fragrant plants of the desert, artemisia, the everlasting flower, and certain dwarf cacti. Trees are scarce, and rarely does one encounter along the streams certain poplars, one species of which, the Canadian poplar (*populus monilifera*), here bears the name of cottonwood, doubtless because the leaves are covered underneath with a white cottony fuzz. The cottonwood is especially dear to the plains hunter and gladly sighted, since, like the palm of the African oasis, it is the tree which announces the presence of water.

Clumps of the river birch mingle with the cottonwood along the streams, a wood valued by those crossing the prairie by wagon train for starting the campfires at night.

The fauna of the great American desert is no more varied than the flora. Everywhere are the buffalo, or bison, enormous bulls with great heads and thick pelt. The Indian hunts the buffalo for food and for hides to tan. The hide, or "robe," serves as a coat or covering for the Redskin, and forms the principal object of commerce with the whites. The tanned hide is used to cover his tent; the flesh, cut out into narrow strips like straps and dried in the sun, lasts indefinitely. The smoked tongue, a delicate morsel, is the only part which the whites willingly eat.

The Indians make spoons and powder horns from the horns of the buffalo; from the bones they make scratching knives, scrapers, to scrape the hides which they tan with the brains of the animal; from the tendons of the muscles they make thread and a lining for their bows, and with the gelatine from the hooves a glue to hold the points of their arrows. The Indian thus finds everything in the buffalo, beginning with his chief diversion, hunting. So he follows it in all his migrations; and there is a saying on the prairies: Where the buffalo is, there is the Indian. The Redskin adds further that a tradition runs through all the tribes, namely, that there will be no more Indians when the day arrives that there are no more buffalo. As in so many other places, primitive man will disappear with the primitive animal. For this reason, the Redskin is so hostile to civilization, which, invading

American bison grazing on the great plains, 1906.

the prairies, disperses the buffalo in all directions and little by little brings about his own disappearance.

Along with the buffalo as the principal animals of the great plains are the beaver, which build their clever dams along the streams, and the prairie dogs, not too unlike the marmot, the cony, and the squirrel, which live in a republic of underground villages covering immense areas. We must add the prairie wolf, or coyote, an ever-hungry meat eater, and the graceful antelope, herds of which go by as swiftly as the wind. The antelope lives, like the buffalo, on the grasses of the desert; turf is nowhere lacking, and the prairie has rightly been named the terrestrial paradise of animals.

As one approaches the mountains, the fauna changes, or rather increases, into new species. There the deer, elk, hart, bear, and wildcat give the resolute hunter something to exercise his skill on.

This digression on the zoology and botany of the Great West has taken me away from Julesburg. I return. This improvised city is at the moment the last railroad station of the Pacific—a title which it will very soon yield to Cheyenne—140 miles to the west and soon to be reached. The iron path advances swiftly here. Originally the land belonged to no one, then nature took care to level it off and give it a gentle ascent, better than the most skilled of engineers could have done. Thus, the grade is gradually prepared from the Missouri to the Rocky Mountains, and up to several kilometers of railroad can be laid daily. Everybody moves west with the railroad; the very inhabitants of Julesburg will little by little abandon that city for Cheyenne.

Only recently it was the railroad which advanced where there were no cities; now the cities precede the iron path, establishing themselves in the midst of the desert and saying to the railroad, "Come to us!" The mysterious advance of the human race, since earliest times in history has always pushed westward; but has it ever been witnessed in a livelier and more striking fashion? Indeed, there is a whole new era revealed in this great labor of the United States, at the very hour when we are discussing the piercing of the Isthmus of Panama. It is the ribbon of iron in our era which will pierce isthmuses; in two years, the iron path of the Pacific will carry those who wish to tour the world in three months. Asia will come to visit Europe, and Europe, Asia by this great commercial route, by way of what has so well been called the center of gravity of the United States.

From Paris one will visit Japan or China in 30 or 40 days by the shortest route, straying very little from the great circle of the terrestrial globe. Two steamboat lines and one railroad, and the thing is done. Le Havre or Brest, New York, San Francisco, such will be the major stops of the journey. But while we await the completion of such a project, let us return to our own more modest one.

Julesburg, where we are, is defended by Fort Sedgwick. We have just visited the fort, where Colonel Heine has discovered several companions in arms, among them General Potter, commandant of the place. The General has had his young wife and children brought in. It takes a certain courage to exile oneself thus in the heart of the desert, but American women do not bargain over their devotion and, besides, are great travelers.

Certain Indians are camped around the fort—Sioux of the Oglala and Brule bands. One sees their conical tents rising in the midst of the prairie. Red Cloud and Red Tail have come with their men to treat with the commissioners of the Union. Peaceful today, these bands may perhaps tomorrow take up again their terrible fight of war.

A few years ago, Fort Sedgwick was surrounded by Cheyennes, Sioux, and Arapahos in league against the whites during the time of the War of Secession. The Redskins had forgotten for the time their former intestine wars and turned their efforts against the common enemy. Emigrants, pioneers, fleeing in fright, took refuge in the fort. The prairies had been set on fire all around. The Indians, to the number of several thousand, threatened to subdue the besieged by hunger. The attackers could be repulsed only by cannon and grapeshot.

But I must leave Julesburg; I hear the continental stage just arriving, the "overland mail."

We have one portion of our journey yet to make, my companions and I, a stretch of 190 miles across the great desert. We have with us an escort of six soldiers, perched on our vehicle, from where they survey the terrain. I shall write you from Denver if we arrive safe and sound, or if we are scalped en route by the Cheyennes or Arapahos, whose territory we cross, and have to buy a wig to adorn our occiput.

My Life on the Frontier

Miguel Antonio Otero

I SHALL NEVER FORGET our first trip from Kansas City to Kit Carson. Of course, we had been following the building of the railroad from the Missouri River to Wallace, Kans., but this was the first through trip we ever made from Kansas City to Kit Carson. More especially do I remember the last day before reaching Kit Carson. Very early in the morning, we sighted an immense herd of buffalo. They were only a short distance south of the railroad track; indeed, many small bunches separated from the main herd were only about 200 yards from our train, but as far as the eye could reach toward the west were buffalo. They were scarcely moving—just grazing along slowly, while many were lying down, apparently unafraid of the train. All day long, our train advanced toward the setting sun, stopping at many stations along the route for wood, water, meals, and orders, and consequently we were always in sight of that same herd of buffalo. It is hard to imagine such a thing today, but it is an absolute fact.

Owing to the great danger of Indians, who were constantly burning the old wooden trestlework bridges, our train did not travel at night, stopping over at a regular station until after breakfast the next morning. We reached Kit Carson early in the day. The large herd of buffalo was no longer in sight, for it had turned south toward the Arkansas River.

We found our new residence quite comfortable and well-located, about 200 yards west of the commission house of Otero, Sellar & Co. Frequently, very early in the morning, I have seen large herds of buffalo lethargically crossing the railroad track, grazing quietly not over 300 yards from our back fence.

During the summer of 1871, my brother Page and I devoted much of our spare time to catching prairie dogs and taming them. This we found was profitable business, for we had little or no trouble in selling them to the tourists. Some account of how we caught these elusive little animals may be of interest. Enlisting the assistance of some of our friends among the freighters, we could borrow a wagon and team, as well as a few teamsters. We would fill the wagon with empty whiskey barrels, and then would drive to the well on Big Sandy Creek, where we filled the barrels with water. Along with the barrels, we would provide ourselves with a number of gunny sacks from the store.

With this equipment, we would proceed to the prairie dog town, which was a few miles west of our home, between Kit Carson and Wild Horse. Then we would start catching the prairie dogs. We would locate a hole into which we had just seen a family of young dogs scurry. It was easy enough to distinguish the young dogs from the old ones by the way they would bark. When a young dog barked, he would leap erect and merely give one bark, whereas the old dogs would first scurry back into their holes with their families and then expose merely the top of their heads and bark continuously until we got too close.

The next thing we would do was to drive the wagon to the hole we had selected and empty about two barrels of water into it, a quantity usually sufficient to fill an ordinary hole. In the course of a minute or so, the little fellows would begin to come out, half-drowned, and then it was a simple matter to grab them by the back of the neck and store them in one of the gunny sacks. Very frequently, they were alive enough to turn and bite our hands, and I do not know of any bite more painful. My hands today show where the prairie dogs took nips more than 55 years ago.

We would carry our captives home and then proceed to tame them. After the taming process was well underway, we would allow the little animals to make homes in our backyard. We would begin the holes for them with our knives, digging to a depth of three feet and leaving it to the prairie dogs themselves to finish the job. They made nice pets, often becoming as affectionate as house dogs. At feeding hours, we would go out into the yard and call them by name, and it was great fun to see them come, all in a bunch, to be fed. In their eagerness for food, they would crawl all over us, poking their heads into our pockets; then when they had finished their meal, they would crawl into our pockets, where they would sleep for some time, never attempting to bite, even when we happened to disturb them during their nap.

On one occasion when we were out catching prairie dogs, I saw the largest herd of antelope that I remember having seen on the western plains; they were

In the 1800s taimed prairied dogs had been sold as pets to tourists visiting the west.

running very fast and it took fully half an hour for the herd to cross the railroad track. They were going south, and we judged that the herd was at least a half-mile wide—they must have numbered up into the millions. Today, there are only 21,000 antelope in the United States!

Another sport we greatly enjoyed was catching buffalo calves. Mounting our horses, we would borrow two or three wagons with good fast teams and would have these follow us as we rode ahead. Each one in the party would have several pieces of quarter-inch rope, about three feet long, which would be tied to the horn of his saddle. Of course, before making these preparations we had already located a herd of buffalo, and when we were all ready, away we would go.

If the herd happened to be on the move, we could with no difficulty ride up to it, or very close to it, before the buffalo would realize what was up, but once they perceived our presence the race would begin in dead earnest. Our horses were trained to their part in the game; we would run them against a calf and down it would go sprawling, the horse stopping dead in his tracks. Then we would jump down beside the fallen calf, which was so clumsy that it would need some time to get on its feet again, and would quickly tie its feet with one of the pieces of rope, leaving it where it fell for the wagon to pick up, while we continued the chase.

We found the sport the more zestful because we had to work rapidly. If a cow happened to recognize her calf among the victims, she might turn and make matters critical for us. We usually escaped such encounters by giving the mother a wide berth and going on after the herd, which was generally too busy to notice the loss of a single calf. If the solicitous mother lingered beside her offspring, the driver of the wagon would usually shoot her and take the meat to the freighters' camp. During one of these calf chases, it was an easy matter to fill all of the wagons with calves, and, this done, we would turn homeward.

We would place the young buffalo in the corral belonging to our father's firm, where we would feed them. Usually, we had a few antelope in the corral, which the herders would bring in with them, capturing them in the tall grass which impeded their escape. We did a good business of selling both our buffalo calves and young antelope to the tourists. We took orders from them, which we promptly filled and shipped by express; usually in the course of time more orders would follow from either our customers or their friends.

Large numbers of wild horses grazed around Kit Carson, but we did not participate actively in capturing any of them. Hunters, however, would go out after them, using a bunch of tame horses, which they would induce to mingle with the wild ones. Then the hunters would start a stampede of the hybrid herd in the direction of the town. The tame horses would naturally head for their accustomed corral and some of their wild mates would follow them into it. I remember one occasion that nearly 50 head of wild horses were caught in this way, and some were really fine animals.

Time Exposure
The Autobiography of William Henry Jackson

William Henry Jackson

WHEN WE REACHED THE TOWN of Fairplay, we found letters from Dr. Hayden and Steveson telling us that they would arrive with the supply train about three days later. Another small division of the Survey was already on hand, and with an unexpected free day before us we proceeded to use it with enthusiasm, if not to anyone's permanent advantage. Fairplay was not quite as wide open as Cheyenne in 1869. But we found what would serve. Purely as a side issue—a sort of constitutional, really—I climbed Mount Lincoln, 12 miles away, and made a few pictures. Among my best early photographs are the ones of the famous Montezuma silver mine near the top.

After Hayden came in, we all spent a week comparing notes, studying our common problems, and mapping our courses for the remaining weeks. My assignment was to cross the Sawatch Range to the Elk Mountain region between the Gunnison River and the Grand (so called until 1921, when it received the name of the great river to which it is a tributary, the Colorado) and then to wind up the season by photographing the Mountain of the Holy Cross.

On July 18, I started from Fairplay with my new instructions, a fresh batch of plates, and Dolly. Dolly was a white mule with cold eyes and a haughty manner. I selected her as a temporary mount in Fairplay after my horse became badly injured, but soon I found her the most docile as well as the most sturdy and surefooted of beasts. For the next five years, as long as I was with the Survey, Dolly was mine, and I rode her in preference to any horse.

Criss-cross and detour were the rule as we struck a northwesterly course toward Holy Cross—there were so many pictures that I *had* to take. Mount Massive—Mount Harvard—Mount Elbert, highest point in Colorado—La Plata—Snowmass—these and many more fell before my camera. But many did not, and I regretted the lost ones deeply. Today, favorable atmospheric conditions—clear sky, bright sun, still air, clouds to punctuate the background—are always desired by the photographer. In the '70s, bright weather was even more important. We had no fast emulsions to counteract the effects of overcast skies or to "stop" wind-driven foliage, and we had no filters to define clouds and horizons against the sky. If the weather was good, I could take as fine a picture as can be made today. But on bad days, much patient manipulation of the chemicals was needed to produce acceptable negatives.

The several parties were proceeding westward in the general direction of Holy Cross along more or less parallel routes. Periodical notes came to me from Dr. Hayden by messenger from beyond some distant ridge. Always, these notes included, among more specific instructions, the urgent plea: "Hurry. You are losing golden opportunities."

Early in August, all of us were together once more, on the high divide between East River and Rock Creek. And the catastrophe struck us. An evil mule named Gimlet slipped his pack and broke many of my exposed plates.

The Doctor himself was the first person to notice what had happened. Following directly behind my party, he found plates along the trail and galloped up to learn the cause. By that time Gimlet had scattered most of his load, and it was too late to do anything except right the pack and go back to pick up the pieces. Many plates were unbroken or but slightly nicked; many more, however, all 11x14s, were irreparably shattered.

I think I have never been so distressed in my life—my finest negatives lost before anyone had even seen a print. Nothing could be done to repair the damage, nothing. Dr. Hayden, who had started in to be severe, quickly realized that it was the fault of no single person; and, as always under trying circumstances, he dropped his customary nervous attitude and became the calmest man in the world. It was unfortunate, he agreed, but by no means disastrous—I could go back and retake the more important pictures. It really didn't matter at all, he assured me; there was plenty of time for all that, as well as for the other work ahead. And so I went back. What is more: Dr. Hayden was right. There was time enough for everything; the new negatives proved to be better than the old ones, and the delay brought me to the Mountain of the Holy Cross at the exact moment when every condition was close to perfection.

In the Middle Ages, there was the legend of the Holy Grail. Sixty-seven years ago in Colorado, there was the legend of a snow cross upon a mountain.

No man we talked with had ever seen the Mountain of the Holy Cross. But everyone knew that somewhere in the far reaches of the western highlands such a wonder might exist. Hadn't a certain hunter once caught a glimpse of it—only to have it vanish as he approached? Didn't a wrinkled Indian here and there narrow his eyes and slowly nod his head when questioned? Wasn't this man's grandfather, and that man's uncle, and old so-and-so's brother the first white man ever to lay eyes on the Holy Cross—many, many, many years ago? It was a beautiful legend, and they nursed it carefully. But anyone who wanted to see Holy Cross could climb Gray's Peak on a clear day and pick it up with field glasses. As one comes close to the cross, it always disappears behind Notch Mountain—and that is how the myth established itself.

After making our way over Tennessee Pass, we followed an old Indian trail right to the base of the Holy Cross. At no time en route had we been able to

William Henry Jackson, pioneer photographer, circa 1939.

distinguish the snowy cross itself, and I confess that I found myself experiencing all the thrill of the old stories. And, I think, the other 15 members of the group present felt very much the same way.

On the morning of August 23, we separated into two parties. The larger—headed by Gardner, Hayden, Professor William Dwight Whitney of Yale University, and William H. Holmes, later the distinguished head of the National Gallery—were off to climb Holy Cross, for the purpose of completing a triangulation from the summit. Coulter and Tom Cooper, one of my packers, went with me to try for some photographs from Notch Mountain across the ravine. Tom carried the cameras, Coulter the plate boxes, and I the chemicals and dark tent. Each man's load weighed about 40 pounds.

When prospecting for views, it was my custom to keep well ahead of my companions, for in that way they could often be spared the meanderings that I had to make. On this day, as usual, I pushed on ahead, and thus it was that I became the first member of the Survey to sight the cross. Near the top of the ridge, I emerged above timberline and the clouds, and suddenly, as I clambered over a vast mass of jagged rocks, I discovered the great shining cross dead before me, tilted against the mountainside.

It was worth all the labor of the past three months just to see it for a moment. But as I sat there waiting for Tom and Coulter to catch up, my instincts came to the fore, and I quickly devoured the hefty sandwich I had brought with me. No art was ever any better because the artist was hungry at his work.

By the time all three of us had arrived at the summit, the sky was too overcast for successful photography. While we waited for a break, we could hear faint voices across the gorge. We were that close to the other party.

Had we not been so engrossed in a single objective, our long wait on top would have been delightful. Below us as well as before us the clouds billowed majestically. Then when the mist was heavy in the valley, the sun came out—not enough for picture-taking, but enough to create a great circular rainbow at our feet. I have never seen another like it.

But we were too impatient to enjoy such idle pleasures. Seething inwardly, and all to no purpose, we watched the evening approach. We *must* have pictures before going down. And we *would* have pictures. Foodless, without blankets or even coats, we determined to spend the night on the peak. Leaving our equipment at the crest, we walked down to timberline and built a fire. There we rested on the stony ground until morning. Across the way, our friends had a fire of their own, and every time it flared up, we hallooed and heard their own halloos in answer.

At dawn, we were cold, stiff, hungry—and elated. The day, or at least the morning, promised to be magnificently clear and sunny. In order not to lose a single moment, I hurried wearily back to the top and set up my cameras. But I need not have rushed. The sun was still too low, even in midsummer, to have melted any snow, and without water, I could do no work.

By the time I had enough to develop and wash a few plates, the long flamelike shadows on Holy Cross were rapidly sweeping down into the valley, and, using two cameras, I had made just eight exposures when they were gone. But, with the early sun, those shadows had already helped me to take the finest pictures I have ever made of Holy Cross.

Since 1873, I have been back four or five times. I have used the best cameras and the most sensitive emulsions on the market. I have snapped my shutter morning, noon, and afternoon. And I have never come close to matching those first plates.

The Cliff Dwellers of the Mesa Verde
Southwestern Colorado
Their Pottery and Implements

Gustaf Nordenskiöld

SPRING HOUSE IS FAIRLY WELL PROTECTED from attack by its site. From the bottom of the canyon, the buildings can be reached only by a difficult and dangerous climb from ledge to ledge; and a very circuitous route, either up or down the canyon, must be taken to scale the mesa from the ruin. This cliff-dwelling does not belong to Wetherill's Mesa, it is true; but I have mentioned it in connection with the ruins of the said tract because our visits to the ruin were made with the camp at the middle of Wetherill Mesa as the starting-point.

Before concluding this chapter, I have still to mention one more cliff-dwelling of some considerable size, and situated in a small cañon that runs from Spring House canyon into Wetherill Mesa. It is rather far from the ruin to a place which offers a practicable ascent to the mesa, and the climb is attended with great difficulties. Most of the rooms in the cliff-dwelling lie between the sandstone cliff and the lower slope of the cañon. The upper part of the ruin is situated on several ledges separated by the perpendicular cliff and in part very difficult of access. The ledge visible to the left of the figure seemed, at first, sight completely inaccessible. The cliffs leant outwards, and there was no spot where any inequalities might afford a footing. But from one of the walls, two beams projected, and round one of these, Clayton Wetherill succeeded by a skillful cast in fastening his lasso. He then clambered up the slender rope to the ledge. None of the lower buildings had apparently been high enough to reach up to this ledge. The communication had presumably been kept up by means of ladders of yucca rope attached to the beams, which had probably been placed there for this very purpose, or possibly by the aid of logs set on end and lashed fast. What can have induced a people to have recourse to dwelling-places so incommodious? This is a question that has undoubtedly suggested itself many times already to the reader. The answer must be that nothing short of the ever-imminent attacks of a hostile people could have driven the cliff-dwellers to these impregnable mountain fastnesses, which afforded a safe refuge, so long as food and water held out.

The Light Shines from the West

Robert C. Baron

THERE WAS SOMETHING SPECIAL about the European Americans who went West, and they went for many reasons: hunger, financial opportunities, land ownership, personal or religious freedom, curiosity, a new start, or—in some cases—because they didn't fit in back East. They were independent, and measured each other based on who they were—not who their ancestors were. Chapters five and six are the story of the westward migration before and after the Civil War. In 1862, President Abraham Lincoln signed the Homestead Act and the Morrill Act, and those had influence on western development.

Women's roles were different in the West than they were back East. In 1900, women had the vote in four states—all of them western. By the time the 19th Amendment granting women the right to vote was passed on August 18, 1920, women had the vote in 23 states—22 of them were Midwestern and Western states. The first women to serve as a congressperson, senator, governor, and Supreme Court justice were westerners. Chapter seven introduces that history.

Since the election in 1928, of Herbert Hoover, an Iowan, to the presidency, two-thirds of American presidents have been born or raised in the West. Political ideas have come from the West, whether from the right with Hoover, Barry Goldwater, and Ronald Reagan, or the left with William Jennings Bryan, Robert La Follette, Hubert Humphrey, George McGovern, and Eugene McCarthy. In the last half-century, political leadership has shifted westward.

Although the growth of western cities since 1940 has been considerable (Utah and Nevada are now 90 percent urban), most of the land in the West remains rural. How does the rural land affect the character of the West?

Isolation and Integration

In the census of 1900, more than half of the American population lived in cities and suburbs, and that trend of increasing urban population continues today. And although it varies among states, four out of five Americans live in an urban environment.

For example, in Arkansas, 34 percent of the population lives in rural areas; in Idaho, it's 4 percent; in Iowa, 36 percent; Kansas, 25.8 percent; Minnesota, 26.7 percent; Missouri, 29.6 percent; Nebraska, 26.9 percent; North Dakota, 40.1 percent; Oklahoma, 33.8 percent; South Dakota, 43.3 percent; Wisconsin, 29.8 percent; and in Wyoming, 35.2 percent.

That is only part of the story, however. People may move, but the land doesn't. In Colorado, for example, there has been a large increase in population on the Front Range—the area bordering the east side of the Rockies between Colorado Springs and Fort Collins. Yet, of the 63 Colorado counties, 34 are called rural or predominately rural by the Census Bureau; in California, 11 of the 58 counties are rural or predominately rural; in Kansas, 85 of the 105 counties; in Nevada, 15 of the 17 counties; in Oregon, 28 of the 36 counties; and in Texas, 121 of the 254 counties are rural. Not everyone chooses to live in a city.

Who are these rural people? Some are ranchers and farmers and the businesses that support them. Some are people who want to raise their children away from the crowds and problems of the large-city schools. Some are small businesspeople who may sell their products to a worldwide market. Some are people who have retired and sold their home for a profit, preferring the neighbors and slower pace of country living.

People have always moved to cities for education and jobs as well as the cultural advantages. Yet there are benefits of living in a city while still being able to easily access rural areas for camping, hiking, biking, climbing, skiing, hunting, fishing, and the benefits of nature nearby. There is a difference between the western cities and suburbs and the rural West. Denver, Omaha, Dallas,

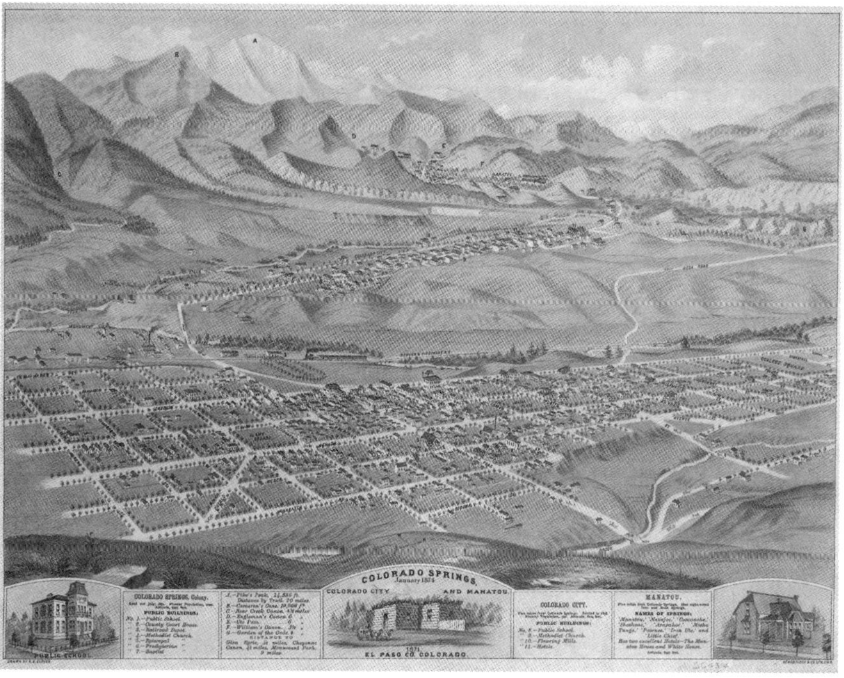

1874 map of Colorado Springs, Colorado City, and Manitou, (El Paso County, Colorado).

Boise, and other cities shared in the technological progress of the 19th and 20th centuries. Rural areas might not have. Most people in the 19th century lived on farms with a small town within riding distance on a horse or buggy. They did not get electric power until the 1940s, good interstate roads until the 1950s, access to radio and television until the 1950s to 1970s, and satellite connection to communication and computer networks until the 1980s or later. The rural West is no longer isolated.

It has been said that the story of the West is the story of water, and whoever controls water controls the region. While this is true, it is not the entire story. It ignores the importance of electric power, since neither cities nor farms can prosper without it. It ignores the importance of communication. An American, no matter where they live, can watch a baseball game or a college basketball team, can read the latest book or see the newest movie, and can even attend a concert by their favorite entertainer or watch an opera broadcast from New York, thanks to modern communications systems.

There was a difference between the pre- and post-Civil War West. There was an even greater change between the pre- and post-World War II West. The following quote by Charles Colton was true when it was written in the 19th century. It is no longer true:

> "If you would be known, and not know, vegetate in a village;
> if you would know, and not be known, live in a city."

Today, rural isolation is no longer always the case. That is why some people who retire are selling their expensive city homes and moving to the country for a better quality of life; they can still visit the city for shopping, cultural events, and medical services. Examples include southern Missouri and Arkansas (the nearest major medical center is Springfield), the mountains of Colorado (the nearest medical center is Denver), or much of rural Utah (the nearest population center is Salt Lake City). Most of the time, however, one is healthy and wants to enjoy the 20 or so years one may have ahead.

SECTION III

Shining Mountains

When It's Springtime in the Rockies

Mary Hale Woolsey

The twilight shadows deepen into night, dear;
The city lights are gleaming o'er the snow;
I sit alone beside the cheery fire, dear;
I'm dreaming dreams from out the long ago.
I fancy it is springtime in the mountains;
The flowers with their colors are aflame;
And ev'ry day I hear you softly saying:
"I'll wait until the springtime comes again."

CHORUS
When it's Springtime in the Rockies,
I am coming back to you,
Little sweetheart of the mountains,
With your bonny eyes of blue;
Once again I'll say "I love you,"
While the birds sing all the day,
When it's Springtime in the Rockies,
In the Rockies, far away.

I've kept your image guarded in my heart, dear;
I've kept my love, for you, as pure as dew;
I'm longing for the time when I shall come, dear;
Back to that dear, old Western home and you.
I fancy it is springtime in the mountains;
The maple leaves, in first sky-green appear;
I hear you softly say, my Queen of May-time:
"This spring-time you have come to meet me here."

The Spell of the Rockies

Enos A. Mills

EARLY ONE SUMMER, while exploring a wide alpine moorland above the timberline, I—and some others—had an experience with one of those sudden stormbursts. The region was utterly wild, but up to it straggling tourists occasionally rode for a view of the surrounding mountain world. All alone, I was studying the ways of the wild inhabitants of the heights. I had spent the calm, sunny morning in watching a solitary bighorn that was feeding among some boulders. He was aged, and he ate as though his teeth were poor and walked as though afflicted with rheumatism. Suddenly, this patriarch forgot his age and fled precipitately with almost the speed of frightened youth. I leaped upon a boulder

Enos Mills, the father of Rocky Mountain National Park, stands in the doorway of his cabin. He built this cabin, located on Longs Peak, while in his teens.

to watch him but was instantly knocked headlong by a wild blast of wind. In falling, I caught sight of a straw hat and a wrecked umbrella falling out of the sky. Rising amid the pelting gale of flung hail, ice water, and snow, I pushed my way in the teeth of the storm, hoping for shelter in the lee of a rock-pile about a hundred yards distant. A lady's disheveled hat blew by me, and with the howl of the wind came almost- drowned, excited human utterances. Nearing the rock-pile, I caught a vague view of a merry-go-round of man and horse, then a glimpse of the last gyration, in which an elderly Eastern gentleman parted company with a stampeded bronco.

Five tourists had ridden up in the sunshine to enjoy the heights, and the suddenness and fierceness of the storm had thrown them into a panic and stampeded their horses. They were drenched and severely chilled, and they were frightened. I made haste to tell them that the storm would be brief. While I was still trying to reassure them, the clouds commenced to dissolve and the sun came out. Presently all were watching the majestic soaring of two eagles up in the blue, while I went off to collect five scattered saddle-ponies that were contentedly feeding far away on the moor.

Though the winter winds are of slower development, they are more prolonged and are tempestuously powerful. Occasionally these winds blow for days; and where they follow a fall of snow, they blow and whirl this about so wildly that the air is befogged for several hundred feet above the earth. So violently and thickly is the powdered snow flung about that a few minutes at a time is the longest that one can see or breathe in it. These high winter winds come out of the west in a deep, broad stratum that is far above most of the surface over which they blow. Commonly, a high wind strikes the western slope of the Continental Divide a little below the altitude of 11,000 feet. This striking throws it into fierce confusion. It rolls whirling up the steeps and frequently shoots far above the highest peaks. Across the passes it sweeps, roars down the canyons on the eastern slope and rushes out across the plains. Though the western slope below 11,000 feet is a calm zone, the entire eastern slope is being whipped and scourged by a flood of wind. Occasionally, the temperature of these winds is warm.

These swift, insistent winds, torn, intercepted, and deflected by dashing against the broken skyline, produce currents, counter-currents, sleepy eddies, violent vertical whirls, and milling maelstroms that are tilted at every angle. In places, there is a gale blowing upward; and here and there, the air pours heavily down in an invisible but almost crushing airfall.

A Lady's Life in the Rocky Mountains

Isabella L. Bird

Estes Park, Colorado, October

* * *

I HAVE NO HEAD and no ankles, and never ought to dream of mountaineering; and had I known that the ascent was a real mountaineering feat, I should not have felt the slightest ambition to perform it. As it is, I am only humiliated by my success, for Jim dragged me up, like a bale of goods, by sheer force of muscle. At the Notch, the real business of the ascent began. Two-thousand feet of solid rock towered above us; 4,000 feet of broken rock shelved precipitously below; smooth granite ribs, with barely foothold, stood out here and there; melted snow refrozen several times presented a more serious obstacle; many of the rocks were loose and tumbled down when touched. To me, it was a time of extreme terror. I was roped to Jim, but it was of no use; my feet were paralyzed and slipped on the bare rock, and he said it was useless to try to go that way, and we retraced our steps. I wanted to return to the Notch, knowing that my incompetence would detain the party, and one of the young men said almost plainly that a woman was a dangerous encumbrance, but the trapper replied shortly that if it were not to take a lady up he would not go up at all. He went on to explore and reported that further progress on the correct line of ascent was blocked by ice; and then, for two hours, we descended, lowering ourselves by our hands from rock to rock along a boulder-strewn sweep of 4,000 feet, patched with ice and snow, and perilous from rolling stones. My fatigue, giddiness, and pain from bruised ankles, and arms half pulled out of their sockets, were so great that I should never have gone halfway,

Isabella L. Bird

had not Jim, *nolens volens*, dragged me along with a patience and skill and withal a determination that I should ascend the peak, which never failed. After descending about 2,000 feet to avoid the ice, we got into a deep ravine with inaccessible sides partly filled with ice and snow and partly with large and small fragments of rock which were constantly giving way, rendering the footing very insecure. That part to me was two hours of painful and unwilling submission to the inevitable—of trembling, slipping, straining, of smooth ice appearing when it was least expected and of weak entreaties to be left behind while the others went on. Jim always said that there was no danger, that there was only a short bad bit ahead, and that I should go up even if he carried me!

Slipping, faltering, gasping from the exhausting toil in the rarefied air, with throbbing hearts and panting lungs, we reached the top of the gorge and squeezed ourselves between two gigantic fragments of rock by a passage called the Dog's Lift, when I climbed on the shoulders of one man and then was hauled up. This introduced us by an abrupt turn round the southwest angle of the peak to a narrow shelf of considerable length, rugged, uneven, and so overhung by the cliff in some places that it is necessary to crouch to pass at all. Above, the peak looks nearly vertical for 400 feet; and below, the most tremendous precipice I have ever seen descends in one unbroken fall. This is usually considered the most dangerous part of the ascent, but it does not seem so to me, for such foothold as there is secure, and one fancies that it is possible to hold on with the hands. But there, and on the final, and, to my thinking, the worst part of the climb, one slip, and a breathing, thinking, human being would lie 3,000 feet below, a shapeless, bloody heap. Ring refused to traverse the Ledge, and remained at the Lift howling piteously.

From thence the view is more magnificent even than that from the Notch. At the foot of the precipice below us lay a lovely lake, wood embosomed, from or near which the bright St. Vrain and other streams take their rise. I thought how their clear cold waters, growing turbid in the affluent flats, would heat under the tropic sun and eventually form part of that great ocean river which renders our far-off islands habitable by impinging on their shores. Snowy ranges, one behind the other, extended to the distant horizon, folding in their wintry embrace the beauties of Middle Park. Pike's Peak, more than 100 miles off, lifted that vast but shapeless summit which is the landmark of southern Colorado. There were snow patches, snow slashes, snow abysses, snow forlorn and soiled-looking, snow pure and dazzling, snow glistening above the purple robe of pine worn by all the mountains; while away to the east, in limitless breadth, stretched the green-gray of the endless plains. Giants everywhere reared their splintered crests. From thence, with a single sweep, the eye takes in a distance of 300 miles—that distance to the west, north, and south being made up of mountains 10, 11, 12, and 13,000 feet in height, dominated by Long's

Peak, Gray's Peak, and Pike's Peak, all nearly the height of Mont Blanc! On the plains, we traced the rivers by their fringe of cottonwoods to the distant Platte, and between us and them lay glories of mountain, canyon, and lake, sleeping in depths of blue and purple most ravishing to the eye.

As we crept from the ledge round a horn of rock I beheld what made me perfectly dizzy to look at—the terminal peak itself—a smooth, cracked face or wall of pink granite, as nearly perpendicular as anything could well be up which it was impossible to climb, well deserving the name of the "American Matterhorn."

Scaling, not climbing, is the correct term for this last ascent. It took one hour to accomplish 500 feet, pausing for breath every minute or two. The only foothold was in narrow cracks or on minute projections on the granite. To get a toe in these cracks, or here and there on a scarcely obvious projection, while crawling on hands and knees, all the while tortured with thirst and gasping and struggling for breath, this was the climb; but at last, the Peak was won. A grand, well-defined mountain it is, a nearly level acre of boulders, with precipitous sides all round, the one we came up being the only accessible one.

It was not possible to remain long. One of the young men was seriously alarmed by bleeding from the lungs, and the intense dryness of the day and the rarefaction of the air, at a height of nearly 15,000 feet, made respiration very painful. There is always water on the peak, but it was frozen as hard as a rock, and the sucking of ice and snow increases thirst. We all suffered severely from the want of water, and the gasping for breath made our mouths and tongues so dry that articulation was difficult and the speech of all unnatural.

From the summit, were seen in unrivalled combination all the views which had rejoiced our eyes during the ascent. It was something at last to stand upon the storm-rent crown of this lonely sentinel of the Rocky Range, on one of the mightiest of the vertebrae of the backbone of the North American continent, and to see the waters start for both oceans. Uplifted above love and hate and storms of passion, calm amidst the eternal silences, fanned by zephyrs and bathed in living blue, peace rested for that one bright day on the peak, as if it were some region.

Where falls not rain, or hail, or any snow,
Or ever wind blows loudly.

Estes Park, December 7

Yesterday morning, the mercury had disappeared, so it was 20 degrees below zero at least. I lay awake from cold all night, but such is the wonderful effect of the climate, that when I got up at half-past five to waken the household for my early start, I felt quite refreshed. We breakfasted on buffalo beef, and I left at eight to ride 45 miles before night, Dr. Hughes and a gentleman who was staying there convoying me the first 15 miles. I did like that ride, racing with the other riders, careering through the intoxicating air in that indescribable sunshine, the powdery snow spurned from the horses' feet like dust! I was soon warm. We stopped at a trapper's ranch to feed, and the old trapper amused me by seeming to think Estes Park almost inaccessible in winter. The distance was greater than I had been told, and he said that I could not get there before eleven at night and not at all if there was much drift. I wanted the gentlemen to go on with me as far as the Devil's Gate, but they could not because their horses were tired; and when the trapper heard that he exclaimed, indignantly, "What! That woman going into the mountains alone? She'll lose the track or be froze to death!" But when I told him I had ridden the trail in the storm of Tuesday, and had ridden over 600 miles alone in the mountains, he treated me with great respect as a fellow mountaineer and gave me some matches saying, "You'll have to camp out anyhow; you'd better make a fire than be frozen to death." The idea of spending the night in the forest alone, by a fire, struck me as most grotesque.

We did not start again till one, and the two gentlemen rode the first two miles with me. On that track, the Little Thompson, there a full stream, has to be crossed 18 times, and they had been hauling wood across it, breaking it, and it had broken and refrozen several times, making thick and thin places—indeed, there were crossings which even I thought bad, where the ice let us through, and it was hard for the horses to struggle upon it again; and one of the gentlemen who, though a most accomplished man, was not a horseman, was once or twice in the ludicrous position of hesitating on the bank with an anxious face, not daring to spur his horse upon the ice. After they left me, I had eight more crossings and then a ride of six miles before I reached the old trail; but though there were several drifts up to the saddle, and no one had broken a track, Birdie showed such pluck, that instead of spending the night by a camp-fire, or not getting in till midnight, I reached Mr. Nugent's cabin, four miles from Estes Park, only an hour after dark, very cold, and with the pony so tired that she could hardly put one foot before another. Indeed, I walked the last three miles.

Specimen Days in America

Walt Whitman

An Hour On Kenosha Summit

JOTTINGS FROM THE ROCKY MOUNTAINS, mostly pencill'd during a day's trip over the South Park RR. returning from Leadville, and especially the hour we were detain'd, (much to my satisfaction,) at Kenosha summit. As afternoon advances, novelties, far-reaching splendors, accumulate under the bright sun in this pure air. But I had better commence with the day.

The confronting of Platte canyon just at dawn, after a 10 miles' ride in early darkness on the rail from Denver—the seasonable stoppage at the entrance of the canyon, and good breakfast of eggs, trout, and nice griddle-cakes—then as we travel and get well in the gorge, all the wonders, beauty, savage power of the scene—wild stream of water, from sources of snows, brawling continually in sight under the dazzling sun, and the morning lights on the rocks—such turns and grades of the track, squirming around corners, or up and down hills—far glimpses of a hundred peaks, titanic necklaces, stretching north and south—the huge rightly named Dome rock—and as we dash along, others similar, simple, monolithic, elephantine.

An Egotistical "Find"

"I have found the law of my own poems," was the unspoken but more-and-more decided feeling that came to me as I pass'd, hour after hour, amid all this grim

A view from Kenosha Pass. Photo by Leander Sylvester Keyser, 1902.

joyous elemental abandon—this plenitude of material, entire absence of art, untrammel'd play of primitive Nature—the chasm, the gorge, the crystal mountain stream, repeated scores, hundreds of miles—the broad handling and absolute uncrampedness—the fantastic forms, bathed in transparent browns, faint reds and grays, towering sometimes a thousand, sometimes two or three thousand feet high—at their tops now and then huge masses pois'd, and mixing with the clouds, with only their outlines, hazed in misty lilac, visible. ("In Nature's grandest shows," says an old Dutch writer, an ecclesiastic, "amid the ocean's depth, if so might be, countless worlds rolling above at night, a man thinks of them, weighs all, not for themselves or the abstract, but with reference to his own personality, and how they may affect him or color his destinies.")

New Senses—New Joys

We follow the stream of amber and bronze brawling along its bed, with its frequent cascades and snow-white foam. Through the canyon we fly—mountains not only each side, but seemingly, till we get near, right in front of us—every rood new view flashing, and each flash defying description—on the almost perpendicular sides clinging pines, cedars, spruces, crimson sumach bushes, spots of wild grass—but dominating all, those towering rocks, rocks, rocks, bathed in delicate tint-colors, with the clear sky of autumn overhead. New senses, new joys, seem develop'd. Talk as you like, a typical Rocky Mountain canyon, or a limitless sea-like stretch of the great Kansas or Colorado plains, under favoring circumstances, tallies, perhaps expresses, certainly awakes, those grandest and subtlest element emotions of the human soul, that all the marble temples and sculptures from Phidias to Thorwaldsen—all paintings, poems, reminiscences, or even music, probably never.

Steam-Power, Telegraphs, &C.

I get out on a 10 minutes' stoppage at Deer Creek, to enjoy the unequal'd combination of hill, stone and wood. As we speed again, the yellow granite in the sunshine, with natural spires, minarets, castellated perches far aloft—then long stretches of straight-upright palisades, rhinoceros color—then gamboge and tinted chromos. Ever the best of my pleasures the cool-fresh Colorado atmosphere, yet sufficiently warm. Signs of man's restless advent and pioneerage, hard as Nature's face is—deserted dug-outs by dozens in the side-hills—the scantling hut, the telegraph-pole, the smoke of some impromptu chimney or outdoor fire—at intervals little settlements of log-houses, or parties of surveyors or telegraph builders, with their comfortable tents. Once, a canvas office where you could send a message by electricity anywhere around the world! Yes, pronounc'd signs of the man of latest dates, dauntlessly grappling with these grisliest shows of the old kosmos. At several places steam sawmills, with their piles of logs and boards, and the pipes puffing. Occasionally Platte canyon expanding into a grassy flat of a few acres. At one such place, toward the end, where we stop, and I get out to stretch my legs, as I look skyward, or rather mountain-topward, a huge hawk or eagle (a rare sight here) is idly soaring, balancing along the ether, now sinking low and coming quite near, and then up again in stately languid circles—then higher, higher, slanting to the north, and gradually out of sight.

America's Back-bone

I jot these lines literally at Kenosha summit, where we return, afternoon, and take a long rest, 10,000 feet above sea-level. At this immense height, the South Park stretches 50 miles before me. Mountainous chains and peaks in every variety of perspective, every hue of vista, fringe the view, in nearer, or middle, or far-dim distance, or fade on the horizon. We have now reach'd, penetrated the Rockies, (Hayden calls it the Front Range,) for 100 miles or so; and though these chains spread away in every direction, specially north and south, thousands and thousands farther, I have seen specimens of the utmost of them, and know henceforth at least what they are, and what they look like. Not themselves alone, for they typify stretches and areas of half the globe—are, in fact, the vertebrae or backbone of our hemisphere. As the anatomists say a man is only a spine, topp'd, footed, breasted and radiated, so the whole Western world is, in a sense, but an expansion of these mountains. In South America they are the Andes, in Central America and Mexico the Cordilleras, and in our States they go under different names—in California the Coast and Cascade ranges—thence more eastwardly the Sierra Nevadas—but mainly and more centrally here the Rocky Mountains proper, with many, an elevation such as Lincoln's, Grey's, Harvard's, Yale's, Longs, and Pike's peaks all, over 14,000 feet high. (East, the highest peaks of the Alleghanies, the Adirondacks, the Catskills, and the White Mountains, range from 2,000 to 5,500 feet—only Mount Washington, in the latter, 6,300 feet.)

The Parks

In the midst of all here, lie such beautiful contrasts as the sunken basins of the North, Middle, and South Parks, (the latter I am now on one side of, and overlooking,) each the size of a large, level, almost quadrangular, grassy, western "county," wall'd in by walls of hills, and each park the source of a river. The ones I specify are the largest in Colorado, but the whole of that State, and of Wyoming, Utah, Nevada and western California, through their sierras and ravines, are copiously mark'd by similar spreads and openings, many of the small ones of paradisiac loveliness and perfection, with their offsets of mountains, streams, atmosphere and hues beyond compare.

One Man's West

David Lavender

LONG AGO DAVID SANG, "I will lift up mine eyes unto the hills."

Their majesty is inescapable, yet very few alpine dwellers ever climb. Mountaineering in many of its aspects entails a devilish amount of work, and those who wring livelihood from the high country already have enough of that.

To be sure, a valley rancher after 40 years in the shadow of some crag may at last want to see what his domicile looks like from above. He inveigles his neighbors into a picnic; they slog up the easiest side of the peak, point out their fence lines to each other, and slog back down. Prospectors occasionally make an ascent while looking for outcroppings, and now and then a sheepherder will assuage boredom by heaping a mound of rocks on top of some pinnacle to show he has been there.

None of these ventures is mountaineering, however. None is undertaken with the idea that spiritual values or even plain fun might lie in them. This viewpoint is reserved for certain city dwellers who physically are by no means as well fitted for it as their country cousins. Nonetheless, climbers during the past half century or so have become an integral part of the mountain scene. Oblivious to the stares of the natives, they clump in growing numbers through the streets of the decaying mining towns, sounding like horses in their hobnail boots. Thousands of them have banded together in clubs which publish bulletins, conduct outings, and lobby vigorously in the legislatures for pet conservation bills. During any week of the summer and many weeks of the winter you are apt to find in some remote, hard-to-reach vale groups of from two to 60 ragged, sunburned people enjoying a side of the mountains that the early pioneers seldom saw. Today they are as real to the high country as the miners or sheepherders, and some of my happiest times were spent in the company of these strangers who my compatriots at the Camp Bird and elsewhere sincerely believed were a little "tetched."

My brother, Dwight, was first infected with the virus, for the mountains had always been a passion with him. We had been born in the mining town of Telluride, Colorado, where the canyon of the San Miguel heads in a U-shaped basin half a mile deep. The boys of the village scrambled about the bases of the bright-colored cliffs as boys elsewhere climb trees and barns. It was an aimless zeal, however, and the idea of focusing it on a peak top never occurred to us until we had theoretically reached the age of better judgment. And then Dwight met some members of the Colorado Mountain Club.

When it developed that the club was planning a weekend assault on Mount Wilson, near Telluride, there was no restraining him. The great day arrived; we threw a pack on an old horse—we were living on the ranch then—and made a two-day ride across the hills to town.

I shall never forget the look on the hotelkeeper's face when we entered the lobby and it dawned on him that we were there to join the mountaineers. He was an odd little man, very frail and very neat, with the thin, high-domed face of an aesthete. His soft eyes peering blandly through thick spectacles made him look as though he should have been on the lecture platform of some university rather than behind the counter of a moribund hostelry. But behind it he had been since the glamour days of gold, when Telluride boasted 26 saloons and no church; a quarter was the smallest coin in circulation and the conductor on the little narrow-gauge railway announced the town by bawling "To Hell You Ride." In those days champagne and caviar and terrapin had been staple items on the hotel menu; officers' wives and mineowners' mistresses had come to its parties in Parisian gowns. Sudden death, sudden fortune, sudden poverty—all this the proprietor had seen and shared. Yet, he looked at Dwight and me as though he could not believe it.

"Are you going with this outfit?" he said, glancing at the climbers. We hung our heads and mumbled an admission. It was a painful moment.

As I recall it, 19 people showed up for the trip, 12 men and seven women. Now, Telluride was not as populous as it had been. The last of the great mines, the Smuggler-Union, had closed down a few years before. However, the town still remained the county seat; here and there a fresh green lawn showed that some stubborn settler was hanging on. A few fat-bellied, rusty-faced politicians wandered through the red sandstone courthouse; mountain ranchers occasionally stopped by to trade, and bewhiskered placer miners still hopefully poked about the dumps. But for the most part the stores were boarded up, and broken windows gaped in the abandoned houses. The arrival of 19 people in a body could not escape note.

The astonished city fathers did their best. They gave us a banquet. A good one, too, with the ghosts of the hotel's old chefs rising nobly to the occasion. Instead of receiving the pieces of high-grade ore that in former days had been passed out to distinguished guests, we were treated to abundant samples of the town's last going industry—brewing. There were speeches. The beauties of the landscape were rhapsodically extolled by men whose axes and dredges and dynamite had done their best to destroy that beauty. The old phrase "Switzerland of America"—every mountain sector of the West calls itself that—was trotted out and dusted off by half-a-dozen willing throats.

Warmed by their own voices and their own beer, the hosts began having a wonderful time. Then, just as the party was taking on a faint blush of former celebrations, the climbers all stood up and went to bed. They were leaving for the assault at four o'clock the next morning and they wanted to leave fresh. Incomprehensibility worse confounded! If the dismayed city fathers needed further evidence of idiocy, here it was.

Four o'clock the next morning was cheerless. Dawn had not yet come, and no stars were visible in the sodden sky. However, weather is one of the accepted hazards of climbing. We piled into cars and away we went along the narrow, breathtaking dirt road that skirts the vast upper gorges of the San Miguel. Eventually, after passing through the huddle of huts which is Ophir and skidding wildly along the greasy branch road that leads to Dunton, we reached a high, alpine vale known as the Dunton Meadows. Here, we left the cars and set out afoot. It was daylight now, but Mount Wilson was not to be seen. Clouds lay on the treetops.

* * *

Our leaders ran the gamut on that Wilson climb. Trail-finding was the worst. At lower elevations, we encountered mazes of timber falls and impenetrable thickets of underbrush. We struggled through what seemed miles of scree and talus, steep slopes of shattered slide rock that have fallen from the cliffs and roll backward under you with every step you take. Rain drenched us; and as we climbed higher, we were presented with the odd spectacle of snow going straight up instead of down.

This phenomenon was occasioned by the wind whipping through the basin below. When it met the towering ridge along whose knife-edged summit we were worming our way it was deflected upward with its burden of sleet. The effect, as we crouched there in our lonely miasma of mist, was indescribably weird. It was also cold. I had no gloves, but for some reason I had slipped an extra pair of woolen socks in my pocket. I put these on my hands. The luxury was wonderful—until I noticed, though I tried hard not to, that one of the ladies of the party was also gloveless. I surrendered my socks. Never have I enjoyed so rich a feeling of chivalry or suffered so from frigid fingers.

* * *

When we finally staggered onto the fog-shrouded summit, it was 6:00 P.M. We had no desire to wolf out the night on the mountaintop, yet we knew that fatalities might well repay any attempt by 19 tired people to descend in pitch-darkness the exposed cliffs we had climbed. Brows knit, the board of strategy went into a huddle. It was decided to select a much longer but safer route to the sheltering timber some 3,000 feet below. Westward, long snow slopes dropped into a basin—Killpacker Basin, some disgusted packer had named it long ago. After reaching its bottom, rounding its southern arm, and then doubling back through the spruce forests, we could, we hoped, regain our cars without breaking our necks.

With 19 ice axes and the ability to use them, the descent of the snow fields could have been accomplished in minutes by a glissade. This is simply skiing without skis. You slide on your feet, crouching with the hip-high, T-headed, steel-pointed axe braced behind you, serving as both rudder and brake. There is nothing more exhilarating; on a 1,000-foot run, you can build up tremendous speed. Like skiing, the glissade is best done with swishing zigzags and swoops and as few cartwheels as possible. Just make sure there are no crevasses in the way.

On this Wilson trip, however, we had only two or three ice axes, which the leaders used for hacking out steps on icy pitches. So we had to creep downward like snails with the freezing night crowding hard on our heels. Suddenly, one of the men flopped in the snow and refused to budge another inch. Nervously, we cajoled him and in desperation even shook him up a bit. In the end, we had to take him by the arms and drag him down the hill. He became violently ill, retching pitifully.

That was a thing which might have happened to any of us. Mountain sickness is no respecter of apparent physical condition. In extreme form it affects the brain, fatally undermining the powers of judgment and has played a tragic part in some of the Himalayan fatalities of recent years. At the lower elevations of American mountains, the results are not so fantastic. Here, headaches, listlessness, nausea, vomiting, cold hands, and cold feet are the main symptoms.

The trouble is apparently caused by insufficient oxygen in the bloodstream. Doctors rising from sea level to 14,000 feet sometimes faint without artificial oxygen and compensation for pressure changes. A climber ascending on foot affords his body more time to adjust itself. Even so, before he rushes his peak he should spend a day or two conditioning himself in a high-altitude camp. He should also take salt. A short teaspoonful the night before an ascent and another at the start will help keep him healthy, for it seems that mountain sickness, like heat prostration, can be aggravated by loss of essential body salts through perspiration.

When we at last reached timber line on Mount Wilson we tried to bivouac, but the ground was a sea of mud, and the smoky, stuttering fire we managed to kindle was inadequate to cope with the mass miseries of nineteen exhausted souls. In despair we blundered on, clambering endlessly through deadfall and underbrush, falling into ravines, tripping on roots, wallowing knee deep in mountain bogs. Toward dawn we located the cars, returned to Telluride, and collapsed into bed. My first organized climb was over.

The next evening, I came down to the hotel lobby, ravenous and creaking in every joint. The proprietor asked, with some maliciousness, I thought, "Well, did you like it?"

I considered. Fortunately, God gave man a poor memory for physical discomfort. The active ingredients which made the hurt so brutal at the moment lose their keen edge in retrospect; we are able to look back on them with certain detachment and even make them subject matter of our dearest conversation pieces. Pleasure is different. Memory fondles it. It becomes a nostalgia, poignant and real and difficult to put into words. And, so, I remembered Mount Wilson. Not the cold and the cruel fatigue but rather the multitude of tiny things which in their sum make up the elemental poetry of rock and ice and snow. The feel of granite under your fingers; the obedient flex of your muscles swinging you upward to the stance you must reach or fail; the taste of a cigarette when you hunker for a moment under a shelving rock. A flash of sunlight; a laugh; an incongruous patch of dwarf flowers at the base of an icy boulder.

"Yes," I said, "I liked it."

Wolf Creek Pass

C.W. McCall

Me and Earl was hauling chickens on the Flatbed out of Wiggins
When we spent all night on the uphill side
of 37 miles of hell called Wolf Creek Pass
Which is up on the Great Divide.

We were sitting there sucking toothpicks and drinking Nehis and
onion soup mix
And I said "Earl, let's mail a card to mother and then send them
chickens on down the other side."
Yeah, let's give 'em a ride.

Wolf Creek Pass way up on the Great Divide
Comin' on down the other side.

Well, Earl put down his bottle,
Mashed his foot down on the throttle,
And then a couple of boobs with a thousand cubes in the 1948 Peterbilt
screamed alive.
We woke up the chickens.
We roared up offa' that shoulder, spraying pine cones, rocks and boulders
And put 400 head of them Rhode Island Reds and a couple of burnt out
roosters on the line.
Look out below, 'cuz here we go

Wolf Creek Pass way up on the Great Divide
Swingin' on down the other side.

Well, we commenced the truckin',
And them hens commenced a cluckin',
Then Earl took out a match and scratched his pants
And lit up the unused half of a dollar cigar.
Took a puff, said, "My, ain't this pretty up here."
I said "Earl, this hill can spill us.
"You'd better slow down or you're going to kill us.
"Just make one mistake and it's the pearly gates for them 85 crates of
USDA
approved cluckers.
"You wanna hit second?"

Wolf Creek Pass way up on the Great Divide
Truckin' on down the other side.

Well, Earl grabbed on the shifter,
And he stabbed her into fifth gear
And then the chromium plated folie aluminated genuine accessory
shiftknob
Come right off in his hand.
I said, "You wanna put that thing back on, Earl."
He was trying to thread it on there when the fire feel of his cigar
And dropped on down and sorta rolled around
And then lit on the cuff of Earl's pants and burned a hole in his socks.
Yessir set 'em right on fire
I looked on outta the window and I started counting phone poles
Going by at the rate of 4 to the 7th power.
Well, I put 2 and 2 together and added 12 and carried 5;
Come up with 22,000 telephone poles an hour.

I looked at Earl and his eyes were wide,
His lip was curled and his leg was fried and his hand was froze to the
wheel
Like a tongue to a sled in the middle of a blizzard.
And I says, "Earl I'm not the type to complain
"But the time has come for me to explain

"That if you don't apply some brake real soon
"They're going to have to take us up with a stick and a spoon."
Well, Earl reared back and caught his leg, stepped down as hard as he could on the brake;
The pedal went clear to the floor and stayed right there on the floor.
… Sorta like steppin' on a plum.
Well, from there on down it just wasn't real pretty,
It was hairpin county and slick back city.
One of them looked like a can full of worms
Another one looked like malaria germs.
Right in the middle of the whole damn show
Was a real nice tunnel now wouldn't you know.
The sign said clearance at the 12-foot line
But the chickens was stacked to 13'9".
When we shot that tunnel at a hundred and ten
Like gas through a funnel and eggs through a hen.
We took that top row of chickens off slicker than a storm off a Louisiana swamp.
Went down and around and around and down.
We run out of ground at the edge of town.
Bashed in at the side of the feed store in downtown Pagosa Springs.

Wolf Creek Pass way up on the Great Divide
Truckin' on down the other side.

Wolf Creek Pass way up on the Great Divide
Truckin' on down the other side.

In the Shadow of the Rockies

Blanche M. Tice, lyrics by Gene Lindberg

Ev'ning shadows falling,
Wandering days are thru.
Soon you'll hear my calling,
Comin' swingin' down a mountain trail to you.

CHORUS
In the shadow of the Rockies.
Blending with the sunset hue.
We discovered love together,
Where the streams sing of dreams come true.
In the Golden West together.
To a "Nest o' Rest" we'll stray.
In the shadow of the Rockies,
At the rose-colored close of day.

Ev'ning breezes humming,
Soft, when day is thru.
Whisper, dear, I'm comin'
Thru the columbines that line the trail to you.

Mount Emma (centered), from Carol M. Highsmith's monumental Library of Congress Collection

Beyond the Aspen Grove

Ann Zwinger

I COUNT THE SPRING YEAR well begun when the aspen dangle their three-inch catkins, fuzzy earrings which dust the cabin deck with pollen. The buds spill them anywhere from late March to the end of April. The catkins appear before the leaves do, open to the pollinating spring breezes. The amount of pollen is prodigious. When I cut a bouquet of spring branches, the table on which they sit is deep in pale sulphur-yellow pollen the next day.

Our log notes the appearance of the first leaves between May 14 and May 20, the third week in May consistent over the years. The leaves are a pale lucid green, circles cut out of green tissue paper and overlaid in shifting patterns. Now is the time to hang out the hammock and feel, in the chill warmth, intimations of summer. A week ago, the light was too bright for reading comfortably in the grove; now, the leaves make kaleidoscopic shadows on the book page.

Lying in the hammock, looking up at the leaves, I can see the gall swellings which appear almost as soon as the leaves open, opaque against the translucent leaf. Galls usually appear in the early leaves, looking like green peppercorns. Leaf miners make meandering mines in the thin galleries between the upper and lower leaf surface when the leaves are larger.

* * *

These young trees sprouted in this area when it was suitable to their needs, just as the annuals and perennials invaded the bare ground of the meadows. The preparation was done by pioneer willows and sedges which created land out of marsh, and by beaver cuttings which let in the light.

As the young trees become established, they begin to infringe upon each other's needed space. Competition shows in the slenderness of trunk and paucity of leaf. Competition begins when the demands of the plants are in excess of the site's ability to fulfill them and is keenest among plants of the same species which have identical requirements. Those trees which survive the competition will have about 50 years of rapid growth and a life expectancy of about 100 years, rarely much longer.

This is one of the reasons aspen is considered a "trash" tree. Not being especially long-lived, the fallen trunks open the ground to erosion. To the lumberman, aspen takes up space that might better be used for more commercially desirable stands. By the time an aspen is large enough to cut for lumber, it is usually infested with heart-rot fungi and is therefore useless. We had to cut down a 20-year-old aspen while surveying; rot had already begun in the heartwood.

Aspen catkins.

Aspen is really useful only for smaller things; young trees make fine fence posts. Susan loves to carve it, and I still have a smooth satiny spoon she made years ago from sapwood. The sapwood in the tree we cut broke like gypsum. It was slippery wet and sweet-smelling with summer, a pale, creamy lemon yellow.

Westerners have a special feeling about aspen that encompasses none of these ideas. It is the only tall deciduous grove-forming tree of the montane area. Alder, willow, dogwood, and mountain maple are all shrubs or shrub-like trees and, on our land, are never over 12 to 14 feet high. Conifers have a majestic monotony, like someone who is always right. They are too timeless to mark the seasons. But aspen has éclat, a glorious brashness in defiance of the rules, the flapper who does the Charleston in the midst of the grand waltz. The landscape would be dull indeed without them.

* * *

In the center of the aspen grove is a small clearing, scarcely big enough to be called a meadow, which in summer is sweet and soft with white clover and edged with black-eyed Susans, lupines, and fleabanes. It is open and sunny and level, large enough to put up a badminton net or for playing volleyball. Herman mows it, bemoaning the fact that without any care it is an impeccable lawn and that his tastefully manicured city front yard often doesn't look as well.

Like the aspen grove itself, it is a people place, and because it is much lived in and played in, some of the happiest memories of Constant Friendship are tied to it.

Some years ago, several families with young children planned an old-fashioned Fourth of July with us, to be shared with other friends who enjoy the out-of-doors. A bachelor brought a boiler-size watermelon. He chose to sleep on the raft in the middle of the lake and nearly congealed in the early morning dews and damps. He was just getting to sleep in the warmth of the sunshine when Herman shot off his carbide cannon announcing breakfast and a glorious Fourth.

There were watermelon-seed-spitting contests and fishing (which was largely unsuccessful due to the noise); there was a one-legged race and a treasure hunt. Susan and her house guest, Jean, planned a flag ceremony which the young children carried out. They requested silence as we crossed the footbridge to the flagpole. Small hands struggled with stiff latches and stubborn grommets. Then slowly and carefully they raised the American flag to catch the morning breeze under a Colorado sky. Beneath it flew the bright blue flag of Constant Friendship with a blazon of five aspen leaves. The dignity and propriety of the boys, stilling the giggles of the girls, invested the mountain clearness with ideals and hopes. There are those moments that we remember with clarity because they epitomize a time or an awareness that by caring for the things close to us we are able then to care for the larger world. No one had to ask for silence back across the footbridge.

The children wove in and out of the day on their own errands. It was as if the adults watched from the wrong end of a telescope trained on a section of stage landscape. Periodically figures came into view, a frieze of youngness running across the set, first from one wing of aspen, then the other of pine, diagonally upstage and down, sometimes stage front, sometimes behind a scrim of aspen leaves, sometimes swiftly, sometimes in a pavane. They belonged to the land that day, not to their parents. They were small sprites of the substance of leaf and shadow, interwoven with the patterns of flickering sunlight. The figures seemed to pause briefly, then rearrange—moments of stop-motion alternating with moments of movement.

Once a tree is grown, there is no return to the seedling stage, and so the adults who watched could only remember and see arabesques of life and sunshine and unaware grace as natural as a flower or branch in the varying small figures. Even out of sight, the sound of their voices came carried on the aspen breeze. They were small exotic creatures at home in a world of wind and light. Here in these mountain meadows and groves, they were all Peter Pans.

And then dinner, complete with fried chicken, corn on the cob, baked beans, salad, sliced tomatoes, cucumber and watermelon pickles, homemade bread, coconut cake decorated with a red, white and blue pennant—all the good things brought and all the good things remembered from an Indiana Fourth of July. After darkness, we went up to the ponderosa hill overlooking the lake. Herman set off fireworks from the lake rock, each shower reflecting in the blackness beneath, hissing upward to drop sizzling into itself. When the last rocket fell, it was hard to know whether it was fireworks or a shooting star.

The Last Midwife

Sandra Dallas

DAWN BROKE ACROSS THE TENMILE RANGE in fiery slashes of red—flaming streaks the color of blood. Sunrise was always violent in the high country. There were no pink-edged clouds or pale patches of lavender. Such softness wouldn't be right in that raw landscape where men in their stampede for precious metals churned up the mountain streams until they were trickles of water through mounds of yellow waste rock and scraped the thin topsoil from the land, leaving it naked, bare of anything that grew.

Tired as she was, Gracy Brookens stopped her buggy to admire the sweep of color that crept over the dark humps of mountains to the east and cast light onto the tips of the peaks with their honeycombed drifts of snow from last winter—or the winter before. It was past starshine now, and the red slashes were edged with gold richer than anything that ever came out of a Tenmile mine. Swatches of blue the color of columbines seeped into the red. The glory of the sky told Gracy there was a Holy Spirit in that land of greed and struggle, particularly on a morning when she had just birthed a baby in Mayflower Gulch. Not that she needed convincing. The birth of a baby was proof enough. Every baby, she believed, was a miracle of God.

The infant had been a tiny thing, no bigger than a gray squirrel, most likely conceived in a mountain meadow, born in a hewn-log cabin with nary a window and only a dirt floor for him to crawl on. He'd be bred in the trees and rocks of the mountain peaks, like any other wild thing, brought up by the girl and boy who were only half grown themselves, young as Gracy's Jeff. It wasn't an easy life ahead. The baby had been born to poverty, would know disease and death, harshness and cold before he was grown, and likely, he wouldn't have much book learning. But he'd have love. Those two who formed him out of themselves had love enough to sell. …

Gracy leaned back against the seat now but did not think of sleeping. It had been a good birth, an easy one, although the girl wouldn't think so. Gracy wondered what number it was. She should have kept track of the babies she'd delivered but she hadn't. She didn't even remember the number of ones who had died, and she thanked God this wasn't one of them.

A little brightness came into the sky now, the sun lighting the tips of ever-lasting snow on the farthest peaks, shining on the late, crimson-tipped Indian paintbrush and tiny yellow wildflowers that shone like drops of molten gold in the green carpet of grass. It was a sunrise that seemed to last forever. Gracy passed a spread of stalks with bright pink blooms—the flowers the women called summer's-half-over. She'd seen them in the moonlight the night before and would have stopped to pick a bouquet for the girl, but she hadn't wanted to waste the time. She wouldn't pick them for herself, because she had flowers at home. …

The heavens lightened, and the red streaks softened, filling the sky between the mountain ranges with color. The sunrise never failed to thrill Gracy, especially in the mornings when she was returning from a birthing. Babies, it seemed, liked to be born in the dark. She stopped the buggy at the overlook, Buddy waiting patiently, for the old horse was used to Gracy's fits and starts. She tightened the shawl around her, because even in midsummer the nights were cold, and she shivered as she got down from the carriage and peered out over the valley, across to Turnbull Mountain. The morning light shone on the glory holes that pitted it, their gouged rock spilling over the hillside.

Minerals of Colorado

Friends of Minerology

Growth of Mineralogic Knowledge

SOME COLORADO MINERALS and mineral deposits were known long before the beginning of the written record. The Native Americans used agate, chalcedony, and other forms of quartz for weapons and tools; they used clay for pottery, and mineral pigments for various purposes. They found and processed turquoise and other gem minerals for particular uses, such as ornamentation and as amulets. After the Native Americans came the predominantly European explorers, trappers, and guides. Although they left no records in the scientific literature, it is known that some of them found gold.

The written public record of the occurrence of minerals in Colorado began in 1858, when gold was first authentically reported. Even then, the record of the first few years was confined to newspapers and personal writings, only a few of which have survived the years. Henderson (1926) gave a carefully documented summary of the beginning of Colorado mining history.

For some time, gold was the only mineral mentioned in the literature, but even the first placer miners must have been familiar with other minerals, for they surely recognized the quartz sand, brilliant garnets, pyrite or "fool's gold," and magnetic concentrates that went through their crude washers. As soon as vein gold was found in 1859 in the Gregory diggings near Black Hawk, the miners, as well as the assayers and others who had a part in the burgeoning mineral industry, began to recognize, and eventually to record, many other metallic and nonmetallic minerals that were in or near the ore deposits. Thus began the literature of Colorado minerals, a literature that has continued to grow, from the times when mining and mineral resources were a mainstay of Colorado's economy to the years of research and development related to demand for specific minerals.

One of the earliest descriptions of minerals other than native gold is that of Whitney (1865), who mentioned the native silver and richly argentiferous galena that had been recently found in the Tenmile district, Summit County. Both in his earliest booklet, which today would be classified as a prospectus designed to attract speculative capital, as well as in a later work (1867), Whitney mentioned other mineral deposits and noted a few minerals, such as "black sulphurets of silver," "ruby silver," "sulphates of copper," "limonite," and others. Few of these notes can be translated with any certainty into terms of modern mineral species. Whitney's 1867 report is useful, however, because it contains lists of the mines and mining districts that were active at that time in Clear Creek, Gilpin, and Summit Counties.

From this early period, the fledgling mining and smelting industries in Colorado, as well as the communities that developed to support them, grew at a rapid rate.

The first known attempt to list the mineral species of Colorado is that of Hollister (1867). He not only reported the early history and status of the mining industry in Colorado but included a list of all the mineral species and varieties known to him at the time, with brief notes on their localities. His list was followed by many others, which vary in the amount of detail and in the character of their documentation. In general, each succeeding list is longer than the previous ones, thus recording the steady growth of the knowledge of Colorado minerals.

Valley of the Dunes

Robert Rozinski and Wendy Shattil (photographs)
Audrey DeLella Benedict (text)

I have always told people that the San Luis Valley is more than home to me. It is a spiritual place unlike any other on earth.

THE SMELL OF THE EARTH and the sight of the mountains at Los Rincones take me back to my childhood, and beyond. My family helped settle the San Luis Valley in the mid-1800s after first helping to settle the City of Faith, Santa Fe, more than 400 years ago. My ancestors traveled north into the Sangre de Cristo Mountains until they came to the valley where my family's ranch still stands today, near the Rio Grande.

One of the strongest impressions anyone takes from the valley is the overwhelming sense of majestic age. The Sangre de Cristos are not young mountains; they have stood silent watch as ages have passed. Emanating from these mountains and clearings, one can feel the wisdom of patience, fortitude, and strength.

But nowhere is that majestic patience more obvious than at Great Sand Dunes National Park and Preserve. These dunes were built grain by grain by the winds blowing hundreds of miles up the valley over tens of thousands of years.

Throughout the years, the Great Sand Dunes have proved more than simply a notable landmark. Their establishment as a national monument and later as a national park has helped stimulate the economy in the San Luis Valley, providing jobs to many of us both at the park and through the generated tourism. They have attracted visitors from around the world, allowing us to share our unique culture and values with all who care to learn.

In 1932, when the Great Sand Dunes were first designated a national monument, the 30-square miles of land were finally protected after a decade of disregard by gold miners flocking into the nearby mountains.

On November 22, 2000, President Clinton signed into law the Great Sand Dunes National Park and Preserve Act. With the stroke of his pen, the monument was expanded into a national park and preserve to include the towering peaks and placid alpine lakes bordering the dunes. The dunes, and their neighbors, were forever protected for all to enjoy.

The Great Sand Dunes were the shifting sentinels of the San Luis Valley: changing yet constant emblems of deliberate creation and a methodical Creator. They are unlike any other place on Earth, as witnessed by the thousands of visitors the dunes receive every year.

I invite you to join us, through the photographs and words in this book, to enjoy the most breathtaking and glorious places in the San Luis Valley. I promise you will be as enrapt as I am, drawn to witness them in person. And then you will begin to understand the majesty of my home.

They say that nothing of beauty can ever be rushed. Truly, the San Luis Valley and the Great Sand Dunes bear witness to this statement. And now you can too.

—Former Senator Ken Salazar, Colorado

* * *

With the coming of spring, the San Luis Valley's wetlands welcome tens of thousands of northbound avian travelers—sandhill cranes, herons, the white-faced ibis, geese, ducks, grebes, shorebirds, and songbirds of every stripe. The skies are alive with continual arrivals and departures, endless lifting and settling of ducks, and the splendid cacophony of a thousand different voices.

My spring ritual—conducted with binoculars in hand—always involved a march migration to Monte Vista National Wildlife Refuge to mark winter's end with a spirit-lifting infusion of sandhill crane music. The refuge, which hosts nearly 20,000 migrating sandhill cranes and has the highest nesting densities of ducks in North America, combines a network of irrigated wetlands and fields planted solely to support resident breeders as well as migrants. For several weeks each spring and fall, the San Luis Valley serves as a staging ground and refueling stop for the cranes along a migratory pathway that may be millions of years old.

The crane family (Gruidae) is one of the oldest bird families in the world, having made its first appearance roughly 65 million years ago. Fossil wing bones of sandhill cranes (*Grus canadensis*), exactly identical to those we see today, have been found in Wyoming and Nebraska and are thought to be at least nine million years old—making the sandhill crane the oldest modern bird species on Earth.

We know that prehistoric people hunted sandhill cranes in the San Luis Valley for thousands of years and that the Spanish explorers referred to the nearby San Juan Mountains as *las sierras de las grullas* or "mountains of the cranes." In a rock shelter above Limekiln Creek, along the southwestern edge of the valley, the image of a large flying bird—undoubtedly a sandhill crane—has been pecked into the smoke-blackened wall of the shelter. Though the age of this rock art panel is unknown, the small geometric design below the bird is thought to be a Puebloan crane clan symbol. Sandhill cranes were held in such high regard by Puebloan peoples up and down the Rio Grande that lessons drawn from the crane's lifeway and habits are found in traditional "teaching" stories told to children. Cranes also play a signal role in secret rituals practiced by the Tewas, the Zuni, and the Hopi.

Though the sandhill cranes are still a long way off, I can hear the first armada before I actually see them, calling—a formidable, dignified procession across the dusk-stilled sky.

Soon, a single trumpet-like horn note reverberates from overhead, and the cranes begin swirling down like parachutists to land in the field directly before me. In the distance I can see and hear hundreds more in the fading light, long wavering lines of cranes coming from every direction to spend the night within the safety of their legions. The sandhill cranes will spend several weeks alternating flights to traditional sites each evening for roosting and to farm fields and meadows each dawn to forage and build fat reserves for the final flight to the nesting grounds. There is much chattering between them as the cranes settle in for the night, the din diminishing as sleep comes to the flock, heads gracefully tucked under their wings. As the moon rises and cold settles like a blanket over the fields, I see thousands of crane shapes illuminated in silvered moonlight, and I leave them to their well-deserved rest.

Voices of the American West

Corinne Platt

Gudy Gaskill: Mother of the Colorado Trail

Now in her mid-80s, Gudy Gaskill still has the energy of her younger years. A longtime member of the Colorado Mountain Club, Gudy has hiked all over the world, climbed all 54 of Colorado's 14,000-foot peaks, and summited several other peaks up to 23,000 feet in elevation.

Gudy is known for her almost single-handed effort in building the Colorado Trail, a 468-mile-long trek between Denver and Durango, one of the longest continuous trails in the United States. For her, it is much more than just a trail; it's a lifestyle. She and her husband, David, live in the foothills west of Golden, Colorado. Here they have easy access to the mountains and two of their eight grandchildren, who live next door.

MY HUSBAND, DAVID, AND I joined the Colorado Mountain Club in the 1950s, after we moved to Denver. In the early '70s, I got wind of plans for a trail between Denver and Durango and was so excited. According to Merrill Hastings, the former publisher of *Colorado Magazine,* the trail was conceived in a conversation between him and Bill Lucas, our Rocky Mountain regional forester at the time. Both were horse riders and were impressed with the extensive trails in Europe. One of them said to the other, "Wouldn't it be nice if we could ride our horses without having to drag the packhorses behind us?" So they conceived of a European-style trail in America.

Bill and Merrill asked many different environmental organizations to participate in the planning of the trail. Those groups helped, but I was the only one who actually stayed with it. I was president of the Colorado Mountain Club. I was also chairman of the Huts and Trails Committee, which was an environmental group that went out and cleaned, picking up after the sixties' children. Between the war and the '60s, they all lived in tents and shared communities. We did a lot of cleaning up after them. Anyway, I was the only woman on the Colorado Mountain Trail Foundation board of directors, and Bill told me they had hired me—for $10 a day—to get the trail started. I never saw any money, but I was asked in 1974 to chair the committee that would develop and manage the building of the trail.

We had to draw the route through 13 different Forest Service districts and try to link existing mining and logging roads. Then we sent the plan to the different districts. If a forester didn't want the trail, I would go down there and try to persuade the district ranger of its value. Most districts were in agreement after a year.

At the same time, I was recruiting and training volunteers, leading trail crews, and purchasing supplies. Over the course of the next 13 years of building the trail, I oversaw over 10,000 volunteers from all 50 states and many foreign countries.

As we were starting the trail, Ed Quillen wrote an article called "Trail to Nowhere" in *Empire* magazine. Fortunately, it caught the attention of Dick and Dottie Lamm; Dick was the governor of Colorado at the time. They came out on the trail and helped put in a new section of trail along Twin Lakes. Dick was so thrilled by the end of the day, he said he wanted to hang out with us all summer. After his experience, he hosted a fundraiser. He actually managed to add a rider to a bill and earmarked $14,000 for the trail. It was a real turning point for us.

Our volunteers were the heart and soul of the trail. I discovered that with volunteer help, the trail could be built for about $500 per mile, compared to the Forest Service's estimated $25,000 per mile. We could build one mile in one week if we had a full crew. And that was a lot of hard work.

We finished the trail in 1987. It was voted by *Backpacker* and *Outside* magazines as the best trail in the West and, by *Backpacker,* as one of the 30 best trails in the world.

Michael Martin Murphey wrote the words to "Along, Along the Colorado Trail" about his time on the trail. He sang with the trail riders every night around the campfire and gave a percentage of the money he raised doing that to the Colorado Trail Foundation. It was just mind-boggling to sit around the campfire and listen to him sing songs. Judy Collins dedicated a song to me and sang it, and it was just beautiful.

I can't believe how many people still hike the trail in the summer. When I hike the whole trail, it takes me six weeks or more, but people have done it in 28 days. For me, it's just leisurely hiking, and I tell anyone who wants to do it to plan on six weeks so they don't miss any of it. A lot of people will walk it for a week one summer and then maybe two weeks the following summer. And there are two couples I know of who hike a section every weekend. They start in different places and cross paths and end up taking each other's cars home. It will take them three summers to complete the trail.

Now, I spend about 12 weeks every summer at the Colorado Trail Foundation facility in the mountains above Lake City, managing the foundation's education and art programs. The cabin is on the Alpine Loop Scenic Byway, right at the foot of Redcloud and Sunshine peaks. We offer classes in wildflowers, painting, geology, storytelling, photography, and wilderness first aid. I buy the food and cook for the students. On Saturday afternoons, when the last guest leaves at the end of one session, I make the two-hour drive to Gunnison to stock up on provisions for the next group and check in on the home we still own there. Then I drive back and get ready for the next group first thing Sunday morning. I love it.

David was always very supportive. I was footloose and fancy-free before we were married. I was afraid my freedom was going to be squelched, so he and I signed a contract saying that we could each do our own thing and the other one could not complain about it unless we really thought that it was destroying the family. He worked on the trail approximately one day.

I didn't build the trail to leave any kind of a legacy. I just did it because I thought it was the most gorgeous scenery I'd ever seen. I wanted other people to be able to see it too. Just to think that other people could share that was incredible. I still get letters all the time from people around the world saying that it changed their lives. It's neat for me to share in those little moments.

David is also in his late-80a. He hasn't been doing much hiking lately. I asked him one day if there was some place in the world he'd like to go that he hasn't gone to. He said he'd like to go hiking in Canada. So, as a Christmas gift, I gave him another hike. We're going up to Banff and Mount Assiniboine. He is helicoptering out when we're done, and I will backpack out the other side. He'll drive around and pick me up, then we'll hike for a few more days. The northern light is wonderful. It changes my attitude about being too old for backpacking anymore.

It's just that I love hiking. I can't stay inside.

Gudy Gaskill fell in love with the Rocky Mountains in the 1930s. In the early 1940s, she and her twin sister, Ingeborg, enrolled at Western State College (WSC). After Gudy earned her bachelor's degree, she married David, also a WSC graduate, and moved to Kansas, where they ran up to 10,000 sheep before their herd was wiped out in a blizzard in the early 1950s. David and Gudy joined the Colorado Mountain Club after moving back to Denver in 1952. By the 1970s, she was leading trips throughout the world. She was named the first woman president of the CMC in 1977. She has won numerous awards, appeared on the Today show, been honored by two U.S. presidents, and was inducted into the Colorado Women's Hall of Fame in 2002. Merle McDonald of the Colorado Trail Foundation said of Gudy, "No person, man or woman, has ever single-handedly had a greater impact on the successful completion of a national treasure as Gudy has with the completion of the Colorado Trail."

SECTION IV

Growing Up with Colorado

The Switzerland of America

Samuel Bowles

Denver, Colorado, September, 1868.

INEXHAUSTIBLE AS IS COLORADO'S mineral wealth; progressive as henceforth its development; predominant and extensive as are its mountains; high even as are its plains—in spite of all seeming impossibilities and rivalries, agriculture is destined always to be its dominant interest. Hence, my faith in its future and its influence among the central states of the Continent. For agriculture is the basis of wealth, of power, of morality; it is the conservative element of national and political and social growth; it steadies, preserves, purifies. Fully one-third of the territorial extent of Colorado—though this third is as high as Mount Washington—is fit, more, rich for agricultural purposes. All the vegetables and the fruits of the temperate zone grow and ripen in it; and through the most of it, cattle and sheep can live and fatten the year round without housing or feeding. The immediate valleys or bottom lands of the Arkansas and Platte and Rio Grande and their numerous tributaries, after they emerge from the mountains, are of rich vegetable loams, and need no irrigation. The uplands or plains are of a coarse, sandy loam, rich in the phosphates washed from the minerals of the mountains, and are not much in use yet except for pastures. When cultivated, more or less irrigation is introduced, and probably will always be advisable for sure crops of roots and vegetables; but for the small, hard grains, I doubt it will be generally found necessary. It is a comparatively dry climate, though showers are frequent, and extend over a considerable part of the spring and summer.

At a rough estimate, the agricultural wealth of Colorado last year was a million bushels of corn, half a million of wheat, half a million of barley, oats and vegetables, 100,000 head of cattle, and 75,000 to 100,000 sheep. The increase this year is at least 50 percent; in the northern counties, at least 100 percent. Indeed, the agriculture of the northern counties, between the Pacific Railroad at Cheyenne and Denver, which has come to be full half that of the whole state, is the development almost entirely of the last three years. South, in the Arkansas and Rio Grande valleys, the farming and population are older, going back to before the gold discoveries. This is the Mexican section, and was formerly a part of New Mexico. Its agriculture is on a large but rough scale, and only the immense crops and the simple habits of the people, chiefly ignorant, degraded Mexicans, permit it to be profitable. The soil yields wonderfully, north and south. There is authentic evidence of 316 bushels of corn to the acre in the neighborhood of Denver this season; 60 to 75 bushels of wheat to the acre are very frequently reported; also

250 bushels of potatoes; and 60 to 70 of both oats and barley. These are exceptional yields, of course, and not of single acres, but of whole fields, and on several farms in different counties. Probably 30 bushels is the average product of wheat; of corn no more, for the hot nights that corn loves are never felt here; of oats say 50, and of barley 40, for the whole state. Exhaustion of the virgin freshness of the soil will tend to decrease these averages in the future; but against that we may safely put improved cultivation and greater care in harvesting.

The melons and vegetables are superb; quality, quantity and size are unsurpassed by any garden cultivators in the East. The irrigated gardens of the upper parts of Denver fairly riot in growth of fat vegetables; while the bottom lands of neighboring valleys are at least equally productive without irrigation. Think of cabbages weighing from 50 to 60 pounds each! And potatoes from five to six pounds, onions one to two pounds, and beets six to 10! Yet, here they grow, and as excellent as big.

* * *

Stock-raising on the Plains is a simple and profitable business. The animals roam at will, and a single man can tend hundreds. The only enemies are the Indians and the diseases that the Texas cattle bring up from the South. But the former are the great evil; the confusion, danger and loss they have created this season sum up a serious blow not only to stock-raising, but to all farming. Even if the evil is suppressed hereafter, this season's raids are a year's loss to the agricultural interests of Colorado. Many farmers have given up in despair from danger and disaster, and retired from the field; others hesitate and refuse to come, who otherwise would be here at once and in force of capital and energy, to enter upon the business.

These great interests of mining and farming shade naturally into others, and already there are the beginnings of various manufacturing developments, as there are the materials and incentives for such undertakings without stint. Some 15 or 20 flouring mills are in operation throughout the state. The Colorado wheat makes a rich hearty flour, bearing a creamy golden tinge; and I have eaten nowhere else in America better bread than is made from it. There is a baker in Georgetown whose products are as rich and light as the best of German wheat bread. The wheat will rank with the very best that America produces, and is more like the California grain than that of "the States." Coal mines are abundant, and several are being profitably worked along the lower range of the mountains; as, indeed, they have been found and opened at intervals along the line of the Pacific Railroad over the mountains, and are already supplying its engines with a most excellent fuel—a hard, dry, brown coal, very pure and free-burning; in Boulder valley and Golden City, iron is being manufactured from native ore; at Golden City, there is a successful manufactory of pottery ware and fire brick; also a paper-mill and a tannery, and saw-mills; the state already supplies its own salt; soda deposits are everywhere, and will be a great source of wealth; woolen mills are few and greatly needed, as wool-growing is the simplest of agricultural pursuits here; a valuable tin mine has been lately discovered and its value proved, in the mountains; and next year the Railroad will be one of Colorado's great interests, and bring harmony and unity and healthy development to all her commercial, material, and political interests. Also, by that time she will be a state, and so responsible for her own government, be it good or bad.

High, Wide and Lonesome

Hal Borland

I WANTED WINTER TO BE EXCITING. I wanted some real storms. Summer storms were fun, and they gave you a shivery feeling sometimes, when the great, towering clouds boiled like foam in a kettle and lightning flashed in all directions and the thunder made the hills bounce. But there weren't many summer storms like that. And with the exception of the Christmas storm, when Dick brought me home from the big sheep camp, last winter hadn't amounted to much. I wanted a real, rip-tearing blizzard.

I got it.

The Saturday when we were all set to try to get to Gary in the buggy, it began to snow in mid-morning. It was just a slow, quiet snowfall with hardly any wind, but Mother said we'd better not start out in it. I thought she was being too cautious, but by the middle of the afternoon I knew she was right. The wind came up, and it really began to blizzard.

* * *

While we ate supper the wind sifted snow in around every window and made eddies in the air so that the flame in the lamp flickered and smoked. We hung quilts over the windows to break the gusts of fine snow and we stuffed a towel under the door. Mother put the hot flatirons in our beds and I tried to read for a while sitting with my feet in the oven. But the fire died, sucked right up the chimney, and I went to bed. The wind was shaking the house so much that the dishes rattled on the shelves.

It snowed and blew all night. When I wakened the next morning there was a drift of snow on the edge of my bed and when I stepped down I went into snow a foot deep on the floor. There was a drift under every window in the house. We ate breakfast before I tried to get to the barn. When I opened the house door I hit a solid wall of snow. The drift there was six feet deep.

We knew it was still blowing. We could hear it. But we didn't know it was still snowing until I tunneled through that drift at the door and got into the open. It took me an hour to get clear, and it was still snowing. It was eleven o'clock when I reached the barn and got the door open there.

Everything was all right at the barn. The snow had banked it and the animals made it almost as warm as the house. I did the milking and rationed out the hay I had got in the day before and started back to the house. I had to dig out every path because they'd all drifted full again. Before I got to the house the milk was full of slush, half frozen though it had been warm when I left the barn.

The wind eased off somewhat that evening, but the snow continued. The second day I had to dig out all over again. And that day I had to water the stock. They couldn't go any longer without it. Mother said she was going to help. She'd seen what the wind could do to her skirts, so she put on a pair of Father's overalls, belted them at the waist, tied them at the ankles, and put on overshoes, coat and scarf. She carried kettles of boiling water and thawed the pump while I got on Mack and broke trail from the barn to the well. When we had a trail opened through the snowdrifts, Daisy and the calves followed to the well, drank, and were very glad to get back in the barn. And that afternoon I had to find some way to get hay. The only way was to dig a path to the stacks, carve off a big slice of one stack with the hay knife, and carry it into the barn.

Before I got the hay into the barn, I began to wonder if I really wanted a blizzard. My arms ached; my ears stung; I was sweating like a horse; and when I stopped to catch my breath, the sweat seemed to turn to icicles in my armpits. But I got the hay in, and I did the evening chores, and I shoveled my way back to the house, where the big bowl of steaming pinto beans was worth all the sweating. The Mexican wants his beans hot with chili peppers. The New Englander wants his beans sweet with molasses and salt pork. We had ours simmered for hours with no seasoning but salt and swimming in their own brown juice. To us, they were bread and butter and meat and potatoes, as they were to many an isolated homestead. On a cold, blizzardy night, they were more than sustenance; they were warmth and comfort and a promise for tomorrow.

That was our pattern for four days: wind and snow and shoveling and pumping and milking and carrying sheep chips. Soft snow turned to ice crystals which, wind-driven, bit cheek and knuckle and made you a sentient part of the storm. It became a kind of game to see how much cold you could take, how much wind you could face, and how much snow you could shovel. And, as the storm progressed, it even added comfort to the house. Until the snow banked the house to the eaves, the stove cast so small a circle of warmth that I could stand with my hip pockets practically on the stove lids and still see my breath. Then we were drifted in, and I could go clear across the room before my breath was visible.

The snow probably stopped on the third day, though we couldn't tell. There were flashes of sunlight, but the air was still full of snow, undoubtedly blown from the hilltops. It seemed impossible that the snow could continue to drift, but it did. It seemed that the drifts had been built as high as they could stand and all the ridges had been swept bare.

But at least the wind eased away and the plains lay white and silent. And new—white, gleaming, pristine new.

* * *

After such a storm, the world of the plains is a strange and magnificent place. It is as though all the earth-shaping forces have been at work on a vastly quickened scale of time. Hills, valleys, hollows and hummocks have all been reshaped to a new pattern. The wind has had its way, at last, the wind that is forever trying to level the hills and fill the valleys. It has been able to work its will with an obediently plastic, though transient, material.

Our wind had been somewhat thwarted, by a fence post, a hay stack, even by a tall weed stem. It had swirled and eddied, and we could see all the swirls and eddies frozen in the snow. Change was everywhere, but there was one constant, the soft curve. You saw it in the eddy around a fence post, the swirl around a hay stack, the shape of a hill, the flow of a valley, and in a thousand variations of the amazing curl of a snowdrift.

The wind had all but obliterated the house, the barn, the fences, the hay stacks. They were still there, but they had been merged into the drifted landscape, their own shapes lost and distorted. There was virtually no trace of human tenancy except the smoke from our chimney. Paths were drifted over. Fences were buried under the drifts. Hay stacks were only larger drifts, as were both the house and the barn. And we, the human survivors, had been driven back, in a way, into a cave; the house was more than a cavern in a hillside of snow. There, we had survived as a kind of outpost in a world suddenly engulfed in a new ice age. An ice age, though, that would retreat and vanish in a matter of weeks rather than centuries and eons.

The initial vacancy of that world was beyond belief. It was a vast white void, no wing in the sky or a moving paw upon the snow. In time, of course, in a day or two, the prairie quail huddled in bunch grass caves beneath the drifts worked their way out. Field mice, tunneling under the snow from one seed head to another, would come to the surface and explore. Jack rabbits would break through the drifts that sheltered them beside the soap weed clumps. Prairie dogs would open their snow-sealed burrows and yelp at the white and hungry world. And coyotes would come from their dens and make lean shadows on the snow and send their hungry yelps.

Round By Round
An Autobiography
Jack Dempsey

WHEN I WAS SEVEN YEARS OLD, in the small town of Manassa in southern Colorado, I had a run-in with a boy named Fred Daniels, about my own size, who went to school with me. Just what started us fighting I can't remember; in fact, it is from my father that the description of the set-to comes—but at any rate, we tangled in one of the wide, dusty, road-like streets of the country town.

We went to it hammer and tongs, as small boys will, with ferocious swinging blows that missed a mile. The noise attracted men from the country store, and a half-circle gathered, amused, to watch us, as they might watch a dogfight. Apparently, in that pioneer atmosphere of the Rockies, nobody thought of interfering. Fred's father was there, and so was mine, laughing and slapping their thighs, watching us.

The going kept getting rougher and rougher. The two of us tried everything we could think of, wrestling and butting and kicking and everything else. Presently Fred's father yelled encouragingly, "Bite him, Fred!"

Everybody laughed, and Fred turned his head to find out what his father had said. It left him wide open, and they tell me I instantly took advantage of it an bopped him on the chin as hard as I could. Over he went! The fight was finished.

Years later, as you will see, that early fight had its influence on many of my battles in the ring. It affected my entire career. …

The whole San Luis Valley in which Manassa lies, was, and still is, exactly suited to fight like that. … When I was born there and christened William Harrison Dempsey, in June 1895, there were only 30 or 40 houses. Picture a flat, high-lying, western valley about 100 miles long and nearly 70 miles across, entirely surrounded by rugged mountains, many of them over 14,000 feet high. Warm in summer, freezing in winter, with lots of snow. Just to the west lies the backbone of the whole country, the Continental Divide. It is still wild, open country, with cattle and sheep ranches, flat meadows and sagebrush between widely separated towns. …

The first white settlers of the valley … were Mexicans, who came up the Rio Grande from the southwest. Most of the towns still have Spanish names—San Acacia, Del Norte, La Garita, Estrella, and La Jara. They contrast sharply with the later names given to other towns by farmers who moved into the valley, following the gold rush, from eastern states—Russell, Center, Henry, Bountiful, and McGinty. Together, these widely differing strains have populated the valley side by side. …

* * *

Manassa was strong on religion. When I was a small boy a great Mormon church was built there and painted white. … Every evening, we had family prayers. A blessing was always asked at the beginning of each meal. Regularly, the Teachers of the Mormon church, corresponding to preachers in other religions, visited our house to see how things were going. They would exhort my father to do right, as they saw the right … but in spite of all the religion, Manassa was like every other pioneer town: tough and ready for anything.

My parents were poor. Although there was plenty to eat, we were otherwise a poverty-stricken household. My father was of a roving, happy-go-lucky disposition. He didn't like to stick to the same job, the same farm. He wanted endless variety. When he had money, he spent it generously, but he rarely had any. He loved to have a good time. He used to play the fiddle, without notes, but with nimble fingers running the same rollicking melody over and over and over—"Turkey in the Straw," "Arkansas Traveller," "The Wild Goose." Occasionally, he'd make up a tune of his own. Sometimes he played for dances.

Any inconsistency between his religion and his manner of living never bothered him. "The Mormon religion," he would explain, "is a good thing. It shows you what you ought to do. That's the main thing, always to know what you ought to do. Of course, you don't always do it. Nobody does. That's human nature. But at least you ought to know what's right. I reckon that's what religion is for." …

My mother was very different. She was much more ambitious than my father. She was scrupulously clean. She was always scrubbing floors, always washing clothes or washing windows or cooking or putting up fruits or vegetables for winter. … Mother had great dreams for all of us. We were all to be well educated and successful, rich and powerful ladies and gentlemen. And above all, "good citizens," whatever that meant. We were to make the country better. My mother wasn't as joyous as my father, but she was more sincere.

* * *

We were always surrounded with horses, cows, pigs and chickens. Also considerable dogs. I learned to ride a horse almost as soon as I learned to walk. One summer, my father took me over to Cumbres Pass with him, when he had a contract cutting out ties for the railroad. I can remember helping my older brothers snake the logs with a mule.

Mostly, during those days at Manassa, my mother was too crowded with work, and my father too busy with his own schemes and expeditions to have much time for us. We had to be shaped by our day-to-day adventures and experiences—the fights with Mexican boys and trying to throw ropes on horses—rather than by much guidance from our parents. … We never had any "store" toys. We had to make our own playthings. Chips of wood became boats, sticks became spears, bits of rope became lariats. We were able to make fairly respectable bows and arrows, and we had a lot of fun with these things.

Looking back at it now, it seems as if I almost always had a good time. The only bad thing was the feeling of being so very poor.

Second Hoeing

Hope Williams Sykes

OUT OF THE CHURCH, dodging and shrinking, trying to avoid the rain of barley corn, and wheat which showered round them from numerous pockets and small sacks, the bridal parry ran to the parsonage to get coats and have witnesses sign the marriage license.

Hannah tried to shake the grain from her clothes. Small red spots showed on her throat where the grain had pelted. She tried to dislodge the last of the seeds as she rode with the bridal parry to the photographer's.

They waited awkwardly for the photographer to get ready. She looked at Henry Goelzer, small, skinny, and loose jointed. Not much like his huge fat mother more like his bullet-headed father. He had the same drooping shoulders, the same watery blue eyes. Henry looked simple, ashamed. No wonder he wouldn't meet her glance.

"Well, that's over." Jake Heist took Hannah's arm and led the way to the car. "Now for the wedding eats. I'm starved." He grinned at them all.

Down through the wide streets of Valley City they went, across the river to the narrow streets and little houses of Shag Town, to the dingy home of the Goelzers.

A group of young men held a thick rope stretched across the gateway.

"You gotta pay to get in," they shouted in unison.

"Open that gate, or I get out and throw you away," one of the bride's boys called loudly from the car.

"One dollar you pay before you get in to eat. You know the bride gotta have some money. She don't feed you for nothin'. One dollar."

"We don't! Twenty five cents is all wc pay," Jakc rcplicd loudly.

The four bride's boys each threw a quarter to the gate keepers, and the rope was lowered.

As the car came into the yard, three old men standing under a tree started playing, "Jesus, now lead on 'til the peace is won." The bass horn, clarinet and cornet sent a high lilting melody across the yard, the bass horn boomed.

Older women came running out of the house to kiss Olinda and shake Henry's hand.

The bridal parry made their way through the crowded Goelzer kitchen. The odor of cooking was thick in the warm air. The old women cooks bustled about in woolen dresses covered by great aprons.

"In the front room," shouted one, motioning.

Stepping sideways, turning and twisting, they made their way.

Hannah stepped over the board seats and slid along until she was beside Olinda at the long bride's table. It was covered with snowy linen and set with thick white dishes.

A cook brought a glass pitcher. "For the bride's flowers," she said, and waited while Olinda soberly placed her pink carnations and sweetpeas within. She placed it in the center of the table directly in front of Olinda, moving the huge bride's cake to one side.

Bowls of butterball soup, with the tin dippers resting in their depths, were brought in by the cooks, and each guest at the bride's table ladled out the delicious yellow butterballs and finely cut noodles into his own individual soup bowl. The great platters of brown and sizzling turkey, goose, and chicken were brought in. The browned potatoes followed with rich dressing, pickles, and homemade bread.

Henry poured a small wine glass of whisky and passed it. The glass was returned, filled again and passed to the next one at the table, and so on until every one had drunk. Soberly, Hannah emptied the glass; stolidly, she set to eating her butterball soup.

Fingers curved around her ankle, then moved on. Hannah felt Olinda move slightly, and sensed that she moved one of her feet backward so that the unseen prowler could not touch it. At the same time, Hannah knew that Olinda put her other foot forward so that her slipper could be taken off, but in such a manner as would give the impression that she didn't want any one to steal her slipper.

One of the cooks came in with her right arm bandaged in a huge white cloth.

"I burn mineself mit the bride's soup," she shouted loudly, holding up her arm for all to see.

"Money, I got have so I pay a doctor. Two, three, might five dollar it take—take up a collection so I pay him," she shouted.

Hannah watched while the fat cook squeezed around people, reaching with a long-handled tin dipper across the table so that the nickels, dimes, and quarters could be tossed in. She slapped some of the men boisterously upon the back, telling them loudly to put in plenty of moneys.

Everyone knew the cook's arm wasn't hurt.

As the men sampled the liquor, talk and laughter flowed louder.

Old lady Heist shouted for silence. She elbowed her way to the tables holding a huge white pillow in a fancy embroidered case. In the center of the pillow was a small paper basket surrounded by great paper roses. Across one corner stood dolls, dressed as bride and groom.

"Money to buy the bride's bedclothes! The bride and her man got have some covers so they don't freeze when they sleep mit each other." Quarters dropped into the elaborate basket.

Hannah woodenly watched the whole procedure.

Daniel Kniemer held aloft Olinda's white bridal slipper. A great pink bow of crepe paper and a pink carnation were tied around the instep.

"You're some bride's boys," Kniemer said in mock severity. "Why don't you take care mit the bride more better? There she sit mit cold feets. You want her to catch cold so Henry lose her right away?" He laughed loudly.

"Well, boys, I got the bride's slipper, here. You wasn't smart enough to keep it for her, so now you got to buy it back for her. You know a bride's got to have her slipper or she don't can dance mit you. If you want to dance mit the bride, she gotta have shoes. You have to pay so you get it back.

"What am I bid for it?"

"Fifty cent," came a call from an adjoining table.

"Just 50 cents for this beautiful bride's slipper? Ach, too cheap. Who'll make it one dollar?"

"Two dollar," came a deep rumbling voice from the other room.

"You make it two dollars?" The auctioneer nodded to the bride's boys. Jake soberly nodded his head, answering for all of them. This was serious business, for the bride's boys had to chip in and buy the slipper at the highest price bid.

Three dollars, four, five, six, seven. Then it jumped to 10 dollars. It sold at 12 dollars. It was too high. It meant that each of the four bride's boys would have to pay three dollars apiece. Resentment boiled up inside of Hannah, but none of the turmoil showed in her face. Then the older women brought out the wedding gifts, placing them on the cleared table.

Henry and Olinda stood up, and according to the custom, Henry unwrapped each present, saying aloud to Olinda the name of the giver. Olinda took the present from his hand, held it aloft, and thanked the giver. She passed it around for each to see and feel, to decide whether it was worth much or little.

Expensive gifts: bedspreads, linens, curtains. Cheaper gifts of dishes, cooking pans, towels and small useful articles from the fifteen cent store. A motto from a sister, "The Lord Is My Shepherd." More suitable, Hannah thought, would have been, "Forgive Us Our Sins." Foolish gifts, a bright pink baby hood in a purple box. Olinda held it up, a faint smile touching her blushing face. The crowd roared, jokes and suggestive stories began.

Jake pressed Hannah's hand, giving her a slight shove. "Come on, let's get out," he whispered.

Daniel Kniemer blocked her way.

"Have a drink, Hannah," he urged, holding up a pitcher. Hannah shook her head and moved around him.

Old lady Kniemer, unable to get out, slid down and crawled under a table. Hannah helped her to her feet.

Hannah stood on the porch. The cool air blew upon her hot, powder-streaked face. The party was breaking up and some of the young people pushed past her.

"Come on—let's ride around a while before we go on to Schreissmillers'," someone shouted.

In the brightly decorated cars, laughing loudly, with horns honking, they tore down the dirt streets. It was four o'clock in the afternoon when they stopped near the Schreissmiller barn.

"Hurry, you don't wanta miss the dance," Jake shouted, pulling Hannah up the rickety ladder to the barn loft.

Benches were ranged along the walls. In one corner, cake, sandwiches, and pies were piled upon boards laid on trestles. This was for the midnight lunch. On one corner of the table was the wedding cake, waiting to be cut into the smallest pieces possible. Each piece would be auctioned off at midnight. Each piece would probably bring from 10 to 25 cents.

In a far corner, near the window, were the two violinists, and Fred Engenboch with his big harpboard, laid on a table in front of him.

Hannah looked at Fred's strong dark face and at his big husky body clad in his best suit. Fred was good looking. No wonder Frieda was proud of him. It was too bad Frieda couldn't be here—her baby had come just a week ago, a puny boy. Fred had had to come. He had the finest harpboard in all the country and played at all the weddings. His harpboard had a six-inch sounding board and was handmade of solid oak, with many wires strung across its broad surface. In the sunlight streaming through the window the brass-bound corners gleamed and many tightly strung wires glistened like silver.

Daniel Kniemer stepped up and held his hand high for silence.

"Everybody's what dance with the bride will have to pin a dollar bill on her dress, or they have to give one silver dollar. The womens can dance for fifty cent." He turned to Fred. "Go on with the dance," he ordered.

Fred struck the wires with two curled, soft-wood sticks. Instantly the room was filled with sound, as though a dozen violins were wailing in slow mournful tones.

Olinda and Henry stood stiff and straight before the harpboard, faces serious, looking down as Fred played the slow music. This was the bride's music. Fred's strong hands flew faster, the music quickened, and the two Schmidt boys raised their violins and joined in the fast and joyous tune.

Henry danced this first dance with Olinda. The older men and women crowded around the open doorways and against the walls. Hannah saw her mother crying. Great tears were splashing down her cheeks and she was wiping them away with her broad hands. Tabia was comforting her, and Lizzie and Mary stood near. Lizzie straight as a rod, Mary dumbly patting Ana's shoulder.

This was the groom's dance, the only time during all the wedding dancing that he had to dance. He had it easy, Hannah thought, and Olinda will be sick. For the bride was compelled to dance every dance that was played.

Olinda had sinned but she would pay, Hannah thought grimly. She watched Olinda dance by with her long white veil tied to her arm by a pink satin ribbon. Rice and grain showered around Olinda and Henry. It fell on Olinda's hair, rattled as it hit the worn boards of the bare floor.

Mrs. Hergenboch, Fred's mother, who was Olinda's godmother, wriggled her way through the packed crowd and, raising her arm high, shouted, "Hockzeit!" (Wedding Time) and dashed a large dish to the floor, where it broke into bits. Olinda and Henry kept on dancing, and the scrunch of the broken dish under the soles of their shoes sent shivers racing up Hannah's back. Some of the older women and men stooped down and picked up the largest of the broken pieces. The smaller pieces were left to be ground into the floor.

Henry danced with Olinda for three rounds before the music stopped.

Jake nudged Hannah's arm. "You dance with Olinda next, Hannah. I'll pay for it."

Hannah started to shake her head, but she saw Ana nod and smile at her, so she consented. Jake pinned the dollar bill to Olinda's dress, Fred struck up the music, slow and mournful, and Olinda and Hannah stood side by side, facing the harpboard. When the music quickened Olinda and Hannah went into the dance. Everyone watched.

Hannah felt that she dared not look at Olinda. She held the pudgy body lightly, but even so it seemed to her that all who danced with the bride must know. Round and round she danced, three whole rounds. It was the custom to allow members of the wedding party three rounds with the bride; all others paid their dollar for but two rounds. When each of the wedding party had danced with the bride, guests were allowed the privilege of dancing with her.

The old women smiled happily as they watched each man pin a dollar bill to the bride's dress. Their jiggling feet kept time to the music. Some of the old men danced with each other, their faces wreathed in smiles.

Whenever the musicians stopped to rest the old men, as well as the younger, stamped their feet on the wide boards of the loft until it sounded like the thunder of stampeding cattle.

Little Britches

Ralph Moody

WHEN WE LIVED in East Rochester, Mother used to let Grace and me take the money to pay the grocery bill every Saturday. Mr. Blaisdell always gave us a little bag of candy when we came in to pay, but since we had moved out to the ranch we never got any. I liked all kinds of chocolate, but I liked the bitter kind Mother used in cakes best. The last Christmas before we came west, she had made fudge with some of it. It was the best candy I ever tasted. I got thinking about fudge, and one night I asked her when she was going to make some more. She said maybe she'd make some when Christmas came, but sugar cost too much to be using it up in candy we didn't need.

The more I thought about fudge, the more I thought about the bar of Baker's chocolate we got with our last groceries, and the more I wanted some of it. Baked beans, pea soup, and fried sidemeat had tasted all right before, but thinking about chocolate, they didn't even make me feel hungry.

The next afternoon when I was helping Father on the winnower, I was thinking of what he had said about going to meet your troubles and how much less they would be. I don't know if I'd even stopped thinking about that when I began dreaming about chocolate again. It was right then I got the idea: If I should whack a chunk off the end of that bar of chocolate, Mother would be sure to miss it. Then, before she had any idea who had done it, I could confess and probably wouldn't even get a spanking for it, any more than I did for going up to Two Dog's.

I waited till she was out feeding the chickens, then told Father I was thirsty and thought I'd go in for a drink of water. All the time I was going into the house and getting the bar of chocolate down out of the cupboard, my head kept wanting to think about tearing boards off my house, but I wouldn't let it, because I told myself that was only when you did things you shouldn't and then lied about it—I wasn't going to lie at all about the chocolate.

I heard Mother coming just when I had the knife ready to whack off the end of the bar, so I had to slip it into the front of my blouse and pick up the water dipper quick. Before I went back to help Father, I went to the barn and hid the piece of chocolate back of the currycomb box.

All the rest of the afternoon, I didn't like to look at Father. I tried to get him to let me go over to see Willie Aldivote, but he wouldn't. Every time he spoke to me I jumped, and my hands got shaking so I couldn't hold the pieces still enough for him to solder. He asked me what was the matter, and I told him it was nothing, that my hands were getting cold. I knew he didn't believe me, and every glance he looked my way my heart started pounding, because he could always tell what was going on inside my head. It seemed it would never come time to go for the cows. I didn't want the chocolate any more; I just wanted a chance to put it back without being caught.

On the way out for the cows, my heart stopped pounding so hard, and I could think better. I hadn't really stolen the whole bar of chocolate, because I had only meant to take a little piece, and that's as much as I would have taken if Mother hadn't come in just when she did. If I put back the whole bar, I wouldn't have done anything wrong at all. I'd nearly decided I would do it, but just thinking so much about chocolate made my tongue almost taste the smooth bitterness of it. It didn't seem as if it would be very wrong if I only took a small piece. Then I got the idea that if I took a sharp knife and cut about half an inch off the end—with a good clean slice—Mother might never notice it.

I was nearly out to where the cows were picketed when I remembered what Father had said when I got my trap: some of the money in his pouch was mine because I had earned it. Why wouldn't it be all right to figure that the bar of chocolate had been bought with my own money, and in that way I wouldn't be stealing at all. That seemed to fix everything, and I got planning how I would go out to the barn every night after school and whittle off a little piece of chocolate.

I could have felt all right about the whole business if it hadn't been for Mother's reading. Sometimes, on Sunday afternoons, she used to read just to Father, but any of us could stay in the house and listen if we wanted to. He often had her read Shakespeare's plays, and the one he liked best was about Hamlet. I liked it, too, and used to listen every time she read it.

I had just pulled the picket pins and was heading the cows home when the bad king's prayer came into my head, and I couldn't get it out. I tried to think about how Hi dived off his horse and came up on his feet, and about Two Dog, and King, and everything else, but my head kept saying, "Oh, my offense is rank," until I thought I'd go crazy.

We were nearly to the railroad track when I decided to leave the hole and twisted out a dried soapweed stalk with seed pods on it. When you threw one of them up in the air it would wobble and twist all around so that you never knew which way it would come down. I told myself that if it came down with the pods to the west, I'd take the whole bar of chocolate back. If it came down pointed to the north, I'd take half an inch off the end, but if it came down pointed to the east, it had been bought with my own money, and it wouldn't be stealing to keep it.

I swung the pod stalk around my head a few times and flung it as high as I could. Then I shut my eyes tight till I heard it land. When I opened them, the pod of the stalk was pointed almost toward the west, but not quite. It was a little toward the south.

There was a bright moon when I went to bed that night, and it was sharp and clear. I couldn't go to sleep and kept trying to remember how much the pod end of the stalk had really been pointing toward the south. At last, I heard Father put the cat outside for the night; and a little later, when I peeked under my curtain, I could see he had blown out the lamp.

I pulled my overalls up over my nightgown and took my shoes in my hand. When I was out in the yard I slipped them on and took the axe from the chopping block. It was good and sharp, and I was sure I could peel off a smooth, thin slice of chocolate with it.

It was dark as tar inside the barn, but I felt along the wall for the currycomb and lifted the chocolate box out from behind it. King had followed me, and I fell over him when I was groping for the door, but it was so light outside you could almost have read a book. I shook the bar out of the box, unwrapped it, and laid it on the lower rail of the corral fence. Just as I was starting to cut it with the axe, Father said, "Son!"

I couldn't think of a thing to say, but I grabbed up the bar of chocolate and shoved it inside the bib of my overalls before I turned around. He picked me up by the shoulder straps—just as he'd have picked up a kitten that had wet on the floor—and took me over to the wood pile. I didn't know anybody could spank as hard as he spanked me with that little piece of board. It felt as if my bottom was going to catch fire at every lick.

Then he stood me down and asked me if I thought I'd deserved it. He said it wasn't so much that I took the chocolate as it was the way I took it, and because I tried to hide it when he spoke to me. But it was the next thing he said that hurt me worse than the spanking.

He said, "Son, I realize a lot better than you think I do that you have been helping to earn the living for the family. We might say the chocolate was yours in the first place. If you had asked Mother or me for it, you could have had it without a question. I won't have you being sneaky about things. Now, if you'd rather keep your own money separate from the family's, so you can buy the things you want, I think it might be a good idea."

I never knew till then how much I wanted my money to go in with Father's. Ever since we bought the cows, I had been able to feel I had a part in all the new things we were buying to make ourselves real ranchers, and it looked as though it were all slipping away from me. I had felt I was beginning to be a man, but I guess I was still just a baby, because I hid my face against Father's stomach and begged him to let me put my money in with his.

Father hadn't been coughing nearly so much that fall as he used to, but he coughed and it seemed as if he choked a little before he answered me. He said he didn't want a sneaky partner, but if I could be open and aboveboard he didn't know a man he'd rather be in business with.

I couldn't help crying some more when he told me that; not because my bottom was still burning, but just because I loved him. I told him I'd never be sneaky again, and I'd always ask him before I did things. We walked to the house together. At the bunkhouse door he shook hands with me, and said, "Good night, partner." When I went to sleep, my hand was still hurting—good—from where he squeezed it when we shook hands.

Founder's Praise

Joanne Greenberg

IT GOT SO THAT THE OLD MAN would sit in his chair by the front window and conduct the storm. When it scoured up from the south, he would dare it to drown them. When the storm lay its gritty black winds about them, he would shake his fists at it. Sometimes the wind would change in mid-storm, layering the colors—gray and black and red, and their own pale earth flung back at them, after a ride to Texas and Oklahoma. It was a game the winds were playing, setting down red dunes with sharp edges in one storm and carrying them off in the next and whipping three years' seeds through air suddenly gone solid.

Now, the ground was so dry that it wouldn't even clump if it was wetted. Inside the houses, the dust that had forced its way through every crack blew the air dark. They wore it, ate it, breathed it, spat it out black from dry throats every morning. "Like livin' in a coal mine," Charlie cursed. "Dark as a mine, even in the daytime."

When the winds were at their worst, there was nothing to do but stay inside. They wore dampened rags over their faces to keep the dust from their lungs. Between the dry storms, they worked until they were exhausted. The old man had dug the house out, Edgar the northeast side of the barn. The wind drove dry branches and the roots of old trees against their fences and piled the rubbish of distant farms against their outbuildings. The well went foul and silted up. There was no water, and they had to haul emergency supplies from town. More and more families packed up and left. There came to be a place in the services on Sunday when one or two or three men would get up and announce that they were leaving. "Anyone feels I got a debt to 'em, come on over and take what's fair. There's tools and things—the wife's got a tea set and a cherry-wood chest." And he might laugh a little, embarrassed, at the joke he had not meant, a laugh that had no humor in it.

The Bissets did not see them go. Their place was east of town and no one went by. The road beside the farm was a minor one, used once and now forsaken for a larger one, a mile or so to the north, that led directly through the town. On this road, people said, the cars and carts and horses and wagons moved in a slow stream. Stopping in town, people would look around through shocked, road-dulled eyes. "We thought it would be better here—they told us it was better here," and they would go on.

It moved Edgar to see his father's rage. The old man had more energy in his body than Edgar did—enough to curse the dunes that danced and changed, east, southeast, south-southeast, back and forth, changing color, as the wind changed direction. He noticed that after every blow the old man would shoulder his shovel and go to the same banked place that buried the front porch, the same drowned fence. Edgar wondered how long the old man's spirit would last. He wondered how long he and Charlie would be kept from insanity, how much less they could eat and not starve to death, how many weeks it was to ruin. He did not speak. He seldom spoke five words at all between sunup and dark.

At the end of March, the winds stopped abruptly and on the third of April it rained. It was a black rain, full of the north-winding dust that had been held in the clouds, and it left black grit wherever it fell. After the rain, Edgar drove the remaining four cows to browse on whatever new grass might have come up. The cows looked skeletal, and they barely had the strength to move. Erosion had made a cleft through what had once been Mutcher's farm, and at the bottom of this draw there was a protected place and the barest haze of new grass. Edgar left them there and went scouting in the arroyos and dry creek beds for whatever else there might be. By noon, he had worked all the way around to the east of the farm without finding anything on which the cows could feed. At lunch, Ralph told Edgar to go on scouting to the south for new grass. He would bring the cows back before dark. It was a scanty meal, barely enough to keep Edgar from cramping as he walked in and out of the eroded places in the vast, flat land. Edgar kept looking up at the sun, which seemed suddenly cold. He walked quickly to keep warm. Here and there he found a web of grass, hair-thin and almost too delicate to see on the south-facing sides of the arroyos. Too little. Too fragile. He noted the places and started for home.

As he walked, he thought of the cows, once good stock. The dust had filtered into their fodder as it had into everything else, and their teeth had been ground down, almost by half. They were so thin—

He was crossing the broom field near home when he saw the old man coming toward him, running, his arms out as though to stop himself from falling. Edgar began to run. As they neared each other, Edgar heard his father yelling his name and he ran faster, until they met between barn and house and Charlie Dace came running up from where he was working.

"Edgar!" the old man gasped. "The cows!"

"What?"

"The cows has been took!"

"What, stolen?"

"Took, took!" The old man coughed, gasping for breath, while Edgar in an agony of frustration almost jumped from one foot to the other.

"The cows has been took!" the old man finally gasped. "Not stole—took—took against nature!" And before he fell, staggering, he led them to the old Mutcher place and the draw.

Looking down the draw, they saw all four cows, wandering aimlessly, having eaten all the grass there was. "You—don't—see—!" the old man gasped. "But I seen. Growin'. Growin' grass. The cows—is growin' grass!"

Edgar caught Charlie's eye. They might have laughed, except that Ralph's voice had hysteria in it, and his face showed terror sharp as the marks of a slap.

"What do you think?" Charlie murmured under his breath. Edgar shook his head. Slowly, they walked toward the bony cows.

"They seem okay," Charlie whispered. "Still got their winter hair, and they are thin, but they seem okay."

Looking back, they could see Ralph standing above them, motionless now.

"Lookin' like he's lost his mind?" Charlie whispered. Edgar said nothing. They went closer.

At first, it seemed like winter hair, a thicker coat against the winds, and then they saw what the old man said was true. The cows were green. Patches of new prairie grass were growing from the backs and down the flanks of Juliet, Pride, and Independence. Movie Star, whose place was near the far wall of the barn, had the left side of her body evenly covered with prairie grass, young clover, and wild oats. Neither of the men wanted to touch the cows—there was a whiff of the old horror in them—but Edgar made himself remember that he had been on battlefields, and seen grass growing between the fingers of a severed hand. After a moment he pushed himself forward and grabbed at Movie Star, raking at the green cover on her side. She lowed and pulled away from him. Charlie, beside him, was cursing in a self-absorbed monotone as he pulled at the green weeds caught among the rotting hair of Independence's back.

"You can't get under it!" Charlie cried. "The dust has been drove up right into the skin and it's all matted in there with roots. These cows must be carryin' 20 pounds of dirt on 'em."

"You ever hear of this before?" Edgar asked him.

"One time, a long time ago, I heard a fellow tell about a tornado come through one year and done like that, drove dirt into cows' hides so hard it couldn't be got out."

"What happened to the cows?" Edgar asked.

Charlie stood, embarrassed, fussing with Movie Star and then Independence. "He didn't say," he muttered.

Edgar sighed. Charlie had kept to himself so long that he had lost the talent for telling a convincing lie.

* * *

The next week, another sandstorm crested and broke on the fields. Ropes of dust were held upright like cobras swaying from a basket. And the old man shouted curses at the storm in his dried-out plains voice. It lasted for four days. The air in the house was gray. The drying, abrading dust found each hair-thin fault and secret path inward to the heart of the house and the men there. They coughed and spat blood. They burned their kerosene lamps all day and still had to grope for doorways.

When the night pots were full, the old man went to dump them out the back door away from the wind, but it saw him and turned and blew his piss—turned black in its moment in the air—back in his face. At the sight of him crusted, black, and dripping, Charlie and Edgar had a fit of hysterical laughter, but they couldn't laugh long because they began to choke—the air had gone solid again.

When it was over, they went out to the barn and slaughtered the cows. The hides were useless; the green patches gone to mold, rotten under the skin. Although the meat was not good, they boiled, smoked, pickled, and oven-dried it. They used every jar that could hold a seal and processed them in the sour water that the well pumped. They were stupid with exhaustion and threw the good parts out with the rotten; there was no time to boil and settle the water they needed. So much was waste and useless that the old man cried in rage.

Butcher's Crossing

John Williams

BY THE TIME HE GOT BACK to the camp, the sun had gone behind the western mountains; there was a chill in the air that went through his clothing and his sweaty skin. Charley Hoge trotted out from the camp to meet him.

"How many?" Charley Hoge called.

"Miller counted 135," Andrews said.

" 'I God," Charley Hoge said. "A big one."

Near the camp, Andrews halted his horse and untied the rope from the saddle horn.

"Nice little calf you got," Charley Hoge said. "Make good eating. You want to dress her down, or you want me to?"

"I'll dress her," Andrews said. But he made no movement. He stood looking at the calf, whose open transparent eyes were filmed over blankly with a layer of dust.

After a moment, Charley Hoge said: "I'll help you fix up a scaffold."

The two men went to the area where earlier Charley Hoge had been working on the corral for the livestock. The corral, roughly hexagonal in shape, had been completed, but there were still a few long aspen poles lying about. Charley pointed out three of equal length and they dragged them back to where the buffalo calf lay. They pounded the ends of the poles into the ground, and arranged them in the form of a tripod. Andrews mounted his horse, and lashed the poles together at the top. Charley Hoge threw the rope, which was still attached to the calf's head, over the top of the tripod, and Andrews tied the loose end to his saddle horn. He backed his horse up until the calf was suspended, its hooves barely brushing the short grass. Charley Hoge held the rope until Andrews returned to the tripod and secured the rope firmly to the top, so that the buffalo would not drop.

The buffalo hung; they surveyed it for a moment without speaking. Charley Hoge went back to his campfire; Andrews stood before the hung calf. In the distance, across the valley, he saw a movement; it was Schneider and Miller returning. Their horses went in a swift walk across the valley bed. Andrews took his knife and put it carefully to the exposed belly of the calf.

He worked more slowly this time. After he had made the cuts in the belly, throat, and around the ankles, he carefully peeled the hide back so that it fell down the sides of the animal. Then, reaching high above the hump, he stripped the hide from the back. It came off smoothly, with only a few small chunks of flesh adhering to it. With his knife he scraped the largest of these chunks off, and laid the skin on the grass, flesh side downward, as he had seen Schneider do. As he stood back, looking down at his hide, Miller and Schneider rode up and dismounted.

Miller, his face streaked with the black residue of powder smoke and smears of red blood, looked at him dully for a moment, and then looked at the hide spread on the ground. He turned and shambled unsteadily toward the campsite.

"Looks like a clean job," Schneider said, walking around the hide. "You won't have any trouble. Course, it's easier when your carcass is hanging."

"How did you and Miller do?" Andrews asked.

"We didn't get halfway through. We'll be working most of the night."

"Wish I could help," Andrews said.

Schneider walked over to the skinned calf and slapped the naked rump of it. "Nice little calf. She'll make good eating."

Andrews went to the calf and knelt; he fumbled among the knives in his case. He turned his head to Schneider, but he did not look at him.

"What do I do?" he asked.

"What?"

"What do I do first? I've never dressed an animal before."

"My God," Schneider said quietly. "I keep forgetting. Well, first you better dress her. Then I'll tell you how to cut her up."

Charley Hoge and Miller came around the tall chimney rock and leaned against a log. Andrews hesitated for a moment, then stood up. He pushed the point of the knife against the breastbone of the calf, and poked until he found the softness of the stomach. He clenched his teeth, and pushed the knife in the flesh, and drew the blade downward. The heavy, coiled blue-and-white guts, thicker than his forearm, spilled out from the clean edge of the cut. Andrews closed his eyes, and pulled the knife downward as quickly as he could. As he straightened up, he felt something warm splash in front; a gush of dark, half-clotted blood had dropped from the opened cavity. It spilled upon his shirt and dripped down upon the front of his trousers. He stepped backward. His quick movement sent the calf rocking slowly on the rope, and the thick entrails slowly emerged from the widening cut. With a heavy, liquid sound they spilled upon the ground; like something alive, the edge of the mass touched Andrews and covered the tops of his shoes.

Schneider laughed loudly, slapping his leg. "Cut her loose!" he shouted. "Cut her loose before she crawls all over you!"

Andrews swallowed the heavy saliva that spurted in his mouth. With his left hand he followed the thick, slimy main gut up through the body cavity; he watched his forearm disappear into the wet warmth of the body. When his left hand came upon the end of the gut, he reached his other hand with the knife up beside it, and sliced blindly, awkwardly at the tough tube. The rotten smell of the buffalo's half-digested food billowed out; he held his breath, and hacked more desperately with his knife. The tube parted, and the entrails spilled down, gathering in the lower part of the body. With both arms, he scooped the guts out of the cavity until he could find the other attachment; he cut it away and tore the insides from the calf with desperate scooping motions, until they spread in a heavy mass on the ground around his feet. He stepped back, pale, breathing heavily through his opened mouth; his arms and hands, held out from his body, dripping with blood, were trembling.

Miller, still leaning against the chimney rock, called to Schneider: "Let's have some of that liver, Fred."

Schneider nodded, and took a few steps to the swinging carcass. With one hand he steadied it, and with the other reached into the open cavity. He jerked his arm; his hand came out carrying a large piece of brownish-purple meat. With a few quick strokes of his knife, he sliced it in two, and tossed the larger of the pieces across to Miller. He caught the liver in the scoop of his two hands, and clutched it to his chest so that it would not slide out of his grasp. Then he lifted it to his mouth, and took a large bite from it; the dark blood oozed from the meat, ran down the sides of his chin, and dropped to the ground. Schneider grinned and took a bite from his piece. Still grinning, chewing slowly, his lips dark red from the meat, he extended the meat toward Andrews.

"Want a chew?" he asked, and laughed.

Andrews felt the bitterness rise in his throat; his stomach contracted in a sudden spasm, and the muscles of his throat pulled together, choking him. He turned and ran a few paces from the men, leaned against a tree, doubled over, and retched. After a few moments, he turned to them.

"You finish it up," he called to them. "I've had enough."

Without waiting for a reply, he turned again and walked toward the spring that trickled down some 75 yards beyond their camp. At the spring he removed his shirt; the blood from the buffalo was beginning to stiffen on his undershirt. As quickly as he could, he removed the rest of his clothing and stood in the late afternoon shadow, shivering in the cool air. From his chest to below his navel was the brownish-red stain of buffalo blood; and in removing his clothing, his arms and hands had brushed against other parts of his body so that he was blotched with stains hued from a pale vermilion to a deep brownish crimson. He thrust his hands into the icy pool formed by the spring. The cold water clotted the blood, and for a moment he feared that he could not remove it from his skin. Then it floated away in solid tendrils; and he splashed water on his arms, his chest, and his stomach, gasping at the cold, straining his lungs to gather air against the repeated shocks of it.

A Tenderfoot in Colorado

Richard Baxter Townshend

ON A BLAZING HOT NOON in early summer, I was riding around over the range looking for a stray horse. The endless rolling surface of the prairie seemed absolutely bare of cattle, so far, at least, as one could depend upon what the eye alone. For it was one of the days when the "smoke" was strong—"smoke" being the name we used to give to the mirage. Out in Colorado, all the baffling uncertainty of vision that makes for mystery, all illusion, all glamour, belong to the dazzling hours of midday and not to the gloaming.

In the early morning, and towards evening, there is no "smoke" and no mystery, for out there on the great plains, 5,000 feet above sea level in the driest part of the American continent, the air is of an incredible transparency. Fifty miles from my ranch, the huge red granite dome of Pike's Peak heaved up its beetling crags against the western sky; and at sunrise, every crack and crevice of the rocks showed as sharp and clear-cut as though they were only half a mile off. Northwards, the stem of one solitary pine, 10 miles away, made a thin black line against the sky, and I once knew a single horseman detected by the keen sight of a frontiersman standing in front of my ranch over on Holcombe Bluffs across a distance of fully two leagues.

But as the summer sun mounted high and poured his scorching rays on the bare ground, there came a change. The lowest layer of air absorbed the heat from the heated soil and presently began to rise up in wavering currents such as one may observe to quiver perpetually over the mouth of a furnace.

Through this flickering veil of mirage, all things were seen distorted, shifting, uncertain. A solitary soapweed 100 yards away might suddenly stand up and develop legs and become a horse; again, the horse's back would swell and arch itself into a great hump, and lo! There stood a buffalo instead; presto! the buffalo would shrink, elongate himself, and be transformed into a thicket of reeds, shaking in the wind, alongside a pool of clear delicious water. And then in a moment, the scene would change back again, the illusion pass, and the common soapweed was a weed once more.

However, I had no time to waste over fancies, but pushed on in search of my stray horse, on whom, if chance willed, and the "smoke" were not too confusing, I might happen at any minute…

* * *

I turned back to the rolling prairie … and as I went I noticed half a dozen dun and brindle Texas cows, who had already slaked their thirst, travelling steadily away from the water in the same direction as myself. A few young heifers and steers accompanied them, though the mass of the cattle, as I well knew, would stay by the water till the heat of the day was over; but this party of long-horned, long-legged Texas ladies clearly had business elsewhere. They struck into one of the innumerable cattle trails leading from the high pastures to the water and pressed up it, travelling one close behind the other at a steady walk that occasionally became a trot. I rode parallel to them, curious to see the goal they were making for so eagerly.

Up we went into the high-rolling sand hills, and there, in the middle of them, in a little cup-like hollow, I saw a regular Texas nursery. Eight little dun-coloured Texas calves lay there, squatted close to the sandy ground with which their coats matched so well, their heads lying out flat, with the chins pressed down on the sand just as little antelope fawns would have crouched. In this pose they were all but invisible. Beside them lay two elderly Texas cows, whose office had been to guard the crèche.

The mothers, who had travelled till now in perfect silence, began to low loudly and lovingly when they caught sight of their offspring, and in a moment each young hopeful had jumped up and rushed to his own dam, where his wriggling tail and nuzzling head, the busy lips frothing with milk, soon showed he was getting the dinner he had waited for so patiently. Meantime, the two guardian cows had risen to their feet and lost no time in starting off in their turn to make their trip to the water, leaving their own two calves safe in the care of the rest of the band.

The system of mutual protection was perfect. Brer' Wolf might prowl around and watch with hungry eyes till his lips watered—there was no chance for him to get veal for his dinner while the sharp horns of those fierce Texas mothers guarded their children. Broadly speaking, one might say the Texas cow, the cow of the wilderness, had evolved an institution that has enabled her and her offspring to survive the dangers of savage life.

This institution has been long superseded by the civilized life of the farm for the well-bred short-horn cow; but take her away from her sheltered surroundings and turn her loose on the range, and she is as helpless as most duchesses would be if left on a desert island. The pedigree daughter of 50 prize-winners must inevitably succumb to the dangers of her new life unless she has initiative enough to revert to the social system of her own primitive ancestors who fought with the wolf and bear in the woodlands of early Britain.

The Cattlemen

Mari Sandoz

Some Dedicated Men

THOROUGHLY DISGUSTED at last, Charlie Goodnight gave up ranching in Texas. Too many Indians and no use begging for help from that Reconstruction gathering of scalawags and carpetbaggers down at Austin. ... But the mining regions of the Rockies seemed to have some money left. Steers worth at the most $8 or $10 in Texas brought $60 up there.

* * *

It would take real time, money, and sand to swing down an unknown trail through waterless country to get around the Comanches, or most of them. Yet, Charlie Goodnight, an old cowman at 30, insisted he was heading for Colorado and going around the south to do it. He gathered up little herds of loose, unmarked cattle here and there ... claiming they belonged to him but with no brand to prove it.

Old Charlie, as some called him now, was convinced by his wartime experience with the Rangers, and since, that any crossing of the Indian country of northwest Texas was to be avoided.

* * *

Goodnight also knew something of the country he would have to cross on the southern swing and the turn westward to the Pecos and up its briny, forbidding canyon and beyond. The reputation of the stretch to the Pecos was bad ever since the first cattle came to Texas with Coronado. The other two ranchers who were to go with Charlie Goodnight to Colorado got scared out just chewing it over. In the end, the old rancher Oliver Loving, who had tried to talk Goodnight against it, too, asked to go along.

* * *

Goodnight had planned his drive in the hope that there was some nice money to be made for beef in Colorado, and certainly there would be grass to hold any stock not readily salable. Now another and—by his planned route, a more immediate—hope came up: the hope of selling beef to fill Indian contracts in New Mexico on the way. There was even a chance of cornering a little of the often-exorbitant prices that some Indian contractors seemed to get.

* * *

So, in 1866, trailing a mixed herd of 2,000 steers, cows, and calves with 18 hands, mostly armed, they set out, the 54-year-old tough and hardened Loving in charge of the herd.

Pulling For New Grass

Perhaps it was true that in Colorado a cattleman could still make a living.

He let his impatient horse out, pointing his hat at arm's length before him, signaling the direction. So Goodnight scouted the trail for water, for range and ground, doubling back to give his signals. Loving, behind him, knew how to get the most from the men and the herd. All but the two point riders, the best men in the outfit, shifted positions daily to relieve those on the dusty side and those riding drag—always keeping the herd strung out well and yet close enough to let them feel each other, hold them in an unbroken file to crawl like a thin, dark, thousand-segmented jointed snake over the rolling prairie. It was a pretty route through the mirage region—the Phantom Hill country. By then, the herd was a fine traveling unit, the leader taking his place every morning, keeping it day after day. As in most herds, the steers had traveling companions and when separated they raised their heads to get wind of each other, bawling until they got together. Each strong young cow gathered her own following within the herd. As in most good-sized drives, there were a few muleys, born hornless, and within a few days these bedded close together, a little apart. As usual, too, there was a loner or two who went prowling up one side of the herd and down the other, apparently searching for the never-lost. Sometimes, there was an outcast, hooked at everywhere, with even the muleys making the homing motion. All these, unless steadied down early, ended up in the drags, with the poor, the old, and the very young.

* * *

Loving had the herd traveling very well in the heat and dust by the time they reached the head of the Middle Concho, where they rested and fed before starting on the dry, horse-killing jump of around 80 miles to the Pecos, with 12, 15 miles considered a good drive in the burning sun. Then, after days without water, and the smell of it from the river to drive the cattle wild, they would have to pass the poison lakes marked by whitened bones long before the first Spaniard rode through that way. They had been warned against the poison lakes, the alkali strong enough to kill everything that drank the water, and just beyond was the Pecos, with most of the banks very steep, the crossing a swift, swimming current.

Goodnight and Loving watered the herd—steers, cows, and calves—with all they could drink and filled the canteens and the water barrels of the grub wagon to overflowing. Then, in the afternoon, they pointed the herd to follow the sloping sun down the pale, baked earth.

They trailed late that first evening, made dry camp, and pushed on early. While stock on the range often went without water for three days, driving dried them out as it did men. The second night the herd was too thirsty to bed down, many would break back as they walked and milled all night so it took most of the men to hold them. Goodnight realized that this wouldn't do—the cattle had walked on the bed ground to take them most of the way to the Pecos. He got the herd started very early, knowing that the cattle would have to be pushed today, the herd whipped up by the sleepy, worn-out cowboys under the sun that glittered in great rippling mirage lakes ahead. The canteens dried up, the water barrels began to rattle in the wagon, and the dust rose in bitter white clouds that choked them all. It cracked the lips under the protecting kerchiefs tied loosely enough to be drawn up over the nose, almost to the hat-brim, the dust-rimmed eyes bloodshot and burning; it stung and burned in the sweated saddle galls.

* * *

Charlie Goodnight was suddenly less angry with Texas, less impatient for a shot at Colorado ranch possibilities. He hurried back on the 700-mile trail to gather another herd for the Indians before winter. He rode ahead, followed by a pack mule carrying the $12,000 in gold.

* * *

Up near Fort Sumner, Oliver Loving put a little meat on the cows and calves the Indian agent had turned back and then trailed them slowly to the Raton Mountains, the Arkansas River, and beyond, blazing the trail most of the way. Near Denver, he sold the whole lot to John W. Iliff for his range in northeast Colorado, in the heart of a new cattle region.

Down in Texas, Goodnight collected his second herd of the summer, 1,200 head, all steers, able to travel fast and strong.

* * *

By now, it was too late for the Indian contracts, and when the herd finally reached Sumner Goodnight headed it on toward Colorado. From the Raton Pass vision he looked down over the mountain slopes to the great fall-yellowed grasslands of the upper Arkansas River so like the cloud-shadowed swells of a green sea. He pointed the herd along the north-flowing creeks and up near the head of one of these, the Apishapa, Goodnight stopped. The canyon was around 20 miles long, not very deep, but with walls steep enough so it was practically inaccessible except at the two ends, which could be kept closed very handily by casual line riding. The creek, between banks lined by box elders, shyly sank out of sight during the day and ran again when the sun settled behind the canyon walls. The cowboys joked about it, glad they could laugh after the very grueling drive.

Here, Goodnight established his ranch in what seemed to him a most beautiful cow country and perhaps his would be the first extensive cattle venture in southern Colorado. At least he had the world to himself again, with, so far as any of them knew, little danger from raiding Indians, probably more danger from outlaws. So they turned the cattle loose and set to cutting pines for a log cabin.

The Contested Plains

Elliott West

THIS WAS THE TRUE MEANING of the power struggle of whites and Indians. In the middle of the 19th century, two cultures acted as two compelling visions in a land that could support only one. The struggle—of both peoples to enliven their dreams, of each to deny the other—was one of the great American stories.

In world history it was the most dramatic collision of two objects that, more than any others, have inspired people to redream their existence. The horse offered spiritual transformation, a union of superior beings, the dream of the centaur: man in flight over the land, in rightful dominion over lesser, leg-bound humanity. Gold was the Great Untarnished, purifier and renewer; God-scant sunlight crumbled and held in your hand.

For North Americans, the story tells of the dynamism unleashed when frontiers rolled into country already tangled in change. The starvation and butchery at the end was part of the horrific consequence of the European importance; but when Coronado crossed the Arkansas, he also (without having a clue what he was doing) triggered the greatest explosion of creative energy the country would ever see. Frontiers were messy, and so are their legacies.

For the United States, these events played an unrecognized part in its own making. As the Union was being confirmed in battle to the east, something similar was happening in mid-America from the discovery of gold and its instant impact on millions of minds. The revision of plains and mountains was a central moment in a nation imagining itself whole. It also had its bloody confirmation. Chivington's march on Sand Creek came as Sherman was slicing Georgia in half. Investigators were taking testimony on the massacre when they heard of Lee's surrender at Appomattox. Until the "disc of howling wilderness" was rethought as a heartland of promise, Lincoln's nation "so conceived and so dedicated" could not be fully comprehended.

As moral entertainment, the history of Indians and the gold rush, when set in the context of the land's antiquity, should be a caution. The whites who celebrated the final crushing of a rival vision were already suffering from the hubris of their own. Of all peoples over the past 12,000 years, they came to the country with the greatest power to stretch the restraints that hem in everyone. They pulled more than anyone ever had from its reservoir of energy. Seeing only the land's seductive abundance, they extended themselves much further toward its maximum generosity. And when the unbending rules of the minimum were inevitably applied, the result was stunning human and environmental calamities. Looking at the region today, the lessons are clear enough.

It is also hard not to wonder how different those years might have been if all sides had used their prodigious imaginations to picture how varied peoples and dreams might occupy the same place. In their purest forms the visions could not coexist, and it may be that no common ground was possible. We shouldn't waste time wishing frogs had wings. But after all, Indians and whites were masters of change. Their performances were so impressive precisely because they could envision other ways and then muster the will to make them happen. Perhaps their failures should push us to reperceive our own neighborhoods—our modern versions of townsites, stream valleys, and cottonwood groves—into more tolerant shapes. We might find guiding stories that allow a fuller human dignity.

Dying for Chocolate

Diane Mott Davidson

WHEN WE ARRIVED at the sliding glass and screen door that opened onto the patio, a drumroll was issuing from the tape recorder. The guests had turned their attention to the pool. Arch was standing on the diving board. I almost dropped the tray. His hands were cuffed behind him.

"Open this door—open this damn door," I demanded of a startled Julian.

"I haven't lit the—"

"Just do it!"

Julian scraped the screen in its tracks. I wiggled through, hurried across the concrete, and slapped the tray down on the buffet table. I sent Arch vibes: *Don't dive off that board with your hands cuffed, don't dive, don't...*

His body lifted and flipped. There was a splash. I counted. *One, two, three, four, five, six, seven ...*

No Arch.

I did what any mother would do. I ran to the pool and jumped in. Water drenched my clothes, pulling me down. I kicked off my shoes, took a deep breath, and went under. Arch was standing on the bottom of the pool, thrashing about with the cuffs. I swam and kicked fiercely until I got to him. I grabbed him under the armpits just as the cuffs came off. Lunging from the bottom of the pool, I tugged him upward as hard as I could.

"Braaugh!" he gargled when we splashed through the surface. He coughed and choked on the water. "Stop!" he shouted. "Stop! What are you doing? Mom! Jeez! You've ruined everything!" He broke away from me and doggie-paddled to the side of the pool.

"I was trying to help you," I sputtered, to no avail.

Effusive clapping greeted us when we climbed up the ladder. Arch gave me his most hateful look.

"You screwed everything up! Why do you always have to embarrass me?"

"I'm sorry. I'm sorry." When I could bear his angry eyes no longer, I stared down. My clothes were soaked. Puddles were forming around my feet.

"Did you plan it that way?" cried Weezie. Her voice was shrill with delight. "That was quite a performance!"

Arch slunk into the house. I went after him and plodded upstairs to change. When I got to the third floor there was a tightness in my throat. Next door, Arch crashed about, looking, I assumed, for dry clothes. I found tissues, wiped my face, and coughed.

All I had ever wanted was to be a good mother. I hadn't thought it would be that difficult. I read the books. I took my child to the pediatrician, the park, and the playground. I read to him and spent time with him and helped with the schoolwork. I'd never even had a regular job until it was a financial necessity. I just wanted to take care of Arch. I thought all I had to do was love him, keep him safe and well, and do the best I could. In turn, he would turn out well-adjusted, happy, and appreciative.

Right.

The sun finished its slide into the mountains. The air was suddenly chilly. When I was putting on a sweat suit and dry sneakers, there was a knock at my door.

"Mom, it's me."

I wrapped a towel around my wet head and opened the door.

He avoided my eyes. His voice was shaky. He said, "Mom, I know you want to help. But it's just not working."

"Honey, please. I thought you were drowning."

"Well ... I just wanted to tell you. I'm definitely going to ask Dad if I can go live with him for a while."

Daze on the Plains

Pat Staten

Cows

COWS ROAM THE LONG, gentle hills of the prairie in herds. Against the clouds and yellow grasses, they move like one creature. On quiet days, they seem to be as permanent and unmoving as trees. Later, I will look up and they've roamed to another part of the pasture, traveling with the imperceptible subtlety of clouds, as the passage of a day.

Their bodies are massive and warm and reassuring. Their eyes are large and easily frightened. They seem to wish nothing more than to wander the plains, chewing grass, drinking water, mating, having babies, drifting into the dreams we cannot dream. They seem to partake of some eternal spirit that's in the land and the space and the clouds. That spirit is a gentle spirit; it wants nothing more than the quiet dream of just living.

On long, quiet, soft days on the endless prairie, I often feel the cows are my only companions. Though I've had a few problems with the gang, we've now settled into an understanding, and they barely note my comings and goings, to the point that they do not rush out of my way on the road even when I toot the horn. They know I'm a bluffer. I've often had to stop the car and get out and pat one on the bottom to get her or him moving along out of the road.

But when I return from town, it's reassuring to see the herd somewhere as I enter the ranch—off in the north pasture, down by the water tank south of the Big House, or occasionally wandering around near the Little House. If I do not see them for days because they've wandered far north to the canyon lands, I miss them and often go off on long walks to find them. I come upon a slight bluff and spot them, looking like tiny toys against this enormous landscape.

Almost every section of the ranch has an assortment of cow bones. The bones remind me of driftwood—dry and bleached by the sun, smooth, white, like wood to the touch, flung about by the elements and scavengers. Hip bones, leg bones, ribs, occasionally a skull, as though the cow's very bones had become its grave marker. As though the haphazard arrangement of these bones would tell the story of the animal's life, if one only knew how to read the language.

If I owned a cattle ranch, I'd probably never be able to take them to slaughter. Most of the ranchers do not see the slaughter. It's done professionally at the slaughterhouses. Thus, the romance continues of cowboy and cow and horse, though the reality isn't at all what the movies would have us believe. Even contemporary movies haven't got a clue as to what goes on out here. But why should they? Reality isn't their business, and rightly so. Nobody would pay to go see reality.

The cows and I had quite an adjustment period, which I never anticipated. Who thinks you'll have to come to social terms with a bovine mentality? But I have often had to come to terms with an intelligence much lower than anything these cows would tolerate, and often it was supervising my workload. I found this social compromise with the cows nearly as complex and exhausting and puzzling as it is with my own species because the cows posed much more profound issues than usual human concerns—those involve your income, your sexual agenda, and whether you like hardwood floors or shag rugs. Once you're through that, you've usually got the whole thing down with people, though a human would never dream of letting it end there. Like dogs with fleas, the scratching and judging and appraising never ends. Nowadays, we all accept that we've got fleas but want to know size, origin, and final body count.

Once the cows seemed to know who I was, the issue did not arise again, which it always does with humans. Who are you? What do you want? Where are you going? Where have you been? Are you into microbiotics, herbs, crystals, numbers, stars, tea leaves, or noodle curls? Are you seeing a shrink, and if so, is he or she Freudian, Jungian, Gestalt, or Hermie Schwartz? Do you like men or women or both or neither or balloons? Do you think I'm wonderful and intelligent and impressive as I do, or do you think I'm stupid and ugly and insignificant as I do? It wears a person down after a few decades.

Ruxton of the Rockies

LeRoy R. Hafen

The Upper Arkansa

OUR COURSE ON LEAVING Red River was due north, my object being to strike the Arkansas near its headwaters, on the other side of the Rocky Mountains, and follow as near as possible the Ute trail, which these Indians use in passing from the Del Norte to the Bayou Salado[1], on their annual buffalo hunts to that elevated valley.

Skirting a low range of mountains, the trail passes a valley upwards of 50 miles in length[2], intersected by numerous streams (called creeks by the mountain

1 Salty Marsh. The term was applied to present South Park, Colorado; at the head of the South Platte River. The early name derives from the salt spring and marsh near the southern end of South Park.

2 San Luis Valley, Colorado, sometimes called the "Roof Garden of America," from its high elevation (about 7,600 feet).

men), which rise in the neighbouring highlands and fall into the Del Norte, near its upper waters. Our first day's journey, of about 25 miles, led through the uplands at the southern extremity of the valley. These are covered with pine and cedar, and the more open plains with bushes of wild sage, which is the characteristic plant in all the elevated plains of the Rocky Mountains. On emerging from the uplands, we entered a level prairie, covered with innumerable herds of antelope. These graceful animals, in bands containing several thousands, trotted up to us, and, with pointed ears and their beautiful eyes staring with eager curiosity, accompanied us for miles, running parallel to our trail within 50 or 60 yards.

The cold in these regions is more intense than I ever remember to have experienced, not excepting even in Lower Canada; and, as a northerly wind sweeps over the bleak and barren plains, charged as it is with its icy reinforcements from the snow-clad mountains, it assails the unfortunate traveller, exposed to all its violence, with blood-freezing blasts, piercing to his very heart and bones.

* * *

Such was the state of congelation I was in on this day that even the shot-tempting antelope bounded past unscathed. My hands, with fingers of stone, refused even to hold the reins of my horse, who travelled as he pleased, sometimes sleuing round his stern to the wind, which was dead ahead. Mattias, the half-breed who was my guide, enveloped from head to foot in a blanket, occasionally cast a longing glance from out its folds at the provoking venison as it galloped past, muttering at intervals, *"Jesús, Jesús, qué carne"*—what meat we're losing! At length, as a band of some 3,000 almost ran over us, human nature, although at freezing point, could no longer stand it. I jumped off Panchito, and, kneeling down, sent a ball from my rifle into the thick of the band. At the report two antelopes sprang into the air, their forms being distinct against the horizon above the backs of the rest; and when the herd had passed, they were lying kicking in the dust, one shot in the neck, through which the ball had passed into the body of another. We packed a mule with the choice pieces of meat, which was a great addition to our slender stock of dried provisions. As I was "butchering" the antelope, half a dozen wolves hung around the spot, attracted by the smell of blood; they were so tame, and hungry at the same time, that I thought they would actually have torn the meat from under my knife. Two of them loped round and round, gradually decreasing their distance, occasionally squatting on their haunches, and licking their impatient lips, in anxious expectation of a coming feast. I threw a large piece of meat towards them, when the whole gang jumped upon it, fighting and growling, and tearing each other in the furious melee. I am sure I might have approached near enough to have seized one by the tail, so entirely regardless of my vicinity did they appear.

A Ditch in Time

Patricia Nelson Limerick with Jason L. Hanson

IN THE EARLY 19TH CENTURY, explorers of the Front Range of Colorado declared that the scarcity of water made conventional American settlement in that locale impossible. In the 21st century, the Front Range is home to a population of millions.

What happened?

An enormous infrastructure rearranged the distribution of water. Dams store spring runoff, capturing water that would otherwise flow downstream and out of the state. Tunnels under the Rockies divert water from the Western Slope to the Front Range. The comparative scarcity of the western water supply did not impose the limits that the early explorers expected because of human engineering skills and because of the creation of an enormously complicated legal and political structure. The belief that aridity in itself would exercise the power to reshape or even prohibit standard American customs of settlement and land use did not turn out to hold water. On the contrary, that power was overruled by the institutions and organizations that acquired, manipulated, and managed water.

For all the distinctive features of this particular place, the transformation of the Front Range of Colorado is one example of a much larger historical process. In a manner unparalleled in most of human history, in the United States in the last half century, millions of people lived in a condition of extraordinary material ease, supplied with an abundance of food, energy, and water by institutions and organizations to which most of the beneficiaries did not pay an ounce of attention. The degree of material good fortune achieved by Americans in this era has only been equaled by the degree of their inattention to its sources. When future historians look back at the United States in the 20th century, if they choose accuracy over graceful phrasing, they will have reason to christen this unusual historical interlude as the *Era of Improbable Comfort Made Possible by a Taken-for-Granted but Truly Astonishing Infrastructure.*

This is a book about one of the organizations that built and maintained this extraordinary, comfort-supplying infrastructure. The founders and leaders of the entity we now know as Denver Water were the opposite of procrastinators. When it came to establishing water rights and building structures to store the water thus obtained, they did not wait for crisis to push them into action. Folklore is full of parables and fables that contrast energetic and foresighted creatures who take action well ahead of need with lazy and complacent creatures who do not look ahead and who thus make it easy for trouble to catch them by surprise. In the water allocation of the American West today, the plot structure of these parables and fables appears in many areas. As the title of this book indicates,* Denver Water took action early and repeatedly to secure and provide water to the citizens in its service area, long before actual shortages could appear. In the last half of the 20th century, as urban and suburban growth rates took off in the Front Range, other, less "proactive" communities found themselves in a pickle, with growing demands for water and a late entry into the scramble for water rights. Very much in the manner of the old fables and parables, the late arrivals looked enviously and covetously at the resources held by the foresighted and farsighted entity named Denver Water. To a remarkable degree, the prospects for future growth in the Front Range in the 21st century *seemed* to be under the control of Denver Water and a few counterpart organizations. The word *seemed* appears in italics because there are compelling reasons to question the extent and scale of Denver Water's imperial power over the water supply of the state of Colorado. A good share of this book conducts an exploration of those reasons.

By calling attention to the history of the Denver Water Department, I aspire to challenge the mental habit that welcomes and relishes natural resources as long as they originate in places and processes that are out of sight and out of mind. As historian Martin Melosi put it: "Service delivery is a 'hidden function' largely because it often blends so invisibly into the urban landscape." Diagnosed and lamented by many observers in recent times, this disconnection or alienation from the sites of production of energy, food, and water has proven to be an effective force for undermining and eroding a sense of responsibility. When people flipped a switch and summoned light or heat or turned a faucet and conjured, at will, a flow of clean water, normal human curiosity—Where did this come from? Who made this happen? What consequences will come from this?—went dead. Events and trends of the early 21st century are, however, bringing that curiosity back to life and also reviving a sense of connection and responsibility. From the volatile price of gasoline to worries about the nation's dependence on imported oil, complacency about the use of energy has been rattled. Anxiety about afflictions carried by food, whether through bacterial contamination or chemical additives, has unsettled the capacity to take the grocery store's offerings for granted. In a similar way, public expressions of alarm over the supply and quality of water have grown in frequency and audibility. A variety of wake-up calls have interrupted the American public's long nap.

When the sites of production are no longer concealed and the connection between our material comfort and a giant network of coal mines, natural gas wells, electrical generating plants, transmission lines, dams, aqueducts, trans-basin tunnels, and treatment plants stands revealed, a common first response has

*For readers whose attention to platitudes may have lapsed, *A Ditch in Time* is a play on the old truism that "a stitch in time saves nine."

been not gratitude, but the condemnation of the individuals and groups who created this network and kept it in operation. Another dimension of this book is a re-examination of that understandable impulse to blame and condemn organizations like Denver Water. Experienced scholars in the field of western water history have urged readers to make fuller reckoning with the benefits and gains, as well as the losses and injuries, produced by the creation of the infrastructure that supports and supplies American communities today. Introducing his history of the Colorado-Big Thompson Project and the Northern Colorado Water Conservancy District, historian Daniel Tyler extended a useful and forceful invitation:

> With all due respect to those who view water projects as the work of evil megalomaniacs, I would ask readers to give some thought to the conditions that fostered the need for supplemental water ... and the vision of [the] men who believed they were taking risks for the betterment of their families, friends, homes and businesses.[2]

Surveying water development on a global scale, writer Diane Ward offered a similar observation: "In times of polarized sentiment about the building of big dams, it has often been forgotten that many dams were built with the best of intentions, by men who genuinely wanted to use them for the betterment of mankind."

Readers may feel an occasional temptation to condemn Denver Water's manipulation and mastery of both nature and other communities in the state. And, yet, there are good reasons to temper that temptation with other recognitions and other appraisals. To contemplate a structure like Cheesman Dam, and to police oneself so closely that disapproval stamps out any spark of admiration, one must undertake an intense treatment program in maintaining a properly dour and somber stance of dismay even when confronted with extraordinary human enterprise. The contemporary need for inspiration—for parables of people facing tough problems, refusing discouragement, and pressing on to solutions and remedies—is the most urgent need of the 21st century. Western American history presents an abundance of such case studies, but all of them come with dimensions of moral complexity and displays of the grimmer aspects of human nature. I invite readers of this book to join me in the invention and refining of methods to extract inspiration from the complicated figures of the past, while fully acknowledging their flaws, failings, and blunt exercises of force and power.

While I am not an apologist for Denver Water, working on this book has left me reluctant to offer a complacent condemnation of the organization and its leadership.

Why?

Because those of us who live in the American West today are dependent on, complicit with, and indebted to the organizations and institutions that disrupted the ecosystems and disturbed the landscapes that, a little late in the game, we came to treasure. This is a paradox that is not going to go away, and it is a source of much mischief if denied and evaded. Handled with honesty, the paradox provides the best footing we have for moving toward a more honest and productive relationship to natural resources and the managers to whom, for so long, we delegated the responsibility to acquire those resources and to supply them to us on demand.

A Ditch in Time also has the goal of acknowledging the historical and contemporary importance of cities in the American West, a region long associated with imagery of open spaces and rural enterprises. The Jeffersonian agrarian dream contributed to the desire to see the West as fundamentally rural, and the imagined West of movies and novels reinforced the preference for open spaces over urban spaces. Western historians, present company included, have displayed their own symptoms of attention deficit when it comes to reckoning with western cities. In the most influential histories of western water, the powerful role of the Bureau of Reclamation in the West understandably led historians to focus on the storage and diversion of water for agriculture. The assumption that the history of water development in the West is a synonym for the history of irrigated agriculture in the West is persistent. In a recent overview of western history, making this assumption explicit, an item in the index reads: "Water supply. See irrigation."

To the degree that urban water development has received the attention of historians, the focus has been on Los Angeles and San Francisco, respectively, on the diversions from the Owens and Hetch Hetchy Valleys. While California case studies make for illuminating comparisons, a study of Denver Water has the advantage of reacquainting everyone—Californians, Coloradans, westerners, and easterners—with the significance of the interior West and of ways in which California patterns both match and differ from patterns elsewhere in the region.

Studying Denver Water enhances our recognition of the importance of cities to regional history while also bringing to our attention a set of unexpected similarities between the eastern and western United States. To many observers of the West, the comparative scarcity of water has been the principal feature of regional distinctiveness. Every map of national precipitation patterns seems to make the case for the uniqueness of the West because of its much lower rates of snowfall and rainfall and much higher rates of solar-driven evapotranspiration. And yet a glance at the water systems of cities of the eastern United States delivers a sharp blow to this assumption of water-defined regional uniqueness. Very much like western systems, the infrastructures delivering water to cities like New York and Boston reach far into the rural hinterland, tapping into waters that are not by any definition riparian (that is, the cities draw on diversions from rivers that do not flow by the land occupied by the cities).

Durango

Gary Hart

THE SOUTHERN UTES, with the actions of Congress and court decisions on resource rights, were on the way in the mid- and late-1990s to the establishment of their resource company Red Willow and were receiving advice on how to manage their new trust fund, whose revenues were beginning to grow. They were being besieged by investment advisors and investment funds, all of whom had elaborate, sometimes baroque, financial systems for maximizing gain. Almost all these schemes were focused on the near term and laid out intricate development plans that, for certain fees, would direct the tribe's newfound wealth into immediate returns for individual tribal members. In every case, the paragraphs regarding fees were near the end of lengthy proposed retainer contracts, and all were in small type.

Leonard Cloud and his tribal council found themselves spending increasing amounts of time with Sam Maynard and his law firm. Having been relative outcasts for well over a century, the Utes now were everyone's new friends, particularly everyone who could smell money. There were enough tribal council members who had been manipulated by one kind of immigrant American or another to make them wary. They trusted Maynard, and they had reason to. He and his partners had always treated them fairly, had never propagated large legal bills, and had shrewdly advised the tribe on a number of occasions of one party or another to steer clear of.

But Cloud and his colleagues were troubled nevertheless. On one occasion in the Maynard law firm, he told Maynard, Every way we look at our development plans, we run up against the water problem. Even though we have the new federal laws about our water rights, having the rights and having the water are two different things.

Sam Maynard nodded. You're right, Mr. Cloud. You've got established rights to the Animas and a lesser amount in the Florida and smaller streams, but it clearly isn't enough to meet the requirements of large-scale mineral development. Some of the proposed technologies are water intensive. Besides, you have downstream obligations to lower-basin users in New Mexico to return some of those flows to the stream.

It gets down to the Animas-La Plata, doesn't it? Leonard Cloud said. It always gets down to that project.

Absolutely, Maynard said. If we can't find a way to restart the project, get some federal construction money, and get it going, the Southern Utes are going to hit their heads on a development ceiling. You'll be better off than you were, but not nearly well enough off to create that trust fund for the future that you've decided on.

After the other council member left, Cloud and Maynard walked across the street for coffee. Leonard Cloud was a placid man, measured and thoughtful, not one to become agitated. But his demeanor now was decidedly edgy. Sam, things aren't good around here these days, he said. He waved in the general direction of the town and beyond. It doesn't seem like Durango these days. The atmosphere is not good.

Right enough on that, Leonard, Maynard said. My family's been here well over 50 years, and I've never seen this place in such an uproar. The longer this project stays unresolved, the more this community becomes a political war zone. We've got neighbors who've lived next door to each other for decades and now won't speak to each other.

Cloud said, I ran into Sheriff Ramsay the other day. He was making his weekly cruise through the reservation, and he stopped in to our council offices. He was pretty casual about it, but he made it clear that there are one or two hotheads that might want to make trouble. He asked the tribal law enforcement team to be on the lookout.

This isn't like Durango, Sam Maynard said. We've had our politics and our campaigns and our debates about this and that. But we're going to have to either build this project or kill it and move on. Otherwise, it's a sore that could become some kind of cancer pretty quick.

What have you heard from the feds? Cloud asked.

Since you and I were back in Washington a couple of months ago, Maynard said, I've kept in touch with the staffs of our congressmen and senators and, though they're committed to helping us, it's a struggle to get the construction money. All they can talk about back there is balancing the budget.

Cloud said, But they've got to understand this project's important. We can't get anything done without it.

Understood, Maynard said. But you've got 500 other people in the Congress who've got some federal project they think is as important as ours. I made your point to Senator Thornton's staff guy and he said, Listen, we can get votes for Animas-La Plata, but you know what that means? It means Thornton has to vote for projects in every state those votes come from—and there goes your balanced federal budget.

So what you're saying is, we're stuck, Cloud said. To get the fed's dollars, our congressional folks have to trade votes, and next election time they get crucified for running up spending.

Sam Maynard nodded. Politically, that's the way it works. But I'll keep in touch with them, and maybe they'll figure something out. In the meantime, though, when any of the congressmen come down here, they get an earful from the project opponents. So they're trapped in the local politics. They support the project and half of southwestern Colorado is angry. They oppose the project and the other half of southwestern Colorado is angry.

That's why we pay them the big bucks, Sam, Cloud said and then laughed wryly.

The Woolly West

Colorado's Hidden History of Sheepscapes

Andrew Gulliford

OF THE HUNDREDS of books about cowboys and cowboying in the American West, there are few volumes on sheep and sheepmen. Cowboys sing to their cows and ride the long circle each night around their herd, but then they return to their bedroll and a sidekick takes over. Not so with sheepmen.

A lone shepherd might be in charge of a band of 900 to 1,000 sheep; and though he may have a horse, it's really his dogs that keep the sheep in line, bed them down, and guard them through the night against coyotes and bears. In the herding tradition, the morning star is the shepherd's star—*La Estrella del Pastor*—because herders rise in the dark. Before sunrise, the flock nibbles away, bunched up, moving always toward water and grass—the two elements essential to sheep grazing as described in pioneer diaries and journals.

Cowboys get the fancy hats and hand-tooled leather boots. Sheepherders wear whatever they can find and carry a staff or crook to catch errant sheep by a rear hoof. It's an ancient practice, far older than nineteenth-century cowboying and trailing cattle north to railroad terminus points as America moved west. Sheepherding stories abound in the Bible and in diverse cultures worldwide, but I wanted to learn about sheep in Colorado—where they came from, how they arrived, who owned them, who herded them, and what impact they have had on the environment for almost two centuries.

Cowboys ride the range together, or at least in pairs. Sheepherders are always alone, visited weekly by a camp tender who brings food and other necessities, perhaps tobacco, a skin of wine, more bullets, fresh peaches, news from home.

As I seek answers and try to understand the language and culture of Basque, Greek, and Hispanic families who still raise sheep and graze them on public land, I am captivated by the carvings, the legacy of lone herders high in Colorado aspen groves, on foot or on horseback, etching names, dates, symbols, portraits of beautiful women, and also the occasional curse ...

A 100-history of sheep grazing on Colorado public land should produce some interesting stories, some deep-seated quarrels, and a new awareness of pioneer families who succeeded because of pluck, perseverance, and a willingness to risk rain, snow, coyotes, and cold nights alone, all in an attempt to raise lambs, put weight on the wethers, and make an income twice yearly—from wool and from meat.

Sheep stories abound. In Walsenburg during the Great Depression, a sheepman had his bank loan called in by the local banker, but the rancher had no funds—only sheep. The banker refused to extend the loan, so the rancher did the only thing he could think of. He brought in his woolly assets on four hooves, surrounded the bank, and closed off streets in town with baaing, bleating sheep. The banker relented and extended the rancher's loan ...

The sheep and cattle wars of the 19th century may become the wolf wars of the 21st century. The battleground will be the alpine tundra and mountain meadows of Colorado's national forests and wilderness areas, where old sheep bridges once positioned across swollen creeks will not be replaced in wilderness areas. Sheep helped settle the West. They provided a food source from the very beginning of Western history. Sheep ranchers and ranching families worked hard to make a living across diverse landscapes of sagebrush, mountain parks, and desert canyons, but what was once rural and remote is no longer. ...

Afternoon storm clouds drift across the Flat Tops, the Elks, and the San Juans. Herders move their sheep for the last round of the day, collies nipping at heels, ewes turning to find lambs, guardian dogs alert on the fringe of flocks. First a few raindrops hit on bare ground and then in tall grass. Aspen leaves tremble, showing their undersides. Spruce limbs begin to rise and fall with the wind. A storm is coming. Change is in the air, but it is not just rain.

Shropshire sheep in Colorado.

The Cowboy
Reflections of a Western Writer

Louis L'Amour

TEDDY BLUE, WHO WAS a real cowboy, said that the only two things a cowboy feared were a decent woman and being set afoot.

Fortunately, due to men like Teddy Blue and 50 others we could mention, we do not have to rely on fiction for our picture of the cowboy. We know who he was and what he was like. We have his picture clearly drawn by men who were cowboys or who were there at the time, by women who loved them, married them, and sometimes survived them.

In fiction, the cowboy is usually portrayed as an illiterate, and no doubt many were, but just as many were not; some had excellent educations, going on to achieve a reputation in other fields. Granville Stuart, Eugene Manlove Rhodes, Charlie Siringo, and many others have told of the cowboy's reading habits.

No other type of man has been the subject of so many written words as the American cowboy. Yet he not only inspired literature and produced literature, he was to a considerable extent a product of his literature. From the very beginning the cowboy was, in the minds of those who wrote about him, a dashing and romantic figure. Moreover, although he would never have admitted it, that was how he saw himself. He knew the realities but believed the illusion. He was, after all, A Man on Horseback.

The Bedouin of the desert, the armored knight, the Cossack—all were figures of romance. The cavalry charge is the essence of poetry; the bayonet charge is not.

A few years ago, an eastern writer with a great air of debunking it all commented contemptuously that a cowboy was nothing but a hired man on horseback. Of course. What else? The cowboy knew his job and was happy with it. In most cases, he wished for nothing more. He wanted, above all, to be considered a top hand.

Give him a job to do while mounted, and he would work from daylight to dark. Ask him to dig a posthole, and you had a sour, discontented man. He would dig the posthole, but he did not have to like it and he did not.

He had to know horses and cattle, and he needed skill with a rope. His average working day during the early years on the range was 14 hours, from can-see to can't-see. His night's sleep was usually six hours; but when driving a trail herd, he could expect to do a stint on night guard, usually about two hours.

His work consisted of rounding up and branding cattle, gathering strays, riding fence, pulling cattle out of bogs, treating cuts or abrasions for screw worms, building and repairing fences, cleaning out water holes, or whatever needed doing.

In the old open-range days, he carried a running-iron and branded whatever he found on the range. If an unbranded calf was running with a branded cow, he usually applied her brand to the calf. If there was any doubt, he branded for the home ranch, whatever it might be. After a few years, when fences became common, the running iron disappeared and the stamp iron was introduced, and most of the branding was done during the seasonal roundups.

Over the years, the character of the cowboy's work changed considerably. In the earliest days, the cattle were Longhorns, and they were unlike any cow critter around today. Longhorns were wild animals. Often, they hid in thick brush, coming out to feed only at night. They were big, strong, and fierce and would fight anything that walked. As long as a rider was in the saddle, he was reasonably safe. Caught afoot, he had two choices—run for his horse and get into the saddle or shoot the steer. Usually he elected to run, as the boss did not look with favor on dead steers, but many a cowhand has blessed the Good Lord and Sam Colt for the pistol he carried.

The saddle stock on most of the ranches consisted of half-broken mustangs. They were small horses, incredibly tough, very agile, and soon developed an instinct for working cattle.

Later, when fences came and ranches became settled operations, horses were bred for the job and the saddle stock became better. It also needed more careful handling. On northern ranges, the horses were larger, for they were often required to buck snowdrifts and harsher conditions.

Stories of the West are said, by those who do not read them, to be about cowboys and Indians. Actually, that is rarely the case. More often the protagonist is a ranch foreman, a town marshal, a Texas Ranger, an army officer, or a scout for the army. When a cowboy is the protagonist, he is usually a drifter, and very rarely is he shown at work, doing what has to be done on a ranch.

Usually, cowboys were between 15 and 25 years of age, although some were as young as 12 or as old as 80. By and large, they were a hearty breed. Their work was hard, brutal, and demanding. Their food was, in the earlier years, largely beef, beans, and cornbread with molasses for sweetening.

The cowboys were, as a rule, Anglo-Saxon or Irish (as were the bulk of the early pioneers), and they came from every state in the Union and a half dozen European countries. The first cowboys were Texans who learned how to handle cattle from the Mexican vaqueros who had begun cultivating the art in the time of Cortez.

Boys from the border states soon added to their number. From Illinois, Iowa, Arkansas, Missouri, and Tennessee, to name a few, boys came to ride north with the trail herds. Boys in those states grew up handling stock, and a point to be remembered is that they grew up hunting meat for the table.

Often those who comment on shooting in the West fail to realize that most boys in the border states grew up shooting. If they did not kill their meat they did not have it to eat, and as ammunition could not be wasted in plinking away at any target that appeared, they took their time and made every shot count. The pioneer boy was usually an excellent shot who wasted no ammunition. Many a girl shot equally well, with Annie Oakley as an example. She began shooting game for her own table and then began hunting for the market.

One professor at a Western university has commented that, "It was generally agreed that the six-gun was a hard gun to shoot accurately." This is absurd. Among the many men I have known who used such guns, none would agree. There are many dead men who wish it had been true.

The six-gun, for its time, was an exceptionally efficient gun, and in the hands of a man who knew his weapon, his bullet would go exactly where he wished. The Grand Duke Alexis, after seeing the Smith and Wesson .44, demonstrated by Buffalo Bill Cody, ordered 250,000 of them for the Russian army.

There are literally thousands of cases to demonstrate the effectiveness of the cowboys' marksmanship. There were bad shots then as there are today, but most of the gunfighters served their apprenticeship as buffalo hunters, practicing their marksmanship day after day. Quanah Parker and his Kiowa-Comanche warriors discovered just how well they could shoot at the Battle of Adobe Walls, where 28 buffalo hunters stood off hundreds of his braves.

Cowboys came from everywhere. Teddy Blue, who left an account of his cowboy life in the western classic *We Pointed Them North*, was born in Norwich, England, and was a typical cowboy. Frank Collinson, whose *Life in the Saddle* is another true story of western life, came from Yorkshire, England. Jeff Milton, a cowboy who became a famous Western peace officer, was a son of the governor of Florida.

Unfortunately, from the very first, the cowboy and the West in general have suffered from the writings of various "authorities" who assumed certain things to be true because they are, to their thinking, logical.

The cowboy's attitude toward women, for example, was far different from present attitudes. If we are to understand his times we must know something of his education, family background, and the customs of his time as to what was acceptable conduct and what was not. The cowboy must always be measured by the standards of his time, not ours. Conditions and manners were vastly different.

Moreover, many who presume to write of the western story take altogether too narrow a view of what is "Western" and what is not. The western story is one of the few truly American forms of literature; no other has so captured the world's imagination, and the stories can be found everywhere.

SECTION V

Mining Towns

Casey's Table d'Hote

Eugene Field

Oh, them days on Red Hoss' Mountain, when the skies was fair 'nd blue;
When the money flowed like likker, 'nd the folks was brave 'nd true!
When the nights wuz crisp 'nd balmy, 'nd the camp wuz all astir,
With the joints all throwed wide open 'nd no sheriff to demur!
Oh, them times on Red Hoss Mountain in the Rockies fur away—
There's no sich place nor times like them as I kin find to-day!
What though the camp hez busted? I seem to see it still—
A-lyin', like it love it, on that big 'nd warty hill;
And I feel a sort of yearnin' 'nd a choking in my throat
When I think of Red Hoss Mountain 'nd of Casey's tabble dote!

Well yes; it's true I struck it rich, but that don't cut a show
When one is old 'nd feeble 'nd it's nigh his time to go;
The money that he's got in bonds or carries to invest
Don't figger with a codger who has lived a life out West;
Us old chaps like to set around, away from folks 'nd noise,
'Nd think about the sights we seen and things we done when boys;
The which is why I love to set 'nd think of them old days
When all us Western fellers got the Colorado craze—
And that is why I love to set around all day 'nd gloat
On thoughts of Red Hoss Mountain 'nd of Casey's tabble dote.

This Casey wuz an Irishman—you'd know it by his name
And by the facial features appertainin' to the same,
He'd lived in many places 'nd had done a thousand things,
From the noble art of actin' to the work of dealin' kings,
But, somehow, hadn't caught on; so, driftin' with the rest,
He drifted for a fortune to the undeveloped West,
And he come to Red Hoss Mountain when the little camp wuz new,
When the money flowed like likker, 'nd the folks wuz brave 'nd true;
And, havin' been a stewart on a Mississippi boat,
He opened up a caffy 'nd he run a tabble dote.

The bar wuz long 'nd rangey, with a mirrer on the shelf,
'Nd a pistol, so that Casey, when required, could help himself;
Down underneath there wuz a row of bottle beer 'nd wine,
'Nd a keg of Burbun whiskey of the run of '59;
Upon the walls wuz pictures of hosses 'nd of girls—
Not much on dress, perhaps, but strong on records 'nd on curls!
The which had been identified with Casey in the past—
The hosses and the girls, I mean—and both wuz mighty fast!
But all these fine attractions wuz of precious little note
By the side of what wuz offered at Casey's tabble dote.

There wuz half-a-dozen tables altogether in the place,
And the tax you had to pay upon vitals wuz a case;
The boardin'-houses in the camp protested 'twuz a shame
To patronize a robber, which this Casey wuz the same!
They said a case was robbery to tax for ary meal;
But Casey tended strictly to his biz, 'nd let 'em squeal;
And presently the boardin'-houses all began to bust,
While Casey kept on sawin' wood 'nd layin' in the dust;
And oncet a trav'lin' editor from Denver City wrote
A piece back to his paper, puffin' Casey's tabble dote.

Restaurant interior from the late 1880s.

A tabble dote is different from orderin' aller cart:
In one case you git all there is, in t'other, only part!
And Casey's tabble dote began in French—as all begin,
And Casey's ended with the same, which is to say, with "vin";
But in between wuz every kind of reptile, bird, 'nd beast,
The same like you can git in high-toned restauraws down east;
'Nd windin' up wuz cake or pie, with coffee demy tass,
Or, sometimes, floatin' Ireland in a soothin' kind of sass
That left a sort of pleasant ticklin' in a feller's throat,
'Nd made him hanker after more of Casey's tabble dote.

The very recollection of them puddin's 'nd them pies
Brings a yearnin' to my buzzum 'nd the water to my eyes;
'Nd seems like cookin' nowadays ain't what it used to be
In camp in Red Hoss Mountain in that year of '63;
But, maybe, it is better, 'nd, maybe, I'm to blame—
I'd like to be a-livin' in the mountains jest the same—
I'd like to live that life again when skies wuz fair 'nd blue,
When things wuz run wide open 'nd men wuz brave 'nd true;
When brawny arms the flinty ribs of Red Hoss Mountain smote
For wherewithal to pay the price of Casey's tabble dote.

And you, O cherished brother, a-sleepin' way out west;
With Red Hoss Mountain huggin' you close to its lovin' breast,
Oh, do you dream in your last sleep of how we used to do,
Of how we worked our little claims together, me 'nd you?
Why, when I saw you last a smile wuz restin' on your face,
Like you wuz glad to sleep forever in that lonely place;
And so you wuz, 'nd I'd be, too, if I wuz sleepin' so.
But, bein' how a brother's love ain't for the world to know,
Whenever I've this heartache 'nd this chokin' in my throat,
I lay it all to thinkin' of Casey's tabble dote.

Beyond the Mississippi

Albert D. Richardson

ON THE MORNING AFTER reaching Denver, we started for the Gregory Diggings, 40 miles to the northwest. Along the bank of the Platte, which bounds the town on the north, immigrant wagons extended for a quarter of a mile, waiting to be ferried across for $2.50 each. The boat was propelled by the current, and its daily receipts were from $200 to $300 dollars.

Immediately, beyond stretched a succession of low sandy hills, entirely destitute of trees, and with thin ashen grass, dreary enough to eyes familiar with the rich green prairies of Kansas and Missouri. But we passed several ranches where idle cattle and horses, whose owners were in the diggings, were kept and guarded by the month at from one to two dollars per head. By day they grazed on the desert and really fattened upon its unpromising diet. At night, they were corralled—driven into enclosures—to prevent them from stampeding and protect them against cattle-thieves, which infest all our frontier regions until exterminated or frightened away by the sudden, decisive administration of lynch law.

From Denver to the foot of the range seemed only a stone's throw, but we found it 15 miles. The only well-defined spur is Table Mountain, which rises 500 or 600 feet from the valley, with symmetric stone walls. It looked down upon two little tents, then the only dwellings for miles; but in the intervening years it has seen a thriving and promising manufacturing town spring up under the broad mountain-shadow.

At its base we found Clear Creek, greatly swollen, so we left the coach, saddled our mules and rode them through the stream amid a crowd of emigrants who sent up three hearty cheers for Horace Greeley. The road was swarming with travel. In the distance, they were clambering right up a hill as abrupt as the roof of a cottage.

It seemed incredible that any animal less agile than a mountain goat could reach the summit; yet this road, only five weeks old, was beaten like a turnpike; and far above us toiled men, mules and cattle—pigmies upon Alps. Wagons carrying less than half a ton were drawn up by 20 oxen, while those descending dragged huge trees in full branch and leaf behind them, as brakes.

We all dismounted to ascend except Mr. Greeley, still so lame that the overtaxed mule was compelled to carry him. The astonished brute yielded to despair and climbed vigorously, experiencing painfully the climax of Ossa upon Pelion.

In an hour and a half, we reached the summit. Far below, on the top of Table Mountain, gleamed a little lake. At the foot of the long hill were the pigmies again, and beyond the valley of the Platte with its dark timber and shining water. Before us, mountain lay piled upon mountain—some grassy and others gaunt and bare. From these rose the pine, spruce, and hemlock in perfect cones, interspersed with quivering aspens; while brilliant flowers clothed the desolate peaks with beauty.

Our road led us past the new-made grave of a young immigrant, one of many victims to the careless use of firearms. Up and down the steep mountain sides, across swift-running, ice-cold streams, over jagged rocks and through deep canyons shadowed by sullen walls, we wound our toilsome way. An eager crowd kept pace with us—some walking, others with ox-wagons, pack-horses or mules, and all pressing toward the mines.

At night, we turned our patient animals out to graze and encamped under a sloping roof of fir and pine boughs. Our cook-elect kindled a blazing fire, by which we sat listening to the conflicting reports of the sanguine or disheartened gold-seekers—those going forward led by buoyant hope, and those coming back bringing dearly bought experience.

Wrapt in our blankets upon the hard ground, we gazed through fir boughs at the far-off stars, until the deep soothing music of the pine, the Eolian harp of the forest, mingled with our dreams.

Sluce box mining in the late 1800s.

The next morning we started early and descending, a steep hill, reached at last the Gregory Diggings. The valley presented a confused and constantly shifting picture, made up of men, tents, wagons, oxen and mules. The first miner we—stranger to us—encountered was digging a hole like a grave beside a little rivulet but told us that he had not yet "struck the color."

Along the rocky gulch for five miles were scattered log cabins, tents, and cabins covered with boards sawn by hand or with pine boughs. At the grocery tents, flour was selling at 50 cents per pound; and beside the stream, women were washing clothes at three dollars per dozen.

After breakfasting in the open air, we went from camp to camp talking with miners, and studying their operations. They found no gold in the stream bed but were washing out the "rotten" quartz which they gathered from narrow crevices in the granite on hillsides. Gregory, Green Russell, and the other old Georgia miners, very expert in detecting lodes, found abundant employment in "prospecting" for newcomers at $100 per day. In our presence, one miner washed $4.50 from a pan-full of dirt and told us that another pan had just yielded him $17.87.

Some 20 sluices were in operation. In gulch or placer-mining, the dirt is shoveled into a long wooden sluice or trough, through which a stream of water pours, washing away the earth and leaving the heavy gold dust at the bottom. The sluices were of lumber, which was cut with hand saws and commanded $100 per thousand. There was much speculation in claims; some were sold as high as $6,000, cash.

Most of the miners were exultant and hopeful; but a few, utterly discouraged, were about to return to the States. There were 5,000 people in the Gregory Diggings, and hundreds more were pouring in daily.

Mr. Greeley, Henry Villard of the Cincinnati Commercial, and myself spent two days in examining the gulches and conversing with the workmen engaged in running sluices. Most of the companies reported to us that they were operating successfully. Then we joined in a detailed report, naming the members of each company and their former places of residence in "the States," (that any who desired might learn their reputation for truthfulness,) and adding their statements as to the number of men they were employing and the average yield of their sluices per day. We endeavored to give the shadows as well as the lights of the picture, recounting the hardships and perils of the long journey, and the bitter disappointment experienced by the unsuccessful many—and earnestly warning the public against another general and ill-advised rush to the mines. Little time is required to learn the great truth; That digging gold is about the hardest way on earth to obtain it; that, in this as in other pursuits, great success is very rare. The report was widely copied throughout the country as the first specific, disinterested, and trustworthy account of the newly discovered placers.

The Snow-Shoe Itinerant
An Autobiography of the Rev. John L. Dyer

John Lewis Dyer

As all the mining was gulch or placer diggings, a great part of the people left fall to winter—some for Denver, others for Cañon City or Colorado City, some for the Missouri River with ox teams. Only a few would come back in the spring; for men did not come to Pike's Peak—as it was called—to stay, but to make a stake, and then go back.

In the summer of 1861, a troop of theatrical performers came across to Summit County and played in all the camps—Sunday morning at one place, and in the evening at another. I thought the devil was traveling the circuit as well as myself. I've thought less of theaters ever since. There is little about them but evil. We had few miners who would go to the dance or theaters.

But the best work done was a revival at Gold Run in the midst of winter. The snow was about six feet deep. We concluded to hold a protracted meeting at the schoolhouse, where we had four members, and only about 25 people, all told. From the first, the meetings were interesting. Irrespective of denominations, all began to work in earnest. Seventeen was the average attendance, and about that number were warmed up, reclaimed, or converted. We called it a good revival on a small scale. A more enjoyable time I have seldom had. Among those present were John McKaskill and wife and J. T. Lynch, the former of whom were in Kansas last I heard, and the latter in Utah.

In March 1863, I received my appointment from Kansas Conference. My work up to this time had been as a supply. Through the presiding elder, L. B. Dennis, I was readmitted. It was a surprise, for I had not made up my mind to stay in the mountains. This decided me to stand the storms and leave the events with God and do the best I could to build up the Church in this wilderness country. I was put down for South Park and on the third day of April left Lincoln City and stopped at Mr. Thorn's in Breckenridge until about two o'clock in the morning, when I took my carpet-sack, well filled, got on my snowshoes, and went up Blue River. The snow was five feet deep. It might be asked, "Why start at two o'clock?" Because the snow would not bear a man in daytime, even with snowshoes. From about two o'clock until nine or 10 in the morning was the only time a man could go; and a horse could not go at all. When about three miles up the Blue River, back of Jud's, the wolves set up a tremendous howling quite near. I was not armed but passed quietly along and was not disturbed. It was not likely, I thought, that the good Lord would let anything disturb a man going in the night to his appointment, although wolves and bears, with some Rocky Mountain lions, were numerous.

I reached Montgomery about nine o'clock in the morning. The snow drifted above the tops of the doors. All along the streets, steps had been made in the snow, and served as stairs to get into the stores and houses. There were some 200 or 300 people in town, among them seven members. I must mention Brother and Sister Gurton and Brother and Sister Fowler. I stayed eight days and held service each evening; on Sunday, twice. Two or three professed to be reclaimed, and all were revived. My circuit embraced the above, with Buckskin Joe, Mosquito Pass, and Tarryall. Buckskin Joe was so called from the nickname given to a prospector wearing a suit of that material.

Tarryall was discovered in 1860. Some very rich claims were opened; and soon, all were taken. The news spread, and prospectors by the thousands came but found no chance to get a foot of ground; so they all tarried, and hence the name Tarryall. From there, the prospectors went every way, and some struck pay dirt in the place and called it Fair Play, as they claimed to be more liberal.

This was a two-weeks' circuit. Brother Wm. Howbert was preacher in charge in part of 1860 and 1861 and Brother Loyd in 1862, a part of the year.

Mosquito got its name from this circumstance: The miners met to organize. Several names were suggested, but they disagreed, and a motion was made to adjourn and meet again, the place for the name to be left blank. When they came together on appointment, the secretary opened the book, and a large mosquito, smashed right in the blank, showed it, and all agreed to call the district Mosquito.

In addition to the above places, I went to California Gulch, as that place was not supplied.

Two Mexicans, called Espanosa, who had become enraged against the government of Colorado, came from near Fort Garland, armed to kill as many Americans as they could find. They struck the Arkansas River at Hard Scrabble, found Judge Bruce and shot and murdered him. Thence they went north to Park County and murdered Mr. Addleman, and from there to near the Kenosha House where they found two men camped and murdered them. Next, about halfway between Fair Play and Alma, they shot down and killed a Mr. Carter in the road. Just after they had rifled his pockets and taken his pistol and most of his clothes, Mr. Metcalf came along with a wagon and oxen, loaded with lumber. As he sat on the load, they shot at him from a tree about 70 yards off and gave him a close call—the ball striking right opposite his heart. But the ball struck a pamphlet in his side pocket and glanced so that it did not hurt him. He of course halloed, and the oxen took fright and ran. They shot again at him, but missed him; and as there was a house within a half mile, he got clear of them. He was the first one that got away from them to describe them. He said they were negroes or men blackened. I suppose he had never seen a Mexican. One of them had a broad-rimmed white hat; and after he was killed, and his hat brought in, Metcalf recognized it as having been worn by the man who shot at him. From the above place, they went east to the Red Hill crossing of the Denver road, where anyone could be seen coming from either way. There they waited until two men came along on their way from Denver to California Gulch. They shot one dead, and it was supposed the other was wounded in the arm. He retreated down the hill to the foot or level, where they caught him and knocked a hole in his skull. This was the last murder they committed. This was late in the spring. The next morning, the word came to Fair Play that just over Red Hill there were two men that had been murdered, lying by the roadside.

At this time, there were a few soldiers at Fair Play. A number were sent to bring in the dead bodies, and try, if possible, to capture the murderers. Just as the soldiers collected the second dead body, they saw a man coming on the road, whom they at first thought to be a traveler. But seeing them about the same time, and having heard of the numerous murders on the road, he thought they would surely kill him; and, dropping his coat in the road, put out south. The soldiers, seeing him run, thought he was the man they wanted and so followed after him at full speed. He, being a man in the prime of life and active, especially on this occasion, made a good race. The word came to Fair Play that they were after the murderer, and another company mounted on horses to try to head him off. But Mr. John Foster—for that was his name—outran them all. At one time his pursuers were very close on him as he passed over a sharp ridge, but he got over before they got quite to the top, and that gave him a chance to turn his course and throw them off his track. After running 15 or 20 miles, he reached Fair Play in his socks, without coat or hat. As the people saw him in his plight, they halloed: "There comes the murderer!" But I recognized him, as he kept a "Methodist hotel" in California Gulch and kept in between them and him until he got to the first house. The door being open, he went in, and it was some time before he could relate his feat, as he was very short of breath and badly scared—and did not know till then, but it was the murderers that had been running him down. After a while his pursuers came, feeling mortified that he got away from them; but when the facts were known, they felt relieved, for although they had been outrun, they had been saved from killing an innocent man.

I shall not forget that week or 10 days of intense excitement. Everybody was excited. The five murdered men were buried at Fair Play. The sickening sight of the dead, and the thought, "Who would be the next?" set the few inhabitants into almost a panic. During the time, word came that a man was harbored at a ranch some 15 miles east, and a company went over about night and demanded him. The family would not let them in. They guarded the house. There was a shot fired from within which killed a mule. When daylight appeared, they gave the inmates just a few minutes to surrender the man, under the alternative of having the house burned. They went in and took the man and made the ranchman give property to the full value of the mule and ordered him to leave. They took the prisoner near Fair Play and, without trial or jury, hanged him, although he denied being guilty of a crime for which he deserved death. But poor Baxter had fallen into the hands of hard men in an evil hour. This was a mob, and nothing better ever comes of mob work.

But to return to the pursuit of the Mexicans. The people started a company on their trail from Red Hill. As they had two ponies, they were easily trailed and finally were overtaken at breakfast in the chaparral. The pursuers waited for them to go out of the brush to get their ponies. At last only one of them went, and John said to Joe: "Can you shoot him?" He said, "Yes," and with his deadly aim brought him to the ground. The Mexican tried to shoot, but was not able to. One of the avengers, whose brother had been shot by them, craved the privilege to finish the wounded man by shooting him in the head. The other Mexican ran and got upon a pinnacle of rocks that hung almost over where they were. As Mr. Lamb, who shot first, was stooping over the dead Mexican to see whether he had shot him as he intended, the other Mexican shot at him from the rocks, the shot passing through his hat rim, ranging down through his clothes but fortunately doing no harm. He then made his escape back to near Fort Garland, but was not long to be seen. He got one of his nephews, and they took up their residence in the mountains for some time. They would come into the settlements on the sly for provisions. A woman found out where they kept themselves, and told it. Mr. Tom Tobin took a company of five or six men and went in search of them. As there was a bounty for their heads, both were shot—the old man falling dead in his tracks, and the young one, although mortally wounded, running some distance before he expired. That ended the Espanosa trouble. What I have given was most of it along my route of travel, so I had a good opportunity to know the facts. It was a sad blow on Park County. One mother yet lives to mourn the loss of her son; sorrowful traces remain in the memory of all the inhabitants. It was a most daring and deplorable outrage.

A Victorian Gentlewoman in the Far West

Mary Hallock Foote

THERE WAS A YOUNG ENGLISHMAN who spent his evenings rather often in the home whom Arthur called Pricey. His name was Hugh Price. He had no "wife" and no special fireside unless it was ours. The other boys teased him about being in our sitting room, always silent and buried in a book; they called it a "free reading room," and he defended himself candidly, to everyone's delight, with the apology: "A man can't sit in his bedroom, you know!" He was a publican's son, an Oxford man, a student in Germany, a traveler—an impecunious one. If he had any remittances, they were small ones. He was a doleful wit when it came to handling things in a laboratory or stepping about among dishes and frying pans at a campfire, but he had read enormously, and when one or two who could catch what he was trying to say in his shy, halting fashion, he was awfully good company.

Every evening in the cabin he took the same chair in the corner by the stove (unfortunately it was a rocking chair) and read and rocked until all the guests were gone. The rocking annoyed Arthur, who was sensitive to little personal habits, and he did not hesitate to correct this habit in Pricey in a somewhat crude manner. One evening when Pricey was deep in a book and the chair in full career, A. stepped behind and slipped a book under each rocker. It surprised Pricey and caused a general laugh, but he took it with touching good nature; he was not thin-skinned like some boys. We had many long quiet talks when the merrier part of the company had gone. His mind was the most abstruse and cultivated and the least available of the younger men's in Leadville.

Yet, he had his happy moments—never indoors! Once when we were riding in the valley—the valley of the little wild Arkansas near its source, with that towering and stainless sky resting on the mountain peaks—he looked up like a worshipper and said in his fine Oxford accent:

'O tenderly the haughty day
Fills his blue urn with fire—

Who in Leadville could have done that but Pricey or would have thought of doing it! But alas! he was one who stayed in Leadville too long. It was the winter after, when we were in New York, A. received a letter from him and laid it down with a queer look. "Either Price was drunk when he wrote that letter or he has gone out of his mind." It was the last he feared, and drink had nothing to do with it. When we returned from Washington in the spring and Van Zandt from his wild trip to New Mexico (of which more later), those two took care of poor Pricey and sent him home to his relatives in England at their own expense. He had been taken up in the streets wandering about insane and lodged in the common jail for mere safety, lacking every comfort or even decency. No one knew him, and he could give no account of himself—so quickly the little fireside groups dispersed in that bleak, rootless place. "The altitude of heartbreak," it was sometimes called.

* * *

The mountains of the Great Divide are not, as everyone knows, born trees, though we always think of them as far above timberline with the eternal snow on their heads. They wade up through ancient forests and plunge into canons thick with watercourses and pause in little gemlike valleys and march attended by winds across high plateaus, but all such incidents of the lower world they leave behind them when they begin to strip for the skies: like the Holy Ones of old they go up alone and barren of all circumstance, to meet their transfiguration.

We spent the early part of the day steadily climbing; our horses had no load to speak of, yet before noon one of them was hanging back and beginning to show signs of that rapid lung fever which, if a horse has taken cold in those altitudes, has but one end. A. thought he might hold out till we reached English George's, but from that point on, the drive was spoiled by seeing the gasping creature kept up to his work. On the last and steepest grade, before you got to English George's, a sharp turn above a precipice on one side narrowed the road suddenly. The view was cut off ahead, and here we met the stage coming down, all six horses at full speed—they had the precipice on their right, we had the bank, and we had to go up the side of it if we were to pass on two wheels, for there was no room to pass. I felt at that moment I would just as soon die myself as see my husband force that dying horse up the bank, but it had to be done. He stood out on the buggy step, throwing his weight on the upper wheels, and laid on the lash; we did not turn over and we did get by, with about six inches to spare. The two men driving exchanged a queer smile—they understood each other; and I am glad I have forgotten what I said to my husband in that moment when he saved our lives, and I hope he has too! The horse died after we got to English George's, and there we hired another, or the remains of one, and he died the day after we reached Leadville. A. paid for both—and how much more those trips cost him I never knew, but that is the price of Romance: to have allowed his wife to come in by stage in company with drunkenness and vice, or anything else that might happen, would have been realism.

We knew that we were nearly "in" when corrals and drinking places and rude shops began to multiply, and rude, jocose signs appeared on doors closed to the besieging mob of strangers: "No chickens, no eggs, no keep folks—dam!" was one that A. pointed out to me. ..."Shall we drive out or walk?—there is a trail?" he asked. ..."Let's walk, of course!"

At a New Mining Camp

Richard Harding Davis

I MET SEVERAL OF THESE prominent citizens were in Creede, and I found them. Billy Woods fights, or used to fight, at 210 pounds and glories in the fact that a New York paper once devoted five columns to his personality. His reputation saves him the expense of paying men to keep order. Bob Ford, who shot Jesse James, was another prominent citizen of my acquaintance. He does not look like a desperado but has a loutish apologetic air, which is explained by the fact that he shot Jesse James in the back when the latter was engaged in the innocent work of hanging a picture on the wall. Ford never quite recovered from the fright he received when he found out who it was that he had killed. "Bat" Masterden was of an entirely different class. He dealt for Watrous and has killed 28 men—once three together. One night when he was off duty, I saw a drunken man slap his face, and the silence was so great that we could hear the electric light sputter in the next room; but Masterden only laughed and told the man to come back and do it again when he was sober. "Troublesome Tom" Cady acted as capper for "Soapy" Smith and played the shell game during the day. He was grateful to me for teaching him a much superior method in which the game is played in the effete East. His master, "Soapy" Smith, was a very bad man indeed, who hired at least 12 men to lead the prospector with a little money, or the tenderfoot who had just arrived, up to the numerous tables in his gambling saloon, where they were robbed in various ways so openly that they deserved to lose all that was taken from them.

There were also some very good shots at Creede and some very bad ones. Among these latter was Mr. James Powers, who emptied his revolver and the Rab Brothers' stove at the same time without doing any damage. He explained that he was crowded and wanted more room. The most delicate shooting was done by the Louisiana Kid—I don't know what his other name was—who was robbed in Soapy Smith's saloon and was put out when he expostulated. He waited patiently until one of Smith's men, named Farnham, appeared, and then, being more intent on showing his skill than on killing Farnham, shot the thumb off his right hand as it rested on the trigger. Farnham shifted his pistol to his left hand, with which he shot fairly well, but before he could fire, the Kid shot the thumb off that hand too.

This is, of course, Creede at night. It is not at all a dangerous place, and the lawlessness is scattered and mild. There was only one street; and as no one cared to sit on the edge of a bunk in a cold room at night, the gambling houses were crowded in consequence every evening. It was simply because there was nowhere else to go. The majority of the citizens used them as clubs and walked from one to the other, talking drums and corner lots and dived down into their pockets for specimens of ore which they passed around for examination. Others went to keep warm and, still, others to sleep in the corner until they were put out. The play was never high. There was so much of it, though, that it looked very bad and wicked and rough, but it was quite harmless. There were no sudden oaths, nor partings in the crowd, and pistol shots or gleaming knives—at least, but seldom. The women who frequented these places at night, in spite of their sombreros and flashy shirts and bells, were a most unpicturesque and unattractive element. They were neither dashing and bold, nor remorseful and repentant.

They gambled foolishly and laughed when they won and told the dealer he cheated when they lost. The men occasionally gave glimpses of the life which Bret Harte made dramatic and picturesque—the women, never. The most uncharacteristic thing of the place, and one which was Bret Hartish in every detail, was a church service held in Watrous and Baumigan's gambling saloon. The hall is a very long one with a saloon facing the street and keno tables and a dozen other games in the gambling-room beyond. When the doors between the two rooms are held back, they make a very large hall. A clergyman asked Watrous if he could have the use of the gambling-hall on Sunday night. The house was making about $300 an hour, and Watrous calculated that half an hour would be as much as he could afford toward the collection. He mounted a chair and said, "Boys, this gentleman wants to make a few remarks to you of a religious nature. All the games at that end of the hall will stop, and you want to keep still."

The clergyman stood on the platform of the keno outfit, and the greater part of the men took the seats around it, toying with the marking cards scattered on the table in front of them, while the men in the saloon crowded the doorway off the swinging-doors to the bar and looked on with curious and amused faces. In the back of the room, the roulette wheel clicked and the ball rolled. The men in that part of the room who were playing lowered their voices; but above the voice of the preacher, one could hear the clinking of the silver and the chips and the voice of the boy at the wheel calling, "Seventeen and black, and 28 and black again—keep the ball rolling, gentlemen—and four and red." There are two electric lights in the middle of the hall and a stove; the men were crowded closely around this stove, and the lamp shone through the smoke on their tanned, upturned faces and on the white, excited face of the preacher above them. There was the most excellent order, and the collection was very large. I asked Watrous how much he lost by not being open.

"Nothing," he said, quickly, anxious to avoid the appearance of good. "I got it all back at the bar."

The Trail of Gold and Silver

Duane A. Smith

THE LAND IS THERE and always will be there; the same cannot be said for Western Slopers. Setting aside the Mesa Verde people and the Ute, settlement covers only a little over one century, hardly a yawn in the total history of the region. In that time span, man has scarred, dug, and tampered with the Western Slope more than his predecessors ever did. How permanent this intrusion will turn out to be cannot be judged. On the other side of the coin—is the impact of the Western Slope on people evident in unique ways? Did the environment produce a Western Sloper? … history supports his contention.

The isolation, the vastness of the land, and the simple fact that the area and its people were left so long to their own devices produced an independent nature. There was a self-reliance, too, as a correspondent from Breckenridge noted in the August 8, 1860, issue of the *Rocky Mountain News*. He observed that the people generally know their own business, attend to it promptly, and "let others alone." Yet, there was an openness, provided the visitor did not infringe upon the right of privacy of others. Well-known Victorian traveler Bayard Taylor, on a Breckenridge visit in the summer of 1866, commented on just that point and said, "I shall always retain a very pleasant recollection of Breckenridge."

Further insight into Western Slopers was furnished by two ministers who knew them in the 1870s and 1880s—George Darley and James Gibbons. Darley, who saw it all, from red-light district crib to church pew, wrote, "nor could a more intelligent, plucky, warm-hearted set of men be found." Gibbons concurred, going on to say that the region attracted "only the energetic and the robust, who have the hardihood to endure the severe cold that prevails in those altitudes [San Juans]."

Western Slopers tend to be optimistic. "Everybody looks forward," wrote Ernest Ingersoll in the early 1880s, referring to mining and the prospects of selling a claim. "Perhaps this delicious uncertainty is a part of the fun." It must have been, because so many prospectors never struck a profitable deal. That characteristic prevailed, whether in miner, farmer, or merchant. Routt County residents agreed with the *Steamboat Springs Pilot* in 1899, when it prophesied that "the dawn of prosperity" was breaking for them. No matter that the editor had said the same thing before and would again. They treasured this faith, this optimism.

Creede

Cy Warman

Here's a land where all are equal—
    Of high or lowly birth—
A land where men make millions,
    Dug from the dreary earth.
Here the meek and mild-eyed burros
    On mineral mountains feed.
It's day all day, in the daytime,
    And there is no night in Creede.
The cliffs are solid silver,
    With wondrous wealth untold;
And the beds of running rivers
    Are lined with glittering gold.
While the world is filled with sorrow
    And hearts must break and bleed—
It's day all day, in the daytime,
    And there's no night in Creede.

The Life of an Ordinary Woman

Anne Ellis

NELLIE SMELTZER WAS the town dressmaker and milliner. As a girl, she had money and some of the good things it brings, such as education and breeding. She always boasted of going to a private school. When quite young, she married a mining man in Georgetown and had followed him from one mining camp to the other. Finally, they came to Bonanza; here, she planted herself and said, "No more moves."

She has often told me of how she shocked the "natives" when she first came to town with her lovely and daring clothes. I think a low-necked, black tarletan dress was the knockout. I know she must have been beautiful in those days, as she always had very good features and such an air—talked with her eyebrows and shoulders. The thing I remember of her was the enticing colored pictures in her windows. She could twist a scarf around a hat and give it *that* look. These pictures in the window attracted me, and I paid her my first visit, finding a fairyland—mirrors, flowers, hats, Japanese parasols, furniture, and pictures. For many years, her house was a stopping place for me, always warm and pleasant. She was a good dressmaker and considered *very* expensive. Once, when we were flush, she made Mama a dress and charged 10 dollars for it; this seemed awful, but in spite of shirrings, ruffles, pinkings, and puffings, a howl went up over it and it was shown to all of the neighbors.

In those days, you never held a dress up so that your friends could see the outside—oh, no! It was the wrong side which was turned outward and examined in the smallest detail. How it was lined and interlined; how bound; how the seams were finished; the smallness and evenness of the stitches; how the steels were put in—there was the test of the dressmaker's art: they should be put up and down each dart and seam, with fancy stitches in bright colored silk thread; from 14 to 17 were required for the usual basque.

In this dress of Mama's, which looked very stylish, the lining in the overskirt was pieced and patched. This ruined it, and many times I have seen it held at arm's length and have heard, "Now, I just wish you would cast your eye over that; the nerve of a woman to charge me 10 dollars for making a gauzy thing like that; it takes the cake, that's all I've got to say." Nevertheless, we children bragged a good deal over the dress that cost 10 dollars to make.

Mrs. Smeltzer got her spring millinery just before the Fourth of July, but that was soon enough, as it was never warm before this, and the Fourth was the event of the year; and if one had a new hat, it would not be worn before this day. And I had many new hats of hers, some paid for (in small "dribs," depending on how the washing came in or how much milk was sold) and some given me. Always, I liked her. She would give me good advice, none of which I remember. Only once, I was asked to eat with her. The linen napkins and the egg cups of silver filigree impressed me very much. She would tell of Paris fashions, the lack of appreciation in Bonanza, of her girlhood, of balls she attended (I only knew dances); of a dead brother she had loved dearly, and of how she tried to talk to him through the spirits; of her stepmother beating her out of her money; of (when I was older) my love affairs, or rather the lack of them. She would say: "Now, Annie, aren't you mashed on any one? Do you know why you haven't as many beaus as the other girls? Your busts are too small; you should eat more butter and eggs."

For many years, she would go on the mountainside, cut huge pine trees and drag or carry them home and put them in holes in front of her house, where they would last for months; strangers wondered why she had such fine shade trees. She always got her own wood off the mountain, hauled it home, sawed and split it. If you think this is an easy job, you should try it once.

The years pass; each day she looks for the return of her husband. But he never comes. She has no intimate friends, neither women nor men, and never seems to feel the want of them. No relative ever came to see her.

She is never talked about, although many men have tried their luck with her and have left sadder but wiser men. One was told to come late at night; he went, tapped gently on the door; it was opened a crack; he stepped eagerly forward, and his eyes filled with red pepper. Another was also told to "come ahead." When he stepped in, a sweet voice whispered, "Come," but a bucket of cold water had been hanging above the door which tipped, drenched him, and cooled his ardor. There was another one whom she enjoyed visiting with, as he was clever, a good talker, and more one of her own kind. By now she was washing, as the sewing had played out, and when this man would come for his washing, he would slip out the back way if he saw any one coming. I expect he wanted the other men to think he was a clear thing. She never said one word, but at the back door was a steep step; she loosened it and slipped so that the next time her friend sidled through her room (so that he could go out the back way—our houses always had the rooms in a row), he fell, heels over head. She lost his washing!

She was one of the proudest persons I have ever known; she would never allow any one to help her or give her anything. When she would be out hunting wood, dressed in gunnysacks, maybe one foot in an old rubber boot and the other wrapped in an ore sack, if you could coax her in, wanting to give her something to eat, you had to make an affair of it and drink tea along with her. One Christmas, we knew she was hungry. They filled a sack with groceries and put it on her doorstep. When she found it, she took it by the bottom and dumped it first to the right, then to the left, threw the sack over the fence, went into the house and closed the door. She held on to one blue velveteen dress, which she wore on town days, when she dressed for the occasion; for years she wore gunnysacks, and sometimes these were very scant, but whatever she wore, she wore it with flair. She even walked with a tripping sort of strut, and each day of her life powdered white as snow, with flour; in later years she was very dirty, but always powdered thick over the dirt.

Once, when a woman whom she disliked very much left town, Mrs. Smeltzer slipped over and hung crepe on the door. Once, while pulling a bale of hay down a snowy, icy street, a young miner, coming off shift, stopped and offered to help. She peered up at him and said, "Young man, I don't want to get you talked about."

She carried her money in her mouth and the store kept a glass of water for her.

She was honest to a degree; I have known her to walk to Saguache to pay her taxes, 17 miles over a high mountain pass. Once she borrowed our cart, piled it high with millinery, put herself in the shafts, and hauled it to Villa Grove, 15 miles away.

A year or two ago, she was brought to the county seat on an insanity charge, and after the jailer's wife had washed her hair, it was lovely. Then they got one of those cheap straw garden hats, and she insisted on a piece of cheesecloth to trim it and finished with a creation. She and I laughed over the charge; one of the complaints was that she kissed her cow! The cow had come to be her only source of livelihood, and she said to me, "She's the only creature who loves me; why shouldn't I kiss her?" It was at this time she gave me this advice: "Annie, don't ask people about their business. If they want you to know, they will tell you, and if they don't, they won't."

During all these years, there was never one word of complaint at an unkind fate. She died as she lived: proud and alone, asking no odds of anyone. At the end, she was with the only things on earth that loved her—the cow and chickens; the chickens roosted on the foot and under the bed and were blinded by the light when brought out. But even to the end, there was a sign creaking above the door: "Fashionable dressmaking"; and ladies, yellow and fly-specked, dressed in beautiful colors, with tiny waists, big sleeves, and long trains, looked and smiled at you from the fashion sheets in the bay window.

Tomboy Bride

Harriet Fish Backus

SHORTLY AFTER THAT Christmas day, I had a new adventure. Johnny Midwinter, the foreman, suggested that he and George take me into the mine. George thought I would enjoy it.

Johnny met us at the entrance. Outfitted in a miner's long rubber coat and sou'wester, I entered the tunnel where Johnny fastened a miner's candlestick in the top on my hat and, with a dramatic gesture of his pudgy hand, lighted the candle.

Possibly, because I had made the effort to send help to the roustabout which prevented an accident, Johnny decided my interest in the mine warranted a wider understanding of its ramifications. After we walked some distance along the main tunnel, he turned to me with a smile and said, "We'll start up this ladder in what we call a vertical raise. Just climb slowly behind me and George will follow you. When we get up to the stope, take the candle out of your hat and carry it straight up and as far from your face as you can."

What did he mean by a *stope*, and would I recognize it when I reached it?

Step by step, clinging to the rungs, we climbed straight up the three by four opening in the rock. As water dripped from above and hit my hat and face, the candle sputtered. I stepped carefully for fear of tripping on my skirt. With the strange feeling of carrying a candle on my head, I stared steadily at the ladder. The flickering light shone dimly on the walls caging us in, three sides of solid rock and the fourth made of timbers for the ore chute alongside. Each rung was a little harder for me to reach and cling to. By the time 50 rungs were beneath us I began to waver, then I hesitated, but remembering that George was close below and might be thrown off balance, I plunged on. After 100 feet of this fearsome climb, we reached the top of the ladder where the rock closed in over our heads.

Even today, many years later, the memory of that moment hits hard at the pit of my stomach!

Broken ore almost completely filled the cross shaft, leaving only a crooked passage to crawl through, two feet wide, three feet high. Faintness and vertigo swept through me. But not for anything would I let George or Johnny know how desperately fear gripped me. I could hardly breathe. There must have been oxygen but I couldn't pull any of it into my lungs. To cover the sick feeling of panic, I made the excuse, which was real enough, that I needed to catch my breath after the exhausting climb. Unable, in that flat space, to sit up, I lay flat on my stomach, resting, doubting that I could go on.

Through the pounding of my heart I could hear myself saying, "Hattie, you *must* go on. You are the wife of a miner. Keep going and get it over!" But my head was swimming and my stomach churning. I lay there until terror subsided somewhat then told Johnny I was ready.

Holding the candle safely before me I inched along, face down, clawing at rocks with my one free hand, dragging my legs forward, my long skirts hampering every move. Only occasionally could I catch the gleam of Johnny's candle ahead. Unable to look back I could hear George calling a word of encouragement as he followed.

But what if the rock overhead should cave in? The thought was torture. I struggled to wipe it from my mind. In the darkness, broken only by a flicker of a nearby candle, I twisted, turned, writhed like a snake, stopped many times to rest and capture a mite of courage.

It was 150 feet of pure hell! Yet I lived through it. We crossed the awful stope and there remained the descent—straight down another 100-foot ladder in a well, scarcely four feet square, cut in solid rock. It seemed easy. I had room to breathe. With each rung lower there was more space above my head. The tunnel at last! I hurried toward the streak of daylight at its mouth and the great outdoors. Heaven!

Cripple Creek Days

Mabel Barbee Lee

THE STORY IN THE *Times* next morning was tantalizingly brief. Every word was burned in my heart:

> Pearl De Vere, madam at the Old Homestead, died early today from an overdose of morphine. According to a denizen in the house, a gay party was in full swing when Pearl excused herself, saying that she felt indisposed. She refused to let anyone go with her to her room. She was in high spirits all evening, a woman said, and never seemed happier or more carefree. No one could offer any reason why the madam should want to end her life. The body was discovered by the wealthy patron of the lavish affair. It was lying across the bed fully clothed in the ball dress that came only last week from a salon in Paris. The name of the patron could not be learned. It was understood that he left suddenly on business in Denver. Funeral arrangements will be announced later pending word from the deceased's relatives in the East.

Kitty's lips tightened as she pushed the paper aside. "Another one of those unfortunates has taken poison," she said grimly. "It's just as well. Places like the Homestead, together with its inmates, should be wiped from the face of the earth."

It was the saddest Christmas of my life. I had no interest in the gifts that lay under our tree, no desire to help Kitty string cranberries and popcorn. The thought of Pearl De Vere cold in death, forsaken and alone in Fairley Bros. and Lampman's back room pulled at my heartstrings. It was all I could do to keep from crying. My mother had no inkling of my grief and if I wept she would grow suspicious and pry out my secret. So I escaped to my retreat at the Lone Pine Shaft on Mineral Hill to sit on the dump and mourn over the tragedy of my idol.

Then a daring obsession began to grip me. It was nothing less than a visit to the funeral parlor to gaze once more on Pearl De Vere's lovely face. I had never seen a corpse; the very word made me shiver with horror. I would cross the street any time rather than pass near a house with black crepe on the door. But my urge to see her was stronger than my fear; and besides, the saying came to me that if you touched a dead person his ghost would never return to haunt you. Even so, several days passed before I could muster sufficient courage to take such a bold step. The arrival of Pearl's sister from the East brought things to a head; now there wasn't a moment to lose.

At first glance, the entry of the mortuary was so inviting that it might have been a parlor in anybody's house. An enormous fern hung down from an iron stand in a sunny window. Green Brussels carpet covered the floor and comfortable chairs were scattered around. I waited at the desk a moment for the undertaker to appear. The place seemed empty. A large glass case on a table caught my eye. It contained mementos of people who had met violent death in Cripple Creek and were laid out at the mortuary. Each bore a typewritten label. There was the lunch bucket of a miner who had been struck by lightning; sidecombs of Two-Go Ruby who had swallowed strychnine; the pistol of a gambler who shot himself through the mouth; a piece of fuse that another used to blow off his head with dynamite. It was the lock of Pearl De Vere's red hair that made me shudder and try to escape through a back door. But instead, I found myself facing the morgue.

Four shadowy coffins stood along the wall of the dimly lit room, and I recalled with a shiver the mine explosion up on Gold Hill. I was tempted to run out before someone discovered me, but all at once low, insistent voices near a far window caught my ear. A thin, sharp-nosed woman and a man in a dirty oilcloth apron were standing alongside a lavender casket. They apparently didn't notice me as I tiptoed up.

"She's dead," the man was saying. "Her sins won't rub off on you now."

"The stain on our family will never rub off," the woman said bitterly. "It is as set as the dye on her hair! You should have told me what she was, the kind of life she had been leading, before I made the long, futile trip to this loathsome place." She, yanking on her gloves, added, "I'll take no further responsibility. I'm washing my hands of the disgraceful business!"

"But she is penniless!" the man urged. "Do you want your sister buried in the pauper's field?"

"This harlot is no sister of mine!" the woman shot back, as she started to leave. I was trembling so that I dropped my new purse. "What're you doing here?" she screamed, seemingly aware of me for the first time. "A fine place this is for a child!" she flung out, slamming the door so hard the calendar on the wall fell to the floor.

"There's a lot a' mean-hearted folks in the world," the man said, shrugging, "but for my money, she takes the cake!"

"Is Pearl De Vere's hair really dyed red?" I asked, struggling with disillusion.

"Sure," he bantered. "That's nothing. All the girls on the row do it. Sometimes it's black, sometimes blond, and now and then it's red, like De Vere"s. I done my damnedest to bleach it before any of her hoity-toity relations got here, but it was no use—came out a dirty pink—the ungodliest sight I ever seen on a cadaver!"

I leaned over the coffin for a better view. She looked so natural that she might have opened her eyes and smiled up at me slantwise through her long lashes. If there had been any stain of wickedness in her face, death had erased it. She seemed younger than my mother; the hurt, wistful expression about the mouth was like that of a girl. "Do you care if I touch her?" I asked, reaching over to brush a pinkish strand of hair from her forehead.

"Go ahead," the man replied, "but make it snappy. I got work to do. Can't hang 'round here all day. Say," he eyed me sharply, "ain't I seen you somewhere? Whose kid are you, anyhow?"

I turned and ran out of the room, afraid that he was one of my father's friends.

The whole town was in an uproar when word spread that Pearl De Vere's sister had disowned her. The editor of the *Times* wrote, "Cripple Creek can bury its own dead!" The Reverend Jim Franklin preached a sermon called, "Let him Who Is Without Sin Cast the First Stone!" And Johnny Nolan, the owner of the camp's biggest gambling rooms, started a movement to auction off the Parisian ball gown and "give the little girl the finest funeral that money can buy!" But before the exquisite shell-pink creation could be handed over to the highest bidder, Fairley Bros. and Lampman announced receipt of a mysterious, unsigned letter. It was postmarked Denver and enclosed $1,000 in crisp new bills to pay all burial costs. The only request was that Pearl De Vere be laid out in the elegant dress in which she had danced on Christmas Eve.

A throng turned out the day of the funeral, mostly children and miners. I watched from the top of a barrel in front of Roberts' Grocery. Somebody claimed he saw ladies from up on the hill sitting in the shadows of upstairs office windows. The Elks Band headed by Joe Moore led the procession, playing the "Death March." Then came the heavily draped hearse with the lavender casket almost hidden under a blanket of red and white roses. Just behind, a man walked solemnly beside an empty rig with the shiny red wheels, driving the span of restive black horses. A large cross of shell-pink carnations lay on the seat.

My throat ached; I swallowed hard to choke back the tears. Now, four mounted police were coming down the avenue, pushing back the crowd to make way for all the lodge members in brilliant regalia trying to keep in step. The sight of those red fezzes, feathered helmets, and gold-braided scabbards, sent thrills of ecstasy through me. Bringing up the rear were buggies filled with thickly veiled women who, a man said, were Pearl's friends from the row.

I ran along the alley to the edge of town where Bennett Avenue narrowed to the mule road to Pisgah graveyard. Except for a few squatters' cabins, that part of camp was barren and windswept. I climbed on a rock from where I could get a clear view of the cemetery. It was late afternoon and the sun had begun to slant toward Pisgah Mountain. I watched a man chopping wood in front of a tar-papered shack. Not far away, a boy was trying to hitch an obstinate burro to a cart while a dog yelped and snapped at the animal. A chicken hawk soared and dipped above an acrid, smoldering dump ground. My feet were getting chilly, and I hugged myself to keep warm.

The last of the procession had passed by and the marchers were gathering around the freshly dug grave. I wondered uneasily if the services would be long. Soon the train would be coming in from Beacon Hill, and Kitty would call me up and down the neighborhood to help her with supper. The thought had scarcely passed my mind when I saw some of the mourners scattering and climbing back into the rigs. But a few of the lodge members had moved in closer to the grave, and one of them seemed to be reading from a book. All at once, through a break in the trees, I caught a glimpse of the flower-laden casket being lowered into the ground; then came the sad, sweet notes of Joe Moore's cornet playing "Good-Bye, Little Girl, Good-Bye." That was too much for me to bear; my heart was broken, and I buried my face in my coat and sobbed.

When I looked up again, the long line of carriages and men had begun to file through the cemetery gate and down the slope back to camp. But the order had been reversed. The women, coming first, had thrown the veils off their faces and were laughing merrily as the trotting horses kicked up dust. Lodge members hurried willy-nilly, flapping their arms up and down, crossing them from side to side to get warm. The driver of the buggy with the shiny red wheels had jumped on the seat, and the frisky steeds galloped wildly while he held the reins with one hand and reached for a bottle from under the seat with the other. Even the hearse had picked up speed and the wheels rattled clumsily over the stones. The musicians came last; and as they approached me, dapper Joe Moore looked over and winked. Then he sounded the whistle; the snare drums rolled, and the whole band burst into "There'll Be a Hot Time in the Old Town Tonight!"

I waited until they were out of sight and the tune had faded in the distance. I felt suddenly weary, older, and more grown up.

Abroad at Home

Julian Street

HOWEVER, WE DID GET TO Cripple Creek, and for all its mountain setting, and all $300 million of gold that it has yielded in the last 20 years or so, it is one of the most depressing places in the world. Its buildings run from shabbiness to downright ruin; its streets are ill paved, and its outlying districts are a horror of waste stacks, ore-dumps, shaft-houses, reduction-plants, gallows-frames and squalid shanties, situated in the mud. It seemed to me that Cripple Creek must be the most ill looking little city in the world, but I was informed that, as mining camps go, it is unusually presentable, and later I learned for myself that that is true.

Cripple Creek is not only above the timberline; it is above the cat line. I mean this literally. Domestic cats cannot live there. And many human beings are affected by the altitude. I was. I had a headache; my breath was short, and upon exertion my heart did flip-flops. Therefore, I did not circulate about the town excepting within a radius of a few blocks of the station. That, however, was enough.

After walking up the main street a little way, I turned off into a side street with flimsy buildings, half of them tumbledown and abandoned. Turning into a cross street I came upon a long row of tiny one-story houses, crowded close together on the block. Some of them were empty, but others showed signs of being occupied. Instead of a number, the door of each one bore a name, "Clara," "Louise," "Lina," and so on, down the block. For a time, there was not a soul in sight as I walked slowly along that line of box-stall houses. Then, far ahead, I saw a woman come out of a door. She wore a loose pink wrapper and carried a pitcher in her hand. I watched her cross the street and go into a dingy building. Then the street was empty again. I walked slowly. As I passed one doorway it opened suddenly and a man came out—a slim man with a drooping mustache. He did not look at me as he passed. The window shade of the crib from which he had come went up as I moved by. I looked at the window, and as I did so, the curtains parted and the face of a negress was pressed against the pane, grinning at me with a knowing, sickening grin.

I passed on. From another window, a white woman with very black hair and cheeks of a light orchid-shade showed her gold teeth in a mirthless automatic smile and added the allurement of an ice-cold wink.

The door of the crib at the corner stood open, and just before I reached it a woman stepped out and surveyed me as I approached. She wore a white linen skirt and a middy blouse, attire grotesquely juvenile for one of her years. Her hair, of which she had but a moderate amount, was light brown and stringy, and she wore steel-rimmed spectacles. She did not look depraved but, upon the contrary, resembled a highly respectable, if homely, German cook I once employed. As I glanced at her window I saw hanging there a glass sign, across which, in gold letters, was the title, "Madam Leo."

"Madam Leo," she said to me, nodding and pointing at her chest. "That's me. Like the lion, eh?" She laughed foolishly.

I paused and made some casual inquiry concerning her prosperity.

"Things is dull now in Cripple Creek," she said. "There ain't much business no more. I wish they'd start a white man's club or a dance hall across the street. Cripple Creek would be booming."

I think I remarked, in reply, that things did look rather dull. In the meantime, I looked in at her little room. There was a chair or two, a cheap oak dresser, and one bed. The room looked neat.

"Ain't I got a nice clean place?" suggested Madam Leo. Then, as I assented, she pointed to a calendar which hung upon the wall. At the top of it was a colored print of some French painting, showing a Cupid kissing a filmily draped Psyche.

"That's me," said Madam Leo. "That's me when I was a young girl!" Again she gave her laugh.

I started to move on.

"Where are you from?" she asked.

"I came up from Colorado Springs," I said.

"Well," she returned, "when you go back send some nice boys up here. Tell 'em to see Madam Leo. Tell them a middle-aged woman with spectacles. I'm known here. I been here four years. Oh, things ain't so bad. I manage to make two or three dollars a day."

As I passed to leeward of her on the narrow walk I got the smell of a strong, sweet perfume.

"Have you got to be going?" she asked.

"Yes," I answered. "I must go to the train."

"Well, then—so long," she said. "So long."

"Don't forget Madam Leo," she admonished, giving utterance, again, to her short, feeble-minded laugh.

"I won't," I promised.

And I never, never shall.

Colorado
Its Gold and Silver Mines

Frank Fossett

SO BENEFICIAL HAVE BEEN found the climatic influences of Colorado that her fame as a sanitarium is becoming world-wide, and the influx of health-seekers is annually becoming greater. The dryness and lightness of the air and its invigorating character, together with the almost constant prevalence of sunshine, impart new energy to the well, and a fresh lease of life for those whose constitutions are impaired. Here in this elevated plateau, far removed from the chilling winds and damp atmosphere of either ocean, all the conditions of life to the newcomer are fresh and inspiring.

This region possesses influences that arrest the tendency to pulmonary diseases. Consumptives who do not put off their coming too long have been cured effectively, while others have had their days prolonged by months or years. Many eastern people have taken up a permanent abode in Colorado because their health would not permit of their living elsewhere. Others have found the results of a sojourn so salutary that they return to stay. A variety of diseases, chronic or otherwise, find a speedy or partial cure in the pure air or in the health-giving mineral waters.

Investigation and long experience by the highest medical authority have summed the advantages of this climate somewhat as follows: To a person in the enjoyment of fair health, the sensations attending a first entrance into this elevated region are always pleasant. The dryness of the atmosphere, together with the electricity therein contained, combined with, perhaps, other peculiarities of climate, excites the nervous system to a peculiar degree of tension. The physical functions which may have for some time been accomplished in a sluggish, inefficient manner, at once assume a vigor of action to which the system is a stranger. The appetite is keen, the digestion is vigorous, and the sleep sound. The result of these innovations is that all lurking ailments are swept away at once, and whatever there is in each individual to enjoy is called into the fullest action. He revels in what might be called intoxication of good health. An unclouded mind partakes of the elasticity of a healthy body, and a newly-aroused desire for activity is manifested, as well as an increased capacity to accomplish. This, in the beginning, is experienced to a greater or less degree by all who visit this section, and the pleasure attendant upon such a beginning will forever render the Rocky Mountains a resort of unequaled attraction for the tourist.

But besides merely pleasure-seeking travelers who come westward every year, there are thousands of invalids, suffering from a wide range of chronic diseases, who come on a pilgrimage in search of health. In many cases, the relief obtained is surprisingly rapid. The asthmatic forgets in the quiet of undisturbed slumber his nightly suffocation. The victim of chronic bronchitis discovers a new lease of life, and after the lapse of a very brief period he finds it hard to realize that he has been so recently afflicted with a cough so distressing, so violent, or so dangerous. The sufferer from malaria, in that most obnoxious form called fever and ague, is glad to have found a land where fever and ague never come.

While the climate is thus referred to in such seemingly flattering terms, the idea is not intended to be conveyed that there is no bad weather in Colorado. There are almost all kinds of climate, according to elevation and locality, from a warm temperate to that of the borders of the frigid zone, the latter being largely experienced on the lofty peaks of the main range of mountains. Under such circumstances, weather, good, bad, and indifferent must be expected. Still, the belt of country skirting the eastern base of the mountains as well as a few other sections, enjoys an amount of sunshine and of delightful weather with a freedom from storms such as is but rarely encountered elsewhere, and in no section between Colorado and the seaboard. The temperature of a large portion of the foothills country, including such places as Central, Black Hawk, Idaho Springs, and Georgetown, is remarkably even for the entire year, there being less cold weather in winter and less warm weather in summer than in any locality of less elevation. ...

* * *

"Infinite" is the term used by an old Coloradan to describe in brief the climate of this region. Infinite it certainly is in variety, purity, and sunshine. But the variety comes from difference in altitude, rather than in latitude. The Italian or Virginian warmth of the plains, and the frigidity of timberline or of the mountain tops, are experienced on the parallel and within 50 miles one of another. It is but a short remove from a northern to a southern temperature, and from either to the eternal snows of the Sierras. Owing to the dry, bracing qualities of the atmosphere, heat or cold are not felt as severely or readily as where there is greater moisture and humidity.

The quantity of the snow-fall is not great, except on the great mountain ranges and higher elevations. It never entirely disappears from altitudes of from 12,000 to 14,400 feet. Elsewhere, the sun's rays are too powerful to admit of snow lying on the ground a great while unless in case of unusually cold weather, and sleighing is of rare occurrence in many mountain towns.

The Willow-Bender

Helen Rich

ON THE DREDGE, THE WINCHMAN coaxed the fouled bucket lines until at last the bucket ladder and its weight of iron scoops drew clear of the green water. It stretched awkwardly, like a man with a stiff leg, part on deck, part over the pond. The grunting shore crews dug new postholes, setting the deadmen, the posts, in them and fastening the shorelines to hold the boat steady as she turned. By the end of the week, floundering, wallowing, McClain's bellows echoing over the camp, she was turned, headed toward Divide Street, her points set, her spud anchored, the buckets let down into the water again.

By the end of the week, men had already cleared the ground as far as the Moffat house. The company owned land to the town limits, and that was where the Moffat house stood, just on the edge. Jett Moffat watched grimly while she packed. Her old mouth quivered sometimes as she saw the lodgepoles rend from their soil and fall, saw the quaking aspens die, took the final bouquet of sagebrush into her wide nostrils.

One day while she watched, she took down a frayed denim jacket that belonged to her husband, Breck, and put it on over her tremendous calico. She jammed her gnarled feet into a pair of Breck's workshoes and clumped out across the flat, her white hair standing about her head like a ragged cloud.

"Here comes old lady Moffat," one of the workmen said, "looking like she's going to sink a pick into somebody."

She had remembered an *albino mertensia* that grew on this land. It was her most tender possession, although it did not grow on her ground. She had found the rare bells years before and never told a living soul where they were, not even Breck, for fear they would be dug up and taken away. She had even concealed the plant, arranging brush so skillfully that it was open to sun and rain yet no one would think to look where it grew.

She strode fiercely up to Lam Hunter, the gang foreman. "If you've gone and tromped my white bluebells, I don't know what I'll do," she said in her mighty voice.

"What white bluebells, Jett?" Lam asked. "Whereabouts would they be?"

"You've already tore away my marks," Jett moaned, "but they'd be about here somewheres if you ain't destroyed them to death." She began searching for the plant. "Oh, the little dear things!" she cried, then shouted at Lam standing close. "You stand back with your great feet! You stand clear back!" She began a slow circle then, her deep eyes probing for the dusty-green plant that would, by now, be bowing with delicate carillon.

She found it while the gang waited anxious and silent, not daring to grub out a clump of sage or put an axe to a tree. Her hands came together in a great clap of thanksgiving. "You fetch me a shovel, one of you!" she called. She dug it up herself, stooped down and widely circled, and when she had delivered it from its birthplace, she took off her jacket and laid the plant on it, the gravelly dirt sifting only a little.

She let the men see it before she gathered the jacket around it. "Why, they's yards of them bells around this country," one of them said.

She looked at him with majesty. "Blue," she said. "Show me white." She bore it then in her great arms, bare to the river wind. When she got back home she planted it in an eight-pound lard bucket to take with her on her migration.

Mountain Woman

Belle Turnbull

God love these mountain women anyway,
Said Mr Probus. Not to say they're fair
Or sleek with oils, for woodsmoke in the hair
And sagebrush on the fingers every day
Are toughening perfumes, and the sunstreams flay
Too dainty flesh. But what remains is rare,
Like mountain honey to the mountain bear.
He finds his relish in a rough bouquet.

Days when their wash is drying, off they'll go
And fish the beaver ponds. Hell or high water
They'll wade the slues in sunburnt calico
Playing a trout like some old sea-king's daughter.
Hell and high water women ... steady now,
Not all of them, he said. One, anyhow.

Stampede to Timberline

Muriel Sibell Wolle

WHEN THE SIGHTSEEING BUS climbed the long, steep mile from Black Hawk to Central City in the midst of the Colorado Rockies, I sat up a little straighter and could hardly believe my eyes. Wooden sidewalks! Gingerbread frets under eaves; hills tier on tier and mine dumps, with rusty shaft houses everywhere.

"What you see here," said the man in the next seat to me, "is what's left of the old West. You won't see it much longer, for it is disappearing fast."

Craning my neck and looking from side to side, I watched the old houses crowded together with the gaping mine tunnels and the monument commemorating the discovery of Colorado's gold on this spot. Still, the car climbed toward more mines. Ahead, to the left, was an empty firehouse with its bell, standing beside a dump down which gray tailings poured, proof that the mines in the distance were working. On the right were streets, one above another, built on terraces cut from the hills, and on one stood the native stone high school from which, I was told, graduated the first trained teachers of the state.

Crowning the hill was another school building, this one surmounted with a cross. "That," said my neighbor, "was St. Aloysius' Academy, and just below it, on Eureka Street, is one of the most famous hostelries in the West—the Teller House. And below it is the Opera House, and beyond it the Gilpin County Courthouse, and farther up the streets, the Brewery, and at the top of the hill, the cemeteries." My head reeled.

Buildings everywhere, many of them deserted and definitely built many years ago. Few people were in sight when we stopped for soda pop and a quick stroll along the main street, and our footsteps echoed as we climbed the wooden steps to the Masonic Lodge, one of the sights of the city. This was Central City, once the biggest place in Jefferson Territory, and in the '60s surpassing even Denver in size. And here *I* was, fresh from the East and surrounded by a culture which flowered in the '70s and '80s and slowly faded in the '90s.

We stayed all too short a time in Central City and were hurried on toward Idaho Springs and our objective, St. Mary's Glacier, where there would be skiing—a great attraction to easterners on the Fourth of July! We climbed the long, curving hill that led out of Central to Russell Gulch and Idaho Springs; and before we reached the top of the grade, I glanced back for a last look at Central City, cupped in a hollow of the mountains and emanating such a strong flavor of the past. The rest of the trip I do not remember. The skiing and the snowballing are hazy recollections, for my whole attention was centered on Central City, and my mind was made up then and there to know more of its history and to return to its picturesque streets and sketch its tumbling buildings and gaping mines.

A year passed before I could carry out my decision—a year spent in New York. But New York had lost its fascination; more and more, I longed for the mountains and the West. And I well remember the day that I walked into the president's office at the art school where I was teaching and tendered my resignation.

"What's this?" said that gentleman. "Are you going to be married?"

"No," I replied with a wicked gleam in my eye, for I knew how he loved the East. "I'm tired of New York, and I want to go west to live."

So, a few months later, having sought positions from Montana to Arizona, I was fortunate enough to find an opening in the Art Department at the University of Colorado, and I knew that my Central City dream was beginning to materialize.

During the summer of 1926, while teaching at the university, I asked questions about Colorado's past, its mining booms and its ghost towns, but my real interest in history began when I returned to Central City to start my pictorial record of the place. As soon as school closed at the end of August, ignorant of the lack of regular transportation in the West to many mountain points at any time, I made plans to spend the vacation in Central City, 40 miles from Boulder, and when I was ready to start, there was no way to go. The sightseeing companies had closed until the following season; the daily stage up the canyon went only halfway—20 miles is a long hike at 7,000 feet elevation. In desperation, I called the local taxi company and presented my problem to them. They seemed a bit stunned at the request but did some quick calculating and announced that the trip would cost $15. Knowing that the canyon stage to Nederland, 20 miles away, cost considerably less, I decided to take it and hunt the rest of my transportation there.

Armed with sketching materials, I set out on Labor Day on what seemed an innocent excursion. I reached Nederland by noon. Surely someone would be willing to drive me to Central City for a modest sum, and I began inquiring at the garages and hotels; but seemingly no one was interested in a trip to Central. Finally, a man agreed to drive me over. "And how much will the trip cost?" I asked. "Fifteen dollars," was his prompt answer. At this point, the hotel proprietor came to my aid by assuring me that if I spent the night in his hotel I might be able to get over the next day with the Boulder bread man, who served the mountain towns once a week and who sometimes took passengers. Such an arrangement seemed worth trying and much more economical; so I settled down to stay in Nederland, a small mining town, which by the '20s had become a summer resort. All afternoon I tramped the streets, sketching the false-fronted stores, the log cabins, and the big tungsten mill on the creek. To the west was the Continental Divide; and up the winding road to the south lay Central City, 20 miles away. From time to time during the afternoon, great roars and cheers came from the baseball park where a game was in progress; and upon inquiry I learned that the Nederland team was playing the Black Hawk club. That was the last I needed to know that Black Hawk was one mile from Central City; and here in front of me were nine men who, in a few hours, would be going to within one mile of my destination while I sat in Nederland waiting for the bread man. But I was from the East, and one doesn't just offer oneself to a ball team and beg transportation. Yet, the more I mulled it over in my mind, the more foolish it seemed to spend the night in Nederland with Central so accessible.

I entered a restaurant for an early supper, perhaps because, parked in front of it, was a car with a Black Hawk license plate. At a table sat a ballplayer with his wife and family, and as I ate, I gathered courage; and as they were leaving, I told them my plight and said that since I saw they were from Black Hawk maybe they would know some way that I might get to Central. This thin disguise worked; and while I ran for my suitcase, they filled the tank of the touring car with gasoline; and in less than five minutes, I was on my way to the Teller House.

It was a ride I shall never forget. The road in those days was steeper than the new highway and was not surfaced. The car pulled slowly but steadily up the twisting grades while the driver told me of seeing some autos which couldn't make it and had to back up the worst hills. All the while, I sat in the backseat between two small boys with a gaily flowered coverlet tucked under our chins to shut out the cold wind of a September evening.

I watched the sunset colors fade as we drove between stands of lodgepole pines and passed occasional ranch houses. Just before dark, we dropped down into Black Hawk with its mills and smelters and its homes perched crazily on the mountainsides. With true Western hospitality, my "benefactors" drove up to Central City and deposited me in front of the Teller House, refusing to take any remuneration for the trip. I thanked them profusely and was so confused at my temerity in thumbing a ride that even their names have escaped me, and to this day I regret that I do not know to whom I am indebted for starting me on my ghost town hobby.

* * *

For four days I explored Central City, returning to the hotel only for meals and to sleep. There was so much to see and sketch that the days were all too short. At noon time, if I were halfway down the gulch, I had only to put my painting paraphernalia in a deserted cabin and climb up the hill to the hotel for lunch knowing that they would be safe during my absence. Children and passersby watched curiously as I worked and made comments about the pictures. One lady admired a watercolor of Eureka Street showing several residences including her own. When her husband returned from work, she brought him to see the picture, and he, seeing her interest, offered to buy it for her. "No," said she emphatically, "I don't want it unless she will paint it again and make our house look bigger."

One morning, I was sitting in an alley making a watercolor of some buildings and a lazy flight of wooden stairs to the next street level when a girl of about 10 came to look over my shoulder; and as we talked, she found that I was an art teacher. Later, she returned with several little friends and, standing just within earshot, said of my work, "It's pretty good for her being just a teacher and not an artist."

Each day was a new experience, and my enthusiasm to capture the town on paper was greater than my resistance to the cold September winds, which swept through the empty streets and up my arms. As a greenhorn, I had not realized how warm the clothing I should have brought for these mountain altitudes. I had planned to spend two weeks in the town, but at the end of five days I had caught a cold on one shoulder and could neither sketch nor move about with any comfort. The Teller House was cold and dank too in those days, and hot water could be gotten only at intervals, brought in a pitcher by a solicitous but elderly bellhop. Plainy, it was time for me to return to Boulder. But how was I to get there? Inquiry after inquiry convinced me that no one ever went to Boulder, and again I was marooned 40 miles from my destination. Then someone remembered the Boulder bread man who was due the following day. Maybe he would take me. I mentally decided that he jolly well would; and an hour before he was due, I was sitting in front of the store where he made his deliveries, my suitcase beside me. He was not too glad to see me, and when I told him of my plight, he did not say that he would take me; so desperately, I insisted, "But I won't take up very much room," and began to shove my luggage toward the automobile. I remember no more except that, in a few minutes, I was riding beside him with my feet braced against the dashboard as we bounded down the canyon toward Boulder. The truck was short on springs and cushions but speedy; and by the time I was unloaded in front of the apartment in Boulder, I felt as if I'd had a thorough osteopathic treatment. Out came the suitcase from the bread wagon, and slowly but gratefully I limped into the house—my first adventure with Central City over.

Dizzying Heights

Bruce Ducker

THE COUNTRYSIDE WAS SPECTACULAR. A maze of extended buttes carved by wind and water into an intricate pattern. To the south and east, the hillsides were barren. But on the windward and northern sides, where snows gathered and held, forests of black-green ponderosa grew—and rivers, the Marvine and the White, the Dolores and the Eagle, all emptying into the mighty Colorado. Waddy's spirit responded to the romance of place, the only flavor of romance on his plate—though he knew if ever presented he would respond equally to the fleshy kind.

"Ye-ee-ee-ee-ss-ss," he shouted to the sky.

Waddy steered off the exit at a quaint little town and took the road that bordered the Roaring Fork River toward the couloirs in which Aspen nestled. The drive was a constant climb, some 50 miles gaining 3,000 feet. Waddy's spirits climbed as he ascended. The mountains grew craggy, their geology newer and the lines more severe, and the houses now larger and more fantastical. Through it all, edging the road, ran a fierce and freestone river.

The setting did not disappoint him. The sky was a color you could use in a program of heaven. I ought to make a note of that, thought Waddy. Heaven as a video game. Until it came to him: He was no longer in the business.

The environs. Giant houses of every architectural excess—Art Deco Moderne, Bauhaus, Provençal, Philip Johnson nihilist, Tudor, PPG-bulk-sale, Michael Graves-end, Darien feudal, even something that looked like Colorado. The higher up on the cols one looked, the larger the houses grew, until in a band at the highest shelf, with its spectacular views of the ski runs and the wilderness beyond, Starwood, the crown in the jewel. There, buildings poised on the fragile ledges like raptors peering down on the scurrying life below.

On Aspen's outskirts, he passed an airport built against the base of a mountain. The craft on the aprons would have made any nation in the world a proud air force: Gulfstreams and Citations and, huddled over by the fuel pumps, infra dig, King Airs and Lears. Most bore no identifier except a tail number. One or two showed a discreet monogram, as might be embroidered on the linen of a peer of the realm.

Thomas Hornsby Ferril and the American West

Thomas Hornsby Ferril

Old Men On the Blue

I KNOW a barn in Breckenridge on the Blue,
In Summit County, Colorado, where
A Ford transmission rots upon the wall
Beside an ox yoke. You can stand inside
The barn and peer like a pack rat through the logs
And see how summertime looks outdoors, and see
A sleigh with hare-bells ringing under it,
And snowy yarrow drifting over the runners.

How high the mountains are behind the barn
Along toward evening nobody seems to know,
And nobody seems to know, how blue they are,
Not even the old men sitting all day long
On a ledge in the shade in front of the general store;
But they watch the gasoline go up and down
In the big glass pump where the white-faced people stop
Who are crossing the Rocky Mountains.

They watch the white-faced people crawl away
Into the hackled fractures of the peaks,
Up where the Mississippi River ends
And the bodies of the frozen dragonflies
Begin to float to the Gulf of California.

The mountain ranges in the evening fill
The sockets of the old men's eyes with blue,
And some of their cheeks are lavender and lilac.
One long day after sunset sunlight poured
Out of the east, from an amber thunderhead,
To make their cheekbones shine like yellow gold.

The old men do not speak while the pump is running,
But when you drive away you can hear their voices,
Like sounds you hear alone at night in a canyon
When pieces of blackness clatter on pieces of water,
And you think if you didn't have the car in low,
You could overhear what the mountains have never told you.

At night the old men sleep in houses that
Will always have geraniums in the windows.

Amidst the Gold Dust

Julie Danneberg

Mrs. Chalmers: Big Thompson Canyon, September 12, 1873

AFORE WE CAME HERE from back east, Mr. Chalmers was sick, laid low by tuberculosis. We heard that the mountain air in Colorado helped people like him get better. We came, and sure'nuf, Mr. Chalmers got well.

When that woman first showed up here, I figured that she was lookin' for the cure, too. But no; she said she came to see the mountains. Can you imagine such foolishness? A grown woman cavortin' around the countryside all alone. Humph! She asked for a room. And though I saw no good in this citified woman's silly travels, I said she could stay for five dollars a week. "As long as you make yourself agreeable," I told her.

Isabella: September 12, 1873

Agreeable? My word! I almost left when that pinched, uneducated woman told me that I had to make myself agreeable in this, the most disagreeable of places. The Chalmerses had a squatter's claim of 160 acres of land and lived here many years under the most uncivilized of conditions. Their family of seven squeezed into a falling-down, two-room log cabin with no beds, no furniture to speak of, and not even a fastening on the door. When I saw this and saw my ride rattle away, faced with the Chalmerses' unfriendliness, I just sat down and knitted. After a while, I regained my composure enough to eat the supper they placed silently beside me—dried beef and milk.

As soon as darkness fell, the family dragged their straw mattresses and blankets outside to sleep under the stars. I preferred inside by the fire. I often heard tiny animals scurrying across the floor, and once awoke to find myself looking into the eyes of a snake. The next morning, in an effort to make myself "agreeable," I offered to do the dishes.

Mrs. Chalmers: September 13, 1873

When that woman asked to wash the dishes, I done shook my head, disbelievin'. I said, "I'm guessin' you'll make more work than you'll do. I see those hands of yours, all smooth and white. Never done a stitch of work, I bet. No, thank you. I'll do the dishes myself."

Isabella: Longmont, End of September, 1873

I stayed with the Chalmerses for over a week and never reached my goal of getting farther into the mountains. Defeated, I returned to a hotel on the prairie.

Platt Rogers:End of September 1873

My friend, Sylvester, and I had long looked forward to our mountain holiday. We were spending the night in Longmont before taking on the last leg of our journey, the long hard ride into Estes Park. The proprietor of our hotel asked us to take along a female hotel guest. Said he'd consider it a personal favor. Naturally, we said yes, although inwardly I feared the presence of a woman might prove a hindrance. "Oh well; maybe she'll be young and beautiful," we comforted ourselves. My hopes were dashed next morning, when I first saw Miss Bird. She wore strange-looking bloomers, rode like a man, and was neither young nor beautiful.

We began our ride, and I was relieved to find that Miss Bird did not slow our progress.

Mountain Jim: End of September, 1873

I met the gracious and lovely Miss Isabella Bird when she first passed my home on her way to Estes Park.

My proper name is James Nugent, but I am known as Mountain Jim, partly because of my skills as a hunter and trapper and partly because of my untamed behavior. My home is at the edge of Estes Park, a wide and wild river valley sitting in the shadow of tall granite mountains. The hunting here is plentiful, and the people are not. That is why I like it.

Isabella: End of September, 1873

On the approach to Estes Park, we passed a rustic cabin that looked more like the den of a wild beast than the home of a human. Lynx, bear, and other furs dried on the roof, while a wisp of smoke puffed leisurely out of the chimney. A deer carcass hung at one end of the cabin. A large collie dog growled our greeting. Out came a rough mountain man dressed in a buckskin suit, a knife tucked in his belt, and a revolver sticking out of his breast pocket. His hair, a messy tangle of long blonde curls, partially hid the scars that rippled half his face. I found out later the scars came from a fight with a bear.

* * *

J.J. Brown: Summer 1886

Right away, I got permission to call on Miss Margaret Tobin. It didn't take long for Maggie to show her true colors. I arrived at her house, hat in hand, full of plans for our first evening together. When she came to the door, Maggie looked past me to my one-horse, rather shabby, proprietary carriage parked in the street. "No, thank you," she said and walked inside.

Margaret Tobin didn't consent to a seat by my side until I came back the next evening driving a much nicer, two-horse carriage. Only 19 years old, and yet she knew exactly what she wanted and wouldn't accept less. I liked that.

Margaret: Summer 1886

I knew what I wanted, and Jim wasn't it. I wanted to marry a rich man, and Jim wasn't rich, not even close. I wanted to marry someone to help me give my parents some of the luxuries they'd missed, working day and night to keep us six children in that tiny house, with food on the table and shoes on our feet.

But it didn't take long for me to fall in love with Mr. J.J. Brown, a poor, hardworking miner. I tried to resist, but finally I figured I'd be happier marrying for love than money. So I married Jim. When I became Mrs. J.J. Brown, I stopped cooking and caring for my brother, moved into my husband's tiny house, and began cooking and caring for him.

SECTION VI

The Tabors

Horace Tabor

Duane A. Smith

> Oro City, December 27, 1876. Is a very shrewd businessman and not liable to lose money, has a good chance to make money as he has no competition. Estimated worth say $15,000.

THIS R.G. DUN REPORT fairly and accurately described the pre-Leadville and Bonanza Horace Tabor. An 1859er who had spent nearly two decades following the will-o'-the-wisp Colorado mining frontier, Tabor was then living and working in out-the-way Oro City, near where Leadville would be one day.

Soon thereafter came the Little Pittsburg silver strike, and Tabor's fortune took flight. Very quickly, Colorado—and the rest of the nation—was hearing about Horace Tabor. "Denver's lucky star was high when Governor Tabor decided to spend his fortune here," praised the *Denver Tribune* (September 7, 1881). The *Leadville Daily Herald* (July 8, 1882) understood his contribution: "Colorado has produced fortunes for many men, but no man who has met with success has so freely made investments in this state, as has Governor Tabor."

The events that followed that amazing silver discovery on Fryer Hill, May 1878, unfolded like a classic Greek tragedy. Tabor weathered them all, and his name has resounded through the succeeding decades. No other Coloradan of his generation is so well remembered, nor does anyone else so typify the tempo of this legendary mining era. While the others—Henry Teller, David Moffat, Jerome Chaffee, Edward Wolcott—have faded in memory, Tabor is still alive, thanks in no small measure to that epoch-capturing opera, *The Ballad of Baby Doe*.

He is perhaps remembered for all the wrong reasons—the love triangle, the divorce, the decline and collapse—rather than for the faith, the optimism, and the investments that built Colorado. Even more regrettable is the fabrication that came to be accepted as fact; as far as can be ascertained, he never told Baby Doe to "hang onto Matchless." Her later life—and death—these are catalyst enough for the legend, without adding a 1938-concocted story that seems unlikely ever to die.

Cabin Life in Colorado

Mrs. H.A.W. (Augusta) Tabor

I WAS THE FIRST WOMAN IN California Gulch. There was only one party of us, one of seven men, and we were to join with them, but I was sick in Denver, and they all went off a few days ahead of us. We were all this time trying to catch up with them. We knew they had gone somewhere into the mountains prospecting—150 miles southwest of Denver. They were prospecting along as they went; tried several gulches before they found California Gulch. When we got to Cachela Poudre, we stopped one month. My husband whip-sawed some lumber to make sluice boxes and put them in. We found plenty of gold, but there was so much black sand, and we did not know how to separate it. We had no quicksilver, so we had to abandon it. I would work all day long picking out with a little magnet; and when night came, I would not have a pennyweight, it was so fine. Afterwards, those diggings turned out to be very rich—if we had stayed right there, we would have had enough. It is owned by capitalists now, 20 miles below California Gulch. The town of Granite is there now. We abandoned Granite. We were the first there and camped there one month. Three gentlemen, Nathaniel Maxey, S. P. Kellogg, Mr. Tabor and me, and my baby, now a young man.

Someone came down California Gulch and reported they had found gold; they were looking us up and wanted to get in supplies. He came to our camp and told us to move up, telling us to go up until we came to the first large bald mountain on the road, then turn up that gulch around the bald mountain; it would take all day to go with the ox team, we would probably see the smoke of their campfire. We went up there and found Slater and Abe Lee. Those were the first men who panned out in California Gulch. They got a dollar to the pan, and that encouraged them right off. We killed our cattle that we drove in and divided the beef among them. We lived on that a few days until the man got back with some Mexicans coming in with flour. They turned to and built me a cabin of green logs—had it finished in two days. We lived there all summer. Mrs. C.L. Hall was the second lady to cross the South Park, now living at 412 Broadway, Denver. Dr. Bond came from Iowa. Had a very interesting wife; he was a gambler. He is blind now, and she has to support him.

In the wintertime, when everything was frozen up, there was no mining, and the men who had a little means would go out to the cities and spend all their money and go back in the spring.

Really, the women did more in the early days than the men. There was so much for them to do—the sick to take care of. I have had so many unfortunate men shot by accident, brought to my cabin to take care of. There were so many men who could not cook and did not like men's cooking and would insist upon boarding where there was a woman, and they would board there all they could.

We arrived in California Gulch May 8th, 1860; and in 1861, we had acquired what we considered quite a little fortune, about $7,000 in money. We came over into Park County, started a store, and stayed there six years. We rode over Mosquito Pass. My husband was postmaster. It was called Buckskin Joe when we lived there. A man who wore buckskin clothes whose name was Joe discovered the first diggings there. There was a little mining excitement, about 200 people were there, so we went over with the rush and started a store there until the mines all played out. Then we went back and opened a place in California Gulch—still continued the mercantile business. My husband kept the post office and express office, and I kept a boarding house in California Gulch. We were in better fix to keep those places, as almost everyone who came in just had a pack on his back. We had a little house and things in shape to keep them.

A man named Wm. Van Brooklyn—who did not like mining, as it was too hard work—said he had a pair of mules and he would start an express and would ride the mules alternately. He brought our letters in, and we paid him 75 cents each for them and paid accordingly for any little express matter he could bring on a mule. He was a heavy man and could not bring much. I kept the express books, started the letters, and took the money. He said if I would board him while he was running the express, he would give me his claim, but I would not board him for it, so he sold it to a man named Ferguson and Stevens—and that summer, there was $80,000 taken out of that claim by those two men. I weighed all the gold that was taken out of the upper end of the gulch that summer. There was many a miner who did not know the first thing about weighing gold. I never saw a country settled up with such greenhorns as Colorado. They were mostly from farms and some clerks. They were all young men from 18 to 30. I was there a good many years before we saw a man with gray hair. They thought they were going to have a second California; they gathered all the knowledge they could from books. Some Georgia miners reported there was gold here, and they came out to search for it. Thousands turned back. We met them every day, and they advised us to go back; but we started with six months provisions and thought, if we did not find anything here, we would go on to California.

When we came here, everybody said nothing would ever grow on this sandy desert, and no one could ever build a railroad in those mountains.

Mr. Tabor supplied the first 300,000 ties to the A.T. & S.F. Railroad. It took five months to get those ties down the mountain. He was under contract to get them down to the road at such a time and was under bonds and he was a man who would not allow his bondsmen to pay. He expected to get them down when the water was high in the spring, but we did not have any snow that spring and could not float them, so he had to hire teams to get them out of that canyon. I stayed at home all that five months and kept the store going. We had a good deal of money to take care of; we had the only safe in the country and had to keep everybody's treasures in that safe, and I was a little afraid for the five months he was gone from home.

A man named Green took the contract to get out the ties for the A.T. & S.F. The ties were got up where California Gulch is. They were owing Mr. Tabor a good deal of money for supplies, and he found out the man was not going to make a success of it and became alarmed, so he took the contract off Green's hands to get his money out of it, and that is where he missed it.

After he got through with the tie business, we found that we had worked two years and had not made a dollar. Had done all the hard work for nothing. He worked hard with the rest of the men. He was terribly pushed to get food enough for them. They would eat an ox at one meal, and more too. All that time, I had the store for him to get money to run those ties through.

He wanted our boy to go into the store, but I wanted him to go to school. I told him I would go into the store and do all the boy could do. I went into the store and he found I was a better hand at keeping the books than he was. I made all the returns for the post office for seven years, and General Adams said that, during the seven years, he only sent back one paper for correction. ...

I have been taken along as a bodyguard a great many times when Mr. Tabor was going to Denver with treasure because he thought he would not be liable to be attacked. I have carried gold on my person many a time. He would buy all the gold that he could and would carry it down ourselves rather than express because our express was often robbed. I have gone across the Mosquito Range with him on horseback. Then we had no road at all. I had the gold in buckskins, then put in gunny bags, then laid on the horse and then my saddle on over the blanket, and bring it that way. Then there would be nothing visible but the saddle. If anyone came along, they would rather search him than me. There were some miles that we could not ride our horses on account of the wind; it blew so fiercely. We had to have our clothes tied on firmly. In some places, it was so steep we had to hang on to our horses' tails. It was all the horses could do to get up.

Silver Queen
The Fabulous Story of Baby Doe Tabor

Caroline Bancroft

Her story had been a drama of contrasts, from rags to riches and from riches to rags again, the whole play enacted against the backdrop of Colorado's magnificent and munificent mountains. But what those ruthless snow-capped peaks give they also take away; and almost as if they are gods, they single out certain characters in history to destroy by first making mad. Mrs. Tabor went to her death in a delusion about the Matchless Mine.

She had lived during the last years of her life largely through the charity of the citizens of Leadville and the bank that held the mortgage on the Matchless. The mine had produced no ore in years and was not really equipped to work, although she could not find it in her soul to admit this harsh fact of reality. She dressed in mining clothes and, off and on during the last 20 years, made a pretense of getting out ore with a series of men she inveigled to work on shares. But she either quarreled with these partners when she became suspicious of their honesty, or the men became disillusioned about the supposed fortune hidden in the Matchless and drifted off.

I only met her once, in the summer of 1927, when I called on her with my father, a mining engineer, who was making a swing around the state to report on the mining situation. Mrs. Tabor, who had known my father for many years, showed us over the premises. She was polite to me but largely ignored me since she was concentrating on my father with the hope he might get her new backing.

The tiny cabin she lived in had been a former tool and machine shop of the Matchless, and the actual shafthouse was perhaps 100 feet or so away. When we entered the shafthouse, it already had an aura of ghosts. Dirt and rust were accumulating from disuse and covered the hoist, cables, and machinery that were still there. It was my father's opinion, voiced to me as we drove off past the Robert E. Lee mine, that quite a lot of machinery had been stolen from the shafthouse without her being aware of it. Or perhaps "the old lady," as he spoke of her, had sold it to get enough to eat and had forgotten the transaction in the forgetfulness of what mountaineers call "cabin fever," a strangeness that overtakes elderly people who live alone.

I was not so interested in the mining aspects of her situation as my father (who was always avid on the scent of ore—gold, silver, copper, tungsten, and at the end, rare minerals such as vanadium, molybdenum, uranium, titanium, and tantalum). What interested me about Mrs. Tabor were her looks and her personality. I studied her quietly while she and my father talked about the glorious riches that would be uncovered if she "could just drift a little further north on the sixth level" or "sink a winze through to that stope on the fourth."

She was a little woman, very withered, and unattractively dressed in men's corduroy trousers, mining boots, and a soiled, torn blouse. She had a blue bandanna tied around her head and when we first drove up back of the Matchless, as close as the car could make it and started to walk to her cabin, she met us halfway, a belligerent expression on her face. My father and she had not met in several years, and it was not until after he gave his name that her manner changed.

She smiled then and said, "Why, of course, pray do forgive me. And what a beautiful daughter you have! It is my lasting sorrow that the Lord's work has taken my own daughter."

I could not have been more startled. The smile, the manner, the voice and the flowery speech were anomalous in that strange figure. Her smile was positively, although very briefly, gay and flashing; the teeth, even and white; and the voice, clear and bell-like; while her manner, I can only describe as queenly despite her diminutive size.

I only remember two other things about that afternoon. After we had spent some time in the shafthouse and walking about outside, while she and my father talked about the direction of the veins and probable apexes, the price of silver and other matters not very interesting to my youthful ears, Father suggested that in the car he had a jug of homemade wine his housekeeper had made. It was during Prohibition, and wine of any sort was a rarity, so that when he invited her for old times' sake, she seemed pleased and asked us up the ledge to her cabin.

While Father went back to the car for the wine, she and I strolled on ahead. I complimented her on the spectacular view of Mount Massive and Mount Elbert, Colorado's highest peaks, off to the west beyond the town of Leadville.

She did not say anything, but she turned her eyes full upon me, the only time I think that she looked directly at me. Again, I was startled. They were very far apart and a gorgeous blue, their unusual color preserved through all the violence and madness and bitterness of her then nearly 70 years.

Her cabin, really no more than a shack, was crowded with very primitive furniture and stacked high in newspapers and mementoes. It was quite neat, although, to my mind, it could have stood a good dusting, and the window panes had evidently not been washed since the winter snows. We drank our wine from an assortment of cups, one of them tin. She apologized for their not being very clean and said something about hauling her drinking water from some distance and using boiled mine water for other purposes.

I did not listen—to my shame, now. While they went on talking, I entertained myself with my own thoughts. I knew almost no Colorado history in those days; I had been out of the state for nine years at school, college, and working in the East—my interests completely disassociated. To me, she was just one more of the queer mining characters my father knew, and he knew dozens. But I lived to regret my youthful ignorance and indifference.

Let's Remember the Real Caroline Bancroft

Sandra Dallas

IN WESTERN HISTORY she was—both literally and figuratively—a giant. Just as she loomed over most women and a goodly number of men in stature, so did Caroline Bancroft, who died recently at 85, tower above other writers of history from this region.

Caroline did a great deal for Western history. She made it palatable. I suspect more people learned Colorado history from her two dozen Bancroft booklets than anything the rest of us wrote. She actually supported herself with her writing, which is more than most Western writers can say.

And she was unfailingly generous, especially to aspiring writers. While many other historians chose to hoard their collections of photographs and make money from them, Caroline long ago turned over her valuable pictures of the Tabors and others to the Western History Department of the Denver Public Library. Anyone who cares about history is indebted to her for saving the stories and recollections of the old-timers she interviewed.

But before we whitewash Caroline Bancroft and bury her with pallid eulogies, we ought to remember her as she was. It wasn't her writing (which wasn't very good) or even her history (which could be thinly researched) that made her a monumental figure. It was Caroline herself.

She was a vibrant, opinionated woman who when stirred showed the wrath of an angry god. She relished her enemies as much as her friends. She loved a good time and, up to the end, had a capacity for liquor that awed even Tom Noel, author of a book on the saloons of Denver. And Caroline had a presence that turned the rest of us into wimps.

I had known her slightly in my childhood as an eccentric family friend who wore orange braids on top of her head entwined with paper flowers. But my first real encounter with her came 20 years ago, when she wrote a withering review of my first book. How, I wondered, could this nice old lady be so brutal? She vilified anybody who made errors—including James Michener after he wrote *Centennial.*

An even worse sin was failing to agree with her. She often wrote in a review that if the author had only read her own writing on the subject, he or she wouldn't have made such a foolish mistake. But when the author did as she suggested, she might charge plagiarism.

Many of us wrote with a sense of Caroline looking over our shoulders, and that was another of her contributions to Western history. More than one author went back to the library to double-check a fact for fear Caroline would catch an error. When I was writing up one of the towns included in my recent *Colorado Ghost Towns and Mining Camps,* I discovered that my date for the town's founding was different from Caroline's. I went back to my source, the autobiography of the town founder, and found I was right. Did I dare stand up to Caroline? Are you crazy? I fudged it.

Caroline's scrutiny and caustic tongue made her many enemies. She relished her feuds. The most famous was with photo historian Fred Mazzulla, who had once been her great "pal," as she dubbed her friends.

As I recall, he said she had swiped a photograph from him; Caroline claimed he had made a pass at her and blamed herself for being indiscreet enough to tell. Whatever it was, neither missed an opportunity to stick it to the other. When the late Olga Curtis wrote an *Empire* magazine article about the two and mentioned that as a young woman Caroline had raced camels in Egypt, Fred wrote a sly letter asking who had won, Caroline or the camels.

While most historians sit on the sidelines and observe life, Caroline lived it. Born into a prominent Denver family—she could get a bit dotty on the subject of the Bancrofts—Caroline shocked her set by going to work for the *Denver Post.* "It was the same as going down to Market Street and working in a house," she liked to say.

She was part of café society, a chum (another Bancroft word) of Evalyn Walsh McLean and Lucius Beebe, and she was even on friendly terms with old Mrs. Crawford Hill, leader of the Sacred 36.

Caroline ("It rhymes with sin, gin or jasmine, take your pick," she would say) also was a friend of Dorothy Parker, and once she and Mary Coyle Chase threw a party for Parker in Denver and invited Denver's underworld. A friend got copies of the invitation and sent them to Denver's upper crust as well, and Caroline had to station someone at the door to turn away the elite.

She never mellowed. That was the reason we all thought she would go on forever. And perhaps she will, since she believed in reincarnation.

But in one lifetime, she had an enormous impact. She won't be remembered as much for her history or her writing as for herself. Like Baby Doe Tabor and Maggie (Molly) Brown, whose lives she chronicled, she was a character. With Caroline Bancroft gone, there aren't many of them left.

SECTION VII

Pikes Peak

America, the Beautiful

Katharine Lee Bates

O beautiful for spacious skies,
    For amber waves of grain,
For purple mountain majesties
    Above the fruited plain!
America! America!
    God shed His grace on thee,
And crown thy good with brotherhood,
    From sea to shining sea!

O beautiful for pilgrim feet,
    Whose stern, impassioned stress
A thoroughfare for freedom beat
    Across the wilderness!
America! America!
    God mend thine every flaw,
Confirm thy soul in self-control,
    Thy liberty in law!

O beautiful for heroes proved
    In liberating strife,
Who more than self their country loved;
    And mercy more than life!
America! America!
    May God thy gold refine,
Till all success be nobleness,
    And every gain divine!

O beautiful for patriot dream
    That sees beyond the years
Thine alabaster cities gleam
    Undimmed by human tears!
America! America!
    God shed His grace on thee,
And crown thy good with brotherhood
    From sea to shining sea!

An Account of Expeditions to the Sources of the Mississippi

Zebulon Montgomery Pike

NOV. 25TH. MARCHED EARLY, with an expectation of ascending the mountain, but was only able to encamp at its base after passing over many small hills covered with cedars and pitch pines. Our encampment was on a [Turkey] Creek, where there was no water for several miles from the mountain; but near its base, found sufficient. Took a meridional observation and the altitude of the mountain. Killed two buffalo. Distance 22 miles.

Nov. 26th. Expecting to return to our camp the same evening, we left our blankets and provisions at the foot of the [Cheyenne] Mountain. Killed a deer of a new species [*Cariacus macrotis*], and hung his skin on a tree with some meat. We commenced ascending; found it very difficult, being obliged to climb up rocks, sometimes almost perpendicular; and after marching all day, we encamped in a cave without blankets, victuals, or water. We had a fine clear sky, while it was snowing at the bottom. On the side of the mountain, we found only yellow and pitch pine. Some distance up, we found buffalo; higher still, the new species of deer and pheasants [dusky grouse, *Dendragapus obscurus*].

The then new species of deer, Cariacus macrotis, *is now known as the mule deer.*

Nov. 27th. Arose hungry, dry, and extremely sore from the inequality of the rocks on which we had lain all night, but were amply compensated for toil by the sublimity of the prospect below. The unbounded prairie was overhung with dense clouds, which appeared like the ocean in a storm, wave piled on wave and foaming, while the sky was perfectly clear where we were. Commenced our march up the mountain, and in about one hour arrived at the summit of this chain. Here, we found the snow middle-deep; no sign of beast or bird inhabiting this region. The thermometer, which stood at 9 degrees above zero at the foot of the mountain, here fell 4 degrees below zero. The summit of the Grand Peak, which was entirely bare of vegetation and covered with snow, now appeared at the distance of 15 or 16 miles from us. It was as high again as what we had ascended, and it would have taken a whole day's march to arrive at its base, when I believe no human being could have ascended to its pinnacle. This, with the condition of my soldiers, who had only light overalls on, no stockings, and were in every way ill provided to endure the inclemency of the region; the bad prospect of killing anything to subsist on, with the further detention of two or three days which it must occasion, determined us to return. The clouds from below had ascended the mountain and entirely enveloped the summit, on which rest eternal snows. We descended by a long, deep ravine, with much less difficulty than we had contemplated. Found all our baggage safe, but the provisions all destroyed. It began to snow, and we sought shelter under the side of a projecting rock where we all four made a meal on one partridge and a piece of deer's ribs the ravens had left us—being the first all we had eaten in that 48 hours.

Nov. 28th. Marched at nine o'clock. Kept straight on down the [Turkey] creek to avoid the hills. At half past one o'clock, shot two buffalo, when we made the first full meal we had made in three days. Encamped in a valley under a shelving rock. The land here very rich and covered with old Tetau [Comanche] camps.

Nov. 29th. Marched after a short repast and arrived at our camp before night; all found well.

Sunday, Nov. 30th. Marched at 11 o'clock; it snowed very fast, but my impatience to be moving would not permit my lying still at that camp. The doctor, Baroney, and myself went to view a Tetau encampment, which appeared to be about two years old; and from their having cut down so large a quantity of trees to support their horses, we concluded there must have been at least 1,000 souls. Passed several more in the course of the day; also one Spanish camp. This day came into the first cedar and pine. Killed two deer. Distance 15 miles.

Account of an Expedition from Pittsburgh to the Rocky Mountains

Edwin James

AT AN EARLY HOUR ON the morning of the 13th [July 1820], Lieutenant Swift, accompanied by the guide, was dispatched from camp to measure a base near the Peak and to make there a part of the observations requisite for calculating its elevation. Dr. James, being furnished with four men, two to be left at the foot of the mountain to take care of the horses, and two to accompany him in the proposed ascent to the summit of the Peak, set off at the same time.

This detachment left the camp before sunrise; and taking the most direct route across the plains, arrived at 11 o'clock at the base of the mountain. Here, Lieutenant Swift found a place suited to his purpose, where also was a convenient spot for those who were to ascend the mountain, to leave their horses in a narrow valley, dividing transversely several sandstone ridges, and extending westward to the base of the Peak.

After establishing their horse camp, the detachment moved up the valley on foot, arriving about noon at the Boiling Spring, where they dined on a saddle of venison and some bison ribs they had brought ready cooked from camp.

The Boiling Spring is a large and beautiful fountain of water, cool and transparent, and highly aerated with carbonic acid. It rises on the brink of a small stream, which here descends from the mountain, at the point where the bed of the stream divides the ridge of sandstone which rests against the base of the first granite range.

The water of the spring deposits a copious concretion of carbonate of lime, which has accumulated on every side, until it has formed a large basin overhanging the stream. This basin is of a snowy whiteness and large enough to contain 300 or 400 gallons and is constantly overflowing. The spring rises from the bottom of the basin, with a rumbling noise, discharging about equal volumes of air and of water, probably about 50 gallons per minute, the whole being kept in constant agitation. The water is beautifully transparent, and has the sparkling appearance, the grateful taste, and the exhilarating effect of the most strongly aerated artificial mineral waters.

Distant a few rods from this is another spring of the same kind, which discharges no water, its basin remaining constantly full, and air only escaping from it. We collected some of the air from both of these springs, in a box we had carried for the reception of plants, but could not perceive it to have the least smell or the power of extinguishing flame, which was tested by plunging into it lighted splinters of dry cedar.

The temperature of the water of the larger spring at noon was 63 degrees; the thermometer at the same time in the shade stood at 68 degrees; immersed in the small spring, at 67 degrees. This difference in temperature is owing to the difference of situation, the higher temperature of the small spring, depending entirely on its constant exposure to the rays of the sun, and to its retaining the same portion of water, while that in the large spring is constantly replaced by a new supply.

After we had dined and hung up some provisions in a large red cedar tree, near the spring, intending it for a supply on our return, we took leave of Lieutenant Swift and began to ascend the mountain. We carried with us, each, a small blanket, 10 or 12 pounds of bison meat, three gills of parched cornmeal, and a small kettle.

The sandstone extends westward from the springs, about 300 yards, rising rapidly upon the base of the mountain. It is of a deep red colour, usually compact and fine, but sometimes embracing angular fragments of petrosilex and other silicious stones with a few organic impressions. The granite which succeeds is coarse and of a deep red colour. Some loose fragments of gneiss were seen lying at the surface, but none in place. The granite at the base of the mountain contains a large proportion of feldspar of the rose-coloured variety, in imperfect cubic crystals, and disintegrating rapidly under the operation of frost and other causes, crumbling into masses of half an ounce weight or less.

In ascending, we found the surface in many places, covered with this loose and crumbled granite, rolling from under our feet, and rendering the ascent extremely difficult. We began to credit the assertions of the guide, who had conducted us to the foot of the Peak, and left us with the assurance that the whole side of the mountain to its summit was covered with loose sand and gravel—so that though many attempts had been made by the Indians and by hunters to ascend it, none had ever proved successful. We passed several of these tracks, not without some apprehension for our lives, as there was danger when the foothold was once lost of sliding down and being thrown over precipices.

After clambering with extreme fatigue over about two miles, in which several of these dangerous places occurred, we halted at sunset in a small cluster of fir trees. We could not, however, find a piece of even ground large enough to lie down upon, and were under the necessity of securing ourselves from rolling into the brook, near which we encamped, by means of a pole placed against two trees. In this situation, we passed an uneasy night, and, though the mercury fell only to 54 degrees, felt some inconvenience from cold.

On the morning of the 14th, as soon as daylight appeared, having suspended in a tree, whatever articles of clothing could be dispensed with, and our blankets, and provisions except about three pounds of bison flesh, we continued the ascent, hoping to be able to reach the summit of the Peak and return to the same camp in the evening. After passing about half a mile of rugged and difficult travelling, like that of the preceding day, we crossed a deep chasm, opening towards the bed of the small stream we had hitherto ascended, and following the summit of the ridge between these, found the way less difficult and dangerous.

Having passed a level tract of several acres, covered with the aspen poplar, a few birches and pines, we arrived at a small stream running towards the south, nearly parallel to the base of the conic part of the mountain, which forms the summit of the Peak. From this spot, we could distinctly see almost the whole of the Peak, its lower half thinly clad with pines, junipers, and other evergreen trees; the upper a naked conic pile of yellowish rocks, surmounted here and there by patches of snow; but the summit appeared so distant, and the ascent so steep, that we despaired of accomplishing the ascent and returning on the same day.

In marshy places about this part of the mountain, we saw an undescribed white-flowered species of Caltha, some Spediculariae, the shrubby cinquefoil (Potentilla *fruticosa, Ph.*), and many alpine plants.

The day was agreeably bright and calm. As we ascended rapidly, a manifest change of temperature was perceptive, and before we reached the outskirts of the timber, a little wind was felt from the northeast. On this part of the mountain, the flowered stone crop (Sedum *stenopetalum, Ph.*) is almost the only herbaceous plant which occurs. The boundary of the region of forests is a defined line encircling the peak in a part which, when seen from the plain, appeared near the summit; but when we arrived at it, a greater part of the whole elevation of the mountain seemed still before us. Above the timber, the ascent is steeper but less difficult than below—the surface being so highly inclined that the large masses, when loosened roll down, meeting no obstruction until they arrive at the commencement of the timber. The red cedar and the flexile pine are the trees which appear at the greatest elevation. These are small, having thick and extremely rigid trunks; and near the commencement of the woodless part of the mountain, they have neither limbs nor bark on the side exposed to the descending masses of rocks. These trees have not probably grown in a situation so exposed, as to be unable to produce or retain bark or limbs on one side; the timber must formerly have extended to a greater elevation on the sides of this peak, than at present, so that those trees, which are now on the outskirts of the forest, were formerly protected by their more exposed neighbours.

A few trees were seen above the commencement of snow, but these are very small and entirely procumbent, being sheltered in the crevices and fissures of the rock. There are also the roots of trees to be seen at some distance, above the point where any are now standing.

A little above the point where the timber disappears entirely, commences a region of astonishing beauty and of great interest on account of its productions; the intervals of soil are sometimes extensive and are covered with a carpet of low but brilliantly flowering alpine plants. Most of these have either matted procumbent stems or, such as including the flower, rarely rise more than an inch in height. In many of them, the flower is the most conspicuous and the largest part of the plant; and in all, the colouring is astonishingly brilliant.

A deep blue is the prevailing colour among these flowers, and the Pentstemon *erianthera,* the mountain columbine (Aquilegia *coerulea*), and other plants common to less elevated districts, were here much more intensely coloured than in ordinary situations.

It cannot be doubted that the peculiar brilliancy of colouring observed in the alpine plants inhabiting near the utmost limits of phaenogamous vegetation depends in a great measure on the intensity of the light transmitted from the bright unobscured atmosphere of those regions, and increased by reflection from the surface of the impending masses of snow. May the deep cerulean tint of the sky be, supposed to have an influence in producing the corresponding colour, so prevalent in the flowers of these plants?

At about two o'clock, we found ourselves so much exhausted as to render a halt necessary. Mr. Wilson, who had accompanied us as a volunteer, had been left back some time since and could not now be seen in any direction. As we felt some anxiety on his account, we halted and endeavoured to apprise him of our situation; repeated calls and the discharging of the rifleman's piece produced no answer. We therefore determined to wait some time to rest and to eat the provisions we had brought, hoping in the meantime he would overtake us.

Here, as we were sitting at our dinner, we observed several small animals, nearly of the size of the common gray squirrel but shorter and more clumsily formed. They were of a dark gray colour, inclining to brown, with a short thick head, and erect rounded ears. In habits and appearance, they resemble the prairie dog and are believed to be a species of the same genus. The mouth of their burrow is generally placed under the projection of a rock, and near these we afterwards saw several of the little animals watching our approach and uttering a shrill note, somewhat like that of the ground squirrel. Several attempts were made to procure a specimen of this animal, but always without success, as we had no guns but such as carried a heavy ball.

After sitting about half an hour, we found ourselves somewhat refreshed but much benumbed with cold. We now found it would be impossible to reach the summit of the mountain and return to our camp of the preceding night, during that part of the day which remained; but as we could not persuade ourselves to turn back, after having so nearly accomplished the ascent, we resolved to take our chance of spending the night on whatever part of the mountain it might overtake us. Wilson had not yet been seen, but as no time could be lost, we resolved to go as soon as possible to the top of the Peak and look for him on our return. We met, as we proceeded, such numbers of unknown and interesting plants, as to occasion much delay in collecting and were under the disagreeable necessity of passing by numbers which we saw in situations difficult of access. As we approached the summit, these became less frequent, and at length ceased entirely. Few cryptogamous plants are seen about any part of the mountain, and neither these nor any others occur frequently on the top of the Peak. There is an area of 10 or 15 acres forming the summit, which is nearly level; and on this part, scarce a lichen is to be seen. It is covered to a great depth with large splintery fragments of a rock, entirely similar to that found at the base of the Peak, except, perhaps, a little more compact in its structure.

By removing a few of these fragments, they were found to rest upon a bed of ice, which is of great thickness, and may, perhaps, be as permanent and as ancient as the rocks with which it occurs.

It was about 4 o'clock P.M. when we arrived on the summit. In our ascent, we had attempted to cross a large field of snow, which occupied a deep ravine extending down half a mile from the top, on the southeastern side of the Peak. This was found impassable, being covered with a thin ice, not sufficiently strong to bear the weight of a man. We had not been long on the summit when we were rejoined by the man who had separated from us near the outskirts of the timber. He had turned aside and lain down to rest and, afterwards, pursued the ascent by a different route.

From the summit of the Peak, the view towards the north, west, and southwest, is diversified with innumerable mountains, all white with snow; and on some of the more distant, it appears to extend down to their bases. Immediately under our feet on the west lay the narrow valley of the Arkansa, which we could trace running towards the northwest, probably more than 60 miles.

On the north side of the Peak was an immense mass of snow and ice. The ravine in which it lay terminated in a woodless and apparently fertile valley, lying west of the first great ridge and extending far towards the north. This valley must undoubtedly contain a considerable branch of the Platte. In a part of it, distant probably 30 miles, the smoke of a fire was distinctly seen and was supposed to indicate the encampment of a party of Indians.

To the east lay the great plain, rising as it receded, until, in the distant horizon, it appeared to mingle with the sky. A little want of transparency in the atmosphere, added to the great elevation from which we saw the plain, prevented our distinguishing the small inequalities of the surface. The Arkansa with several of its tributaries and some of the branches of the Platte could be distinctly traced as a map by the line of timber along their courses.

On the south the mountain is continued, having another summit (probably that ascended by Captain Pike) at the distance of eight or 10 miles. This, however, falls much below the High Peak in point of elevation, being wooded quite to its top. Between the two lies a small lake, about a mile long and half a mile wide, discharging eastward into the Boiling-Spring creek. A few miles farther towards the south, the range containing these two peaks terminates abruptly.

The weather was calm and clear while we remained on the Peak, but we were surprised to observe the air in every direction filled with such clouds of grasshoppers, as partially to obscure the day. They had been seen in vast numbers about all the higher parts of the mountain, and many had fallen upon the snow and perished.

It is perhaps difficult to assign the cause which induces these insects to ascend to those highly elevated regions of the atmosphere. Possibly, they may have undertaken migrations to some remote district, but there appears not the least uniformity in the direction of their movements. They extended upwards from the summit of the mountain, to the utmost limit of vision; and as the sun shone brightly, they could be seen by the glittering of their wings, at a very considerable distance.

About all the woodless parts of the mountain, and particularly on the summit, numerous tracks were seen resembling those of the common deer, but they most probably have been those of the big horn. The skulls and horns of these animals are repeatedly seen near the licks and saline springs at the foot of the mountain, where they are known to resort principally about the most elevated and inaccessible heights.

The party remained on the summit only about half an hour. In this time the mercury fell to 42 degrees, the thermometer hanging against the side of a rock—which in the early part of the day, had been exposed to the direct rays of the sun. At the encampment of the main body in the plains, a corresponding thermometer stood, in the middle of the day, at 96°, and did not fall below 80° until a late hour in the evening.

Great uniformity was observed in the character of the rock about all the upper parts of the mountain. It is a compact, indestructible aggregate of quartz and feldspar with a little hornblende in very small particles. Its fracture is fine granular or even; the mass exhibits a tendency to divide when broken into long, somewhat splintery fragments. It is of a yellowish-brown colour, which does not perceptibly change by long exposure to the air. It is undoubtedly owing to the close texture and impenetrable firmness of this rock that so few lichens are found upon it. For the same reason, it is little subject to disintegration by the action of frost. It is not improbable that the splintery fragments which occur in such quantities on all the higher parts of the Peak may owe their present form to the agency of lightning; no other cause seems adequate to the production of so great an effect.

Near the summit, some large detached crystals of feldspar, of a pea-green color, were collected. Also large fragments of transparent, white and smoky quartz, and an aggregate of opaque white quartz with crystals of hornblende.

About five in the afternoon, we began to descend, and a little before sunset arrived at the commencement of the timber; but before we reached the small stream in the bottom of the first descent, we perceived we had missed our way. It was now become so dark as to render an attempt to proceed extremely hazardous; and as the only alternative, we kindled a fire and laid ourselves down on the first spot of level ground we could find. We had neither provisions nor blankets, and our clothing was by no means suitable for passing the night in so bleak and inhospitable a situation. We could not, however, proceed without imminent danger from precipices; and by the aid of a good fire, and no ordinary degree of fatigue, we found ourselves able to sleep during a greater part of the night.

A Bloomer Girl on Pikes Peak, 1858

Julia Archibald Holmes

AUG. 5—WE LEFT SNOWDELL early this morning for the summit, taking with us nothing but our writing materials and Emerson. We deviated somewhat from our course in order to pass the rim of Amphitheater Canyon. Here, on the edge of perpendicular walls, were poised stones and boulders of all sizes, ready to be rolled, with a slight effort, into the yawning abyss. Starting these stones had been a favorite amusement with those who ascended before us, and it savored somewhat both of the sublime and the terrible. When a stone was started it seemed first to leap into the air, and passing from sight nothing would be heard of it for several seconds. Then would come a crashing, thundering sound from the hidden depths below, which seemed to continue until lost in the distant lower region. From these hollow distant sounds, some of the men had supposed the existence of an inaccessable cave below. As we proved yesterday, however, nothing but a tremendous circular chasm exists. After enjoying this sport a short time, we proceeded directly up towards the summit. Arriving within a few hundred yards of the top, the surface changed into a huge mass of loose angular stones, so steep we found much difficulty in clambering up them. Passing to the right of a drift of snow some three or four hundred yards long, which sun and wind had turned into coarse ice, we stood upon a platform of near 100 acres of feldspathic granite rock and boulders. Occasionally a little crevice among the rocks might be found in which had collected some coarse soil from the disintegration of the granite, where in one or two instances we found a green spot about the size of a teacup from which sprung dozens of tiny blue flowers bewitchingly beautiful. The little ultramarine-colored leaves of the flower seemed covered with an infinitude of minute sparkling crystals—they seemed children of the sky and snow, conseq(u)ently our view was not so extensive as we had anticipated. A portion only of the whitened back-bone ridge of the Rocky Mountains which forms the boundary line of so many territories could be seen, 50 miles to the west. We were now nearly 14,000 feet above the sea level. But we could not spend long in contemplating the grandeur of the scene for it was exceedingly cold; and leaving our names on a large rock, we commenced letters to some of our friends, using a broad flat rock for a writing desk. When we were ready to return, I read aloud a few lines from Emerson.

* * *

Aug. 2d, 1858

Dear Mother: I write this to you sitting in our little house among the rocks, about one hour's walk from the summit of Pike's Peak. It is a curious little nook which we have selected as our temporary home, formed by two very large overhanging rocks, and enclosed by a number of smaller ones, while close beside it is a large snowbank which we can reach with ease. Our couch is composed of a large quantity of spruce boughs (cut with that little knife which you have used so much). These we arrange on the rock, upon which we spread our quilts—reserving others for covering—and by the help of a good fire, which we keep burning all night, we can manage to keep the cold off very well.

Two days of very hard climbing has brought me here—if you could only know how hard, you would be surprised that I have been able to accomplish it. My strength and capacity for enduring fatigue have been very much increased by constant exercise in the open air since leaving home, or I never could have succeeded in climbing the rugged sides of this mountain. There were some steep climbing the first day, and I would sometimes find it almost impossible to proceed. I was often obliged to use my hands—catching now at some propitious twig which happened to be within reach, and now trusting to some projecting stone. But fortunately for me, this did not last more than a mile or so.

We have brought about a week's provisions, purposing to remain here and write some letters, &c. This is the most romantic of places. Think of the huge rocks projecting out in all imaginable shapes, with the beautiful evergreens, the pines, the firs, and spruces, interspersed among them; and then the clear, cold mountain stream, which appears as though it started right out from under some great rock—and on it goes, rushing, tumbling, and hissing down behind some huge rock, and now rising again to view, it rushes on, away down, down, until at length it turns a corner and is lost to our sight. Then think of the fragrant little flowers—so many different kinds, and some of them growing within reach of our snowbank—I will send you some of the different kinds. There is one little blue flower here which, for some reason, I cannot tell exactly what—whether it is the form, color, or fragrance, but it has had the effect to carry me back in imagination to the days of my childhood, in my far-down Eastern home.

But I shall not write any more now, for I mean to finish this on the top of the mountain.

After reaching the topmost part of the Peak, Mrs. Holmes continued her letter as follows:

Pike's Peak, Aug. 5, 1858

I have accomplished the task which I marked out for myself, and now I feel amply repaid for all my toil and fatigue. Nearly every one tried to discourage me from attempting it, but I believed that I should succeed; and now, here I am, and I feel that I would not have missed this glorious sight for anything at all. In all probability, I am the first woman who has ever stood upon the summit of this mountain and gazed upon this wondrous scene which my eyes now behold. How I sigh for the poet's power of description so that I might give you some faint idea of the grandeur and beauty of this scene. Extending as far as the eye can reach, lie the great level plains, stretched out in all their verdure and beauty, while the winding of the great Arkansas is visible for many miles. We can also see distinctly where many of the smaller tributaries unite with it. Then the rugged rocks all around, and the almost endless succession of mountains and rocks below, the broad blue sky over our heads, and seemingly so very near; all, and everything, on which the eye can rest, fills the mind with infinitude, and sends the soul to God.

Post card featuring the summit of Pikes Peak, circa 1902.

South By West

The Rev. Charles Kingsley

Colorado Springs, Colorado, Nov. 1871.

"DEAR ***, —HERE I AM 'LOCATED' at last, and the best thing I can do is to describe my arrival here and my first impressions, which, to say the least, are novel.

"We pulled up at a log cabin by the side of the track, and from the doorway came a voice, saying, 'Dinner's on table.' Out we all got, and I thought—surely we can't be going to dine in this place. But M. took me round to the back door and into a parlour, where he told me to wait while he saw to the luggage. In a few minutes, he returned and took me into the dining room, where I found, to my amazement, two large table on one side and four small on the other, with clean linen, smart waiters, and a first-rate dinner, far better than any we had had on the Kansas Pacific. I was in a state of complete bewilderment, but hunger soon got the better of surprise, and we were doing ample justice to oyster soup and roast antelope when in came General and Mrs. P. It was pleasant to find well-known faces among so many new ones.

"You may imagine Colorado Springs, as I did, to be a sequestered valley, with bubbling fountains, green grass, and shady trees, but not a bit of it. Picture to yourself a level elevated plateau of greenish-brown without a single tree or plant larger than a Spanish bayonet (Yucca) two feet high, sloping down about a quarter of a mile to the railroad track and Monument Creek (the Soda Springs being six miles off), and you have a pretty good idea of the town-site as it appears in November 1871.

"The streets and blocks are only marked out by a furrow turned with the plough and indicated faintly by a wooden house, finished, or in process of building, here and there, scattered over half a mile of prairie. About 12 houses and shanties are inhabited, most of them being unfinished or run up for temporary occupation; and there are several tents dotted about also.

"On the corner of Tejon and Huerfano Streets stands the office of the Denver and Rio Grande Railway, a small wooden building of three rooms in which all the colony work is done till the new office is finished. It is used besides as post office, doctor's shop, and general lounge for the whole town. My house stands next to it: a wooden shanty, 16 feet by 12, with a door in front and a small window on each side—they are glass, though they do not open. It is lined with brown paper, so it is perfectly windproof and really quite comfortable, though it was ordered on Thursday and finished on Saturday. M. has now put his tent up over the front of the shanty, with a rough board floor, and it serves for our sitting room by day and his bedroom at night, so we can warm both tent and room with a stove in the former. But on Monday, we forgot to bring the stove down from Denver, and I had to do without it as well as I could. In one corner of the shanty we put my little camp-bed and my trunk in the others. Our furniture had not arrived from Denver, so M. found an old wooden stool, which had been used for mixing paints upon, tacked a bit of coloured calico over it, deposited upon it a tin basin, and there was an impromptu wash-hand stand. A few feet of half-inch board were soon converted into corner shelves; and, with warm yellow and red California blankets on my bed, and a buffalo robe on the floor, my room looked quite habitable. In the tent, we have put the stove, a couple of wooden kitchen chairs from the office, and a deal table; M.'s bed makes a comfortable sofa by day; and over the door into the shanty hang two bright curtains Dr. B. has brought me from Denver, as a contribution to our housekeeping. In the corner by the stove stands a pail of water, and over it hangs an invaluable tin dipper, which serves for saucepan, mug, glass, jug, cup, and every use imaginable.

"Monday night, after paying one or two visits, we went to the office and had a game of whist with Mr. N. and Dr. G., who has been burnt out of Chicago and come down here to settle. Then I locked myself into my strange new abode, with M.'s revolver as protection against imaginary foes; and by dint of buffalo robes and blankets and heaps of flannel, managed to keep tolerably warm; though my breath condensed on the sheets, and when I got up, the bucket had a quarter of an inch of ice on it.

"This is how our day goes, now that we have got everything 'fixed' properly: Get up at 7 A.M. in the cold, frosty air. M. comes in and lights the stove, heats some water, and by eight we are ready for a walk of nearly half a mile down to the restaurant (the log cabin), with a fine appetite for breakfast. The food is good and plentiful. Beefsteak or venison; biscuit—as they call hot rolls out here;—hot buckwheat cakes eaten with butter and molasses or honey; and the whole washed down with bad tea or excellent rich milk. Then, if there is time, we take a stroll and look for seeds and stones. There are all sorts of stones and crystals to be found here, and I hear of amethysts up the Monument. On Monday, Dr. G. brought me a lump of rock crystal as large as a man's fist, which he picked up close to our tent, and it serves me for a paper weight.

"At nine, work begins, and I attend to my household duties, sweeping the room, etc., and then am ready to help M. in writing out agreements for lots and memberships. At 12:30, the train comes in, and we go down to dinner. At 5:30, it is almost dark; supper is at six, and then we shut up our tent and spend a cozy evening."

SECTION VIII

Good Times

A Fish Dinner

Joseph Addison Thatcher

WE WERE TELLING STORIES which seemed to interest the cowboy, but he never made a remark—some were pretty highly overdrawn, too. Finally, I said, "Boys, I don't think I ever told you my experience fishing in the North Platte. Well, the fishing was rather poor that summer up there. One morning I took my steel rod, a buttered sandwich in my basket, and set off, expecting to be out all day. About noon I had a half-dozen nice trout in my basket, and a severe rainstorm, with terrible thunder and lighting, came up.

"I left the creek and started across a clear place of ground for a clump of trees to get out of the rain. I was running with a rod held up in my right hand when a streak of lightning struck the steel rod, darting me senseless to the ground. I came to in a short time, found I was not hurt, and looking around saw that my creel upon the ground was a bed of live coals, and there were my trout lying upon the coals beautifully broiled. My sandwich was ready toasted; and, to show you the eccentricity of electricity, the bones had been taken out of the fish and made into toothpicks and laid beside the fish. A more dainty lunch I never had. What do you think of that?"

The cowboy couldn't stand this last story and turned on his side, laid his hand on his pistol, and said, "I will bet a dollar that's a lie." I turned to him and said, "My friend, I don't want to win your money by betting on a sure thing—but if old Bill Shakespeare was alive, I could prove it by him. Did you know him? The cowboy said, "No; where did he range his cattle? There was a silence in the tent; then turning, he said good evening, and went out into the night.

Glass lantern slide of lightning. By William N. Jennings, Lightning Photograph, 1885.

Newport in the Rockies

Marshall Sprague

THERE IS NO QUICK WAY to bring General Palmer to the start of his story in '69. He was born in 1836 on a farm in Delaware near Delaware Bay, but he was raised by his parents, Matilda Jackson and John Palmer, in Quaker Philadelphia where he got a grade school education, and a touch of high school. At 17, he was quietly precocious and only a desultory Quaker. He had a large, handsome head, curly brown hair, and a slight wiry frame perhaps five feet eight inches tall. He loved cricket, pretty girls, and arguing about Abolition, anti-Catholics, and freedom of the press. He was even then a sort of self-made Philadelphia aristocrat—a bit stiff and reserved on the outside but diffident, good-humored, and kind within. He was enormously persistent to achieve his own ends which had to do with a dream of building around him a neat, trim, happy, sensible world.

He turned railroader and, at 19, went abroad for his coal-mining uncle to see how coal burned in English and French locomotives. He sailed home eight months later full of bright ideas and a conviction that "Paris is the most wonderful city in the world." In 1857, still under 21, he became private secretary to another Quaker, J. Edgar Thomson, president of the Pennsylvania Railroad. Two years later, he was out west with Andrew Carnegie to decide for President Thomson where the Pennsylvania should go next from Pittsburgh—to St. Louis or Chicago.

Soon, Fort Sumter fell, postponing the question, and it took Will Palmer about two weeks to decide that he had to defend the Union even if he were a pacifist Quaker. But not as a railroader. No office war for him. He read up on pack trains, mules, and litters, got a captain's commission, and recruited a carefully picked troop of proper young Philadelphians, the nucleus of his beloved 15th Pennsylvania Volunteer Cavalry. Palmer wasn't a snob, exactly, in his recruiting. He just felt that people with superior brains and energy ought to hang together and run things.

* * *

The year 1866 was release time for young Americans, a time for exploding of creative energies held in check by the war. General Palmer, aged 30, had been trained well in railroading by J. Edgar Thomson of the Pennsylvania. He knew where to explode—west of Kansas City where new railroads could turn worthless mountains and plains into high-priced real estate. He knew that capitalists were everywhere with tons of cash to invest—dollars in Philadelphia and New York, pounds in London, guilders in Amsterdam. In 1855, he had seen for himself the land hunger of Englishmen, obsessed by fears of running out of pasture on which to feed their cattle and sheep in England.

And so Palmer began his slow demarch on his future Colorado Springs by getting the job to build the Kansas Pacific Railroad west from Kansas City. This political sop of a line was projected originally to join the Omaha-based, California-bound Union Pacific in western Nebraska, but its directors soon forgot its branch role and decided to go to California, too, through New Mexico. In June of '67, these directors in St. Louis ordered General Palmer to make a survey of southern routes through the western wilderness to San Francisco from the railhead at Salina, Kansas.

News of the proposed Kansas Pacific survey got around even to an international conclave of doctors in St. Louis who were attending a lecture series on homeopathic medicine. This homeopathy was all the rage and had to do with giving to patients pills containing minute toxins to counteract the germs which bothered them. Among those at the conclave was a small, bubbling youngster of 26 from London named Dr. William Abraham Bell, who had barely finished his medical training. Bell had journeyed to St. Louis at his father's request. Dr. William Bell, Senior, was one of England's most famous physicians, a man whose bedside charm brought him the trade of everybody who was anybody. He wanted fresh data on homeopathy just to be sure that he wasn't putting the wrong toxins into the stomachs of England's social and business elite.

Young Dr. Bell was pure Irish by birth, but he drank his tea at five o'clock precisely like an Englishman. Medicine, oddly, did not interest him. What he loved was horses and adventure, and when the Kansas Pacific news reached him in St. Louis, he dropped homeopathy—and medicine in general, for that matter—forever. He applied at K.P. headquarters to go on the survey and took the only job left, photographer, after three days of learning how to be one. He met General Palmer in August of '67 in the Raton Mountains part of the Maxwell Grant, 140 miles inside of Pike's Peak. The ensuing survey gave the K.P. party nine months of excitement, danger, and hardship. It involved Indian battles, threats of starvation, lost trails, desert heat, and sub-zero snow storms on the passes as the men moved 5,000 miles through the Southwest to San Francisco and back to Kansas by way of Salt Lake, Cheyenne, and Denver.

Before the trek ended in March of '68, the cavalry hero, Will Palmer, and the effervescent tea-drinker, Willie Bell, had become close friends. They had become also two of the sturdiest males in the Southwest with vast knowledge of what the Rocky Mountains were all about. Back in St. Louis, Palmer urged that the Kansas Pacific should run to California over Raton Pass and on through northern New Mexico. But Congress refused to make any more huge gifts of land to help railroad promoters, and nothing came of the General's suggestions. Young Dr. Bell went back to England to report belatedly to his father on homeopathic pills and to write a remarkable book, *New Tracks in North America,* wound up unhappily building the Kansas Pacific into Denver. There, in August, 1870, it met the Denver Pacific which ran north to join the transcontinental Union Pacific at Cheyenne, Wyoming Territory.

Failure of his K.P. hopes put the General to planning a railroad of his own. It would be, naturally, a neat, trim, orderly affair staffed by 15th Pennsylvania officers and other true-blue friends like Willie Bell. It would be a "North and South" road, from Denver south and over the Sangre de Cristos to the Rio Grande River in the San Luis Valley and on down to Texas and Mexico, to be fed enroute by all future east-west railroads that crossed its right-of-way. It would be a complete novelty, having a three-foot narrow-gauge track which would permit it to make sharp curves and to climb steeply in the Rocky Mountains. It would be much cheaper to build than a line with tracks fourfeet-eight-and-a-half inches apart.

But there was a great difficulty. The government's free-land-for-railroads policy was no more. Eastern and European investors would have no interest in Palmer's proposed line unless it owned a great deal of land the value of which could be expected to increase hugely when the railroad ran through it. The government's preemption price now for Rocky Mountain wilderness was $1.25 per acre—far too high for promoting a railroad. Palmer's problem, then, was to find cheaper land.

One day it occurred to him where to find it—in that Raton Pass region which he and Dr. Bell had examined during the Kansas-Pacific survey. It consisted of two Mexican estates known as the Sangre de Cristo and Maxwell (originally Beaubien-Miranda) Grants. Governor Manuel Armijo had doled them out in the 1840s before the Mexican War, and Dr. Bell's father was physician to many of the British plungers who had money in them—men like William Blackmore, a brother of R.D. Blackmore whose novel *Lorna Doone* was about to become a classic. William Blackmore had put two of his alcoholic brothers on the Sangre de Cristo Grant to straighten them out, and Willie Bell believed that many rich Englishmen would pay for ranches where they could send their black sheep.

* * *

On the basis of these complicated facts, Palmer made a few simple deductions. It was plain to him that the two grants had cost their European owners only a few cents an acre. He had in England two influential friends—the Drs. Bell, Junior and Senior. Suppose the Bells called on the owners and suggested to them that General Palmer was about to build a railroad which just might run through the grants—if the owners took up his railroad bonds? Surely the Europeans would see their opportunity. Palmer's proposed railroad would quadruple overnight the value of these remote 2,752,942.47 acres along the Colorado-New Mexico border below the Spanish Peaks. Even small mortgages on the grants would raise enough capital to build the railroad at least from Denver to the Rio Grande!

At this critical point, in the spring of '69, a cataclysm occurred. Palmer had boarded the Pennsylvania at St. Louis on his way East to look up a friend of William Blackmore's, and he began describing his Colorado and Mexico railroad scheme in a palace car to a fellow passenger who introduced himself as William Proctor Mellen, a New York lawyer. Mellen revealed that he had studied law in Cincinnati as the protégé of Salmon P. Chase, who became Lincoln's Secretary of the Treasury. Both Chase and Mellen, Palmer discovered, knew William Blackmore and other British financiers who were interested in the West. Mellen suggested that he himself might be useful to Palmer in his Western ventures.

The two men were joined in the car by Mellen's 19-year-old daughter, a small demurely elegant, snub-nosed creature with a low musical voice. Her name was Queen. Palmer looked at her once and was lost—the typical total love-fall of a t32-year-old bachelor who gazes upon a soft thing of 19 and realizes with the suddenness of a thunderclap how empty his life has been without her. Before the train reached Cincinnati, the normally composed General was just another frantic suitor.

Some weeks later, Queen told him that she was his. Whether she loved him deeply is a moot point, but there is no doubt about her filial devotion. Queen had been raised mostly by her father, with some help from her stepmother who was also her aunt. She knew that Mellen had made unfortunate investments after the Civil War, that he was discouraged about his career in New York, that he was past his prime at 53 years of age, and that his health was poor. She did not mind, therefore, when Palmer combined his love-making with the acceptance of W. P. Mellen as his close business associate in the Rockies.

The wedding, Queen and Will Palmer decided, would take place at the home in Flushing, Long Island, after Palmer finished building the Kansas Pacific to Denver. By June of '69, he was back at the K.P. railhead—Sheridan, Kansas—writing sonnets by the yard and seeing Queen all over the prairie. His world was upside down. Queen had upset it and he asked himself incessantly how he could bring a refined girl who was used to places like Flushing, Newport, and Saratoga to the bawdy-house environment of a place like Sheridan, or even to raw Denver.

And so—by way of two Mexican land grants and a love affair—we reach the circumstances which resulted in Colorado Springs. Before Queen came into Palmer's life, he had visualized the usual rough railroad towns which he would found along his "North and South" line at intervals to be determined by prospects for agriculture and mining. But Queen split him into two people—the tough empire-builder determined to conquer the wilderness and the Arthurian cavalier shielding his gentle lady from the facts of life. The problem was intricate. Queen, he knew, held deep prejudices against the West, derived from the frontier trials of her maternal grandparents and from the fact that her uncle, Malcolm Clarke, had been killed by Indians in Montana.

To soothe Queen, Palmer had promised to consider settling down in New York City as the eastern officer of the Kansas Pacific, even though he knew that was impossible. He had seen too much of the mountains. The tonic climate and elated air of the Rockies, their majesty and friendliness and simplicity, the heady freedom and infinite horizons, had spoiled him forever for the cramped and soggy East.

Somehow, he would have to make Queen love the mountains, too. This imperative preoccupied him in July of 1869 as he scouted for a section of his "North and South" line, circling from Sheridan, Kansas, up the Arkansas and by moonlight up Fountain Creek where the plains met the Front Range and the Spanish Peaks showed darkly to the south. On the early morning of July 27th, the General, wrapped in blankets on top of his Concord coach, passed Pike's Peak for the first time. He bathed at dawn in the sandy, ice-cold Fountain, breakfasted in moldering Colorado City, and toured that cathedral park of violent reds and deep greens which Pike's Peak pioneers had been calling the Garden of the Gods since 1859.

He loved everything—the soda springs at the foot of Ute Pass, the gray-green mesas and grassy valleys of Fountain and Monument creeks, and the deep, cool canyons smelling of spruce and pine. And Pike's Peak over all. This noble presidence, he knew, had always been the greatest of Rocky Mountain landmarks through immemorial ages of changeless mankind. It was a kingdom in itself of huge jutting spurs and majestic ridges and forested knobs—of vast secret parks and lakes. Soaring a mile above its square-mile mass was the brown 14,000-foot summit—snow-streaked, friendly, and placid.

On that day, Palmer believed that he had the answer to his problem. Here was the one spot in the whole Wild West fit for Queen Mellen of Flushing, Long Island. And after all, he planned to have some sort of town every 10 miles along his railroad. Why not build a very special one at Pike's Peak—an attractive place for well-to-do people on the order of Newport or Saratoga? Next day in Denver, he told Queen about it, but furtively as to what he really had in mind. "I am sure there will be a famous resort here soon," he predicted. And a little further on: "I somehow fancied that an exploration of the Monument or the Fountain might disclose ... perhaps some charming spot which might be made a future home."

The Wildest of the West

Forbes Parkhill

FROM CAPITOL HILL to Holladay Street, all Denver was atwitter with the news. Oscar Wilde was coming! The apostle of aestheticism was booked to bring culture to the uncouth Queen City of the Mountains and Plains in two easy lectures at the gorgeous new Tabor Grand Opera House on June 13 and 15, 1882.

* * *

Among those who pondered the problem of aestheticism were Madame Minnie Clifford and her boarders. Her establishment occupied the site of the original stagecoach stables of the Leavenworth City & Pikes Peak Express Co. Minnie had bought it December 23, 1880, and had converted it into a maison de joie. ...

Minnie Clifford and Emma Nelson and the rest of the girls had no use for effeminate lily-lovers. They much preferred Western he-men who might better be symbolized by the tough, gaudy, rugged sunflower, whose acrid emanations lacked something of the fragrance of the lily.

On the afternoon of April 5, Minnie and a group described by the newspapers as "a number of her subjects" set out to promenade the length of Larimer Street, then Denver's principal business thoroughfare. Minnie's bonnet was adorned with an enormous sunflower the size of a dinner plate. Emma sported a "very intense lily."

Police Officer Thomas O'Connor was pacing his beat in front of the Windsor Hotel. Prancing up to him with mincing steps Emma Nelson, cribbing an expression attributed to Oscar, observed in a shrill feminine falsetto:

"Oh, Officer O'Connor, in that new helmet you look too, too divine! Yes, indeed—too, too!"

The sunflower-sporting Minnie bellowed, "I know what makes the wildcat wild. But who makes Oscar?"...

* * *

The lecturer was booked for a return engagement in Denver Saturday night, April 15. O.H. Rothacker, president of the Denver *Tribune*, had planned to take him for a tour of the city in Rothacker's "six-horse drag" or tallyho. After the lecture he was to be guest of honor at a dinner of leading citizens at the Denver Club.

At the suggestion of Charles E. Locke, Wilde's advance man and press agent, Rothacker had assigned his most brilliant reporter to cover the story of the Irishman's arrival. The reporter was none other than Gene Field, who recently had joined Wilde's *Tribune* wall staff.

Eugene Field was assigned by the Tribune *to cover Oscar Wilde (who is pictured here) on his trip to Denver, but instead Field impersonated Wilde as a hoax.*

Wilde's train was late. The welcoming committee adjourned to a Larimer Street saloon. Between drinks, press agent Locke remarked that it was a shame to deprive the waiting throngs of a spectacle. Field agreed to impersonate Wilde, and the nearby hairdresser who supplied the Holladay Street trade provided him with a wig resembling Oscar's flowing locks.

Wearing a wide-brim hat and an overcoat and sporting a lace handkerchief in his sleeve, Field was driven triumphantly through the streets of Denver by the press agent. For the benefit of the crowd, the pseudo-aesthete languidly fluttered his fingers in his best lackadaisical la-de-da manner at the gaping throngs. There was no applause. One disgusted newsboy shouted, "Shoot Oscar!"

A huge crowd awaited the arrival of the celebrity at the *Tribune* office. On the steps stood dignified F.J.V. Skiff, the *Tribune* business manager, later to become director of the World Columbian Exposition and the St. Louis World's Fair.

Suddenly, the crowd was paralyzed with horror when Skiff, instead of shaking hands, angrily threw a broom at the city's distinguished guest. The broom knocked off the wig, exposing the hoax. Skiff had, of course, recognized the masquerading *Tribune* reporter.

Impressions of America

Oscar Wilde

FROM SALT LAKE CITY, one travels over the great plains of Colorado and up the Rocky Mountains, on the top of which is Leadville, the richest city in the world. It has also got the reputation of being the roughest, and every man carries a revolver. I was told that if I went there, they would be sure to shoot me or my travelling manager. I wrote and told them that nothing that they could do to my travelling manager would intimidate me. They are miners—men working in metals, so I lectured to them on the Ethics of Art. I read them passages from the autobiography of Benvenuto Cellini, and they seemed much delighted. I was reproved by my hearers for not having brought him with me. I explained that he had been dead for some little time which elicited the enquiry, "Who shot him?" They afterwards took me to a dancing saloon where I saw the only rational method of art criticism I have ever come across. Over the piano was printed a notice:

PLEASE DO NOT SHOOT THE PIANIST.
HE IS DOING HIS BEST.

The mortality among pianists in that place is marvellous. Then they asked me to supper; and having accepted, I had to descend a mine in a rickety bucket in which it was impossible to be graceful. Having got into the heart of the mountain, I joined supper, the first course being whisky, the second whisky, and the third whisky. I went to the Theatre to lecture and I was informed that just before I went there two men had been seized for committing a murder—and in that theatre, they had been brought on to the stage at eight o'clock in the evening, and then and there tried and executed before a crowded audience. But I found these miners very charming and not at all rough.

Among the more elderly inhabitants of the South, I found a melancholy tendency to date every event of importance by the late war. "How beautiful the moon is to-night," I once remarked to a gentleman who was standing next to me. "Yes," was his reply, "but you should have seen it before the war."

So infinitesimal did I find the knowledge of Art, west of the Rocky Mountains, that an art patron—one who in his day had been a miner—actually sued the railroad company for damages because the plaster cast of Venus of Milo, which he had imported from Paris, had been delivered minus the arms. And what is more surprising still: He gained his case and the damages.

Colorado Owns a Chunk of Glenn Miller

Frances Melrose

GLENN MILLER, WHO DIED in a 1944 plane crash in the English Channel, was once the highest-paid band leader in the world.

In 1944, it was estimated that one of every three nickels dropped into the nation's jukeboxes played a Glenn Miller record. In a *Downbeat* magazine poll, Miller collected more votes for swing and sweet music combined than any other orchestra leader. Benny Goodman got more for swing.

Miller always has had a special place in the hearts of Coloradans, not so much for his band's renditions of "Old Black Magic," "Tuxedo Junction," "Chattanooga Choo Choo," and the Miller theme song, "Moonlight Serenade," as for the fact that he went to high school in Fort Morgan and then attended the University of Colorado at Boulder. In fact, he worked his way through CU playing a trombone in the college band.

The university was so proud of him that a campus ballroom built in 1953 was named the Glenn Miller Ballroom. Many of these details are in the movie, *The Glenn Miller Story,* which first appeared in 1953. (Miller was born in 1904 in Clarinda, Iowa.)

Miller, who became famous both for his trombone playing and for his distinctive arrangements, earned his first instrument by doing odd jobs when he was 14. He played in bands in Fort Morgan and, after graduation, joined the Boyd Senter Band which traveled in Western states.

By 1923, however, he had decided college was important, and he enrolled at CU. In Boulder he joined the Holly Moyer Orchestra, a dance band that played three nights a week at Citizens' Hall where college students hung out. He was serious about a career as a musician and declined to play football for fear of having his teeth knocked out, disastrous for a trombonist.

He was tall and thin and was not a warm personality. Before long, he had earned the nickname "Gloomy Gus" because of his serious air and strict personal discipline. He also was so shy that, when he organized his own band, it was difficult for him to get up in front to lead it; but he loved the music so much that he made himself stand there.

He stayed at Boulder for a year then left school because he wanted to get started on his musical career. For several years, he worked for different bands, both on the West Coast and in New York, as trombonist and arranger.

In 1928, he married his college sweetheart, Helen Burger, in New York.

About that time, Ray Noble asked Miller to help him put together an orchestra and do the arranging for it. Most of the nation knew this orchestra on Ray Noble's *Coca-Cola Hour.*

Still itching to be on his own, Miller organized a combination of "strings and swing" that recorded for Columbia Records in 1935. Miller's big band was formed in 1937, but a year later he disbanded it and started over. By 1939, the band was a national hit, playing in the famed Meadowbrook Roadhouse and the Glen Island Casino. His band's recording of "Tuxedo Junction" in 1939 was the first million-disc seller in nearly 10 years.

Then came radio's *Chesterfield Show,* which starred the Miller Band.

In 1942, Miller turned the band over to Harry James and enlisted in the Army Air Force. He was appointed conductor of the Army Air Force Band and given the rank of major.

The Air Force Band was playing in Paris in December 1944. Miller was flying ahead of his group to another engagement in France when his plane disappeared over the English Channel. No trace was ever found.

The movie stars James Stewart as Miller and June Allyson as his wife. Henry Morgan had the role of Miller's buddy, "Chummy" MacGregor.

Much of the filming was done on location in the Denver area in 1953. About 3,000 airmen from Lowry Air Force Base performed as extras in a scene showing a USO performance in England in December 1944. Although it was an extremely hot July in Denver—and the temperature inside the hangar was around 100 degrees—the airmen wore heavy wool winter uniforms.

Another day's shooting took place on the CU campus in Boulder. In later years, Miller had remembered his college days by playing songs of the university on his radio program and by making an occasional appearance at the college with his famous orchestra.

About 5,000 Denverites were extras for scenes filmed at Elitch Gardens Trocadero Ballroom, which was torn down in 1975. Stewart's wife, the former Gloria McLean, was in the crowd.

Miller"s 82-year-old mother, Mattie Lou Miller, who lived in Greeley, came to watch the ballroom scenes being filmed and met Stewart.

"He's a fine actor," she commented, "but he doesn't look a thing like my boy."

Civic Center was the locale of another scene, showing Miller stopping to make a phone call from a booth in 1926. Antique car collector Arthur Rippey provided the vehicles for the scene.

September 22, 1985

CZ
The Story of the California Zephyr

Karl R. Zimmermann

PROTEAN CZ: IT CERTAINLY WAS a train that meant different things to different people. For the Interstate Commerce Commission, it was a puzzlement and perhaps its hardest "train-off" decision ever. The railroads felt it a thorn in their collective sides, although for rail enthusiasts it was the great hope, the proof-positive of the popularity of the well-run passenger train. Newsmen and editorialists found in it a cause ill-starred, the best kind. Thousands of Americans whose sense of transportation esthetics had not been dulled by the jet age saw it as a straw to clutch. To children, it was heaven, to the unions, gravy.

And to me? To me it was the final and ultimate train, the point where schedulers and designers, surveyors and engineers, dietitians and personnel men could have said "Stop! We've got it." To be sure, other railroads had rolling stock equal that of the *California Zephyr*. The Union Pacific's dome diners were just about the finest place to sup on earth, let alone on rails. The Santa Fe's Pleasure Domes, the Milwaukee's Super Domes and Skytops were plush and distinctive. The deep-windowed step-down observations of the 20th Century Limited were classic, and who could forget the *Broadway Limited's Pullman* observations *Tower View* and *Mountain View*?

But the CZ's Vista-Dome lounge-observation was no ugly stepsister to any of these, nor were the rest of the CZ's cars, especially when you consider what there was to be seen from the windows. No other train had the Colorado Rockies and California's Feather River Canyon. And five domes from which to view this splendor was hard to beat. So were the food and the service.

Still, for anything to be truly grand, the whole must be greater than the sum of its parts. So it was with the CZ, which built a reputation and established an aura few other trains could touch. In part this was no doubt inherited through the rich Zephyr lineage of its Burlington Route predecessors. Certainly the CZ continued their honorable tradition in all important ways save the emphasis on speed.

And the *California Zephyr* was a pretty train, don't forget that. Pretty, it can't be denied, in a conventional, familiar way, not much different from the other Zephyrs, but pretty from any angle. From high atop the south rim of Gore Canyon: the train was a silver snake, sinuously inching its glittering way along the opposite face of the chasm as if in slow motion. From trackside at Williams Loop: the Sierras' early-morning sun sidelit the Western Pacific's feather-emblemed

F's and spiraling consist, making all seem crisp and fresh an invigoratingly new. From the dome of the *Silver Sky*: the entire train stretched gracefully ahead, then corkscrewed into another cut as Glenwood Canyon towered by. From the station platform at Salt Lake City: the consist stood quietly hissing in the cool dark, windows of Pullmans glowing a welcome.

* * *

We sometimes judge people by the way they die; why not trains? Many great trains have languished in their last years, losing their fine equipment and prestige, until little remained but a name. Though its name too lingered on, the CZ was largely spared this degradation. Instead, it went out looking much as it had in its youth. The lounge-observation was not amputated to simplify switching. Service in the diner remained up to snuff until the end; the carnations in the vases never turned to plastic. Admittedly lateness was the rule in the last years, but no one seemed to mind much, unless it was so extreme that darkness fell on the more spectacular scenery. After all, the CZ was a "cruise train."

Or was it? "Cruise" implies going nowhere fast, and the California Zephyr went lots of places, although relatively slowly. It never stopped being transportation, and this sense of movement and purpose was central to the pleasures experienced aboard the train. Both ocean liner and streamliner lose their majesty when they idle; grandeur accompanies function and direction and urgency on the high seas and high iron alike. The CZ took you somewhere, but it did so in the most civilized possible manner, and that takes time.

* * *

The *California Zephyr* died on March 22, 1970, when the Western Pacific was allowed to discontinue its portion of the run. Any consists that have operated since under the illustrious CZ name are imposters, and must be regarded as such. And when the CZ died, the death knell was rung for the transcontinental passenger train operated in the grand manner, Amtrak notwithstanding. For if the *California Zephyr* was not worth saving at all costs, what running on long-distance rails really is?

A 21-year history is not a long one. But the CZ's career, brief as it was, had everything to delight the chronicler: glamour, warmth, drama, and controversy. Millions rode the train and loved it. Thousands spoke up in protest as it was allowed to roll to its death. It had made a lot of friends, and that in itself tells a story.

The Color Orange

Russell Martin

YOU REALLY COULDN'T HELP but be impressed by the meteorological portent, by the way the weather presaged the start of the season. On Friday, the city was hot and strangely still, the sky blue above the smog. Then on Saturday came a great drum roll of thunder and a spare and promising rain—the dark skies lowering the morning light, the chill wind abetting the nervous anticipation of the two hundred or so fans who milled, umbrellas open and jackets buttoned tight, at the edge of the turf at Mile High Stadium in Denver, waiting for a minor ritual to begin—the taking of the team photograph, annually executed the day before the Broncos' home opener, before new jerseys lost their luster, before injuries and expediencies inevitably began to change the faces in the photograph.

At last, large men in Popsicle-orange jerseys with white numerals wider than pie tins began to amble out of the locker room and onto the field. Helmetless, wincing against the weather, and hunching their huge padded shoulders, they milled near the four rows of risers where they would pose, shouting, "Sheee-it, it's cold," kidding each other about their ugliness, slapping each other's butts, and bouncing on the balls of their feet.

The fans, held at a distance by a harried team PR man, pulled cameras with long lenses from the cover of their coats, aimed them at the men in orange and

Mile High Stadium's last remodle was in 1986, and it was home to the Denver Broncos until 2001 when it closed. The Broncos then moved to a newer stadium, Empower Field at Mile High.

chattered excitedly, the cold—at least for a few moments—no longer a concern. They watched and waited while Dan Reeves, the Broncos' 42-year-old head coach, took on the frustrating task that thousands of grammar school teachers know too well—trying to get his players to line up properly (in their jerseys' numerical order), to bunch up a bit, to move over this way just a little, to drop the rabbit-ears fingers they held behind each other's heads, to stop making silly faces. When Reeves made it clear that everyone could go back inside as soon as the photos were finished, his players quickly simmered down. They stiffened up and looked straight ahead, Reeves and his assistants standing attentively behind them now in matching sport shirts, nearly five dozen all told—players and coaches and trainers—hollering "cheese" in the same instant, then "cheese" three more times to be sure, before they bolted for the locker room, the fans breaking toward them then as if intent on some open-field tackling. But the contact was light, nothing more than the pressing of pads of paper into the players' chests; the fans—suddenly intimidated by the sea of orange and, my God, by the size of these men, and surely by their local celebrity—blurting only "Would you...?" or "Please?" as they held pens up to the players' eyes.

I wiped the rainwater off an aluminum bench and sat down, the only spectator among 75,000 empty seats. I had never been in this place before, this colossal horseshoe painted in section-coded colors—yellows, blues, oranges, and reds—some sort of outsized theater in the round, all seats focusing on a distant stage that was simply a rectangular strip of grass, a place that, even in its emptiness, offered a vision of drama, a heady sense of coming attractions. Mile High Stadium, cobbled and riveted through four series of renovations since it first served as a baseball park in 1948, had been sold out for every regular-season home game of the Denver Broncos since the beginning of the 1971 season—15 years, 117 games, 120 if you count the three play-off games played here in 1977, 1978, and 1984. Tomorrow it would be sold out again as 75,000 blue-capped and orange-shirted football fans, no, Broncos fans, streamed into this stadium to pledge their allegiance, to scream their hearts out, to die with every Denver turnover, to know true exaltation if their guys were ahead at the end of the game.

The Broncos were my team, too, if the truth were told. After 94 years of American professional football, they were still the only team anchored between the Sierras and Kansas City—the only game in the Great American West save the teams scattered along the Pacific Coast, which somehow didn't count. Growing up in a rat-ass town located where the Rockies descended to the Navajo desert, I had become a Broncos fan in the years during which they were indisputably the worst team trying to play the game. They wore silly vertically striped socks, their helmet logo was a dumb cartoon depiction of a bucking horse, and—back then—a .500 season would have been something worthy of wild celebration. But the Broncos were likable. Actually, they were lovable—lovable in the way that a dog who just can't manage a trick is lovable. They reminded us of ourselves, I suppose—our unabashed optimism somehow always countered by a bare reality. Throughout the mountain West, the Broncos were the boys we worried about on tattered stools in small cafés, the team we lambasted on job-site lunch breaks, the team we coached brilliantly over beers and whiskeys then gamely cheered through the subsequent losing effort. Perhaps we cared about them so much simply because they so often broke our hearts.

After 11 losing seasons (44 wins, 105 losses, and 5 ties), the 1971 Broncos were nonetheless, and for no discernible reason, able to sell out every home game. To no discernible effect: The team barely mustered a 4-9-1 record that year.

In 1972, things began to get a bit better. In their first year under former Stanford University head coach John Ralston—a Dale Carnegie advocate and a shrewd judge of football talent—the Broncos went 5-9. Then in 1973, while the rest of the nation focused on a minor skirmish called Watergate, football fans in the Rockies reveled in—can you imagine it?—a winning season, 7-5-2. It had taken 14 years to achieve, but we are a patient people, those of us who live in the American outback. Broncomania, the term for the condition that had afflicted long-suffering fans, came into common usage, and there was indeed a growing, nearly epidemic, mania about this laughing stock football team that had finally found a way to win. Four years and three more winning seasons later, the meek inherited the earth and the 12-2 Broncos, coached by a fireplug named Red Miller, went to the Super Bowl. But because life has little meaning, the 1977 season ended in defeat. In Super Bowl XII, the Wild West Bowl, the Dallas Cowboys corralled the Denver Broncos, and 40,000 visiting Denver fans milled through New Orleans's French Quarter in dazed and dangerous post-game depression. Back in the Rocky Mountains, everybody—except those who were in comas and had good excuses not to have watched the game—turned off the television, sighed a great collective sigh, and averred in a voice sad and deflated, "Well, what'd we expect? Shoot, we're talking *Broncos*, after all."

Yet despite that game's bitter lesson, it was a kind of watershed. Never again could the Broncos simply be lovable losers. The very fans who had become devoted to them because of their strange socks, because of their succession of aging and unathletic quarterbacks, because of their penchant for snatching defeat from the pendulous jaws of victory, now demanded something better, more than mediocrity, something akin to excellence.

The national sports media, on the other hand, and football fans elsewhere in the country really didn't give much credence to the Broncos' ascendancy that year. They didn't suppose it would last long. One hinterland team or another always seemed to be able to pull off a Cinderella season. But for the Broncos' owners, coaches, players, and for their much-abused fans, .500 seasons would never again be adequate achievements. The vertically striped socks had long ago been burned in a pre-game ceremony. Now it was time to incinerate an image—one of a team, and a town, that simply didn't amount to much.

During the decade that followed the Super Bowl season, the Broncos were a good football team. Twice they won the American Football Conference's Western Division. They recorded at least ten victories per season in all but the strike-shortened 1982 season. Under current head coach Dan Reeves, the team had won 45 games, losing just 28. Only two other teams posted better records during that decade. Yet at the start of the 1986 season, a remnant of the Broncos' first incarnation remained, some long-standing and latent suspicion of ineptitude: The Broncos had played in four post-season playoff games since that trip to the Superdome. They weren't super, or even adequate to the task, in a single one of them.

As the 1986 season was set to open, everyone's annual anxieties were compounded by a strange new reason to worry. In addition to all the usual concerns about the adequacy of the offensive line, and the utter absence of a running game, there was this to worry about: Five national magazines that are prone to make such prognostications had recently made the Broncos their pick to be representing the American Football Conference in Super Bowl XXI in Pasadena—a few months and a dozen and a half football games down the road. For crying out loud! Not only was the upcoming schedule a virtual minefield; not only was the running offense its usual suspect self; now there were these crazy expectations to contend with.

Sitting in the autumnal gloom on a hard seat in that silent stadium, I was eager for some football finally to be played, whatever the four-month succession of games might bring—a season unparalleled or a season like so many others. I had come to the city from the hard-scrabble sticks to observe firsthand what theretofore I had only gleaned from Sunday afternoon television and the sports pages of Denver's dailies. I wanted to get some measure of what fed this football mania, to try to understand why this team could captivate so many dissimilar people. The Broncos were the great democratizer in Denver, the one safe but shared and passionate conversation between the rich and the poor and the sea of people in the economic middle ground, between people who were white and brown and black.

Still, football was only a game—a diversion, an entertainment, as simple and artificial and ultimately unimportant as a Saturday schoolyard match played between neighborhood boys. And this was what intrigued me. How was it that a series of games, of contests between mercenary athletes, which had no real or concrete connection to the lives of the rest of us, could assume such vital importance? Why did the weekly fate of Denver's football team—or of other teams in other cities—garner the kind of attention that might otherwise have been given only to a summit between the superpowers? What was it, for heaven's sake, that football offered us?

Colorado
A Liquid History & Tavern Guide to the Highest State

Thomas J. Noel

El Ortiz Tavern

AFTER DAYS ROUSTING about the Rainbow Trout Lodge, I joined Julio Archuleta, Little Ernie Marquez, and other employees for visits to the El Ortiz on Antonito's faded Main Street. Even back then, the El Ortiz usually looked deserted. A "For Sale" sign shared the front window with tubs of geraniums whose riotous red blossoms meant that Angie was still there.

Angie Ortiz had geranium-red hair and a sunny smile. She struck me as the brightest and fastest talker in town. And she ended her dances with a cartwheel. "I married Ricardo Casias," Angie explained once, "because he was the best dancer in Antonito."

Angie and Ricardo made the tavern a dance club, and, on occasions, a dinner club with Angie cooking on the huge old cast iron range. The ancient building had been Ira Green's dry goods store until Angie's father, Gaspar Ortiz, bought it. He helped Angie and Ricardo switch to wet goods.

Angie put a sign over the doorway, *Peace To All Who Enter Here*, and called everyone honey. Yet, she could throw out a troublemaker in seconds, usually out shouting them in the process. She kicked them out in either English or Spanish, allowing the customer to pick the language of eviction.

Rarely did Angie turn gloomy, but late one night, when I was the last customer, that angel behind the bar sighed: "Tomas, the El Ortiz will always be in limbo. I will never be able to escape it. No one's ever offered me even one peso for this place. Antonito is doomed."

It all started, she explained, back in the 1850s when the first New Mexican settlers came up the Rio Grande into Colorado. They hoped for a more promising place than the high, dry desert of the San Luis Valley. But the lead mule stopped and would not budge. The New Mexicans pulled and they pushed. They kicked and swore and prayed. But it just stood there, stubborn as a jackass. Finally someone noticed that the statue of Nuestra Señora de La Guadalupe had fallen off the creature's back and landed on the banks of the Rio Conejos. ...

The ultimate fate of a town founded by rail and real estate developers instead of by heavenly guidance also troubled Gaspar Ortiz, founding father of the El

Ortiz Tavern. A wiry man with a wispy moustache, he leaned against the high-backed booth. His dim eyes grew sharper as he looked into the past:

"My great-grandfather came from Spain. My father, Gaspar Florentino Ortiz, was here when the railroad came down from Alamosa. The Spanish people didn't want the railroad. They thought it would bring in bad people. They were right. Once the railroad came, we lost this land."

My father was postmaster here, and he named the little town south of us for our family, Ortiz. Once Antonito was rich with sheep. I was born in 1886 and can remember driving thousands of sheep down Main Street to the railroad cars headed for Denver. Sheep were to us what buffalo were to the Indians. The people of the San Luis Valley ate lamb, wore wool, slept in wool blankets, and even made the windows of their homes out of sheepskin. Those were the happy days. Millions were made in the sheep business. But little stayed in Antonito."

Last time I visited Antonito, the El Ortiz was closed.

The Governor's Chessboard

Richard D. Lamm

I CAME TO THE STATE permanently in November of 1961, not knowing a soul, and a year later I was president of the Denver Young Democrats. Five years later, I was elected to the Colorado legislature; six years later, I was elected assistant minority leader; and 13 years later I was elected governor. In the process, I had authored and shepherded through the legislature the nation's first liberalized abortion bill and led the successful campaign to bring the 1976 Winter Olympics to Colorado. Conventional wisdom on both these issues at the time, I was told, was that I was committing "political suicide."

I see the Democratic Party as a special interest party, and while I am glad it is a party of compassion and generally favors working people, it also has been captured by many special interests, including the teachers' union and the trial lawyers (to name only two). It is financed by special interest money, and while Democratic special interests are less venal than Republican interests, they are still special interests. ...

Community is both ancient and fluid; doing good—but we cannot take "community" for granted in the United States. We have too much evidence that we are unraveling and becoming unglued. There is too much tension, too much misunderstanding. Too many separate tribes yelling at each other. Our civic dialogue is too often a "dialogue" between the blind and the deaf.

The Song of the Lark

Willa Cather

On the Art of Fiction

ONE IS SOMETIMES ASKED about the "obstacles" that confront young writers who are trying to do good work. I should say the greatest obstacles that writers today have to get over are the dazzling journalistic successes of 20 years ago—stories that surprised and delighted by their sharp photographic detail and that were really nothing more than lively pieces of reporting. The whole aim of that school of writing was novelty—never a very important thing in art. They gave us, altogether, poor standards—taught us to multiply our ideas instead of to condense them. They tried to make a story out of every theme that occurred to them and to get returns on every situation that suggested itself. They got returns of a kind. But their work, when one looks back on it, now that the novelty upon which they counted so much is gone, is journalistic and thin. The especial merit of a good reportorial story is that it shall be intensely interesting and pertinent today and shall have lost its point by tomorrow.

Art, it seems to me, should simplify. That, indeed, is very nearly the whole of the higher artistic process: finding what conventions of form and what detail one can do without and yet preserve the spirit of the whole—so that all that one has suppressed and cut away is there to the reader's consciousness as much as if it were in type on the page. Millet had done hundreds of sketches of peasants sowing grain, some of them very complicated and interesting, but when he came to paint the spirit of them all into one picture, *The Sower,* the composition is so simple that it seems inevitable. All the discarded sketches that went before made the picture what it finally became, and the process was all the work. The white ribbons were never realities to her after all. She did not believe in them. It was only in attitudes of protest or reproof, clinging to the cross, that human beings could be even temporarily decent.

Preacher Kronborg's secret convictions were very much like Anna's. He believed that his wife was absolutely good, but there was not a man or woman in his congregation whom he trusted all the way.

Mrs. Kronborg, on the other hand, was likely to find something to admire in almost any human conduct that was positive and energetic. She could always be taken in by the stories of tramps and runaway boys. She went to the circus and admired the bareback riders, who were "likely good enough women in their way." She admired Dr. Archie's fine physique and well-cut clothes as much as Thea did, and said she "felt it was a privilege to be handled by such a gentleman when she was sick."

Soon after Anna became a church member, she began to remonstrate with Thea about practicing—playing "secular music"—on Sunday. One Sunday, the dispute in the parlor grew warm and was carried to Mrs. Kronborg in the kitchen. She listened judicially and told Anna to read the chapter about how Naaman the leper was permitted to bow down in the house of Rimmon. Thea went back to the piano; and Anna lingered to say that, since she was in the right, her mother should have supported her.

"No," said Mrs. Kronborg, rather indifferently, "I can't see it that way, Anna. I never forced you to practice, and I don't see as I should keep Thea from it. I like to hear her, and I guess your father does. You and Thea will likely follow different lines, and I don't see as I'm called upon to bring you up alike."

Anna looked meek and abused. "Of course all the church people must hear her. Ours is the only noisy house on this street. You hear what she's playing now, don't you?"

Mrs. Kronborg rose from browning her coffee. "Yes; it's the *Blue Danube* waltzes. I'm familiar with 'em. If any of the church people come at you, you just send 'em to me. I ain't afraid to speak out on occasion, and I wouldn't mind one bit telling the Ladies' Aid a few things about standard composers." Mrs. Kronborg smiled, and added thoughtfully, "No, I wouldn't mind that one bit."

Anna went about with a reserved and distant air for a week, and Mrs. Kronborg suspected that she held a larger place than usual in her daughter's prayers; but that was another thing she didn't mind.

Although revivals were merely a part of the year's work, like examination week at school, and although Anna's piety impressed her very little, a time came when Thea was perplexed about religion. A scourge of typhoid broke out in Moonstone and several of Thea's schoolmates, died of it.

Early in July, soon after Thea's 15th birthday, a particularly disgusting sort of tramp came into Moonstone in an empty boxcar. Thea was sitting in the hammock in the front yard when he first crawled up under the fence. He had a bundle wrapped in dirty ticking under one arm, and under the other he carried a wooden box with rusty screen handles. He had a hungry face covered with black stubble, and he smelled of fried potatoes and onions and coffee. He sniffed the air greedily, slowing and slowing. Thea saw him, and she hoped he would not stop at their gate, for her mother never turned any one away; but this was the dirtiest and most utterly wretched-looking tramp she had ever seen. There was a terrible odor about him, too. She caught it even at that distance, and put her handkerchief to her nose. A long shiver ran through her, for she knew he had noticed it. He looked back at her sharply, and she flushed and hurried into the house.

A few days later Thea heard that the tramp had camped in an empty shack over on the east edge of town, inside the ravine, and was trying to give a miserable sort of show there. He had told the boys who went to see him that he had travelled with a circus. His bundle contained a filthy clown's suit and half a dozen rattlesnakes.

Saturday night, when Thea went to the butcher shop to get the chickens for Sunday, she heard the wail of an accordion and saw a crowd before one of the saloons. There she found the tramp, grotesquely attired in the clown's suit, his bony white face shaved and painted—the sweat trickling through the paint and washing it away—and his eyes were wild and feverish. Pulling in the accordion in and out seemed to be almost too great an effort for him, and he'd pant to the tune of "Marching Through Georgia." After a considerable crowd had gathered, the tramp exhibited the box of snakes, announced that he would now pass the hat, and that when the onlookers had contributed the sum of one dollar, he would eat "one of these living reptiles." The crowd began to cough and murmur, and the saloon keeper rushed off for the marshal who arrested the wretch for giving a show without a license and hurried him away to the calaboose.

The calaboose stood in a sunflower patch; it was an old hut with a barred window and a padlock on the door. The tramp was utterly filthy and diseased. The town had made no provision to grub-stake vagrants, so after he had been detained for 24 hours, the marshal released him and told him to get out of town, and get quick. The fellow's rattlesnakes had been killed by the saloon keeper. He hid in a boxcar in the freight yard, probably hoping to get a ride to the next station, but he was found and put out. After that he was seen no more. He had disappeared and left no trace except an ugly, stupid word chalked on the black paint of the 75-foot standpipe which was the reservoir for the Moonstone water supply; the same word, in another tongue, that the French soldier shouted at Waterloo to the English officer who bade the Old Guard surrender; a comment on life which the defeated, along the hard roads of the world, sometimes bawl at the victorious.

A week after the tramp excitement had passed over, the city water began to smell and to taste. The Kronborgs had a well in their back yard and did not use city water, but they heard the complaints of their neighbors. At first, people said that the town well was full of rotting cottonwood roots, but the engineer at the pumping station convinced the mayor that the water left the well untainted. Mayors reason slowly, but, the well being eliminated, the official mind had to travel toward the standpipe—there was no other track for it to go in. The standpipe amply rewarded investigation. The tramp had got even with Moonstone. He had climbed the standpipe by the handholds and let himself down into seventy-five feet of cold water, with his shoes and hat and roll of ticking. The city council had a mild panic and passed a new ordinance about tramps. But the fever had already broken out, and several adults and half a dozen children died of it. ...

One evening when she was haunted by the figure of the tramp, Thea went up to Dr. Archie's office. She found him sewing up two bad gashes in the face of a little boy who had been kicked by a mule. After the boy had been bandaged and sent away with his father, Thea helped the doctor wash and put away the surgical instruments. Then she dropped into her accustomed seat beside his desk and began to talk about the tramp. Her eyes were hard and green with excitement, the doctor noticed.

"It seems to me, Dr. Archie, that the whole town's to blame. I'm to blame, myself. I know he saw me hold my nose when he went by. Father's to blame. If he believes the Bible, he ought to have gone to the calaboose and cleaned that man up and taken care of him. That's what I can't understand; do people believe the Bible, or don't they? If the next life is all that matters, and we're put here to get ready for it, then why do we try to make money, or learn things, or have a good time? There's not one person in Moonstone that really lives the way the New Testament says. Does it matter, or don't it?"

Dr. Archie swung round in his chair and looked at her, honestly and leniently. "Well, Thea, it seems to me like this. Every people has had its religion. All religions are good, and all are pretty much alike. But I don't see how we could live up to them in the sense you mean. I've thought about it a good deal, and I can't help feeling that while we are in this world we have to live for the best things of this world, and those things are material and positive. Now, most religions are passive, and they tell us chiefly what we should not do." The doctor moved restlessly, and his eyes hunted for something along the opposite wall: "See here, my girl, take out the years of early childhood and the time we spend in sleep and dull old age, and we only have about 20 able, waking years. That's not long enough to get acquainted with half the fine things that have been done in the world, much less to do anything ourselves. I think we ought to keep the Commandments and help other people all we can; but the main thing is to live those 20 splendid years; to do all we can and enjoy all we can."

Dr. Archie met his little friend's searching gaze, the look of acute inquiry which always touched him.

"But poor fellows like that tramp—" she hesitated and wrinkled her forehead.

The doctor leaned forward and put his hand protectingly over hers, which lay clenched on the green felt desk-top. "Ugly accidents happen, Thea; always have and always will. But the failures are swept back into the pile and forgotten. They don't leave any lasting scar in the world, and they don't affect the future. The things that last are the good things. The people who forge ahead and do something, they really count."

Backroads of Colorado

Boyd & Barbara Norton

Greeley to Dearfield

THE TOWN OF GREELEY, at the juncture of U.S. highways 85 and 34, has an interesting history. In 1869, a group of people gathered at the Cooper Institute in New York to hear Horace Greeley, owner of the *New York Tribune*, talk about forming a cooperative farming community, to be called Union Colony, in Colorado. Before the evening was over, several memberships at $15 each had been sold. The only two stipulations were that a member had to be of good moral character and had to abstain from drinking any alcoholic beverage.

Though it was named for Greeley, the town was founded by the *Tribune's* agricultural editor, Nathan C. Meeker, in 1870. When Isabella Bird visited the community three years later, it had 3,000 inhabitants. She called it "the most prosperous and rising colony in Colorado" but complained that it was hot and full of bugs. This could explain why Horace Greeley visited the town but never lived there. Meeker's home is now a museum, preserving many of his effects and other historical mementos. Incidentally, there is a Colorado town named after Meeker, along the White River (described earlier). He's the Indian agent killed in the Ute uprising (the "Meeker Massacre") when he headed the White River Agency.

From Greeley turn east on U.S. 34, a long stretch of which roughly parallels the South Platte. Where the river makes a loop south and then through to the road, look for a highway sign indicating the site of Dearfield, another farming commune.

This cooperative farming venture was started by O.T. Jackson and a tiny band of followers in 1910. It became successful, the new farmers learning as they went about such things as soil conservation and dry farming. Around 1920, the community of Dearfield (so named because the fields had become dear to the inhabitants) could boast a population of 700. By 1929, it was being advertised as a resort—with a lodge, dance pavilion, lunchroom, filling station, with lakes nearby as well as proximity (only 70 miles) to Denver.

Then came the depression and the drought and dust storms of the 1930s. By 1940, the community had dwindled to 12 people. The founder finally gave up too and moved back to Denver, where he died in 1949. Dearfield became a ghost town.

Dearfield's story is much more typical of communes in Colorado than is Greeley's. But there's one thing that sets it apart from the others. Dearfield was settled by and for blacks.

Today, there's a working gas station here. The ruins of the lunchroom and several old houses are still to be seen. They're all that remain of one black man's dream of making it in a white society.

Marmalade and Whiskey
British Remittance Men in the West

Lee Olson

ONE COMMON STORY was that the arriving outcast had lost his sweetheart to another, so he left home to become a hermit. Some tales were salacious: "He had an affair with a married woman," or "The upstairs maid had his baby."

Locals also bestowed gratuitous titles, such as Sir or Lord, when in fact few remittance men had them. As younger sons, they rarely qualified for a title. But while a good many were simply on a lark, the Canadian rancher noted correctly that a great many had intentions of becoming ranchers with help from home.

But there was another, less obvious reason for migration—physical defects and disease. It is impossible to overstate the impact on the West of tuberculosis or realize today how deadly it was. While the ugly lesions of smallpox, the gasping of diphtheria victims, and the shaking chills of malaria were better known, the quiet killing of the tubercle bacillus surpassed them all. Fever, malaise, coughing, and weight loss—these were the symptoms—and then slow death. Poor nutrition and urban crowding, fed by the Industrial Revolution, made tuberculosis the top killer in the eighteenth and nineteenth centuries.

In his book, *Rocky Mountain Medicine*, Dr. Robert H. Shikes points out that the disease did not spare the countryside or the privileged classes. Victims in England included Keats, Shelley, the Brontë sisters, and Elizabeth Barrett Browning. It struck mansions as well as hovels.

Thus, upper-class families filled the resorts of Italy, France, and Switzerland. A mild climate and open air were believed helpful—and they were. But although the bacterium that causes tuberculosis was discovered in 1882, no single magic bullet emerged as a cure. The boom in health spas continued to expand in the American West. Like Europeans, Americans worshipped at the shrine of a dry climate, and railroads circularized eastern cities with brochures advertising the Western spas, mainly in Colorado. A doctor who had toured Europe proclaimed in the *New York Tribune* that "Colorado Springs is the best resort on the face of the globe for an invalid with lung disease."

Coincidentally, the great outflow of moneyed young Britons for economic reasons occurred at this same time period—the late 19th century. Sometimes the motivations were joined. Ambulatory tuberculosis victims sought opportunity in the West where the health-giving climate would also clear their lungs. For many it worked. But these were hard years: One of every three Coloradans had active tuberculosis, and one of every four Coloradans died of it.

The result was that Colorado and neighboring mountain states became the most British of American states, at least for a time. Colorado Springs became "Lil' Lonnon" because there were so many Britons among the "lungers" who came to seek the gift of life from the dry, light air at six thousand feet. (As capital city, Denver recognized that the new sanatoria were rivaling its profits as a mining supply center.) Problems emerged as thousands of patients arrived, many of them destitute. Aware that the disease was spread by contagion, the Colorado General Assembly debated—but did not pass—a bill requiring consumptives to wear bells around their necks so healthy citizens could steer a wide berth. Signs discouraging spitting were posted throughout Denver.

Among the British health seekers was a young physician from London, Dr. S. Edwin Solly, who came to Colorado Springs because either he or his wife suffered early symptoms of the disease. Educated at Rugby and the Royal College of Surgeons, he arrived in 1874, when the cause of tuberculosis was unknown. But he realized that the Colorado climate benefited lung sufferers, along with good nutrition, hygiene, and bed rest. He founded Cragmoor, a sanitarium for the wealthy. But he overcharged his rich patients enough so that for every 100 paying admissions he could accept 500 indigents. Dr. Solly is a visible example of Britons who came to stay and make substantial contributions to the region's culture, education, and progress. There were hundreds of others—educated Easterners as well as Europeans—who came as patients and provided capital and leadership for the Rocky Mountain West.

Tuberculosis wasn't the only ailment that responded to climatic treatment. Isabella L. Bird, plucky daughter of a British clergyman, was prompted to ride horseback through Colorado's Front Range because of fear of an incipient spinal disease diagnosed in Britain. *A Lady's Life in the Rocky Mountains*—a classic book of Western history—was the result.

In the early 1900s tuberculosis patients lie in beds on the porch of a building at the Jewish Consumptive Relief Society (J.C.R.S.) sanatorium, 1600 Pierce Street, Lakewood, Colorado.

SECTION IX

Hard Times

Emily

Emily French

February, Wednesday 26, 1890

I UP; SO SICK; I could not eat. John Clibon came to see if I could go to wash at their in-laws for them all. I promised if I should be able. I took the rug in the basket; went over to Mrs. F. I had a chill; in about one hour, I had to lie down. Joe Berg came while I was there; he stayed that night. I slept on the lounge. I coughed so hard she fixed me some ginger tea; done all she could. I took red pepper, worked on her rug, cut the scallops all ready to sew.

February, Thursday 27, 1890

Got up; built both of Mrs. Frick's fires. The children came out; Florence helped start the breakfast—coffee and meat and pancakes. Old Isenberg is lazy; not up till it was on the table. He don't amount to nothing; sets and talks German. I sat on my false teeth; heard them break as I sat down to grind her coffee. Oh dear; if only I could get through and go away from all this awful life. God, in his mercy, do help me; I am so sick, not able to wash for Agnes. & I had said I would. I took a lot of pepper tea; washed the dishes sat by the fire and worked on the rug. I must get done if I can today, sure, Mrs. F. tries to be kind. She got a good dinner—eggs, coffee and meat, crackers, &c. Hellgate came; staid all night. Mrs. Baltzell came to see why I did not go to wash for Agnes; I to sick. I went over to see Agnes in the cold, told her I would try to wash tomorrow if she & John would help me.

February, Friday 28, 1890

I up but oh so sick; coughed an hour. Mrs. Frick trying to get breakfast, I done all I was able to help. Isenberg still there. I could not eat anything, so I put on my things to go. Mrs. Frick said I ought not do such work. I washed at Joseph Oaks, the big days work. Agnes and John helped me good, I could not have done it if they had not. 2 ticks, a quilt, the stained clothes, all that a death can cause. I washed all day; so tired & cold. Laura & Jim went over to Mrs. Reeds, not a good place for them. I put on Mrs. Oaks cloak; came home. So cold & tired; Annis had a fireplace all nice for me. I sat down a little while, but I had to go to bed. Old Ric I fed good; she so thin. Mr. Oaks brought feed, now she will get all she can eat.

March, Saturday 1, 1890

A still day, awful sick all day. Oh dear; what shall I do; Old Ric, she will have to go hungry; I am not able to feed her.

March, Sunday 2, 1890

I lay still for fear of having a coughing spell. Sick & sore; Annis sleeping so sound; she is a careless *nobody*. Oh why am I left with only her for a companion. I called her, then had a hard coughing spell. She made a fire in the grate or fireplace; it smokes so in the stove. She got her own breakfast. The wind not blowing for a wonder. I called Old Ric & gave her a feed of oats. She looks so much better, the sore on her back nearly healed, has one now on her neck. I crawled to bed; oh dear, I am so sick; won't somebody come, I fear not. My feet are cold. Oh, why cannot I have some care when I always have done all in my power for others, must I suffer here alone & make no *sign*. God send me relief.

March, Monday 3, 1890

I felt very bad when I awoke. Annis crawled out; made a fire; got a little to eat. I lay still, had a hard coughing spell. What will I do, no rest; I am so sore, my kidneys are so weak, I must go see Dr. Higgins, maybe he will do something to relieve me. I had a fire in the fireplace, it smokes so in the kitchen. I tried to sew, cannot do anything. I am perfectly miserable, what shall I do. Does a kind providence send this terrible affliction for my good, or am I to do something that now I cannot seem to see or understand. My good old faithful horse Ric she must have some hay.

* * *

November, Saturday 15, 1890

Thy kingdom come—Amen

Yes, the talk at the table shows they are going to move. She is so cross I shall go unless she treats me different sure. I cannot stand such talk as she gets off about my knowing so much. All I try to do is to please her. I am to go with her to the Cinderella Matinee to care for Maurice. I know she will abuse me; this will be the last time sure. We were just in time for the car, I run to hurry her. I carried the big boy, was worried and tired as we went up the stairs in the 15th St. Theatre. I dropped off his cap, it is so very big for him. Such talk, she abused me as much as she dared. I am going now, on the way home, I see it was to be hotter than ever. I told Mr. Mauck he might pay and I would go, such a scene, she charged me $1.35 for the bonnet we had made. I must stay awhile, I used reason.

November, Sunday 16, 1890

Thy will be done

I got sick, she had said finally I could go to church, but I am sick. I took all the Epsom salts there was, no use, I am near blind with the headache. I done the work all day, took care of the boys, they went out to ride. I lay down on the hall seat upstairs, got to sleep. I have done up the supper work, am now ready to go rest. She is kind now as she can be, I should not mind it if she would be so all the time. She fried the corn, and they eat their supper. I lay down on the sofa where I sleep. They after supper pulled all the tacks out of the carpets upstairs and down. My head feels some better.

November, Monday 17, 1890

On earth as it is in heaven

I up at five, he called, they expect a day's work. I am no more to them than an old horse. They are going to move today in a house, 2922 Downing Ave., where there is a good barn too; they can keep their horses now, he pays $20 per month for its keep. She is not so cross this morning, but she expects me to git all the same. I got breakfast over, then washed out the didies, she packing upstairs, I downstairs, hard at it. The big wagon came at 11, $3 for piano and all. He had three loads in his plumbing wagon, every scrap is to go, she was sure to give that order. I gathered kindling wood, all then went over to the place and worked till 11 hard, three of the carpets down and a good many things straightened. I had to sleep yet on the sofa in the parlor, such a hard bed, she seems not to care. The body lice, such a long siege as I have had.

November, Tuesday 18, 1890

Give us this day our daily bread

Yet we must work. I don't feel as if I could do scarce a thing I had to, life so hard. On the base burner, it is so very heavy, has to be cleaned, 'tis covered with hen droppings and rust, has been in the barn all summer, such a nice stove ruined. I do wish I could have such nice things, but me. Mrs. Mauck is jawing away and in a big ugly fit. Must I go through more of her abuse, yes, she won't try to get the bedstead set up in the back room, I would get a good night's rest; that she don't wish.

November, Wednesday 19, 1890

Again I am serving up a nice hot breakfast to a pair of such ingrates. He is the best of the two, that is not saying much. Cleaned the kitchen. She is cross, went to take him to a job; she goes and takes him and brings him home, I have the cross boys to take care of and work. We put down the last carpet and set up the bedstead. I must take that crosspatch of a Maurice in my bed, oh dear, won't I be glad when this is over.

November, Thursday 20, 1890

And forgive us our debts as we forgive our debtors

I up and breakfast at six, he cross, says two old women and nothing done, she put him up a nice lunch. I hurried to get the water over & things ready for a washing. We will have a big one sure. She says I must do it all winter for her, she left the boiler till Monday. Tired tonight. Cleaning the base burner and scouring the black kitchen floor, three meals a day she will have. She twits me of getting $20 per month but says of late more about my earning it. Yes, I guess I do, I am so tired when night comes. Such a big time tonight, Olive came to see me, Mrs. Anfinger has gone to abusing her, refused her the use of the water closet, such a mean trick. She wanted to see if I was willing for her to leave, yes, she need not take a bit of her abuse—wheeling the old broken baby buggy, getting turnips, hurrying them on, making pie and biscuits, &c—she comes in, commences to abuse me, tells Maurice to strike me, he threatens to do.

Mollie

Mollie Dorsey Sanford

May [1865]—Camp Weld

ON THE MORNING of the 19th, about three o'clock, the night watchman at the corral came pounding on our door with the startling cry, "Get up. There is a flood in Cherry Creek, and hundreds of people are drowning." We could not believe but that he was fooling, until we heard the distant roar and the shouts of men like the coming of a mighty tempest. By hurriedly dressed and started away. I could not leave my sleeping boy. He came back, and said I must see it. I would never probably see so awful a sight again. We bundled up Bertie and, coming over to the creek, found hundreds of people staring and shivering, some half dressed, *and* all in a state bordering on frenzy. Great inky waves rolled up 10 or 15 feet high carrying on their crests pieces and parts of houses, cattle, and for all we know human beings too. In the low places, the soldiers on horseback were rescuing families, risking death to save women and children, and fighting with a foe not easily vanquished. It was the chill hour of morning, hardly daylight, but huge bonfires were lighted all along the banks where drenched and half-drowned people were warmed and dried. In the confusion, families were divided, and plaintive cries were heard above the roar, "O, where is my husband," or, "Where are my children," or "family."

Very little if any loss of life occurred, but homes were swept out of existence. Buildings had been erected on the sandy channel of the creek that were carried away. I came back to our shanty, got a bite of breakfast, and again we went to the scene of desolation, trying to be of some assistance. By was off on duty with the soldiers, a few only who are at Camp Weld. About nine o'clock, I heard a commotion. A man came galloping along, shouting, "All that live on the river bottoms, look out. The Platte is booming," and looking toward my shanty, I could see the water spreading like a mighty lake and knew that all *we* had in the world was in danger. Giving Bertie to a trusty friend, I rushed on to my little home, only to find the banks of the big ditch this side had burst, and water was rushing downhill to meet the coming tide from the Platte. I could go no further but could see that the boys from the corral were loading my things into the wagon. They had to swim the horses before they got through, and here *we* were in a bad plight ourselves. We were kindly taken in by a friend whose home was high and dry and remained several days. The vacant rooms at the barracks were thrown open to the homeless, and here we are again in our quarters where little "Bert" was born. Where we used to walk over to the east side on dry sand or elevated foot bridge, or wagon bridge, now runs a mighty torrent, spanned by a rope extension bridge. A ferry has been built across the Platte, and scenes of disorder and destruction are everywhere. People are groping in the slime and mud of the receding waters for their things, as most of the houses were left standing in the inundated district.

I have not had any of my queer impressions for a long time, until the other night, after I had gone to bed, I seemed to feel there was going to be a fire! I could not sleep and could not impress By at all. He snored away while I laid in fear and trembling. I actually got up and put my valuables and a little money we had under my pillow, fixing my clothes ready to jump into, even placing my shoes and stockings on a chair in easy reach, then crept back to bed, feeling foolish enough, and had just gotten into a sleep, when the cry of "Fire! Fire!" startled us, and all was hurry and confusion; I exclaiming, "I knew it all the time!" The large commissary building, where a large amount of government stores are kept, burned to the ground, doing no further damage, so all we had to do was to go back and settle our scattered household goods again. It seems there is one excitement after another, until I wonder I'm not white-headed. We are hearing of Indian depredations and scouting parties are out now from the barracks. Co. "H" is now and has been for some months stationed at Fremont's Orchard to guard the settlers. Bro. Sam is a member of that company. We stopped overnight with them as we came from Neb. City. There had been a light engagement, and I am all the time looking for news of another, as the Indians are no longer peaceable.

We have had a few weeks of comparative quiet with only occasional rumors of Indian troubles. We had always felt secure here in Denver but were aroused from that feeling by one night of horror. On the evening of the 19th, By, with almost all of the men from the barracks, had gone up to Denver to a political meeting. I sat in our room with the surgeon's wife, reading aloud some thrilling story from the *N.Y. Ledger*. Our babies were sweetly sleeping and all was quiet and serene. It was about 11 o'clock that a horseman, one of our soldiers, came tearing up the road, dismounting before our door. He knocked furiously. I opened it, expecting something had happened, but what was my horror to hear him gasp out, knees knocked together, and his eyes almost starting from their sockets, "Wimmen! Run for your lives—the Injuns are coming 3,000 strong! Run to the brick building at Denver! Governor's orders! But don't get skeered." (I already about paralyzed.) "Mrs. Sanford, you tell the folks down the row while I go around," and away he went to the outside quarters. Mrs. Towles immediately went into hysterics, while I started to give the alarm; but when the woman came to the first door I went to, I could not utter a word. My tongue had cleaved to the roof of my mouth. By this time, I could hear the shrieks of women and children as the flying messenger went his rounds. By an effort of will power, I overcame my terror and was soon back to my room, where my friend was wringing her hands in agony. I could hear bells ringing and the distant sound of confusion. In a very few moments the barracks were empty, the people on the road to Denver. I knew that By would come to me; and if I started, he could not find me. Beside, I could not leave my friend with her two babies nor could I run with mine, so we concluded to stay where we were for a while, thinking it as safe there as on the road to town alone. Very soon, By came. He did not seem so excited, as he hardly believed it, but he said we had better go, as there was not a living soul left at the barracks, as probably if there was an attack they would come here first to seize ammunition and arms. We picked up a few little things for the children, and putting the babies in their buggy, started walking quietly along; and by this time, I had gotten over my fright and did not care for the rumor much. It was so dark we could hardly see an object. We had nearly reached the town when we heard a quick volley of shots, then shouts, and then a mighty rush of horsemen toward us. I dropped on my knees, expecting my time had come at last, when just ahead of us passed a band of loose mules that had stampeded. We came on then to the brick buildings only to find them crowded to suffocation. Fearing a collapse of the building, we went with a friend into her cottage nearby. By was put on patrol duty, his beat being directly in front of the house. Time went by, and no Indians came.

Scouts had been sent out in every direction, alarming settlers as they went; and by daylight, the streets were filled with families who had fled from their homes. The returning scouts had found no traces of the Indians, and finally this and the returning daylight gave us the feeling of security, and the "scare" was over; and in due course of time, people returned to their homes. It all came from some old people living out a few miles, imagining some Mexican cattle drivers to be Indians and, in their fright, running two miles to the stage station, where the alarm was sent to the Governor. It only developed the fact that had there been an attack such confusion and panic ensued that the Indians could have wiped out the town.

Life of George Bent

George E. Hyde

DAWN ON THE MORNING of November 29, I was still in bed when I heard shouts, the noise of people running about the camp. I jumped up and ran out of my lodge. From down the creek, a large body of troops was advancing at a rapid trot, some to the east of the camps, and others on the opposite side of the creek, to the west. More soldiers could be seen making for the Indian pony herds to the south of the camps; in the camps themselves, all was confusion and noise—men, women, and children rushing out of the lodges partly dressed; women and children screaming at sight of the troops; men running back into the lodges for their arms; other men, already armed, or with lassos and bridles in their hands, running for the herds to attempt to get some of the ponies before the troops could reach the animals and drive them off. I looked toward the chief's lodge and saw that Black Kettle had a large American flag tied to the end of a long lodgepole and was standing in front of his lodge, holding the pole, with the flag fluttering in the grey light of the winter dawn. I heard him call to the people not to be afraid, that the soldiers would not hurt them; then the troops opened fire from two sides of the camps.

The Indians all began running, but they did not seem to know what to do or where to turn. The women and children were screaming and wailing, the men running to the lodges for their arms and shouting advice and directions to one another. I ran to my lodge and got my weapons, then rushed out and joined a passing group of middle-aged Cheyenne men. They ran toward the west, away from the creek, making for the sand hills. There we made a stand, but troops came up on the west side of the creek and opened a hot fire on us; so after a short time we broke and ran back toward the creek, jumping into the dry bed of the stream, above the camps. Hardly had we reached this shelter under the high bank of the creek when a company of cavalry rode up on the opposite bank and opened fire on us. We ran up the creek with the cavalry following us, one company on each bank, keeping right after us and firing all the time. Many of the people had preceded us up the creek, and the dry bed of the stream was now a terrible sight: men, women, and children lying thickly scattered on the sand, some dead and the rest too badly wounded to move. We ran about two miles up the creek, I think, and then came to a place where the banks were very high and steep. Here, a large body of Indians had stopped under the shelter of the banks, and the older men and the women had dug holes or pits under the banks, in which the people were now hiding. Just as our party reached this point, I was struck in the hip by a bullet and knocked down; but I managed to tumble into one of the holes and lay there among the warriors, women, and children. Here, the troops kept us besieged until darkness came on. They had us surrounded and were firing in on us from both banks and from the bed of the creek above and below us; but we were pretty well sheltered in our holes; and although the fire was very heavy, few of us were hit.

When the soldiers first appeared, Black Kettle and White Antelope, who had both been to Washington in 1863 and were firm friends of the whites would not believe that an attack was about to be made on the camps. These two chiefs stood in front of their lodges and called to their people not to be afraid and not to run away; but while they were still trying to quiet the frightened women and children, the soldiers opened fire on the camps. Black Kettle still stood in front of his lodge, holding the lodgepole with the big American flag tied to its top. White Antelope, when he saw the soldiers shooting into the lodges, made up his mind not to live any longer. He had been telling the Cheyennes for months that the whites were good people and that peace was going to be made; he had induced many people to come to this camp, telling them that the camp was under the protection of Fort Lyon and that no harm could come to them; and now he saw the soldiers shooting the people, and he did not wish to live any longer. He stood in front of his lodge with his arms folded across his breast, singing the death-song:

"Nothing lives long,
Only the earth and the mountains."

while everyone was fleeing from the camp. At length the soldiers shot him and he fell dead in front of his lodge. Black Kettle stood in his camp until nearly everyone had gone, then took his wife and started up the creek after the rest of the people. Soldiers kept firing at them, and after a while Black Kettle's wife fell. He turned and looked at her, but she seemed to be dead; so he left her and ran on up the creek until he came to the place where the people were hiding in the pits. After the soldiers had withdrawn about dark, the chief went back down the creek to find the body of his wife, but he found her still alive, although wounded in many places. He took her on his back and carried her up the creek to where the rest of us were waiting. Her story was that after she had fallen and her husband had left her, soldiers rode up and shot her several times as she lay helpless on the sand. At the peace council in 1865, her story was told to the peace commissioners and they counted her wounds, nine in all, I believe.

Most of us who were hiding in the pits had been wounded before we could reach this shelter; and there we lay all that bitter cold day from early in the morning until almost dark, with the soldiers all around us, keeping up a heavy fire most of the time. If they had been real soldiers they would have come in and finished it; but they were nothing but a mob, and anxious as they were to kill they did not dare to come in close. They finally withdrew, about five o'clock, and went back to spend the night in the Indian camp. As they retired down the creek, they killed all the wounded they could find and scalped and mutilated the dead bodies which lay strewn all along the two miles of dry creek bed. Even this butchers' work did not satisfy them; and when they reached the Indian camp, they shot Jack Smith and wished to shoot my younger brother Charlie. These two young men (they were half Cheyenne and half white) had remained in the camp when the Indians fled and had later surrendered to some soldiers they knew. Old John Smith was trading in our camp and remained with his son when the Indians fled. When the whites came back to camp after dark, an officer came and told old John that some of the Denver roughs (100-day volunteers) were talking of shooting his son Jack. Smith induced some officers of the Fort Lyon garrison who were his friends to go to Colonel Chivington and ask him to save Jack, but Chivington in the morning had given orders to take no prisoners, so when these officers came in and asked him to prevent the shooting of young Smith, he told them roughly that he had given his orders and had nothing further to say. Old John was sitting in his lodge, waiting for the return of the officers, when shots rang out close by. Then men came into the lodge and told him that his son was dead. The Denver men then wished to shoot my brother also, but Charlie had fallen into the hands of some

Painting of the Battle of Washita (River)—Sand Creek Massacre by Frederic Remington.

New Mexican scouts belonging to the Fort Lyon garrison men who knew all of us Bent boys and who had known our father for years so when the Denver crowd wished to take Charlie out and shoot him, as they had just shot young Jack Smith, the New Mexican men ordered them off and threatened to shoot any of them who attempted to touch Charlie.

After the troops withdrew to the Indian camp, we lay in our pits for some time, suspecting that the whites might come back; but they did not return, and at last we crawled out of the holes, stiff and sore, with the blood frozen on our wounded and half-naked bodies. Slowly and painfully, we retreated up the creek, men, women and children dragging themselves along, the women and children wailing and crying, but not too loudly, for they feared the return of the whites. After a long time, we met Indians with horses. These men had gone out before dawn to see that the herds had not strayed; and reaching the herds just before the troops came up, they succeeded in getting away with some of the animals before the soldiers surrounded the rest of the herds. On seeing the soldiers coming, these Indians had thrown themselves upon the first ponies they could catch and had then rounded up as many more as they could and driven them up the creek. They went away up the creek and waited until the firing stopped after dark, then came cautiously back to see what they could learn, and this was how they happened to find us. They helped the wounded upon the ponies. One of my cousins was with them and gave me a pony to ride, but my hip was so stiff and sore that I could not mount and had to be lifted on the animal's back. After meeting these young men with the horses, our party went on up the creek a few miles farther, moving very slowly, and then, as the wounded and the women and children could go no farther, we all bivouacked on the open plain for the night.

That was the worst night I ever went through. There we were on that bleak frozen plain, without any shelter whatever and not a stick of wood to build a fire with. Most of us were wounded and half-naked; even those who had had time to dress when the attack came had lost their buffalo robes and blankets during the fight. The men and women who were not wounded worked all through the night trying to keep the children and the wounded from freezing to death. They gathered grass by the handful, feeding little fires around which the wounded and the children lay; they stripped off their own blankets and clothes to keep us warm, and some of the wounded who could not be provided with other covering were buried under piles of grass which their friends gathered, a handful at a time, and heaped up over them. That night will never be forgotten as long as any of us who went through it are alive. It was bitter cold, the wind had a full sweep over the ground on which we lay, and in spite of everything that was done, no one could keep warm. All through the night, the Indians kept hallooing to attract the attention of those who had escaped from the village to the open plain and were wandering about in the dark, lost and freezing. Many who had lost wives, husbands, children, or friends, went back down the creek and crept over the battleground among the naked and mutilated bodies of the dead. Few were found alive, for the soldiers had done their work thoroughly; but now and then during that endless night, some man or woman would stagger in among us, carrying some wounded person on their back.

At last we could stand the cold no longer, and although it was still pitch-dark and long before dawn, we left that place and started east, toward the headwaters of the Smoky Hill, where we knew Indians were encamped. It was 50 miles to the nearest of these camps, and we could go but slowly, most of the people, and even many of the wounded, being still on foot. Then we had to dread the pursuit which would probably begin as soon as the coming of day made it possible for the troops to follow our trail, and we knew that if the troops overtook us on the open plain, barely a handful of us could hope to escape. But luckily for us a few of the men who had escaped on their horses at the beginning of the attack had made straight for the nearest camps on the Smoky Hill; and riding all day, they had reached these camps about dark with the news that our camp had been surprised by 1,000 white men. Large numbers of men had at once set out from these camps on the Smoky Hill, bringing led ponies with them loaded with blankets, buffalo robes, and food; and soon after day broke, these people began to join us in little groups and parties. Before long, we were all mounted, clothed, and fed, and then we moved at a better pace and with revived hope; but it was late in the day when we reached the first camp on the Smoky. As we rode into that camp, there was a terrible scene. Everyone was crying, even the warriors and the women and children screaming and wailing. Nearly everyone present had lost some relations or friends, and many of them in their grief were gashing themselves with their knives until the blood flowed in streams.

The Sand Creek Massacre was the worst blow ever struck at any tribe in the whole plains region, and this blow fell upon friendly Indians. The hostiles were camped on the Smoky Hill and Republican, far away from the troops, and our camp would never have been where it was if the chiefs and people had not been assured that peace would probably be made soon and that in the meantime they need fear no attack. From a third to a half of these friendly Indians were butchered in the attack, and of those who escaped very few were without wounds. The women and children were by far the heaviest sufferers.

Colorado Without Mountains

Harold Hamil

WHEN MEMBERS OF our class of 1924 at Sterling High School got together for our 50th anniversary reunion, we could claim at least one distinction. Ours was the only class ever graduated at Sterling with hooded members of the Ku Klux Klan joining in the services.

There were many, of course, who looked upon the Klan as an intruder rather than a participant, but the drama and tension of the occasion could not be denied. This was one aspect of our commencement weekend that everyone seemed to recall in detail after more than 50 years.

Those who have dug into the history of the Klan say that 1924 was the year of its largest national membership. The surge of enthusiasm for the organization was apparent around Sterling, and some of the talk in school corridors had suggested that fathers of some members of the class of 1924 were active in the local unit.

There was a baccalaureate service at the First Presbyterian Church the Sunday evening before the actual graduation program at the high school. We seniors, some 80 of us, sat in our caps and gowns in the front pews.

At a point about midway in the service, there was a commotion at the rear door and concerned looks on the faces of members of the choir who looked out on all that went on.

The presiding pastor, somewhat awkwardly and uneasily, tried to carry on as though nothing was happening. Glancing over our shoulders, we ultimately caught the outlines of peaked hoods in the rear doorway.

I could never believe that the appearance of these Klansmen, about eight in number, was a complete surprise to everyone, but it was obvious that nobody had tipped off the ushers. They had taken a firm position against any interruption of the program and therefore the commotion. Finally, though, somebody passed the word along, and the intruders marched in single file to the front of the church and lined up before the pulpit.

The minister asked if any member of the group had something to say, and one came forward and handed him an envelope. There was a mumbled exchange, and if the minister had been taken by surprise, what he heard seemed to answer all his questions. The visitors marched silently to the exit; the minister put the service back on track, and all of us relaxed.

While the Klan engaged in all kinds of double-talk as to its ideals and purposes, there was a general presumption that its prime concern was to press the interests of white Protestants over those of Negroes, Catholics, and Jews. (I was to learn, many years later, that some of the Protestant German-Russians in Logan County felt the Klan was antagonistic toward them.) There were no Negroes in our class and, to the best of my recollections, no Jews. But there were a half-dozen or more Catholics, and I could detect an obvious uneasiness on the part of a Catholic girl in my pew. If the truth were known, though, the uneasiness was shared by most everyone. This was our first view of the Klan in action. One could not help pondering the ability of such performers to strike terror into the hearts of persons who knew they were on the "enemies" list.

There was much talk around school the next day about our unexpected guests. The minister, as I recall, made known that the envelope he received contained a cash gift and a note of appreciation of his services to the community. Classmates were calling off the names of persons who might have been behind the hoods. One was of a very large man, and one was of a fellow with a missing finger.

Most members of the faculty indicated disgust with what had happened. But one teacher, T.L. Girault, was openly scornful. He denounced the Klan and all it stood for. At the moment, he seemed to make more of the incident than it deserved. Some of us, I am sure, were inclined to think it would have been a pretty dull evening if the Klan hadn't appeared.

About six weeks later, a black touring car drove into the hayfield where Father, two hired men, and I were working. Four men, all in white shirts, got out and went to serious conversation with Father. They stayed for about an hour. On the way to the house that evening, nothing was said about the visitors. But when Father started off to care for the hogs—a chore he reserved for himself—he asked me to join him. This was unprecedented, almost, because I was supposed to milk cows.

As we dipped half-bushel buckets of corn from the granary and spread it on the concrete feeding floor, Father explained that his afternoon visitors had come from Sterling to suggest he be a candidate for the Republican nomination for sheriff. They had known, perhaps, of his plans to leave the ranch and of his hankering to get back into county politics after one term as county commissioner. They had brought assurance of powerful support for his candidacy. But he would have to agree to join the Klan. And the question he finally put to me, in tones that carried a surprising hint my decision might be binding, was whether he should accept the offer and the conditions.

I surprised myself with the promptness of my reply. I told him I was opposed to the Klan and what it stood for in words that I had not repeated since hearing them from T.L. Girault and other teachers following our baccalaureate service. All of a sudden, I realized that I was subscribing fully to opinions I had heard but hadn't taken the time to consolidate into my own thinking.

Whether Father was merely asking me to confirm a decision he already had made is a secret he took to his grave. He didn't run for sheriff.

I went off to college in the fall and was not around to witness other activities of the Klan in Logan County, but I did observe a big Klan rally at Hastings, Nebraska, that fall. Delegates came from a large section of Nebraska and staged a parade that stretched for at least a mile. There were hooded men on horseback and floats depicting little red schoolhouses and other symbols of solid American tradition.

Those who have traced the history of the Klan say that what we witnessed in 1924 was the high-water mark of the organization. It remained but never enjoyed the widespread popularity that it enjoyed for a brief period in the mid-1920s.

T.L. Girault, who taught for many years in the Denver schools before retiring, came to Sterling for our 1974 reunion, and I couldn't help telling him about how his forthrightness helped me make up my mind on what seemed to be a pretty important issue back there in 1924.

Summer Etchings in Colorado

Eliza Greatorex

IN THE GAY PARTY ASSEMBLED for an excursion to Pueblo and the coal mines, I had good fortune to be included. The feelings of our entire company are expressed in a letter of warm and sincere thanks to General Palmer and the officers of the Central Colorado Improvement Company, for their many kindnesses and courtesies.

On that trip, I first comprehended the luxury of travelling by a "special" train, resting in an easy chair, listening to stories of long ago in these regions, when railroads were unthought of—rushing at a speed of 40 miles an hour but stopping at will wherever scenery or incident invited our stay. This was the very poetry of motion, or, at least, the refinement of steam traveling. As we approached Pueblo, a great change was apparent in the character of the scenery. Pike's Peak was grander, the Spanish Peaks and Cheyenne Range more lofty and varied in outline, the Arkansas more rapid and winding, with the added beauty of tall, graceful cottonwood trees rising to a great height on its banks.

Pueblo, now a bright and growing business town, is new and fresh in almost all its streets and buildings. A few of the low *adobe* houses, which were once the only dwellings of the town, still remain at the entrance; but the new city has taken its station on a high, breezy bluff, one of the loveliest possible sites. From Pueblo to the coal mines is the wildest sort of country I have yet seen. The climate in winter is very fine, and there is a large hotel projected close to a spring of iron and soda where invalids may pass the whole season in comfort of sky and sunshine, both of which we nearly forget as we enter the mines. By the twinkling lamps carried in the miners' hats, we see and wonder at all the dark processes of mining. A friend wrote for me some of the salient points in the history of these mines and of the miners; and, only that my space is too small, I would gladly transcribe his letter. The men whose lives are spent in these sad underground shades can have but gloomy and cheerless lives. He says: "The work is very hard. Often the 'cuts' are made by the miner while lying on his side, the pick used by working it over the shoulder, the hole drilled, filled with powder, and blasted, the daring workman still in this uncomfortable position. Some compensation they do manage to find in the spending of their hardly-earned wages." Beef, mutton, vegetables, and pudding, cloth, muslin, silk, and shoes are their ideas of "comfort of life!" As we emerged from the black pit into the day, made dazzling by contrast, a huge miner, who had been our guide and general informant, calls out to "Dave," to know if the new beer had come. Now, "Dave" has been pointed out to us as *the* character of the place—I should say, Dave and his mule, as the two are but parts of one character, whole and indivisible. The *Dave* part is a hunchback, the mule a marvel of strong thews and long ears. Dave's voice is as the herald and proclaimer of all mining movements, heard long before even the ray of his lamp or the tip of the mule's ear reach the mouth of the mine. They bring out the coal and, blessed compensation, bring in the beer. "Who will you have to bring in this beer?" calls General Palmer down the shaft. A great shout from mingled voices answers, "Dave!" and Dave responds lustily, and the mule rattles his bell gayly, as both disappear with the refreshing can. We turn away from these living tombs with a little glow of comfort in our minds, as we know that there is still even that compensation left to the hard lives passed in the Pueblo Coal Mines.

1874 photo of Elanore Gretorex

King Coal

Upton Sinclair

"THERE WAS ANOTHER WAY, Old Mike explained, in which the miner was at the mercy of others; this was the matter of stealing cars. Each miner had brass checks with his number on them, and when he sent up a loaded car, he hung one of these checks on a hook inside. In the course of the long journey to the tipple, some one would change the check, and the car was gone. In some mines, the number was put on the car with chalk; and how easy it was for some one to rub it out and change it! It appeared to Hal that it would have been a simple matter to put a number padlock on the car, instead of a check; but such an equipment would have cost the company one or two hundred dollars, he was told, and so the stealing went on year after year.

"You think it's the bosses steal these cars?" asked Hal.

"Sometimes bosses, sometimes bosses' friends—sometimes company himself steal them from miners." In North Valley it was the company, the old Slovak insisted. It was no use sending up more than six cars in one day, he declared; you could never get credit for more than six. Nor was it worth while loading more than a ton on a car; they did not really weigh the cars, the boss just ran them quickly over the scales, and had orders not to go above a certain average. Mike told of an Italian who had loaded a car for a test, so high that he could barely pass it under the roof of the entry, and went up on the tipple and saw it weighed himself, and it was sixty-five hundred pounds. They gave him thirty-five hundred, and when he started to fight, they arrested him. Mike had not seen him arrested, but when he had come out of the mine, the man was gone, and nobody ever saw him again. After that they put a door onto the weigh-room, so that no one could see the scales.

The more Hal listened to the men and reflected upon these things, the more he came to see that the miner was a contractor who had no opportunity to determine the size of the contract before he took it on, nor afterwards to determine how much work he had done. More than that, he was obliged to use supplies, over the price and measurements of which he had no control. He used powder, and would find himself docked at the end of the month for a certain quantity, and if the quantity was wrong, he would have no redress. He was charged a certain sum for "blacksmithing —the keeping of his tools in order; and he would find a dollar or two deducted from his account each month, even though he had not been near the blacksmith shop.

Let any business-man in the world consider the proposition, thought Hal, and say if he would take a contract upon such terms! Would a man undertake to build a dam, for example, with no chance to measure the ground in advance, nor any way of determining how many cubic yards of concrete he had to put in? Would a grocer sell to a customer who proposed to come into the store and do his own weighing and meantime locking the grocer outside? Merely to put such questions was to show the preposterousness of the thing; yet in this district were fifteen thousand men working on precisely such terms.

Under the state law, the miner had a right to demand a check-weighman to protect his interest at the scales, paying this check-weighman's wages out of his own earnings. Whenever there was any public criticism about conditions in the coal mines, this law would be triumphantly cited by the operators; and one had to have actual experience in order to realise what a bitter mockery this was to the miner.

In the dining-room Hal sat next to a fair-haired Swedish giant named Johansson, who loaded timbers ten hours a day. This fellow was one who indulged in the luxury of speaking his mind, because he had youth and huge muscles, and no family to tie him down. He was what is called a "blanket-stiff," wandering from mine to harvest-field and from harvest-field to lumber-camp. Some one broached the subject of check-weighmen to him, and the whole table heard his scornful laugh. Let any man ask for a check-weighman!

"You mean they would fire him?" asked Hal.

"Maybe!" was the answer. "Maybe they make him fire himself."

"How do you mean?"

"They make his life one damn misery till he go."

So it was with check-weighman—as with scrip, and with company stores, and with all the provisions of the law to protect the miner against accidents. You might demand your legal rights, but if you did, it was a matter of the boss's temper. He might make your life one damn misery till you went of your own accord. Or you might get a string of curses and an order, "Down the canyon!"—and likely as not the toe of a boot in your trouser-seat, or the muzzle of a revolver under your nose."

Buried Unsung

Zeese Papanikolas

THEY LIVED ABOVE THE town's one drugstore in rented rooms. The rooms were almost empty. A few pots and pans, thin beds, and a few Greek newspapers. It was no poverty. It was simply a kind of austerity born out of a lifetime of habit. And what would they spend money for anyway, these two old men, in Oak Creek, Colorado? For these were men who pressed very lightly on the world. Their rooms had a look of being somehow improvised, temporary, as if at any minute one of these old bachelors could stuff a few shirts into a suitcase and disappear down the canyon with no mark of his passing left behind. Barba John Tsanakatsis, with his round peasant face, his sporty cap and marvelous laugh, went to Las Vegas toward the end of October to get warm. Old Mr. Papadakis stuck it out through the winter, a few miles up the road from the ski resort with its bars and restaurants and new plywood chalets for those comfortable enough to play with the season. In Mr. Papadakis' room there was one obvious center. It was not the bed or the table or the gas stove, but a steamer trunk. He opened it for me, showed me its elaborate compartments, its pressers for trousers and suits. He had bought it in the '30s for his first trip back to Crete.

"He used to have some new suitcases," Barba John said, winking slyly, "for the airplane. The best."

"I give them up," Mr. Papadakis said. "They were light, you know. Special, made for the airplane. There was something about them. I just didn't like them." The few possessions in Barba John's room had been tumbled about in a genial disorder. Mr. Papadakis kept his room immaculate. He was a few years older than Barba John, a slender man with a white mustache. He held himself straight. When he spoke English, the words had a tart Cretan twang to them. That afternoon Barba John and I had driven down the canyon looking for him. We found him a few miles out of town where the remains of the mines stuck out of the brush and scrub oak, a rusted coal car, the stump of the tipple, here and there the black smudge of a dump. He was gathering chokecherries to make into wine. He was 85 years old.

We sat in his room drinking the sweet homemade wine, and he was telling me what he knew of the man I was searching for.

"... There was not too many of us speaking very much then. Louis, he didn't speak very much neither, but good enough to get by. But there was not too many to take the speakers' stand and speak and all that. Louis, he done pretty well. He got the appointment around Denver. I don't know who appointed him."

"Did you know him before?"

"I seen him, but I didn't know too much about him. A young, nice, pretty man, that's all I can say."

"So anyway, he was sort of your spokesman?"

"Yes. More like he give us the dope and mix with the higher-ups, you know, and talk things over."

Barba John laughed and pushed back his cap and adjusted his thick glasses to look at the photograph I handed him. "Yes, yes, yes," Barba John said with a devilish chuckle, "here he is. Sure I knew Louis. Had a little coffeehouse in Denver."

"That was on Market Street?"

"Yeah, Market Street."

"What kind of place was it?"

"A coffeehouse. Like them coffeehouses. Maybe you seen them coffeehouses? Have you? Chairs, you know, couple of tables. Serve coffee, little *ouzo*, stuff like that. ..."

"No *ouzo*," Mr. Papadakis interrupted. It was important to him for things to be accurate.

"Sometimes," Barba John went on, "sometimes they have a dance, you know. Let them play the *laouto*. ... Have that two, three times. ..."

Five men drinking coffee.

Out of the Depths

Barron B. Beshoar

MORE THAN FOUR DECADES have passed since the memorable Colorado coal strike of 1913 to 1914, an industrial struggle that left an indelible imprint on the civilized world. Labor and capital have come to grips on many occasions since those historic years, but, except for isolated instances which were little more than repeat performances, the differences have not been so broad in scope or so far reaching in their consequences. It was on the field of Ludlow, where the blood of strikers, their women and children, was shed by a subsidized soldiery, that labor established its right to share in such basic American principles as those of religious and political liberty, free speech and free assembly, and economic freedom. The 1913-1914 strike was not a purely Colorado matter, as the state was merely the testing ground for two divergent principles of life. On the one hand, firmly entrenched and in full power and strength, were those who held to the theory that all benefits properly trickle down from above, and on the other were those who devotedly maintained the democratic proposition that men and women who toil with their backs and hands are entitled to share in the fruits of their productive labor.

Colorado was the testing ground for several reasons. The great corporations of the East seized control of the natural resources of the state during its early, formative years. They invested their surpluses in the isolated holdings as business conditions warranted and they sought through crafty political arts a perpetuation of their absentee landlordism without regard for the desires of the people or the welfare of their own employees. That their policies and methods, which reached such full flower in Colorado, were both unbusinesslike and unmoral, has been demonstrated time and again in the years since 1913. It is a sad commentary on human intelligence and decency to record that it took a bloody war to expose the errors in all of their hideous implications and institute corrective measures, just as it required a war between the states to settle the slavery and federal questions.

Any story of the 1913-1914 strike must, of necessity, be the story of John R. Lawson who was the outstanding labor leader of the day. There were others who outranked him in the United Mine Workers of America but none who equaled him in strike leadership or in the love and respect of the Colorado coal miners. He stood for the best in the union movement and has remained through the years a personification of honest, intelligent, and capable leadership. While many of his colleagues, who held positions of trust and importance, sold themselves to the enemy or sought glory and personal power at the expense of the miners, John

Lawson remained faithful to an ideal and devoted himself exclusively to the welfare of those who placed themselves under his care. His story and that of the strike are inseparably interwoven, so much so that the one cannot be told without the other. Much credit is due the United Mine Workers of America as an organization for the work it did in Colorado in 1913-1914. It spent much treasure, effort and blood in a glorious crusade, but John Lawson remains an outstanding figure. To him, both as a representative of the United Mine Workers and as an individual, the coal miners and labor generally owe the greatest measure of gratitude, respect, and honor.

The record shows that the 1913-1914 strike was lost by the United Mine Workers, but in reality it was won. It is true that the great strike was brought to an end by the organization before its objectives were achieved; but public opinion, which had been aroused as never before or since in an industrial dispute, battered down the gates of the coal operators and in the end the miners and citizens of Colorado were the victors. It is fair to say that the citizens of the state shared in the victory because through it they were freed from a political domination that was as close to absolutism as anything ever attempted in a nation founded on such documents as the U.S. Constitution and the Bill of Rights.

If the account seems biased in favor of labor in general and the coal miners in particular, the reader is asked to remember that it deals with a period in our industrial history when the gun, the club, and the fist were often the sole methods of management-labor communication. Certainly, the Colorado record of that decade is clear and sustaining insofar as labor is concerned; it has been substantiated, not once but many times, by courts of record and the earnest findings of impartial, honest investigators.

The material contained herein is not fiction. It is factual. Perhaps, at times, coal operators and their henchmen will appear too devilish and the coal miners too angelic. Obviously neither side had a monopoly on honesty and morals; and just as obviously, each camp had its share of dishonesty and greed, of lust and envy. However, the opposing principles that motivated the coal operators and the miners give an implication to the story of 1913-1914 that is inescapable in any honest presentation.

Many of the coal operators believed their system was fundamental and necessary. They were sincere in their fear that union organization would spell the end of business enterprise and industrial freedom of the type cherished by boards of directors. Their psychology was not unlike that of the ruling class of a monarchy or a kingdom of a century ago. Most of them had appropriated or inherited their wealth and believed it well within the realm of possibility for any deserving man to do likewise. It is charitable to believe that few of those who sat on the boards of the powerful coal corporations had any understanding of the lives and problems of their workers.

If the mine guards and detectives, the mercenaries who served as the Gestapo of the coal districts, appear to be scoundrels who sold themselves and their fellowmen for a few corporation dollars, the author will consider them adequately presented.

In preparing this volume [Beshoar's], the author had the generous assistance of many men and women who lived through the hectic days of 1913-1914 and knew their events at first hand. I am forever indebted to my own father, Dr. Ben B. Beshoar, who served as the United Mine Workers physician in Trinidad and Las Animas County during those turbulent and dangerous days. I have a vague, small-boy recollection of riding in the back seat of a touring car while he drove, without lights, up the river at night to see a sick miner. And above Trinidad, the night sky was filled with the white beams of search lights sweeping restlessly back and forth, seeking out striking miners, seeking out the young doctor at the wheel of his Overland car, seeking out the little boy in the back seat, the little boy who knew from his father's face that those hard lights were to be feared but was completely unaware that behind those luminous eyes were Rockefeller machine guns that could and would spit death if the lights caught our movement on the bumpy road. And I have other recollections, some dim, some sharp, of cavalrymen with gleaming sabres herding the people along Main and Commercial streets in Trinidad. Of militiamen searching our house for guns and dumping the contents of bureau drawers on the floor while my mother watched them with loathing and contempt. Of miners with red handkerchiefs around their necks and rifles in their hands who hailed my father with jovial but foreign-sounding cries that sounded like "Hello, Doc Bee-shoo."

In another scene, way back in the chambers of memory, I see my Uncle John standing in the laboratory of his dental office in Trinidad, patiently instructing an Austrian miner who spoke little English, in how to shoot out a CF&I searchlight with a beautiful hammerless Savage rifle he was graciously lending to the cause.

And I have an immeasurable debt to John R. Lawson for his assistance, though I must say his innate sense of modesty made him a reluctant and oftentimes unwilling witness to the events of 1913-1914 where John Lawson was directly concerned. One of the things in life that I cherish most was a close personal relationship with John and Olive Lawson. The Lawsons exemplified such virtues as love of freedom, love of fellow man, love of decency, and love for one another. I think of them always with affection and admiration and respect. The world could well use many more Lawsons.

Amache
The Story of Japanese Internment in Colorado During World War II

Robert Harvey

POSSIBLY THE MOST POPULAR program at Amache was the high school intramural sports program. Evacuees followed their teams with intensity.

And these teams were good. Playing other high school teams from Lamar, Denver, La Junta, and Las Animas, Amache squads always ended their seasons at or near the top. Playing teams from less-populated areas provided an edge for Amache's teams. An edge that rankled some.

Throughout the 1944 football season, Wiley's high school football team had fought hard for an undefeated season. But Amache stood in its way. Although a loss to Amache would not keep Wiley from a playoff bid, it would certainly ruin a perfect season. Some said Wiley could outmatch Amache anytime. Many weren't so sure. After all, Amache was a much bigger community with a larger pool to draw talent from. So, by early November—with only Amache remaining as a serious threat—Wiley prepared to meet the camp's team in a classic matchup between the two powerhouse football teams.

Amache's team had anticipated the game for weeks. Players had spent hours of practice for this matchup, for the center's team had found itself with a near perfect season. A knock-off of Wiley might even lead Amache to be declared the unofficial southeastern champs. To this end, coaches endlessly drilled players. Critical plays were honed to perfection. As game day approached, Amache players itched for the chance to show their stuff.

But only days before the two powerhouses were to meet, a handful of parents from Wiley's team filed formal protests. They refused to allow their boys to play against "Jap" boys at the Wiley football stadium. America was at war with Japan, they reasoned. Such activities would not be in standing with patriotism. The parents' protest brought an end to the game, and Wiley's football team would never face Amache in what remained of the 1944 season.

The effects of this cancellation were deep. In a letter to Superintendent of Schools Dr. Lloyd A. Garrison, one young player wrote:

> "We really thought a lot about the game and practiced a pretty lot for it; but rather then feeling disappointed over the waste of our many practices, I am rather more disappointed in the five

> boys' parents who would not permit their sons to play against us because we were Japanese Americans. I and many others interested sports fans, who were eagerly waiting for that game, took this pretty hard and now hold a grudge against the parents of those boys, which I think is only natural.
>
> "I remember last year I, with the varsity basketball team, went to Wiley to play, and we enjoyed it very much. The hospitality and sportsmanship they showed us does not match the reason for Wiley's cancellation of the game. I think Wiley would like it very much to play us and haven't any hard feelings toward us because we are of Japanese parentage. It's a pity to think what a little bunch can do to disappoint over 1,000 spirited students because of race and color.
>
> "Victory over Wiley would have put Amache in a pretty high place in the field of sports, and we could have been recognized as the unofficial Southeastern Champs. I hope someday we or the next year squad can have better luck and chance."

Because of the protest, Amache teams would be forced to play the remainder of the football season as well as the entirety of the basketball season at home.

Did the parents of the five boys protest to keep Wiley's team undefeated? No one can really be sure. But, to the evacuees of Amache, the incident proved once again that their worth was based on ethnic background, not accomplishment. The incident also reminded evacuees just how tenuous their place in American society really was. Plans were made and opportunities were sought, but the ultimate decision to do anything was still influenced heavily by an Anglo-American public.

Granada Relocation Center, Amache, Colorado. December 1941.

Children of the Storm

Ariana Harner and Clark Secrest

ONE DAY: THURSDAY, MARCH 26, 1931. Three places: the blizzard-swept plains of extreme southeastern Colorado, the palatial mansion of Frederick G. Bonfils in Denver, and the USS Arizona steaming north from Puerto Rico.

Onboard the Arizona, President Herbert Hoover enjoyed the day sailing through what *The New York Times* described as "slightly rolling turquoise seas in warm brilliant sunshine." After visits to the Virgin Islands and Puerto Rico, he was returning home to face choppy economic waters, which he tried to calm by preaching "mobilized voluntary action" as a cure-all for the Great Depression. Such rhetoric failed to impress millions of unemployed Americans who believed that the president was at best inept, at worst inhumane. His advisers urged him to demonstrate his humanity and searched for opportunities that would enable him to do so. Hoover listened because he wanted a second term.

The Denver Post for March 26, 1931, reported frigid temperatures in the city and even harsher weather outside of it. Still, the *Post* proclaimed " 'Tis a Privilege to Live in Colorado." Frederick Bonfils, the paper's publisher, knew that his readers liked good news, heartthrob headlines, and sensationalism. On March 26 he gave them doses of each: a gangland story, reports of men getting drunk on radiator alcohol, the saga of a sleepwalking boy, and the marital woes of a would-be beauty queen. That he lived in one of the city's grandest mansions, that he was among Denver's richest men, and that his paper sold more than 300,000 copies each Sunday was not enough. Good stories made money. Bonfils wanted more.

On the eastern plains of Colorado that Thursday, twenty children—ordinary children who had likely never been in a mansion or seen a great ship except perhaps at a movie—struggled to keep from freezing to death in a stranded makeshift wooden school bus. Their lives and deaths (such good human stories) were soon caught in the webs spun by Frederick Bonfils and Herbert Hoover, who exploited the calamity without apparent concern for compounding it.

In *Children of the Storm: The True Story of the Pleasant Hill School Bus Tragedy*, Ariana Harner and Clark Secrest skillfully recount the Pleasant Hill disaster and its aftermath. Many details of the initial event have been told or mistold before. The scope of what happened afterward has not been related until now. Bonfils died in 1933, Hoover in 1964. Some of the survivors of the Pleasant Hill bus tragedy are still alive. Perhaps the truths brought out in *Children of the Storm* will help both the living and the dead rest in peace.

—Stephen J. Leonard

Metropolitan State College, Denver, October 1999

* * *

The First Day

On the flatness of Pleasant Hill, there were twenty children marooned in a drafty school bus with wet cardboard window replacements that were now flapping at the edges, and temperatures that would continue to drop for another twenty-four hours.

After his fruitless attempt to restart the engine, Carl Miller recognized the peril. He summoned Bryan Untiedt, the oldest boy, to help him drain the radiator so it would not freeze. When they returned, they were grateful that although the interior was a little warmer than the outdoors, most of the wind's violence was kept outside. The cold seeped in through the boards and the gaps in the wall joints.

Perhaps a fire would keep everyone warm for a while. Trying to be cheerful, Miller rallied the children to help him gather fuel from within the bus. He retrieved the milk can lid from the bus's running board and placed it in the aisle between the facing wood benches. Children handed him pages from their notebooks and textbooks. Someone pried shards of wood from the driver's splintered seat.

Miller lighted the wood and paper, but the flame was small and the paper, taken from small damp hands, would not burn. Acrid smoke billowed up and filled the bus interior, and the youngsters coughed. They reopened the driver-side window to let the smoke out. And besides, how large of a fire could a can lid contain? Certainly not enough to make a difference in the growing cold.

Miller knew he must keep the children moving to fight off sleep. He widened the aisle one foot by shoving the benches flush against the walls. He told the young people to hop up and down, wave their arms, and mock fight each other. They had set out from the school two hours earlier, surely the storm would ease up before supper. The younger children, who in their naivete still believed it all just an adventure, happily followed his instructions.

The snow swirled ruthlessly around the lonely bus-a wooden box on wheels, a mere speck in the blizzard. No other human beings knew it was there, lost and motionless. Untold millions of tiny particles of frozen water held it captive—life-sustaining water, sometimes scant on their semiarid prairie. Now in its solid form, that same sustenance threatened the lives of the twenty-one people.

The cardboard pieces covering the two broken rear-side windows were becoming increasingly flimsy from the relentless wind and wet snow. Suddenly the wind tore one from the window frame and flung it onto the wooden floor. The gale blasted through the opening, and snow hurled inside. Miller shouted over the noise of the wind that the youngsters must *keep moving! Keep moving, no matter what!*

Chief Left Hand
Southern Arapaho

Margaret Coel

JOHN MILTON CHIVINGTON lived 30 years beyond Sand Creek, but the vitriolic congressional reports and public censure dogged his life. In 1867, his son drowned in the South Platte, and Chivington left Denver for San Diego soon afterwards. By 1872, he was back in Ohio managing a newspaper. At one point, he ran for Congress only to have the shadow of Sand Creek cast upon his campaign, forcing him to withdraw. In 1883, he returned to Denver where he became undersheriff and, later, coroner.

Until his death on October 4, 1894, Chivington justified his attack on Sand Creek in speeches to churches, or any other organization that would listen, as the necessary punishment of hostile Indians. He could never understand why the delivery of that punishment had not brought him the glory and promotion similar attacks had brought other military leaders.

Following Chivington's speech to the Eastern Star in Denver, one day, a woman steered him over to a small, dark woman saying, "Mrs. Prowers, do you know Colonel Chivington?" Amache, the daughter of One-Eye, drew herself up with that stately dignity, peculiar to her people, and ignoring the outstretched hand, remarked in perfect English, audible to all in the room, "Know Colonel Chivington? I should. He was my father's murderer."

Depiction of the Sand Creek Massacre by Cheyenne eyewitness and artist Howling Wolf, circa 1875.

Killing for Coal
America's Deadliest Labor War

Thomas G. Andrews

WHEN THE SOUTHERN COLORADO colliers went on strike in 1919, 1921, and 1922 under the United Mine Workers, and again in 1927 in a dispute involving the more radical Industrial Workers of the World, they ensured that the Great Coalfield War would mark not the endpoint of class conflict in the region but rather the most dramatic moment in an ongoing history of struggle that carried on through the New Deal. Memories of the massacre continued to loom large, informing the Rockefeller Plan, inspiring the state to create a board of labor arbitration, and steeling the American labor movement in its fight to secure the rights for which the martyrs of Ludlow had given their lives. In different ways and to varying degrees, each of these uses of the past—enlisting the history of the coalfield war in the politics that corporations, unions, and the state adopted to champion their respective interests—cut the events of April 20, 1914, off both from their deep context of nearly half a century of contentious relationships between workers, capitalists, and the natural world and from the ensuing workers' uprising, which still remains the most violent American labor rebellion of the post-emancipation era!

A service is held outside for victims of the Ludlow Massacre, 1914.

First of State

Robert Greer

AS HE STEPPED OFF the number 15 RTD bus at the intersection of Colfax Avenue and Larimer Street to head for GI Joe's, a Lower Downtown Denver pawnshop, he took a long, deep breath. When the word "home" briefly crossed his mind, he broke into a nervous, uneasy smile, teased a cheroot out of the soft pack he'd taken out of the pocket of his peacoat, and toyed with the miniature cigar. He hadn't been a smoker when he'd left for Vietnam in the fall of 1969. Now he was. Slipping the cheroot loosely between his lips, he thought about the rare antique license plate he'd pilfered from a GI Joe's display case two years earlier and hidden behind three loose wall tiles next to the groutless seam of an electrical box. He'd uncharacteristically acted on this impulse three days before he'd shipped out for Vietnam, and he wondered if his hidden treasure would still be there.

He couldn't be certain that the Larimer Street pawnshop would even still be standing; many Lower Downtown buildings and dozens of neighboring structures for blocks around had been bulldozed as part of Denver's ongoing Skyline Urban Renewal Project while he'd been gone. But if the pawnshop was there, he had the feeling that the valuable porcelain license plate he'd stashed would still be there as well. There to soothe his fragile psyche, to offer him a belated welcome home.

Fire Line
The Summer Battles of the West

Michael Thoele

DEATH IS NOT COMMONPLACE in the summer battles of the West. It comes, sometimes in horrendous numbers—75 firefighters in the Northern Rockies fires of 1910, 25 in the Griffith Park Fire of 1933, 15 in the Rattlesnake Fire of 1953, a dozen in the Loop Fire of 1966, and 14 at South Canyon in 1994. But more often, across thousands of fires large and small, the West loses six or seven firefighters a season. And some years, none at all. Still, risk defines experience. And the knowledge that the ultimate price is sometimes exacted on the fire lines stands always in the background, a defining shadow for those who speak of forest fire as the moral equivalent of war.

South Canyon, near Glenwood Springs, Colorado, was a small fire that exploded in moments to become a huge and historic one. It delivered the largest set of firefighter fatalities in more than 40 years and shook the wildland fire community to its foundations. In a summer in which new fire starts seemed always to exceed available crews and resources, the fire sprang from a lightning bolt that nailed the mountain's flank in early July. Smoldering small and innocuous in oak brush on the steep, dry slope, the fire was monitored but not fought for several days because larger Colorado fires were threatening homes and resources were in short supply. It was still small, about 30 acres, when firefighters got to it on July 5. The following day, when it had swelled to 50 acres, a reinforced contingent of 49 smokejumpers, hotshots, helitack firefighters, and BLM and Forest Service groundpounders took it on.

In late afternoon, with the fire still growing, a cold front with stiff winds blew down on nearby Storm King Mountain. It triggered a blowup that sent flames hooking beneath the firefighters on a steep canyon slope cloaked in brushy Gambel oak. Within moments, a wall of flame 300 feet tall and a quarter-mile wide funneled up the canyon.

Nine members of Oregon's Prineville Hotshots and three Forest Service smokejumpers—from McCall, Idaho, and Missoula, Montana—were caught in the fire's path on a section of steep upslope. For crucial moments, they had not been able to see the approaching fire. Too late, they sensed their predicament. Too late, they found themselves in the race that could not be won. The fire rocketed 1,200 feet in two minutes. It overran them as they sprinted and tried to deploy fire shelters in the final, heartbreakingly steep stretch below the ridgetop. Nearby, the flame front cascaded over an adjoining ridgeline and chased down two firefighters from a BLM helitack crew that was based in Grand Junction, Colorado. Fleeing the fire, they died when a steep rocky chute, 50 feet deep, cut off their escape route.

As always, the tragedy was followed by an investigation. It concluded much like investigations of other fatal and near-fatal wildland fire incidents. The rules of engagement for wildland fire are simple and broad. Organized as ten Standard Fire Orders and 18 "Watch-Out" situations, they are, in effect, a safety code. But veteran firefighters can debate like Torah scholars over precisely how the rules should be applied in given tactical situations. So, like all of the world's fundamental codes, from the Ten Commandments to the Bill of Rights, the simple precepts become the mother of debate, and interpretation goes on forever. The difficulty is in the details. Will this chosen escape route actually work if the fire blows up? In tough, uneven terrain, how many lookouts must you post to be certain that you really know what the fire is doing? And how do you come to terms with risk, how do you strike the balance that resolves the counterpoised yin and yang of Fire Order No. 1, "Fight fire aggressively but safely?"

SECTION X

The Underside

Roughing It

Mark Twain

REALLY AND TRULY, two thirds of the talk of drivers and conductors had been about this man Slade, ever since the day before we reached Julesburg. In order that the Eastern reader may have a clear conception of what a Rocky Mountain desperado is, in his highest state of development, I will reduce all this mass of overland gossip to one straightforward narrative and present it in the following shape:

Slade was born in Illinois, of good parentage. At about 26 years of age, he killed a man in a quarrel and fled the country. At St. Joseph, Missouri, he joined one of the early California-bound emigrant trains and was given the post of trainmaster. One day on the plains, he had an angry dispute with one of his wagon drivers, and both drew their revolvers. But the driver was the quicker artist, and had his weapon cocked first. So Slade said it was a pity to waste life on so small a matter, and proposed that the pistols be thrown on the ground and the quarrel settled by a fistfight. The unsuspecting driver agreed and threw down his pistol—whereupon Slade laughed at his simplicity and shot him dead!

He made his escape and lived a wild life for a while dividing his time between fighting Indians and avoiding an Illinois sheriff, who had been sent to arrest him for his first murder. It is said that in one Indian battle he killed three savages with his own hand and, afterward, cut their ears off and sent them, with his compliments, to the chief of the tribe.

Slade soon gained a name for fearless resolution, and this was sufficient merit to procure for him the important post of overland division-agent at Julesburg, in place of Mr. Jules, removed. For some time previously, the company's horses had been frequently stolen and the coaches delayed, by gangs of outlaws, who were wont to laugh at the idea of any man's having the temerity to resent such outrages. Slade resented them promptly. The outlaws soon found that the new agent was a man who did not fear anything that breathed the breath of life. He made short work of all offenders. The result was that delays ceased, the company's property was left alone, and no matter what happened or who suffered, Slade's coaches went through every time! True, in order to bring about this wholesome change, Slade had to kill several men—some say three, others say four, and others six—but the world was the richer for their loss. The first prominent difficulty he had was with the ex-agent Jules, who bore the reputation of being a reckless and desperate man himself. Jules hated Slade for supplanting him, and a good fair occasion for a fight was all he was waiting for. By and by, Slade dared to employ a man whom Jules had once discharged. Next, Slade seized a team of stage horses which he accused Jules of having driven off and hidden somewhere for his own use. War was declared; and for a day or two, the two men walked warily about the streets, seeking each other—Jules armed with a double-barreled shotgun and Slade with his history-creating revolver. Finally, as Slade stepped into a store, Jules poured the contents of his gun into him from behind the door. Slade was plucky, and Jules got several bad pistol wounds in return. Then both men fell and were carried to their respective lodgings, both swearing that better aim should do deadlier work next time. Both were bedridden a long time, but Jules got on his feet first, and gathering his possessions together, packed them on a couple of mules and fled to the Rocky Mountains to gather strength in safety against the day of reckoning. For many months, he was not seen or heard of and was gradually dropped out of the remembrance of all save Slade himself. But Slade was not the man to forget him. On the contrary, common report said that Slade kept a reward standing for his capture, dead or alive!

After a while, seeing that Slade's energetic administration had restored peace and order to one of the worst divisions of the road, the overland stage company transferred him to the Rocky Ridge division in the Rocky Mountains to see if he could perform a like miracle there. It was the very paradise of outlaws and desperadoes.

* * *

Slade took up his residence sweetly and peacefully in the midst of this hive of horse thieves and assassins; and the very first time one of them aired his insolent swaggerings in his presence, he shot him dead! He began a raid on the outlaws, and in a singularly short space of time, he had completely stopped their depredations on the stage stock, recovered a large number of stolen horses, killed several of the worst desperadoes of the district, and gained such a dread ascendancy over the rest that they respected him, admired him, feared him, obeyed him! He wrought the same marvelous change in the ways of the community that had marked his administration at Overland City.

* * *

In the fullness of time, Slade's myrmidons captured his ancient enemy Jules, whom they found in a well-chosen hiding place in the remote fastnesses of the mountains, gaining a precarious livelihood with his rifle. They brought him to Rocky Ridge, bound hand and foot, and deposited him in the middle of the cattle yard with his back against a post. It is said that the pleasure that lit Slade's face when he heard of it was something fearful to contemplate. He examined his enemy to see that he was securely tied, and then went to bed, content to wait till morning before enjoying the luxury of killing him. Jules spent the night in the cattle yard, and it is a region where warm nights are never known. In the morning, Slade practised on him with his revolver, nipping the flesh here and there, and occasionally chipping off a finger, while Jules begged him to kill him outright and put him out of his misery. Finally, Slade reloaded, and walking up close to his victim, made some characteristic remarks and then dispatched him. The body lay there half a day, nobody venturing to touch it without orders, and then Slade detailed a party and assisted at the burial himself. But he first cut off the dead man's ears and put them in his vest pocket, where he carried them for some time with great satisfaction. That is the story as I have frequently heard it told and seen it in print in California newspapers. It is doubtless correct in all essential particulars.

* * *

In due time, we rattled up to a stage station and sat down to breakfast with a half-savage, half-civilized company of armed and bearded mountaineers, ranchmen and station employees. The most gentlemanly appearing, quiet, and affable officer we had yet found along the road in the Overland Company's service was the person who sat at the head of the table, at my elbow. Never youth stared and shivered as I did when I heard them call him SLADE!

Here was romance, and I sitting face to face with it!—looking upon it, touching it, hobnobbing with it, as it were! Here, right by my side, was the actual ogre who, in fights and brawls and various ways, *had taken the lives of 26 human beings*, or all men lied about him! I suppose I was the proudest stripling that ever traveled to see strange lands and wonderful people.

He was so friendly and so gentle-spoken that I warmed to him in spite of his awful history. It was hardly possible to realize that this pleasant person was the pitiless scourge of the outlaws, the raw-head-and-bloody-bones the nursing mothers of the mountains terrified their children with. And to this day, I can remember nothing remarkable about Slade except that his face was rather broad across the cheekbones, and that the cheekbones were low and the lips peculiarly thin and straight. But that was enough to leave something of an effect upon me, for since then I seldom see a face possessing those characteristics without fancying that the owner of it is a dangerous man.

The coffee ran out. At least it was reduced to one tin-cupful, and Slade was about to take it when he saw that my cup was empty. He politely offered to fill it, but although I wanted it, I politely declined. I was afraid he had not killed anybody that morning and might be needing diversion. But still, with firm politeness, he insisted on filling my cup, and said I had traveled all night and better deserved it than he—and while he talked he placidly poured the fluid to the last drop. I thanked him and drank it, but it gave me no comfort, for I could not feel sure that he would not be sorry, presently, that he had given it away and proceed to kill me to distract his thoughts from the loss. But nothing of the kind occurred. We left him with 26 dead people to account for, and I felt a tranquil satisfaction in the thought that in so judiciously taking care of No. 1 at that breakfast table I had pleasantly escaped being No. 27. Slade came out to the coach and saw us off, first ordering certain rearrangements of the mail bags for our comfort, and then we took leave of him, satisfied that we should hear of him again, some day, and wondering in what connection.

Strip Search

Rex Burns

WAGER STEERED THE WHITE sedan through the tangle of heavy traffic near the state capitol and its oval of dimly lit trees and paths. The area was now known as Sod Circle because of the male prostitutes who strolled these paths to pose and smile at the cruising cars. A monument to Colorful Colorado and the equality and majesty of the laws Wager was sworn to uphold. He turned onto East Colfax, one of the fibers of the city that still held life after dark, and joined the slowly moving cars going down the tunnel of neon and pin spots that made headlights unnecessary. Colfax Avenue was one of the longest sex strips in the country. The west end went seven miles toward the mountains and was dotted with drive-in restaurants, a beautiful scattering of bars, and a line of motels that did business by the hour rather than by the night. It was mostly the teenie's drag strip. The east end was called adult—adult films, adult bookstores, adult arcades, adult live shows. It went across the prairie in the direction of Kansas, leaving Denver around mile eight, and then staggering on as far again before fading into the bug-spattered neon of all-night truck stops and cut-rate gas stations with their scratched and scarred "adult dispensers" on the grime-streaked walls of men's rooms.

At this, the lower end of the strip, a short walk from the capitol, the Cinnamon Club's glowing pink-and-green sign hung out over a sidewalk crowded with night people. The car glided past a Laundromat, half-filled at 1:30 in the morning with customers hunching their shoulders against one another. Across the street, a dark-colored van sat in the unlit parking lot of a small group of closed shops. Around the van, half a dozen men of various ages clustered, wearing the street uniform of the dope world: tattered fatigue jackets, Levi's; hats of several styles; vests. One, standing at the open door, carefully counted out his money while the driver, dancing anxiously at Wager's unmarked car, snapped his fingers.

"You recognize that dude?"

Axton craned his neck. "No. New pusher in town."

Wager tried to see the plates on the van, but they had been bent and smeared with dirt; besides, it was an item for Vice and Narcotics. If they had the time, if they had the manpower, if they had the interest, Vice and Narcotics might set the dealer up for a buy-and-bust. Had Wager and Axton swung around to arrest them for what was plainly a rolling dope market, the money and the dope would disappear into the vehicle, and so would the case—in some kind of constitutional infringement. It wasn't enough anymore to witness a crime in progress; you had to get a warrant to investigate a homicide if it was on private property. There was a lot of talk about some pendulum swinging back toward law enforcement, but Wager hadn't seen it yet.

He pulled into a yellow zone near the corner, half-aware of the cautious eyes slanting their way from the strolling crowd. Their car caused a subtle undertow among the people walking or standing and talking, or alone and watching the action along the street. A teenaged whore in white shorts turned away abruptly to wander toward the other end of the block, her legs awkwardly thin and bony on tall sandals. From the shadowy landing of a stairway leading up to the cheap apartments above the stores, a figure withdrew into the darkness. Wager and Axton locked the car's doors and walked toward the glare of light. Along the curb, eyes slid away from them, and a grimy pair of panhandlers eased out of their path.

The Cinnamon Club advertised its shows as Sweet-n-Spicy. A glass case brightly lit the entry, showing a fly-specked collection of nude girls standing at the top of a stage, smiling regally down at the camera. At the top, near the center, was one who looked like Annette Sheldon; it was hard to tell, though, because the poses and the harsh light made them all look alike, except for the various hairs.

"Let's get some culture," said Max.

The Case of Alferd Packer

Paul H. Gantt

LARRY DOLAN WAS the first man uptown from the courthouse after sentence had been passed. He hurried to his favorite resting place, the saloon.

"Well, boys, it's all over. Packer t'hang!"

Pressed for particulars by the *habitue*s of the saloon, Larry took an appropriate attitude before his motley audience and delivered his version of the sentence:

The Judge says:

"Stan' up, yah voracious man-eating son of a bitch, stand up!"

Then, pointing his trembling fingers at Packer, so raging mad he was, says:

"They was sivin Dimmicrats in Hinsdale County, and ye eat five of them, G-- d-- ye!

"I sintins ye t' be hanged by the neck until ye're dead, dead, DEAD, as a warnin', ag'in reducin' the Dimmycratic population of th' state."

In this distorted form the "judgment" against Packer spread like wildfire over the West and became known all over the United States. It does great injustice to Judge Melville B. Gerry, a man of the highest type, a Southern gentleman of the old school from Macon, Georgia, a jurist of great learning and knowledge of the law.

The Beast

Ben B. Lindsey and Harvey J. O'Higgins

"ONE WINTER AFTERNOON, after I had been listening for days to one of these cases— if I remember rightly, it concerned the ownership of some musty old mortgaged furniture that had been stored in a warehouse and was claimed by the mortgagee on the mortgage and by the warehouseman on a storage lien—the Assistant District Attorney interrupted the proceedings to ask me if I would not dispose of a larceny case that would not take two minutes. I was willing. He brought in a boy, whom I shall call "Tony Costello," and arraigned him before the court. The Clerk read the indictment, a railroad detective gave his testimony; the boy was accused of stealing coal from the tracks, and he had no defence. Frightened and silent, he stood looking from me to the jury, from the jury to the attorney, and from the attorney back to me—wide-eyed and trembling—a helpless infant, trying to follow in our faces what was going on. The case was clear. There was nothing for me to do under the law but to find him guilty and sentence him to a term in the State Reform School. I did so, and prepared to go back to the affair of the second-hand furniture.

There had been sitting at the back of the courtroom an old woman with a shawl on her head, huddled up like a squaw, wooden-faced, and incredibly wrinkled. She waddled down the aisle toward the bench, while papers of commitment were being made out against the boy, and began to talk to the court incoherently, in an excited gabble which I did not understand. I signed to the counsel for the warehouseman to proceed with his case; he rose—and he was greeted with the most soul-piercing scream of agony that I ever heard from a human throat. The old woman stood there, clutching her shawl to her breast, her toothless jaw open, her face as contorted as if she were being torn limb from limb, shrieking horribly. She threw her hands up to her head, grasped her poor, thin gray hair, and pulled it, yelling, with protruding eyes, like a madwoman. When the bailiff of the court caught hold of her to take her from the room, she broke away from him and ran to the wall and beat her head against it, as if she would batter the court house down on us all and bury our injustice under the ruins. They pulled her out into the hall, but through the closed door I could still hear her shrieking—shrieking terribly. I adjourned the court and retreated to my chambers, very much shaken and unnerved; but I still heard her, in the hall, wailing and sobbing, and every now and then screaming as if her heart was being torn out of her.

I did not know what to do. I thought I had no power, under the law, to do anything but what I *had* done. The boy was guilty. The law required that I should sentence him. The mother might scream herself dumb, but I was unable to help her.

She continued to scream. Two reporters, attracted by the uproar, came to ask me if I could not do something for her. I telephoned the District Attorney and asked him whether I could not change my order against the boy—make it a suspended sentence—and let me look into the case myself. He was doubtful—as I was—about my right to do such a thing, but I accepted the responsibility of the act and consented to it. After what seemed an hour to me—during which I could still hear the miserable woman wailing—the boy was returned to her and she was quieted.

Then I took the first step toward the founding of the Juvenile Court of Denver. I got an officer who knew Tony, and I went with him at night to the boy's home in the Italian quarter of North Denver. I need not describe the miserable condition in which I found the Costellos living—in two rooms, in a filthy shack, with the father sick in bed, and the whole family struggling against starvation. I talked with Tony and found him not a criminal, not a bad boy, but merely a boy. He had seen that his father and his mother and the baby were suffering from cold, and he had brought home fuel from the railroad tracks to keep them warm. I gave him a little lecture on the necessity of obeying the laws, and put him "on probation." The mother kissed my hands. The neighbours came in to salute me and to rejoice with the Costellos. I left them. But I carried away with me what must have been something of their view of my court and my absurd handling of their boy; and I began to think over this business of punishing infants as if they were adults and of maiming young lives by trying to make the gristle of their unformed characters carry the weight of our iron laws and heavy penalties.

Going to Go Meet a Man

William M. King

AS THE HOUR DREW closer still, people poured over the adjacent western slope on which were seated singly and in groups hundreds of [persons] who had come out for the show. Not even the trees in the creek or along its banks were spared, as many men and boys nested in their branches for an elevated view of the proceedings. "The branches were black with swarming human beings, and the most prominent personage among them was an old gray-haired man, whose position was the envy of all observers." Throughout the crowd were many blacks, leading one paper to comment that, "The colored people are largely represented, especially the female portion, and many seemed to regard the day and the event as peculiarly their own." The *Rocky Mountain News* wrote of an "old aunty" who said she was a friend of Andy Green, "but who also claimed that he ought to be hanged, and if nobody else would hang him she would herself." Earlier on, she had gone to the jail but was refused permission to see him. After several unsuccessful attempts to get inside "she sat down in the yard and gave herself up to meditation and song." In a low, hushed key, rocking back and forth with her hands locked about her knees, she chanted,

> Brudder, yo' troubles will soon be over.
> Brudder, yo' troubles will soon be over.
> Brudder, yo' troubles will soon be over.
> And I'll meet you bye and bye.

Every so often a loud howl would escape her lips, announcing a rite de passage from disparate periods of black history. And yet, the *News* continued, she had been eager to arrive at the place of execution. Finding a spot near the barrier rope surrounding the gallows, she defended her fief with ferocious tenacity. "A small barefoot boy crossed 'aunty's' path, and she immediately grew wrathy. She descended like a cyclone on the boy, who was badly scared, and proceeded to mop the earth with him. After she had swept up several bushels of sand in her neighborhood and tossed the boy headforemost into the crowd, she sat down complacently and fanned herself." After the boy was rescued, wrote a *Tribune-Republican* reporter at the scene, the crowd quieted again, having been provoked by the incident.

Measured in hours, Andrew Green's last day had actually begun the previous morning, on Monday, 26 July 1886. In a composition written especially for the *News* and sanctioned by the Reverend Gray, of whom the paper said, "Green followed with child-like obedience in his last moments," Green told the public how his final hours had been spent. First, there had been religious services led by the Reverend Gray and others, which had lasted until 12:30 P.M. and then resumed at about 2:30 that afternoon. These continued, interspersed with visits from numerous folk, until almost midnight. A reporter from the *Tribune-Republican* wrote that, "[Green's visitors'] departure seemed not to affect him. His face was wreathed in smiles as he lightly trod the corridor in front of his cell chatting good humoredly with the guards. This manner was continued until daybreak. His last night on earth had been a sleepless one for Andy Green."

Was he mad? Afraid and afraid to show it? A posturing fool? Who can truthfully say what was the state of Green's mind as his last hours passed away? Some indication of what he was feeling might be found in his farewell poem, published in the *Rocky Mountain News* on the day of his death:

My name 'tis Andrew Green, that name I'll never deny,
I left my aged parents in sorrow for to cry;
Little did they think that this should be my doom,
To die upon the gallows, all in my youth and bloom.

My parents nursed me tenderly, as you can plainly see,
And always gave me good advice to shun bad company;
To leave off night walking and shun bad company,
Else state prison or the gallows my doom would surely be.

But bad company and liquor was all of my delight,
All of my companions invited me out at night;
Said if I commit a murder hung I never shall be,
Take warning boys take warning take warning from me.

Me and my companions went out here not very far,
I had to kill the driver in my object to rob the car;
Then I drew the fatal pop and shot him to the heart,
Leaving his dear little wife a protector from her to part.

Afterwards I was compelled to run to make my escape,
But Providence was above me: alas! it was too late!

Now I am a prisoner and this to be my doom—
To die upon the gallows, all in my youth and bloom.

The day of my execution the people will draw nigh,
My father will come from the East to take his last view of me,

He'll weep and fall into my arms and bitterly will cry:
"Dear son, my darling boy, this day you are doomed to die."

Denver

John Dunning

THEY CALL THIS SKID ROW: a 10-block area of lower downtown, where 50-year flophouses that had once been grand hotels stood crumbling in the sun. In newspaper lingo, the Lowers. You can find the same street in Chicago or San Francisco, the liquor stores with plate windows barred against the night—the 50-cent rooms, the pawnshops, and the whorehouses. Here, men fought for the food they ate, for the cheap wine they drank, for the right to sleep out of the snow, on a roach-infested piece of floor that someone else had paid for. They came to Denver under trains, riding the rods in during the warm months of July and August. They camped in tree groves near the railroad yards, leaving behind piles of bottles and bean cans. Some of them left with the first snow. Those who stayed looked for shelter inside the hotels along the Lowers. They camped under dark staircases, sat through the night four-deep in shower stalls, and flopped and slept wherever there was a bare space. There were men who would kill for a bottle of watered whiskey.

It was a savage place, a place where a whore walking alone was fair game, not for her flesh but for what she had in her purse. Where glass is broken in the night and men scuffle in a deadly dance behind a neighborhood bar. Where the answer is quick and the scream is brief, as though life itself isn't worth the effort.

A savage world, the world of the Lowers. The new world of Tom Hastings.

People called him Hasty down here. He sat alone in the dark, the bottle clutched tight in his fist. It was still half-full, the first good whiskey he had had in a week. Between then and now there had been plenty of bad. He knew some of it had been made with denatured alcohol. After a while you reached the point where, just by putting a drop on your tongue, you could tell good whiskey from bad. Little it mattered: You always drank it anyway and hoped tomorrow's would be better. In the old days, he had heard some bad stories of whiskey poisoning and was almost afraid to drink out of any bottle without a label. People said you could go blind. There were newspaper stories of whole parties being poisoned on bootleg gin. Now he drank anything that had even the suggestion of alcohol. After that first greedy gulp, it didn't matter what it was. If it was good whiskey, you appreciated it all the more. If it was bad, as the old saying about sex went—it was still pretty good.

He was staying at the Silvercliff, a ramshackle place in the heart of the Lowers. It was owned by a Japanese-Hawaiian family named Taketa and was managed by the eldest son, Jon. Taketa had been his best source of human-interest material when he'd been covering the Lowers for the *Post* years ago. Taketa ran a store across from the Silvercliff, which had decayed year by year until it was now the city's worst flophouse. The Silvercliff had gotten so bad that even Taketa didn't go there. He had given Tom an old army cot and permission to use one of the rooms in return for Tom collecting his weekly rents. Three dollars a week, payable in advance. He dunned those who paid late; threw out those who didn't pay at all. Once a room was bought and paid for, what they did with it was none of his business. They could sleep 12 to a room for all he cared, as long as somebody was responsible for the rent next Friday. He knew Taketa didn't care either. Two or three times a week, to help keep him on his feet, Taketa gave him a dinner of old bread and thin soup.

Taketa liked to drink too. He was lively as hell for a Jap. Tom had never met an Oriental quite like Taketa. Usually they were such solemn bastards. But Taketa was cheerful and full of interesting talk. He had a fierce loyalty to his family. Talking about it made Tom think of his family. He looked at Taketa's telephone and thought about trying the old man's estate, just to see if they were there. He thought about Golden and the night Paul had gotten Havana on his wireless, and he'd think, *Jesus, I really should call, let the kids at least know their old man's alive.* He would do that. Pull himself together, starting tomorrow morning. Wash up and go back to Capitol Hill, if Georgeann had saved any of his things. Put on some clothes and catch the trolley for west Denver. Eat dinner tomorrow night with Anna and David. Take a week to dry out; never touch another goddamn drop as long as he lived. When he felt good about himself again, he'd put on his best coat and hat, tie his tie, slip into his good boots, and take himself a little walk downtown. Confidence was what counted in this game. Walk into the *Post* and give Bonfils one chance to hire him back; and if he didn't know a good thing when it walked right up to him, so be it. There were three other papers in this town and half a dozen press agencies. But that afternoon, he'd seen Mallo passing the alley behind the hotel, and he knew it wasn't that simple. And now, looking up at Taketa's smiling face, he said, "Christ, Jon, I really need a drink." And Taketa poured generously from his bottle of good Canadian bourbon because it had been a good day for him. His daughter had gotten married off and was off his hands forever. When Tom left, Taketa gave him the bottle.

He had been sitting on the floor of his room, nursing it for two hours.

He heard a noise outside his door, the sound of several men walking. Whoever it was had stopped just outside his door. His groping fingers found the cork, pushing it into the bottle, and tucked the bottle behind him in a corner. He felt around on the floor until he found his stick.

It was heavy, cut from a green elm tree. He always slept with it close by and had never had to use it. For perhaps a minute he heard nothing. Then came a soft knock on his door. He didn't move. Hardly breathed. Again the knock, this time

louder. One man spoke in Spanish, and the doorknob turned. He heard the click of a tool, a jimmy against wood, and he got to his feet slowly as the wood split and the door swung in.

Three of them stood in the dim hallway. He had never seen any of them. The one nearest the door peered in, then moved inside.

"That's far enough, pilgrim," Tom said.

"Just a little whiskey, friend." The voice had a soft texture, lulling, and a slight Mexican accent. The three of them came in and began to fan out in the dark.

"I said that's far enough."

"Just a drink from your bottle. One drink and we'll go away."

"Not too likely, Mexican."

It was over in less than a minute. The three men backed him into the corner. The bottle crouched between his legs like a frightened child. He heard the snap of a switchblade, saw the gleam, and met the man as he lunged. He swung the stick into the black face, feeling the crunch as it smashed the nose flat. The man dropped at his feet, and Tom finished him off with a kick in the ribs. It was like letting the air out of a balloon.

The others hung back, suddenly wary. Tom pushed the fallen one with his foot. "Get him out of here. Come on, pick him up before I give you a taste of it too. Next time watch whose room you break into."

The Shining

Stephen King

THE ROCK WALL FELL away on their right, disclosing a slash valley that seemed to go down forever, lined a dark green with Rocky Mountain pine and spruce. The pines fell away to gray cliffs of rock that dropped for hundreds of feet before smoothing out. She saw a waterfall spilling over one of them, the early afternoon sun sparkling in it like a golden fish snared in a blue net. They were beautiful mountains, but they were hard. She did not think they would forgive many mistakes. An unhappy foreboding rose in her throat. Further west in the Sierra Nevada, the Donner Party had become snowbound and had resorted to cannibalism to stay alive. The mountains did not forgive many mistakes.

With a punch of the clutch and a jerk, Jack shifted down to first gear and they labored upward, the bug's engine thumping gamely.

"You know," she said, "I don't think we've seen five cars since we came through Sidewinder. And one of them was the hotel limousine."

Jack nodded. "It goes right to Stapleton Airport in Denver. There's already some icy patches up beyond the hotel, Watson says, and they're forecasting more snow for tomorrow up higher. Anybody going through the mountains now wants to be on one of the main roads, just in case. That goddam Ullman better still be up there. I guess he will be."

"You're sure the larder is fully stocked?" she asked, still thinking of the Donners.

"He said so. Wanted Hallorann to go over it with you. Hallorann the cook."

"Oh," she said faintly, looking at the speedometer. It had dropped from 15 to 10 miles an hour.

"There's the top," Jack said, pointing 300 yards ahead. "There's a scenic turnout, and you can see the Overlook from there. I'm going to pull off the road and give the bug a chance to rest." He craned over his shoulder at Danny, who was sitting on a pile of blankets. "What do you think, doc? We might see some deer. Or caribou."

"Sure, Dad."

The VW labored tiredly on up. The speedometer dropped to just above the five-mile-an-hour hashmark and was beginning to hitch when Jack pulled off the road.

("What's that sign say, Mommy?" "SCENIC TURNOUT," she read dutifully.) and stepped on the emergency brake and let the VW run in neutral.

"Come on," he said, and got out.

They walked to the guardrail together.

"That's it," Jack said, and pointed at 11 o'clock.

For Wendy, it was discovering truth in a cliché: her breath was taken away. For a moment, she was unable to breathe at all; the view had knocked the wind from her. They were standing near the top of one peak. Across from them—who knew how far?—an even taller mountain reared into the sky, its jagged tip only a silhouette that was now nimbused by the sun, which was beginning its decline. The whole valley floor was spread out below them, the slopes that they had climbed in the laboring bug falling away with such dizzying suddenness that she knew to look down there for too long would bring on nausea and eventual vomiting. The imagination seemed to spring to full life in the clear air, beyond the rein of reason, and to look was to helplessly see one's self plunging down and down and down, sky and slopes changing places in slow cartwheels, the scream drifting from your mouth like a lazy balloon as your hair and your dress billowed out. ...

She jerked her gaze away from the drop almost by force and followed Jack's finger. She could see the highway clinging to the side of this cathedral spire, switching back on itself but always tending northwest, still climbing but at a more gentle angle. Further up, seemingly set directly into the slope itself, she saw the grimly clinging pines give way to a wide square of green lawn and standing in the middle of it, overlooking all this, the hotel. The Overlook. Seeing it, she found breath and voice again.

"Oh, Jack, it's gorgeous!"

"Yes, it is," he said. "Ullman says he thinks it's the single most beautiful location in America. I don't care much for him, but I think he might be ... Danny! Danny, are you all right?"

She looked around for him and her sudden fear for him blotted out everything else, stupendous or not. She darted toward him. He was holding onto the guardrail and looking up at the hotel, his face a pasty gray color. His eyes had the blank look of someone on the verge of fainting.

She knelt beside him and put steadying hands on his shoulders. "Danny, what's—"

Jack was beside her. "You okay, doc?" He gave Danny a brisk little shake and his eyes cleared.

"I'm okay, Daddy. I'm fine."

"What was it, Danny?" she asked. "Were you dizzy, honey?"

"No, I was just ... thinking. I'm sorry. I didn't mean to scare you." He looked at his parents, kneeling in front of him, and offered them a small, puzzled smile. "Maybe it was the sun. The sun got in my eyes."

"We'll get you up to the hotel and give you a drink of water," Daddy said.

"Okay."

And in the bug, which moved upward more surely on the gentler grade, he kept looking out between them as the road unwound, affording occasional glimpses of the Overlook Hotel, its massive bank of westward-looking windows reflecting back the sun. It was the place he had seen in the midst of the blizzard, the dark and booming place where some hideously familiar figure sought him down long corridors carpeted with jungle. The place Tony had warned him against. It was here. It was here. Whatever Redrum was, it was here.

Blood Betrayal

Ausma Zehanat Khan

A LITTLE ANXIOUSLY, she drove down the East Colfax area strip, searching for the cannabis dispensary. She wanted to get a feel for where the shooting had taken place. It was a typically seedy strip, though the cannabis dispensary was new, a squat, square, glass-fronted store with the windows of its upper story shuttered. Not blacked out but closed by painted green shutters that gave it a look of class. It stood out against its neighbors—a strip club called Shotgun Willie's; a few pawnbrokers with giant WE BUY YOUR GOLD signs; two liquor stores on either side of the street with graffiti marking up their storefronts. Right across from the dispensary was a fast-food falafel joint and beside that a building without windows in the front. Unusually, the windows ran along the side of the building, and she saw that it was a nightclub, the name "The Black Door" stenciled in silver on an imposing black door, the "D" a stylized slash of red. She also noted that the building's main door was painted a discreet red. No lights, no silhouettes of nudes or exotic dancers—nothing flashy that drew the attention.

Blood on the Tracks

Barbara Nickless

CLYDE HAD ONCE been the canine equivalent of a Navy SEAL. His training had gone beyond even the rigorous preparation given a normal military multipurpose dog and made him worth a small fortune. I'd only been able to adopt him because Dougie's death had so destabilized him that he'd been declared unworkable. Now, as a railroad K9, he had decent training. But I had not kept his skills to the level he'd once known. It had never seemed necessary. Nor did he enjoy the work anymore.

Something was broken inside of Clyde. I doubted he'd ever be the dog he'd been with Dougie. Any more than I would again be the bright, fearless woman whom Dougie had loved.

Chasing rabbits, though. That was a new low for us both.

At the suspension bridge, we picked up our pace. The viaduct hung over a sand-choked gully that had been carved out by flash floods. Clyde and I fell into a rhythm as our feet hit the ties.

Half a mile on the other side, we cut right. Twenty feet from the tracks, I gestured Clyde down and then lay flat on the ground next to him. The earth was still damp from the last snow. The Kevlar vest ground into the soft flesh under my chin, and Dougie's ring dug into my breastbone. I wriggled around, trying to get comfortable.

Clyde settled himself companionably next to me, tongue lolling, happier than I'd seen him in a long time. His Kevlar vest didn't bother him at all. Business as usual for a military dog.

"This is like a vacation for you, isn't it, Clyde?"

He yawned.

"That rabbit means we're losing our edge. Getting soft. We need to start training again."

He paid me no attention whatsoever.

We waited. The smells of damp earth and sage wafted up, mingling with the sharp tang of creosote from the railroad ties. A lone crow circled overhead, and I followed it with my eyes, feeling some part of me up there with it, remote and unattached, free of asshole sheriffs and nightmare memories and war-shattered vets. Free of weight.

"Five minutes," the dispatcher said in my ear.

From the south, Engine 158346 was now visible, her headlamp and ditch lights burning brightly in the clear day like a star hooked to a workhorse. She was a 4,000-horsepower war-bonnet, 12 feet wide, 15 tall, and weighing 200 tons. Part of the Powder River run, she'd been built to build America.

But she was also a danger. Flat out, she could go 60 miles an hour. Get too close, and her slipstream would drag you under her wheels. Cross her path, and her driver would not see you. And even if he did, it would take him a mile and a half to stop.

By then, there would be nothing human about you except your DNA.

I could hear her now. The steady thrum of her engine, and beneath that vibrant hum, the clack of her wheels like blood thumping in iron veins. The radio burst with static as everyone down the line confirmed their position. Next to me, Clyde tensed. I re-snapped his lead and pulled him close, wrapping an arm around him.

Railroad dispatch buzzed in my ear. "One minute."

The tunnel vision of combat closed in, shutting out everything but the train. No smells or sights, no sound or sense of touch, other than what rolled in with Engine 158346.

Our Lady squealed over the bridge, tossing off velocity, shrieking to a halt in a way that said stopping was all wrong, that the rhythm of the tracks should never be disrupted. Her steel sides swept by like a leviathan breaching, her wheels screaming in fury. Sparks kicked up from the rails, and it looked like she would sail right on past. Stopping wasn't what she was built for.

But, finally, heavily, she conceded. She dragged to a halt, her brakes whooshing. The air stayed up, just as Albers had promised, and Clyde and I sprang to our feet. We sprinted across the grass then bounded up the stairs and into the cab, me shouting my name as I ran so the crew wouldn't think I was a trespasser.

Albers was sitting in the console behind the controls, his shotgun leaning against the wall within easy reach. The conductor, Greg Walters, sat to his left, wide-eyed and pale. Walters rose and grabbed my arm as soon as I entered the cab.

"Who is this guy, Sydney?" he asked. "I think I saw SWAT out there."

"He's just a trespasser," I told him. "No worries. But we're going to be cautious. I want both of you down, out of sight."

"What? Why?" Walters asked even as he crouched on the internal stairs leading down to the head.

"Bullets will be flying," Albers answered gleefully. He clearly itched to be part of the action. But when I glared, he complied with my order, hunkering near Walters on the stairs and snugging the shotgun up to his chest like a lover.

"Don't even think of using that," I told him.

I removed Clyde's lead and gave him the order to stay with the men. Then I clambered to the top of the locomotive so that I could watch for anyone approaching.

SECTION XI

Diversity

Harvey

Mary Chase

ACT TWO: SCENE TWO

* * *

ELWOOD: I am trying to be factual. I then introduced him to Harvey.

WILSON: To who?

KELLY: A white rabbit. Six feet tall.

WILSON: Six feet!

ELWOOD: Six feet one and a half.

WILSON: O.K.—fool around with him, and the doctor is probably some place bleedin' to death in a ditch.

ELWOOD: If those were his plans for the evening he did not tell me.

SANDERSON: Go on, Dowd.

ELWOOD: Dr. Chumley sat down in the booth with us. I was sitting on the outside like this. (*Shows.*) Harvey was on the inside near the wall, and Dr. Chumley was seated directly across from Harvey where he could look at him.

WILSON: (*Crosses a step* R). That's right. Spend all night on the seatin' arrangements!

ELWOOD: Harvey then suggested that I buy him a drink. Knowing that he does not like to drink alone, I suggested to Dr. Chumley that we join him.

WILSON: And so?

ELWOOD: We joined him.

WILSON: Go on—go on.

ELWOOD: We joined him again.

WILSON: Then what?

ELWOOD: We kept right on joining him.

WILSON: Oh, skip all the joining.

ELWOOD: You are asking me to skip a large portion of the evening.

WILSON: Tell us what happened—come on—please—

ELWOOD: Dr. Chumley and Harvey got into a conversation—quietly at first. Later it became rather heated and Dr. Chumley raised his voice.

WILSON: Yeah—why?

ELWOOD: Harvey seemed to feel that Dr. Chumley should assume part of the financial responsibility of the joining, but Dr. Chumley didn't seem to want to do that.

KELLY: (*It breaks out from her*). I can believe *that* part of it!

WILSON: Let him talk. See how far he'll go. This guy's got guts.

ELWOOD: I agreed to take the whole thing because I did not want any trouble. We go down to Charlie's quite often—Harvey and I—and the proprietor is a man with an interesting approach to life. Then the other matter came up.

WILSON: Cut the damned double-talk and get on with it!

ELWOOD: Mr. Wilson, you are a sincere type of person, but I must ask you not to use that language in the presence of Miss Kelly. (*He makes a short bow to her.*)

SANDERSON: You're right, Dowd, and we're sorry. You say—the other matter came up?

ELWOOD: There was a beautiful blonde woman—a Mrs. Smethills—and an escort seated in the booth across from us. Dr. Chumley went over to sit next to her, explaining to her that they had once met. In Chicago. Her escort escorted Dr. Chumley back to me and Harvey and tried to point out that it would be better for Dr. Chumley to mind his own affairs.

WILSON: Does he have any?

ELWOOD: Does he have any what?

WILSON: Does he have any affairs?

ELWOOD: How would I know?

KELLY: Please hurry, Mr. Dowd—we're all so worried.

ELWOOD: Dr. Chumley then urged Harvey to go with him over to Blondie's Chicken Inn. Harvey wanted to go to Eddie's instead. While they were arguing about it I went to the bar to order another drink, and when I came back they were gone.

WILSON: Where did they go? I mean where did the doctor go?

ELWOOD: I don't know—I had a date out here with Dr. Sanderson and Miss Kelly, and I came out to pick them up—hoping that later on we might run into Harvey and the doctor and make a party of it.

WILSON: So you satisfied? You got his story—(*Goes over to* ELWOOD, *fists clenched.*)—O.K. You're lyin' and we know it!

ELWOOD: I never lie, Mr. Wilson.

WILSON: You've done somethin' with the doctor and I'm findin' out what it is.

SANDERSON: (*Moving after him*). Don't touch him, Wilson.

KELLY: Maybe he isn't lying, Wilson.

WILSON: (*Turning on them, furiously*). That's all this guy is, a bunch of lies! You two don't believe this story he tells about the doctor sittin' there talkin' to a big white rabbit, do you?

KELLY: Maybe Dr. Chumley *did* go to Charlie's Place.

WILSON: And saw a big rabbit, I suppose.

ELWOOD: And why not? Harvey was there. At first the doctor seemed a little frightened of Harvey, but that gave way to admiration as the evening wore on. The evening wore on! That's a nice expression. With your permission I'll say it again. The evening wore on.

WILSON: (*Lunging at him*). With your permission, I'm gonna knock your teeth down your throat!

ELWOOD: (*Not moving an inch*). Mr. Wilson—haven't you some old friends you can go play with? (SANDERSON *has grabbed* WILSON *and is struggling with him*; KELLY *dials phone.*)

WILSON: (*Being held, glares fiercely at* ELWOOD; KELLY *dials phone*). The nerve of this guy! He couldn't come out here with an ordinary case of D.T.'s. No. He has to come out with a six-foot rabbit.

ELWOOD: (*Rises—goes toward desk* L). Stimulating as all this is, I really must be getting downtown.

KELLY: (*On phone*). Charlie's Place? Is Dr. Chumley anywhere around there? He was there with Mr. Dowd earlier in the evening. What? Well, don't bite my head off! (*Hangs up.*) My, that man was mad. He said Mr. Dowd was welcome any time, but his friend was not.

ELWOOD: That's Mr. McNulty the bartender. He thinks a lot of me. Now let's all go down and have a drink.

WILSON: Wait a minute—

KELLY: Mr. Dowd—(*Goes over to him.*)

ELWOOD: Yes, my dear—may I hold your hand?

KELLY: Yes—if you want to. (ELWOOD *does.*) Poor Mrs. Chumley is so worried. Something must have happened to the doctor. Won't you please try and remember something—something else that might help her? Please—

ELWOOD: For you I would do anything. I would almost be willing to live my life over again. Almost. But I've told it all.

KELLY: You're sure?

ELWOOD: Quite sure—but ask me again, anyway, won't you? I liked that warm tone you had in your voice just then.

SANDERSON: (*Without realizing he is saying it*). So did I. (*Looks at* KELLY.)

WILSON: Oh, nuts!

ELWOOD: What?

WILSON: Nuts!

ELWOOD: Oh! I must be going. I have things to do.

KELLY: Mr. Dowd, what is it you do?

ELWOOD: (*Sits, as* KELLY *sits* R. *of desk*). Harvey and I sit in the bars, and we have a drink or two and play the jukebox. Soon the faces of the other people turn toward mine and smile. They are saying: "We don't know your name, Mister, but you're a lovely fellow." Harvey and I warm ourselves in all these golden moments. We have entered as strangers—soon we have friends. They come over. They sit with us. They drink with us. They talk to us. They tell about the big terrible things they have done. The big wonderful things they *will* do. Their hopes, their regrets, their loves, their hates. All very large because nobody ever brings anything small into a bar. Then I introduce them to Harvey. And he is bigger and grander than anything they offer me. When they leave, they leave impressed. The same people seldom come back—but that's life, my dear. There's a little bit of envy in the best of us—too bad, isn't it?

SANDERSON: (*Leaning forward*). How did you happen to call him Harvey?

ELWOOD: Harvey is his name.

SANDERSON: How do you know that?

ELWOOD. That was rather an interesting coincidence, Doctor. One night several years ago I was walking early in the evening along Fairfax Street—between 18th and 19th. You know that block?

SANDERSON. Yes, yes.

ELWOOD. I had just helped Ed Hickey into a taxi. Ed had been mixing his rye with his gin, and I felt he needed conveying. I started to walk down the street when I heard a voice saying: "Good evening, Mr. Dowd." I turned, and there was this great white rabbit leaning against a lamppost. Well, I thought nothing of that, because when you have lived in a town as long as I have lived in this one, you get used to the fact that everybody knows your name. Naturally, I went over to chat with him. He said to me: "Ed Hickey is a little spiffed this evening, or could I be mistaken?" Well, of course he was not mistaken. I think the world and all of Ed, but he was spiffed. Well, anyway, we stood there and talked, and finally I said—"You have the advantage of me. You know my name and I don't know yours." Right back at me he said: "What name would you like?" Well, I didn't even have to think a minute: Harvey has always been my favorite name. So I said, "Harvey," and this is the interesting part of the whole thing. He said—"What a coincidence! My name happens to be Harvey."

SANDERSON (*Crossing above desk*). What was your father's name, Dowd?

ELWOOD. John. John Frederick.

SANDERSON. Now, Dowd, when you were a child you had a playmate, didn't you? Someone you were very fond of—with whom you spent many happy, carefree hours?

ELWOOD. Oh, yes, Doctor. Didn't you?

SANDERSON. What was his name?

ELWOOD. Verne. Verne McElhinney. Did you ever know the McElhinneys, Doctor?

SANDERSON. No.

ELWOOD. Too bad. There were a lot of them, and they circulated. Wonderful people.

SANDERSON. Think carefully, Dowd. Wasn't there someone, somewhere, sometime, whom you knew—by the name of Harvey? Didn't you ever know anybody by that name?

ELWOOD. No, Doctor. No one. Maybe that's why I always had such hopes for it.

SANDERSON. Come on, Wilson, we'll take Mr. Dowd upstairs now.

WILSON. I'm taking him nowhere. You've made this your show—now run it. Lettin' him sit here—forgottin' all about Dr. Chumley! O.K. It's your show—you run it.

SANDERSON. Come on, Dowd—(*Pause; putting out his hand.*) Come on, Dowd—

ELWOOD (*Rises*). Very well, Lyman. (SANDERSON *and* KELLY *take him to door.*) But I'm afraid I won't be able to visit with you for long. I have promised Harvey I will take him to the floorshow.

(*They exit* U.C. WILSON *is alone. Sits at desk. Looks at his watch.*)

WILSON. Oh, boy! (*Puts head in arms on desk.* DR. CHUMLEY *enters* L. WILSON *does not see him until he gets almost* C. *stage.*)

WILSON (Jumping up, going to him). Dr. Chumley—Are you all right?

CHUMLEY. All right? Of course I'm all right. I'm being followed. Lock that door.

WILSON (*Goes to door* L.; *locks it*). Who's following you?

CHUMLEY. None of your business. (*Exits into office* R.; *locks door behind him.*)

(WILSON *stands a moment perplexed, then shrugs shoulders, turns off lights, and exits* U.C. *The stage is dimly lit. Then, from door L., comes the rattle of the doorknob. Door opens and shuts, and we hear locks opening and closing and see light from hall on stage. The invisible Harvey has come in. There is a count of eight while he crosses the stage, then door of* CHUMLEY's *office opens and closes with sound of locks clicking. Harvey has gone in—and then—*)

CURTAIN

The Life and Legend of Gene Fowler

H. Allen Smith

THERE WAS ALWAYS a poker game in progress at the Press Club. It ran night and day, seemingly without recess, and there were some who said it had gone on without interruption since the siege of Vicksburg. Players arrived and sat in for a few hours and then departed, to be replaced by other players.

The Press Club was quartered in a downtown office building, then moved to another downtown office building, and finally settled in its own two-story structure across from the Denver Athletic Club. Legend out of the heroic age tells us that when the moving vans arrived at the second location, six players were engaged at stud poker. They refused to get out of their chairs. They refused to abandon the table. After much yelling and cursing, a compromise was reached. The movers picked up the chairs and table and carried them quickly out to the van. The players followed, carrying chips and cards and whiskey glasses, and the stud game continued inside the van while it rumbled through the streets en route to the club's new quarters.

A chief fixture at the club's poker table was Colonel Gideon B. McFall, associate member. As a general rule, press clubs in American cities take in press agents, advertising blokes, politicians, and other riffraff, charging them heavily for the privilege of belonging, and of saying they belong. If it were not for the dues of these non-journalists, few clubs would be able to survive.

Colonel Gideon B. McFall was one of the members who had no connection with newspapers or other periodicals. Little was known about his history. It was a sure thing that he could pay his immoderate club dues out of his poker winnings and have enough left over to buy Elitch Gardens and the Brown Palace. He often referred to himself as a southerner, raised on a great plantation in Mississippi. Someone once investigated this julep-y claim and established the fact that the colonel had his origin on a pig farm near Ottumwa, Iowa.

As long as anyone could remember, Colonel McFall had been banker of the Press Club poker game. He looked more like a banker than an Iowa farm boy, and Gene Fowler said he had one of the two finest heads of silvery hair in the city—the other belonged to the County Coroner. Almost everybody on every newspaper in town owed the colonel money.

On a starless Saturday night in December, the two most inept poker players west of St. Louis, Fowler and Lee Casey, made their way to the Press Club bent upon losing their paychecks to Colonel McFall or anyone else who might be around. They found the poker game overcrowded, and even the colonel had withdrawn temporarily to stretch his legs and take on a ham-and-cheese sandwich. While Colonel McFall chewed at his supper, he stood with Fowler, Casey, and police reporter Jack Carberry.

"There is a smell of snow in the air," said the colonel, "and I have a great idea. Let us repair to my little cottage in Park Hill where I have an adequate supply of drinkin' whiskey and a large stack of firewood. The hell with frivoling away an entire night at the gaming table in this sordid den when we can settle down to a long evening of pleasant talk."

Fowler, Casey, and Carberry agreed with the stipulation that they be permitted to purchase a spare case of Wilson's whiskey, and the colonel, with his customary high-flown Dixieland style, ordered a horse-drawn cab. No plebeian streetcars for gentlemen when McFall was host.

The brougham had no more than got started up 17th Street when snowflakes the size of potato chips began to swirl upon it and a few blocks farther on it became almost impossible to see through the storm. Then a faint "halloo" sounded in the night, and a ghostly figure came groping through the snow. The figure turned out to be Charlie Carson, foreman of the *News* stereotype room. He stumbled his way up to the door of the carriage, peered within, recognized the occupants, and cried out: "You fellas on your way to a whorehouse?"

They hauled him in out of the storm, and he announced firmly that he was going home to his wife with his paycheck intact; and just because it was a Saturday night, by God, he wasn't going to no bookshop nor neither was he going to throw his hard-earned money away on drinking and gambling. "You fellas got a drink with you?" he asked, though he really didn't need one.

At the colonel's cottage, Charlie resumed work on the Wilson's while the others were divesting themselves of their outer garments. He was soon asleep. The colonel got into his red velvet carpet slippers, stirred up the fire, and meanwhile, reaching for his pipe tobacco, his hand by accident fell upon a deck of playing cards.

"Egad!" he exclaimed. "This smacks of Kismet! Oh, well, why not? Just a little sociable hand or two by way of preliminary—then the good talk."

There would be no good talk.

They played all night and up to noon the next day, and after that they began playing in relays, taking catnaps and partaking of snorts. Lee Casey, a worrier, discovered that the snow was up to the window tops and the doors could not be opened. He made telephone contact with the *News* and was told that Denver was in the grip of the worst blizzard since the second year of the Pony Express. Following which the lines went down, and the little group of hardy and heroic souls played on in utter isolation from the world.

Early on the third morning, the firewood ran out. The whiskey supply was still ample. The players donned overcoats and hats and continued the game; but after a while, Fowler made mention of the cold. He got up and inspected two wooden chairs that stood against the back wall. He broke the chairs into pieces and put them on the dying fire. From time to time more furniture was broken up and fed to the flames and then books and old newspapers—anything that would burn. By the next day, the Donner Party of Park Hill was down to the oaken table in the middle of the room and the four chairs around it. These were shattered and tossed into the fireplace, but the game did not end. Colonel McFall, Fowler, Casey, and Carberry stretched themselves on the carpet and continued with stud and draw. Charlie Carson woke up long enough to crawl closer to the fire and then resumed his sleep.

Early on Thursday morning, the fire department clawed its way through the snowbanks and rescued all hands. The booze was gone, there was no food in the house, and the poker players were tired. Before departing the cottage, Colonel McFall totted up the reckoning. For the first time in recorded history, the silver-haired cavalier from Ottumwa was a heavy loser.

"Pay up!" cried the others, proud of their achievement.

"Hold!" protested McFall. "You lads have forgotten something."

He quickly penciled out an inventory of those possessions that had been burned in the fireplace. He calculated the fair market value of furniture, books, clothing, and carpeting, then prorated the damage three ways. And he made it stick.

Recalling those fine days and nights when he worked for the *Rocky Mountain News*, Fowler said:

"It seemed that I never could have lived anywhere else in my youth but in an untamed town. I have to laugh at my own naivete, for I had thought that the mad behavior of Denver, shortly after the century dawned, was the norm for the entire world. Both my great joys and supposedly great sorrows came from this childish credo when I finally pranced along the avenues of New York and the Left Bank of Paris. Of course, I now know that a man who dares laugh or pursues his own simplicities is bound to be kicked to death. This does not deter me."

Timberline

Gene Fowler

MRS. BROWN WAS 39 years old when she left Liverpool for New York on the *Titanic's* maiden voyage. Instead of a girlish slimness, she now was rugged and generously fleshed. Nevertheless, she still bubbled with a seldom-varying vitality.

She sang in the ship's concert and was popular with the traveling notables despite her growing eccentricities. She amused some and terrified others with pistol feats, one of which consisted of tossing five oranges or grapefruits over the rail and puncturing each one before it reached the surface of the sea.

Although she spent great sums on clothes, she no longer paid attention to the detail or how she wore them. And, when she traveled, comfort, and not a desire to appear *chic*, was her primary consideration.

So, when Molly decided to take a few turns of the deck before retiring, she came from her cabin prepared for battle with the night sea air. She had on extra heavy woolies, with bloomers bought in Switzerland (her favorite kind), two jersey petticoats, a plaid cashmere dress down to the heels of her English calfskin boots; a sportsman's cap, tied on with a woolen scarf, knotted in toothache style beneath her chin, golf stockings presented by a 70-year-old admirer, the Duke of Charlot of France, a muff of Russian sables, in which she absent-mindedly had left her Colt's automatic pistol—and over these frost-defying garments, she wore a $60,000 chinchilla opera cloak!

If anyone was prepared for Arctic gales, Mrs. Brown was that person. She was not, however, prepared for a collision with an iceberg.

In fact, she was on the point of sending a deck steward below with her cumbersome pistol when the crash came.

In the history of that tragedy, her name appears as one who knew no fear. She did much to calm the women and children. Perhaps she was overzealous, for it is recorded that she refused to enter a lifeboat until all other women and their young ones had been cared for, and that crew members literally had to throw her into a boat.

Once in the boat, however, she didn't wait for approval—she seized command. There were only five men aboard and about 20 women and children.

"Start rowing," she told the men, "and head the bow into the sea."

Keeping an eye on the rowers, she began removing her clothes. Her chinchilla coat she treated as though it were a blanket worth a few dollars. She used it to cover three small and shivering children. One by one she divested herself of heroic woolens. She "rationed" her garments to the women who were the oldest or most frail. It was said she presented a fantastic sight in the light of flares, half standing among the terrified passengers, stripped down to her corset, the beloved Swiss bloomers, the Duke of Charlot's golf stockings, and her stout shoes.

One of the rowers seemed on the verge of collapse. "My heart," he said.

"God damn your heart!" said The Unsinkable Mrs. Brown. "Work those oars." She herself now took an oar and began to row.

She chose a position in the bow, where she could watch her crew. Her pistol was lashed to her waist with a rope.

The heart-troubled rower now gasped and almost lost his oar. "My heart," he said. "It's getting worse!"

The Unsinkable one roared: "Keep rowing or I'll blow your guts out and throw you overboard! Take your choice."

The man—who really did have a *fatty* condition of the heart—kept rowing. Mrs. Brown sprouted big blisters on her hands. But she didn't quit. Then her palms began to bleed. She cut strips from her Swiss bloomers and taped her hands. She kept rowing. And swearing.

At times, when the morale of her passengers was at its lowest, she would sing.

"The God damned critics say I can't sing," she howled. "Well, just listen to this ..."

And she sang from various operas.

"We'll have an Italian opera now," she said at one time. "Just let anyone say it's no good."

She kept rowing.

And so did the others. They knew she would throw anyone overboard who dared quit, exhaustion or no exhaustion.

She told stories. She gave a history of the Little Johnny. She told of the time she hid $300,000 in a camp stove and how it went up the flue.

"How much is $300,000?" she asked. "I'll tell you. It's nothing. Some of you people—the guy here with the heart trouble that I'm curing with oars—are rich. I'm rich. What in hell of it? What are your riches or mine doing for us this minute? And you can't wear the Social Register for water wings, can you? Keep rowing, you sons of bitches, or I'll toss you all overboard!"

When they were picked up at sea, and everyone was praising Mrs. Brown, she was asked:

"How did you manage it?"

"Just typical Brown luck," she replied.

"I'm unsinkable." And ever afterward she was known as "The Unsinkable Mrs. Brown."

At the End of the Santa Fe Trail

Sister Blandina Segale

GOOD FRIDAY, 1873.—Sisters Marcella, Fidelis, and myself went up the mountainside to see the Penitentes make the "Way to Calvary." About one hundred took part in it. They walked in twos, faces covered, backs bared. Each had several branches of long, bruised cacti, with which they lashed their backs as they slowly ascended the spur. At each lash they said, *"Yo penitente picador"* (I, a repentant sinner). When the one dragging the cross reached the summit of the spur, some of the Penitentes helped to raise the cross he alone had dragged. It seemed impossible for any one man to have accomplished such an act, but we saw him do it. We were several miles from Trinidad and wanted to reach our convent home before the lighter of our globe threw his golden rays to warn us that he soon would retire.

Easter Sunday, 1873.—I must tell you what information I received concerning the *Penitentes*. The Way of the Cross, of course, was taught the natives by the good Franciscans; so also penance was preached to them. When the Franciscans were obliged to leave the Southwest, it naturally fell to the stronger-minded and piously inclined to perpetuate what had been taught them, but in this teaching each leader followed his own idea; hence, we find that whilst the members of some lodges are perfectly docile to the teachings of the Church, other lodges have not the least conception of the correct spirit of Catholicity, though they consider themselves good Catholics.

The *Penitentes* in this vicinity do not even make their Easter duty. They do not scruple to abstract cattle from another man's ranch on the Easter Monday, after having scourged themselves on Good Friday and called themselves "repentant sinners." This reminds one of the private interpretation of the Bible. The *Penitentes* interpret the teaching of the Franciscans in their own way. The initiation to these lodges varies also. Here is one form: Ridges are made from neck to waistline with sharp stones. By privilege, I was allowed to visit one of their lodges—it was literally bespattered with blood—side, walls, and ceiling, too—yet the members of the lodge visited are adroit pilferers of any branded domestic animals seen on the plains. These same members never approach the Sacraments.

Easter week.—Here is a tragedy which took place this week. An elderly lady and gentleman—Americans—residing a few miles from Trinidad, were found murdered in their home. Suspicion at once pointed to the natives as the perpetrators of the horrible deed. Small groups of men were sent out to capture the murderers. One posse trailed four Mexicans, and because they would not acknowledge the deed, they were hanged on the first tree to which they came.

Afterwards, the corpses were huddled into a wagon, brought to Trinidad in triumph and thrown into an old vacant adobe hut, 12 feet from the graveyard near the Convent. Can you imagine how we felt! Two days later, the real murderers were captured and confessed the crime. They were outlawed Americans!

Cousin Jack (or English) Pasties

Ladies of Monte Vista

FOR CRUST, TWO AND one-half cups flour, three-fourths cup chopped suet, pinch of salt, and about one tablespoon lard mixed with the other ingredients to form a dough like ordinary pie crust. Roll out one-half inch thick and the size of a dinner plate; on half of this, place a layer of sliced onion (one small onion) or turnip, a good layer of sliced raw tomato—and, on top, a layer of small pieces of raw meat (beef or pork), one pound for two pastries, sprinkle with pepper, salt and bits of butter; fold the other half of the crust over this, and crimp the edges as in a turnover.

—Mrs. Parmenter

Wah-To-Yah and the Taos Trail

Lewis H. Garrard

THE MORNING CAME, and we were somewhat occupied in trading, but robes scarce, the buffalo hair not being in prime order.

We were invited to Gray Eyes' lodge, to a feast, early in the day. Sitting down after shaking hands, a wooden bowl of choice pieces of fat meat was set before us. We used our own knives and fingers. Gray Eyes has two wives and 12 children, two of whom—fine-looking boys of 15 and 13 summers, respectively—were in the lodge; their father's eye beamed on them fondly when he spoke of their killing buffalo from horseback with bow and arrow. The eldest had an open, frank countenance—the reverse of his father, whose features plainly showed duplicity, and his small gray eyes—hence his cognomen—twinkled replete with rascality, for which he is noted.

It is Indian custom that whatever is set before the guest belongs to him; and he is expected to take what he does not eat home with him; so we stuck our knives in some of Gray Eyes' fat slices when the pipe was finished.

Smith's son Jack took a crying fit one cold night, much to the annoyance of four or five chiefs who had come to our lodge to talk and smoke. In vain, did mother shake and scold him with the severest Cheyenne words, until Smith, provoked beyond endurance, took the squalling youngster in hand; he shouted, and shouted, and swore, but Jack had gone too far to be easily pacified. He then sent for a bucket of water from the river and poured cupful after cupful on Jack, who stamped, and screamed, and bit, in his puny rage. Notwithstanding, the ice-cold stream slowly descended until the bucket was emptied; another was sent for, and again and again the cup was replenished and emptied on the blubbering youth. At last, exhausted with exertion and completely cooled down, he received the remaining water in silence, and, with a few words of admonition, was delivered over to his mother, in whose arms he stifled his sobs, until his heart-breaking grief and cares were drowned in sleep. What a devilish mixture Indian and American blood is!

The Indians never chastise a boy, as they think his spirit would be broken and cowed down; and instead of a warrior, he would be a squaw—a harsh epithet, indicative of cowardice—and they resort to any method but infliction of blows to subdue a refractory scion.

Jack has three names: that of Jack, so called by the whites, and two Indian ones—Wo-pe-kon-ne and O-toz-vout-si—the former meaning "White Eyes"—a nickname—the latter, his proper title—"Buck Deer."

For pastime, I began a glossary of the Cheyenne tongue to facilitate its acquirement; the visitors, thinking me a queer customer (mah-son-ne—"a fool"—as they were pleased to denominate me and my vocabularic efforts), replied willingly to my inquiries of *"Ten-o-wast?"*— "What is it?"—at the same time pointing to any object whose name I wished to know. I wrote their answers according to the pronunciation. The squaws of our lodge gave me words, purposely, not easily articulated or written; my attempts at correct enunciation were greeted with lively sallies of laughter. Our conversation was carried on in broken—very broken—sentences; and, I must say, the part that they too ably sustained was not of the most refined character. No person so young as myself had ever visited the Cheyennes, and the gentle fair seemed glad to meet one divested of the trader's assumed consequence.

The visits of the Indians were divided between Mr. Bent's lodge and our own; but we saw as many as we wished, for our coffee and sugar cost us a dollar a pound. To secure the good will and robes of the sensitive men, we had to offer our dear-bought Java at mealtime—the period of the greatest congregation. Still, their company was acceptable, as their manners, conversation, and pipes were agreeable.

So complete and comprehensive is their mode of communication by signs that they can understand each other without a word being said and with more facility than with the lips.

I had a small box in which were shirts, tobacco, a backgammon board, and a few books; one of them from Harper's series of the Family Library on the heavenly bodies. The plates were incomprehensible to the natives; and with all my efforts, I could but imperfectly make myself understood, even on most commonplace matters. Some of the chiefs, having seen this book, would not be put off without an answer to their queries; and it brought all my ingenuity into play to make suitable similes between the plates and things within their knowledge; consequently, great perversion of Dick's celestial geography took place.

A chief, named Mah-ke-o-nih or the "Big Wolf," professedly took a great liking to me. We went, by his invitation, one day, to a feast, guided by his youngest son, where we found Mah-ke-o-nih in a small lodge. After the customary salutations, we sat down to a bowl of dried stewed pumpkin, with a horn spoon sticking in it, from which we partook by turns. The spoon was a curiosity in its way, manufactured from the horn of a Rocky Mountain sheep and holding at least a pint. The childish hint, "take a spoon, pig," would not help the matter much if these kinds were in use.

The meaning of *feast* (a term much in vogue with the traders) is anything set before one, by invitation, be it much or little, rare or common.

Mah-ke-o-nih was in mourning for the loss of a near relative; and, to show the outward customary signs of grief, he lived in a small lodge. He is now old; but, in his younger days, the name of Mah-ke-o-nih was well known as that of a brave, and in later years, as a fearless warrior of unspotted fame. Now he is honored and respected for his Indian virtues.

I gave him a bent piece of hickory from an ox yoke with which to make a bow. As hard wood is scarce, and as the chief knew that I had been offered, several times, a robe for it, he was much pleased by my preference; and, in return, gave me his title. After this circumstance, I was known among the Cheyennes as Mah-ke-o-nih—sometimes as Veheo-kiss, or the "Young Whiteman."

In this village were more than a hundred dogs—from the large half-wolf down to the smallest specimen. Often, during the night, they broke forth in a prolonged howl, with the accompanying music of hundreds of prowling wolves making a most dissonant, unearthly noise. And such a fuss! Everyone ceased talking until the Voices of the Night were hushed. In our lodge were three huge curs and four cross-feists; and whenever the signal for a general bewailing was given by some superannuated mother of many canine generations, out, pell-mell, tore our loud-mouthed curs and the snarling squaw-pets to join the doggish revelry.

The love of gaming seems inherent in our very natures; as a proof of this, it was ever a favorite amusement with the Cheyennes and other Indians long ere they became acquainted with the whites. Their game, however, is simple, though not the less injurious in its effects. It is played by the young men and women, who, sitting in a circle, and with a rocking to-and-fro motion of the body, accompanied by a low quiet chant, increased in vigor as the game progresses, hold a bit of wood, cherrystone, or anything small in the hand; and after a series of dexterous shiftings, so as to deceive, hold them out while the singing stops, for the players to bet in which hand is the stone. So soon as they say, the object is shown; the fortunate ones sweep the stakes; the stone is given to the next, in order of rotation, the chant again strikes up—other trinkets are put up, and the betting recommences. They laugh and get much excited over their primitive game; and, often, an unlucky maiden rises from her amusement without the numerous bracelets, rings, and beads with which she came gayly decked to the meeting lodge.

This morning was one of November's most genial days. About 10 o'clock, I walked out and sat on a dry cottonwood log to admire the rural and domestic scene. The grass was green in many places—the majestic cottonwoods, not yet entirely robbed of their foliage, upreared their imposing trunks, while the branches gracefully overhung the clean, wind-swept grass.

The yellow, cone-shaped lodges looked like so many pyramids. Near them were industrious squaws, bringing, by dint of constant exertion, buffalo skins down to the required thinness by means of the dubber, which, as it struck the hard and dry robe, sounded like the escapement of steam from a small pipe. The valley was partly locked in by a low range of hills, on whose sides numerous bands of gay-colored horses were luxuriating on the fine, nutritious verdure. Around the lodges, troops of boys were shooting at marks with bow and arrow or tumbling on the grass in childish sport. Dignified chiefs walked with stately step and erect heads to grave council or taciturn smoke.

I sat long—collecting and embodying the thoughts and actions of the past four months, summing up the whole, with a glance at my then present situation. My companions were rough men—used to the hardships of a mountaineer's life, whose manners are blunt, and whose speech is rude—men driven to the western wilds with embittered feelings—with better natures shattered—with hopes blasted—to seek, in the dangers of the warpath, fierce excitement and banishment of care. The winter snow wreaths drift over them unheeded, and the night wind, howling around their lonely camp, is heard with calm indifference. Yet, these aliens from society, these strangers to the refinements of civilized life, who will tear off a bloody scalp with even grim smiles of satisfaction, are fine fellows, full of fun and often kind and obliging.

Early Days on the Western Slope of Colorado

Sidney Jocknick

IN THE YEAR 1881, Ouray paid his last visit to Washington. He took his wife Chipeta with him. She was in those days a remarkably handsome woman. Ouray was very much devoted to her. They remained a month in Washington and had frequent interviews with the President and with the Secretary of the Interior, Carl Schurz. Of the impressions which Mr. Schurz received of Ouray, I will here quote from his "Private Memoirs:"

"Ouray and Chipeta often visited me at my home, and they always conducted themselves with perfect propriety. They observed the various belongings of the drawing room with keen but decorous interest, and were especially attracted by a large crystal chandelier which was suspended from the ceiling. They wished to know where such a chandelier could be bought, and what it would cost; it would be such an ornament to their home.

"In official conversation, his talk was quite different from that of the ordinary Indian chief. He spoke like a man of a high order of intelligence and of larger views, who had risen above the prejudices and aversions of his race, and expressed his thoughts in language clear and precise, entirely unburdened by the figures of speech and superfluities commonly current in Indian talk.

"He had evidently pondered much over the condition and future of the Indians of North America and expressed his mature conclusions with the simple eloquence of a statesman.

"He comprehended perfectly the utter hopelessness of the struggle of the Indians against the progress of civilization. He saw clearly that nothing was left to them but to accommodate themselves to civilized ways or perish. He admitted that it was very hard to make his people understand this; that so long as they did not fully appreciate it, they should, as much as possible, be kept out of harm's way; that it was the duty of influential chiefs to cooperate with the Government to make the transition as little dangerous and painful as possible; that he, therefore, recognized the necessity of removing the Utes from Colorado, hard as the parting from their old haunts might be, and that he depended on me to bring about that removal under conditions favorable to his people.

"Ouray was by far the brightest Indian I have ever met.

"After the conclusion of our negotiations, which resulted in the restoration of peace and in the eventual removal of the Utes to a reservation in Utah, Ouray returned to his Western home. Soon after, he fell ill and died. Then something of a very touching nature happened.

"Some time after Ouray's death, I received from a government agent on the Ute reservation a letter which Ouray's widow, Chipeta, had dictated to him. In it, she told me that I had been her departed husband's best friend. He had said so. I had also done much to save his people from grave disaster and was therefore their best friend. She wished to give a memory of her husband as a present—the things he valued most. Would I accept the present?

"I thereupon wrote the agent asking him to inform himself whether my accepting a present would have a good effect with the Utes, and also whether my acceptance were thought advisable, whether it would be the proper thing on my part to send a present in return, and—if so—what should it be.

"A few weeks afterward, I received a box containing the clothes Ouray had worn while negotiating the treaty with me in Washington and, in addition, his tobacco pouch and an old powder horn which he used in his younger days.

"This was Chipeta's present. It was accompanied by a letter from the agent, giving me from Chipeta this message: If I accepted the present, to keep it while I lived and for my children, it would be regarded by Chipeta and her people as a proof of true friendship on my part, and they would esteem that friendship very highly. But if I made a present in return, it would be understood by them as signifying that I did not value their friendship much and simply wished to get rid of an obligation and be quits with them, and this would make them sad. Chipeta, therefore, hoped I would accept the present and let our friendship stand.

"It will be admitted that greater delicacy is seldom met with, even in the most refined society. It must be added, however, that this was an exceptional case. Ordinarily an Indian, when he makes a present to a white man, expects one in return, and his equanimity is by no means disturbed when that which he received is much more valuable than that which he has given. Nor does he differ very much in this from a majority of the civilized race.

"What I wish to show is that the noble savage, with chivalrous impulses and fine sentiments, as he occasionally appears in romance, should not be regarded as a mere figment of the imagination. He has existed, and no doubt he exists even now. It should, indeed, be remembered that the same superior Indians are, at the same time, in many respects, not above the barbarous habits and the ways of thinking of their tribes."

Wait Until Spring, Bandini

John Fante

HE CAME ALONG, kicking the deep snow. Here was a disgusted man. His name was Svevo Bandini, and he lived three blocks down that street. He was cold and there were holes in his shoes. That morning, he had patched the holes on the inside with pieces of cardboard from a macaroni box. The macaroni in that box was not paid for. He had thought of that as he placed the cardboard inside of his shoes.

He hated the snow. He was a bricklayer, and the snow froze the mortar between the brick he laid. He was on his way home, but what was the sense in going home? When he was a boy in Italy, in Abruzzi, he hated the snow too. No sunshine; no work. He was in America now, in the town of Rocklin, Colorado. He had just been in the Imperial Poolhall. In Italy there were mountains, too, like those white mountains a few miles west of him. The mountains were a huge white dress dropped plumb-like to the earth. Twenty years before, when he was 20 years old, he had starved for a full week in the folds of that savage white dress. He had been building a fireplace in a mountain lodge. It was dangerous up there in the winter. He had said the devil with the danger because he was only 20 then, and he had a girl in Rocklin, and he needed money. But the roof of the lodge had caved beneath the suffocating snow.

It harassed him always, that beautiful snow. He could never understand why he didn't go to California. Yet he stayed in Colorado, in the deep snow, because it was too late now. The beautiful white snow was like the beautiful white wife of Svevo Bandini, so white, so fertile, lying in a white bed in a house up the street. 456 Walnut Street, Rocklin, Colorado.

Svevo Bandini's eyes watered in the cold air. They were brown; they were soft; they were a woman's eyes. At birth, he had stolen them from his mother—for after the birth of Svevo Bandini, his mother was never quite the same, always ill, always with sickly eyes after his birth, and then she died, and it was Svevo's turn to carry soft brown eyes.

A hundred and fifty pounds was the weight of Svevo Bandini, and he had a son named Arturo who loved to touch his round shoulders and feel for the snakes inside. He was a fine man, Svevo Bandini, all muscles, and he had a wife named Maria who had only to think of the muscle in his loins and her body and her mind melted like the spring snows. She was so white, that Maria, and looking at her was seeing her through a film of olive oil.

Dio cane. Dio cane. It means God is a dog, and Svevo Bandini was saying it to the snow. Why did Svevo lose 10 dollars in a poker game tonight at the Imperial

Poolhall? He was such a poor man, and he had three children, and the macaroni was not paid, nor was the house in which the three children and the macaroni were kept. God is a dog.

Svevo Bandini had a wife who never said: Give me money for food for the children, but he had a wife with large black eyes, sickly bright from love, and those eyes had a way about them, a sly way of peering into his mouth, into his ears, into his stomach, and into his pockets. Those eyes were so clever a sad way, for they always knew when the Imperial Poolhall had done a good business. Such eyes for a wife! They saw all he was and all he hoped to be, but they never saw his soul.

That was an odd thing because Maria Bandini was a woman who looked upon all the living and the dead as souls. Maria knew what a soul was. A soul was an immortal thing she knew about. A soul was an immortal thing she would not argue. A soul was an immortal thing. Well, whatever it was, a soul was immortal.

Henry Williams etching, 1877.

Second Banana

Dottie Lamm

For all those spouses married to Top Bananas in politics, art, medicine, business, academia, or life in general—

> The attention going to him did not threaten me. What did threaten me was that I was not doing anything. I didn't like being Mrs. Charlton Heston. I was Lydia Clark.
>
> —Lydia Clark Heston

Anxiety Lurking in "Second Banana"

BY EVERYONE'S MEASURE, the weekend was a happy one—packed snow, bright sunny weather, and two children who acted as if their parents not only existed but somehow were salvageable human beings.

V.I.P. day at Beaver Creek, a new Colorado ski area officially opened, featured in *Sports Illustrated*, and praised by all. From a former U.S. president to the newest and youngest ski operator, all cogs in the wheel of the area's success congratulated each other with smiles. Smiles. Chatter. More smiles. Jokes. A weekend of public and private acclaim. No booing. No family traumas. Not even a marginal inconvenience.

After each descent from the chair at the top of the mountain, the small group gathered to exchange stories and vignettes. The snow crackled as the skiers stamped their fiberglass, their wood, and their metal on its polished surface. Poking their poles in the snow for emphasis, they shifted weight from side to side with a kind of stationary swagger. The anticipation of skiing combined with entrepreneurial success created a "macho" aura and demeanor, even in the women.

A good weekend. A great weekend! A weekend I wouldn't have missed. Why then, the Monday morning blues? Why the exhaustion? The quiet depression? Why the feeling of relief to be home, as if the weekend had been a colossal burden instead of a darned good vacation?

I run to my office as if to embrace its musty clutter. I wrestle, I muse, I reflect. I try to work on an article regarding fashion which somehow feels lifeless, trivial? Good, however, just to be here. Calmer after working, I reflect again on the past 48 hours.

Why was all the smiling, the constant attention so debilitating? Aren't I proud of my husband's success? Yes. Can't I see that I have at least some part of it? Yes. Am I resentful? Sometimes. But isn't he considerate? Usually. Then aren't I just "grousing" unnecessarily? Maybe.

"Second banana." The phrase pops into my consciousness unexpectedly. Second banana. First encountered in a speech by actress Linda Lavin, the term encompasses the stilted passivity syndrome which can suddenly engulf the spouses of notable achievers.

For second bananas, so much time seems to be spent in limbo—waiting, smiling, waiting. A 20-minute wait after the speeches. A five-minute wait for pictures. At least 10 minutes of socializing after each ride on the lift, foot stamping at the chill when the sun slips behind a cloud.

The governor comes in for lunch. Pictures. Waiting. Lunch. Talk. More waiting. Sunny ski minutes slip away. The family is dancing on a string of the father's position. The children have skied away on their own by mid-morning with my encouragement. But I remain, caught in the middle.

Caught in the middle—sniffing out the social expectations of others as I sniff in the exhilarating air. Would I cause concern or resentment if I skied off alone? Would I even be missed if I skied off a cliff?

Caught in the middle of a three-person chairlift for three long rides between people who talk over my head about issues of only peripheral interest to me. Caught in the middle. I hurry my daughter out of the ladies' room. "The governor is waiting," says the State Patrol driver pointedly, hovering over us as we exit. Big deal, I think, but I say nothing.

In time spent waiting, perhaps only one full ski run was lost. Did it really matter? Not much. The day was pleasant enough to stand and enjoy the view. And a full day of "public relations" on skis can hardly be considered a hardship compared with how most people in the world spend their workdays!

But "second-bananaing" becomes debilitating in any setting when it seems as if it will go on endlessly. By Monday morning, the retreat to the world of words that I alone weave and the attention to letters from readers directed just to me is a welcome respite.

And I wonder about all other spouses married to strong attention-getting others, who not only create their own wavelengths but also find that three-fourths of the world moves with them. How do those spouses survive if they don't have some escape, some activity which is theirs alone?

The weekend. What do I wish could have been different? I smile as I write all of this out of my system. Nothing specific, really. Nothing at all. But a general wish, yes, I do have one.

I wish that someday for some whole 24-hour period, all the "top bananas" of the world would walk in the shoes and feel the psychic vibrations of the "second bananas." Just for a day.

Champion of the Great American Family

Congresswoman Patricia Schroeder

WITHOUT FAIL, every year, some organization has a new idea for a cookbook and asks me to contribute a favorite recipe. I have to laugh because I really don't prepare meals beyond the hunt-and-gather stage. My "cookbook" consists of a list of the phone numbers of every carry-out restaurant within a 15-minute radius of my house. When people insist on a recipe, here's the one I send for breakfast: "Find a bowl. If it's on the floor, wash it because the dog was probably using it last. Find a box of cereal, preferably sugar-coated so you won't have to find the sugar. Find the milk, but check the spoil date before pouring. Then assemble."

* * *

When I first ran for Congress in 1972—as I have said—the chances for a successful Democratic candidacy in Denver did not look too good. Nationally, Richard Nixon was on his way to burying George McGovern in what was, at the time, the largest landslide victory in presidential election history.

In Denver, the prospects for a Democrat's winning the city's seat in Congress were so dim that no one wanted to run. Mike McKevitt, a popular Republican district attorney, had won the seat in 1970 after a bitter Democratic primary in which an antiwar challenger defeated the 10-term incumbent, thereby splitting the Democratic party. Worse, the 1971 redistricting had shifted a chunk of Democratic neighborhoods into an adjoining suburban district, thus improving McKevitt's chances.

A group of young, liberal Democrats, including my husband, caucused through the spring of 1972 to try to recruit a candidate. After a lot of discussion back and forth, the talk turned to running a woman. In the old days, there were two ways for a woman to run for Congress: as the widow of an incumbent or as a challenger in a hopeless race. Scenario number two was how I was chosen to run.

Jim stayed out late one night and came home just as I was getting into bed. "Guess whose name came up as a candidate for Congress," he said.

"I don't know."

"Guess."

"I don't know," I said, slightly irritated.

Jim said, "Yours."

I stared at him blankly.

"Somebody's got to run in this one, Pat. And none of the men want to go it. Larry Wright [a friend and a prominent Colorado Democrat] said, 'Let's get someone a little different. How about your wife, Jim?' "

"What did you say?" I asked.

" 'How about *your* wife?' "

I did end up running, but throughout the primary and the general race, I continued working at my part-time jobs teaching law, as hearing officer for Colorado's state personnel system, and as a volunteer counselor for Planned Parenthood. I spent little time wondering what life as a congresswoman would be like. There didn't seem to be much point. The one trip we made to Washington to raise money and support from the Democratic National Committee had been fruitless. I wanted to run a campaign on the issues—the Vietnam War, housing, the environment, children, the elderly. The DNC didn't think I would win that way—or any way—and they sent us home empty-handed.

So we raised money the same way we organized, at the grass roots. We had thousands of campaign posters printed on bright-colored paper because we "got a deal." It turned out that the bright colors were almost as controversial as the posters themselves. Few candidates defy the unspoken rule that campaign literature be printed in red, white, and blue, and that it show the candidate in front of the Capitol dome with his family and the dog. (Republicans would always insert a horseback shot in their brochures and the Democrats a bike-riding scene, to show their love of the outdoors.) Not only was the color of our paper unorthodox, my face didn't appear on any of my posters. Instead, one poster showed a field of tombstones in Arlington Cemetery with the headline: "Yes, some American troops have already been withdrawn from Vietnam." Another had a picture of a young Hispanic child with the caption: "This radical troublemaker wants something from you. Hope."

I discovered early in that first campaign that I enjoyed talking to people one-on-one, and I did a lot of it. Because they thought victory was a sure thing, the local Republican party kept my opponent in Washington for all but the last month of the campaign. That gave me a great head start. I began to relax and enjoy myself, whether I was going from door to door, from living room to living room, or from community center to community center.

Maybe I was good at campaigning because when I was a child, my family moved around a lot. Between the time I was born in Portland, Oregon, and my graduation from high school in Des Moines, Iowa, we had moved from Kansas City, Missouri; to North Platte, Nebraska; to Sioux City, Iowa; to Dallas, Texas; to Hamilton, Ohio. Starting at three, whenever we moved, I had to find kids to play with in the new neighborhood, so as soon as the moving truck pulled away, I would line up my toys on the sidewalk and sit down next to them. It worked. The toys were like flypaper! I made friends almost at once.

Although I became an adept campaigner, I was so busy juggling campaign, part-time jobs, and family that I was taken by surprise when, on election day in November 1972, I won 52 percent of the vote. I wasn't expecting the victory, and I certainly wasn't ready for what this would mean for me or my family. Jim wisecracked, "Well, you can't call a press conference now and say, 'I was only kidding.' "

Asians in Colorado

William Wei

A Profile in Courage

DURING THIS DARK CHAPTER in American history, Colorado had a shining light—Governor Ralph L. Carr. In a nation gripped by war hysteria, Carr stood virtually alone among public officials in his opposition to the wholesale incarceration of Japanese Americans in concentration camps. In doing so, he defended the civil rights of all Americans. With singular moral courage and at the cost of his political career, he affirmed anew the American pledge of liberty and justice for all. Yet, except to the Japanese Americans whom he helped and students of Colorado history, Carr remains largely unknown.

On February 29, 1942, Carr publicly declared that Colorado was willing to provide temporary quarters for Italian, German, and Japanese refugees from the West Coast. He admonished Coloradans against engaging in attacks on these groups and pointed out, "They are as loyal to American institutions as you and I. Many of them have been born here—are American citizens, with no connection

Colorado Governor Ralph Carr, 1940.

with or feeling of loyalty toward the customs and philosophies of Italy, Germany, and Japan." They were, in a word, trustworthy.

To show in a personal way that he meant what he said, Carr invited a Japanese American into his Denver home. He hired Wakako Domoto to work as his house girl. She was an exemplary student at Stanford University before being forced to leave with her family for Amache. Initially, she refused to accept the position with Carr because of fears about leaving Amache and facing angry Coloradans, who might abuse, beat, or even lynch her, a treatment some Coloradans suggested for all "Japs." To allay her forebodings, Carr personally went to Union Station to escort her to his home. He also arranged for her to take courses at the Emily Griffith Opportunity School and provided room and board as well as a salary of $35 dollars a month.

Carr's willingness to accept Japanese Americans into Colorado subjected him to intense public pressures. He regularly received hate mail. As Carr confided to his friend James F. Lockhart in Los Angeles, he got "oodles" of scathing letters that "took [his] hide off." Some writers accused him of being Japanese or "merely" in love with them. Critics demanded that he use force to prevent them from entering Colorado. His political nemesis, U.S. Senator Edwin "Big Ed" Johnson (Democrat), wanted him to use the National Guard to close the borders to Japanese American migrants, whether citizens or not. (Having himself used the National Guard earlier to block the entrance of migrant sugar beet workers when he was governor of Colorado, Johnson knew that it could be done.)

Governor Carr's perspective on the treatment of Japanese Americans was complex. While he was ambivalent about the questionable orders of the president and American military authorities to imprison Japanese Americans and restrict their freedoms, he nonetheless followed those directives for the same reason that he defended the rights of Japanese Americans—loyalty to the country and the ideals of Americanism.

He was acutely aware of the injustice of imprisoning Japanese Americans in concentration camps without a fair hearing. Carr saw the clamor for incarcerating Japanese Americans for what it was—intolerance. He recognized that they were entitled to equal protection under the law. Besides the inherent immorality and illegality of such treatment, he understood the appalling implications of the federal government's action. The failure to defend the rights of the Japanese Americans would imperil the rights of all Americans. In explaining his offer to welcome the West Coast refugees, Carr warned: "I am not talking on behalf of Japanese, of Italians, or of Germans as such when I say this. I am talking to ... all American people, whether their status be white, brown, or black, and regardless of the birthplaces of their grandfathers, when I say that if a majority may deprive a minority of its freedom, contrary to the terms of the Constitution today, then you as a minority may be subjected to the same ill-will of the majority tomorrow."

God Is Red

Vine Deloria Jr.

UNTIL 1890, American Indians played a critically important role in American domestic affairs, symbolizing the vast wilderness and frontier that Americans wished to tame. From the 1890s until the 1960s, Indian were truly the "Vanishing Americans," and most people believed that the tribes had largely been exterminated. There were token Indians present at Columbus Day and Thanksgiving celebrations and some Indian women sitting at the Santa Fe railroad stations selling pottery; but for most Americans, Indians had ceased to exist.

It is difficult to describe just how America began to embrace Indians again in recent years. When the Indian protests began in the 1960s, white Americans learned that in the remote canyons of the West, the swamplands of the Great

Studio portrait of a Plains Indian, circa 1860.

Lakes, and the southeastern United States were seemingly thousands upon thousands of Indians. Perhaps their first response was a sense of outrage and shock. Where were these angry Indians coming from and what was their gripe? They soon discovered that Indians had enjoyed treaty rights for nearly a century. They learned that as resources had been gobbled up by urban America, they were now in conflict with American Indians over the remaining natural resources of the continent, the best of which were in Indian hands.

The initial tendency of many whites was simply to demand that these resources also be taken and that Indians be moved into the mainstream of white society thereby removing their legal rights to these lands. Needless to say, these same officials did not demand that African-Americans or Chicanos or Hispanic Americans be given the same rights as whites; they were not sitting on oil, water, and mineral resources. White America only agitated to take away whatever rights Indians still had. Always, this pressure was disguised under the argument that all people, being citizens, should enjoy the same basic rights. Thus, where Indians had preserved hunting and fishing rights, the right to self-government, tax exemptions on land, and the power to zone reservation lands, the cry was to bring about equality. At the county and town level, where Indians did not have employment, housing, equal criminal justice, and social equality, there was no corresponding effort to provide these things that allegedly all Americans enjoyed.

In the 1860s, conditions were terrible for American Indians. The California Indians, for example, had been systematically neglected by generations of state and federal bureaucrats. In the 1850s, the federal government had signed a series of treaties with the bands and communities of Indians in California. These treaties gave the Indians clearly defined reservations in certain areas of the state, primarily in places not wanted by the whites or, at that time, inaccessible to them. But as gold fever grew in intensity and mining technology grew more sophisticated, arriving settlers began to prowl the length and breadth of the state looking for gold. The miners' objections to the federal effort to preserve the Indian ancestral lands were loud and violent.

Colorado's Japanese Americans
From 1886 to the Present

Bill Hosokawa

ONE DAY IN FALL 1944, Schluter asked one day whether they had to farm in Colorado and, if so, how much money it would take to own a farm or buy one.

Bob replied, "I guess we could scrape up about $1,200. We never had almost all of it." He thought a while and went off to camp. They waited until the following spring to act on the matter.

He heard no more. Schluter sat down and said something like, "Tell your folks to come out of Brighton. I've just bought you a farm—40 acres with good water rights here on the outskirts. The price is $6,000—$150 an acre—and you can pay me a bond whenever you can."

The land had been planted largely in sugar beets. Bob used the family's savings to buy a team of horses and a 10-year-old tractor, equipment needed to turn the beet fields into a vegetable farm. The first crop included tomatoes, cucumbers, and green beans. The soil was fertilized chemically, in addition to using barnyard manure as commonly used by other farmers. Harry bought supplies and took the produce to the Denargo wholesale market in Denver where grocers and brokers came to stock their bins. The Sakatas astounded Schluter by repaying the loan, plus interest, after the second harvest.

Early on, Bob detected a significant trend in the vegetable market. The corner grocery stores that required only small amounts of any one vegetable were being replaced by huge supermarket chains whose buyers wanted to be assured of a steady supply of produce of uniform quality. The era of food factories in the field had arrived, and Bob realized he would have to gear up his operations to succeed.

After the untimely deaths of his father and Harry, Bob found support and counsel in Frank Nakata, among the younger Issei in the Brighton community, and set out alone to expand his fields as rapidly as he could afford it. Today, Bob, with his wife, Joanna, and son, Robert, as partners, owns Sakata Farms, more than 3,000 acres in the Platte River Valley around and north of Brighton. (*American Vegetable Grower* lists it as the 15th largest in the Southwest region.) Sakata's land is in a patchwork pattern, partly because he acquired smaller farms as they became available and partly because he scattered his holdings over a large area to minimize the danger of an entire planting being wiped out by summer hailstorms. He was particularly happy to buy farms whose owners were nearing retirement. "They were going out of business anyway," Sakata explains, "and I could assure them a comfortable income for the rest of their lives."

Without an adequate supply of water, farming is impossible in the semi-arid West. Sakata made sure the farms he bought had ample water rights. When shares in water distribution companies became available, Sakata was quick to purchase them. As his operations expanded, Sakata found himself spending more and more time at a drawing board and in his maintenance shop as he designed new machines to speed up soil preparation, seeding, cultivating, harvesting, and packing his crops. One of his inventions is a giant machine that harvests an acre of corn in an hour, doing the work of 24 men handpicking the ears. His wife, who as a bride had worked alongside her husband in the fields, took charge of the expanding office chores. Their son, with degrees in microbiology, chemistry, and psychology, became general manager.

Sakata has made time to be more than just a farmer. He has been a bank director and member of the Brighton School Board. He helped found the Brighton Community Hospital and served nine years as its president. He served two terms as president of the National Sugar Beet Growers, served as president of the National Onion Growers Association, was named one of four outstanding young American farmers by the United States Junior Chamber of Commerce, was one of five members of the Agricultural Commodity Credit Board under Presidents Ford and Nixon, and is an elder at Brighton's First Presbyterian Church.

Sakata's agricultural know-how has gone international. He has been a consultant with the Hokkaido Sugar Company and the Takii Seed Company in Japan and the Sakata (no relation) Seed Company of Kyoto. He advised the Kubota Tractor Company on ways to adapt their machinery for the U.S. market and was a consultant to Mitsubishi Heavy Industries on development of a central pivot irrigation system and improvements on forklift trucks.

All his consulting with Japanese firms is without charge. Sakata says, "It's certainly debatable whether there is any advantage to our company in return for all the time I am spending in sharing my ideas and views on technology for improving food production, but I get a good feeling to know that I may be contributing towards the betterment of society."

One of his rewards was a Japanese decoration, the Order of the Sacred Treasure, Gold Rays with Rosette, in 2000. But equally important to him is the friendship and respect of the people who work for and with him in Brighton. An honor he cherishes especially is induction in 1999, together with Joanna, to the Colorado Agricultural Hall of Fame.

In contrast to Sakata's focus on farming, Shunso Matsuda's family built a successful company farming and raising livestock. Almost immediately after war broke out in 1941, federal agents arrested Matsuda, an Issei from Hiroshima who had risen to farm foreman near Salinas in California's Monterey County. Like other Japanese American community leaders, he had been picked up for no reason other than that he was a Japanese immigrant who had gained some prominence in the community. When all persons of Japanese ancestry were ordered out of the West, his wife, Chie, and their children left to join friends in Las Animas in Colorado's Arkansas Valley. In time, the oldest of the sons, Sam, joined the Army, studied at the Military Intelligence School and was sent to Tokyo where he served as interpreter in the war crimes trials.

Meanwhile, when the Matsudas learned that the Great Western Sugar Company was opening a plant at Hereford, close to the Wyoming line and east of Fort Collins, they moved there to find work. By 1970, Great Western's magazine, *Through the Leaves*, reported that the three Matsuda brothers—Tosh, Sam, and Dick—in partnership with Dick Woods, owned the Buckeye Land and Livestock Company. They grew sugar beets, corn, and alfalfa; fattened some 35,000 lambs each year on their Colorado property; and operated a ranch on leased land northeast of Casper, Wyoming, where 12,000 ewes and 2,000 cattle were pastured. The story also said the Matsudas set a record for their area by delivering 60 truckloads of sugar beets in one day to the Buckeye shipping station. As this is written, Sam Matsuda is retired in Wellington, and his son, Dave, farms some 700 acres in the area, custom feeding lambs and growing sorghum for dairymen.

A Nisei who decided there was a better way to make a living than farming—and succeeded eminently—is Jim Kanemoto of Longmont. He was born in 1917 to Goroku and Setsuno Kanemoto, immigrants from Hiroshima, who were farming near LaSalle, Colorado. In 1935, Jim was living in the Denver Buddhist Temple dormitory and attending Manual Training High School when his father died in an automobile accident. Jim hurried home to take over the family's 80-acre farm on rented land just outside of Longmont. Goroku, by law, could not own land. But Jim, as a citizen, could, and he saw no advantage in continuing to be a renter. Shortly, he and his brother George, younger by two years, contracted to buy 140 acres off South Main Street on what was then Longmont's southern outskirts. Eventually, their holdings grew into a 350-acre vegetable farm with a retail market on South Main.

By 1944, Jim felt secure enough to marry Chiyo Miyasaki from another Colorado farming family. (And four years later, George married Chiyo's sister, Jane.) "We worked hard together," Jim recalls. "Sometimes, when I was extra busy in the fields, Chiyo would help load up the truck, drive a load of vegetables to the Denargo market in Denver, sell the produce, and then buy fruits and other stuff to sell at the market we were running."

In winter, when there was time to spare, Jim tinkered with ideas for improving farming methods. One was a portable dam that could be placed in an irrigation ditch to regulate the volume of water diverted to the fields. Kanemoto patented it and, in 1960, founded the Kane Manufacturing Company to manufacture and market it.

All That is Secret

Patricia Raybon

November 1922

THE LITTLE BABY WAS four hours old. Still unwashed. Barely crying. But Joe Spain's old ears recognized the sound. A human infant. Somebody's mistake left in the Colorado cold to die.

He twisted his mouth, pulled the reins on his cutting horse, Barrel, and turned into the freezing wind. Barrel's ears stood straight up, trembling. The horse heard it too. On the cold, open plains, the wide early morning silence rendered every sound bigger, as if magnified.

The cry was half a mile away. But Spain still heard it clear as a bell.

"C'mon, girl," he said to Barrel. "We best go see."

He let the big horse pick her way through the frozen scrub and prairie grass. A light snow the night before had dusted the ground, leaving a far and white horizon under the blinding blue sky.

The horse was fresh and eager, but already both of them were breathing hard, their breath turning to white vapor in the sharp, bracing frost.

Spain, a part-time cowboy, stood up in his stirrups and scanned the prairie with narrowed eyes, peering in all directions. His lean body, still skinny after 60-odd years, steeled itself against the cold. As a Negro man, he knew some considered him out of place in such environs. But he had known no place better or longer than these High Plains, and the pure respect he felt for the rough landscape bordered on its own kind of adoration, if not sheer awe.

Scanning the terrain, he stood in the freezing wind, the brim of his worn wool Stetson pulled low and humbled in the shining, cold glare.

Then he saw the tracks. Footprints in light snow. He looked beyond the traces and saw the county road. Right away, he figured what had happened. Before daybreak, somebody drove their vehicle down the road until it turned to dirt. Then they hopped the low, barbed-wire fence that bordered the road, trekked a cold mile into Lazy K pastureland, and looked for a dip in the flat landscape.

There in the open, in a draw in the middle of the range, they left the child. No attempt to bury it. Coyotes would eat the evidence. Or a family of foxes.

As for the snowy footprints, they would melt in the dry air and blazing sun—just as they were doing right now. By noon, the cold prints would all be gone.

Spain nosed the horse to follow the tracks toward the sound. If the child was going to make it, he'd have to find it now.

Sure enough, the cry was growing fainter. Barely a whimper now. But finally he saw the bundle, wrapped in a torn piece of dirty tarp.

The horse saw the dark bulge and pulled up, dug her hooves into the cold ground.

"It's okay, girl," Spain said. He patted the animal's neck, slid out of his saddle, and dropped the reins. Barrel stood alert, agitated but waiting.

Sighing, Spain crunched across the frozen grass and looked down at the tarp. He pushed the hat back on his head and knelt in the snow. Pulling back the tarp, he felt his gloved hands go cold.

It can't be. Not again.

The tiny child was wrapped in a man's white dress shirt and nothing else. Blood on its slick black hair had started to ice. The baby was shivering, lips almost blue. A low moan, no longer a cry, emerged from its tiny, perfect mouth.

"*Lord Jesus,* pretty little baby," Spain said.

He reached down, picked up the child, flicked the bloody ice off its head, letting the tarp fall off. "Good grief, what a hateful way to enter this ol' world."

He opened his old shearling jacket, pressed the baby onto his chest, breathed hot breath on its face, took off his gloves with his teeth, and rubbed his large hands on the baby's ice-cold back. Coaxing it. Scolding it. "C'mon, little bit. Ol' Joe's got you."

A lone rider by simpleinsomnia.

"The Utes Must Go!"

Peter R. Decker

THE U.S. GOVERNMENT, however, had not yet finished reconfiguring the Ute reservations. In 1886, in a move to save administrative and military costs, Washington combined the Ouray and Uintah Reservations into one unit, insensitive to the disparate histories and cultures of the three Ute bands, all the while keeping an eye on them from Fort Thornburgh. When well over half of the Uncompahgre and White River bands, unhappy with their land and irregular rations, made an effort to move to the Cheyenne River Indian Reservation in South Dakota, the army hunted them down and drove them back into their Utah pen. In 1887, Congress finally enacted its allotment policy, so dear to Schurz and Indian reformers, with passage of the Dawes Act. It proved to be as unpopular as it was ineffective. The Utes, as well as other tribes, quickly discovered that as much as Washington wished to push the Indians toward "the habits of civilization," it was difficult to sustain a livelihood on semiarid parcels too small and dry to sustain a prairie dog colony. In addition, the entire concept of individual ownership violated the Utes' concept of tribal holdings. In 1895, the Weeminuche band, under Chief Ignacio's leadership, found the

A depiction of the Ghost Dance of the Sioux Indians in North America. Originally published in the Illustrated London News, *1891.*

allotment idea so alien to their tradition that they moved to the western end of the Southern Ute Reservation, where they established their own Ute Mountain Reservation. They refused to accept any allotments. In Utah and within the remaining portion of the Southern Ute Reservation, where allotments were made and often forced upon individual Utes, the parcels carried the prohibition against selling the land for 25 years. Lands not allotted, or about 85 percent of the reservation, were declared "excess" by Washington and thrown open to white settlers. It is no wonder that the Utes, along with other tribes, took to the soon-to-be-banned Ghost Dance, which promised to the faithful a better life and an empowerment to rid the world of whites. And to further convince the Utes that agreements were made to be broken, Washington lopped off more than 50,000 acres from the Southern Ute Reservation to carve out Mesa Verde National Park and another million acres from the combined Uintah/Ouray Reservation to create the Uintah National Forest. The Utes did receive some compensatory lands and cash in the 1930s and 1950s, but the payments, said the Utes, failed to match the government's original promises.

Ironically, the Southern Utes today are recognized primarily for their wealth. The 1,400-member tribe sits on one of the biggest supplies of natural gas in the United States. The Utes retained the mineral rights on the entire reservation, including "excess" lands sold to whites, creating immense legal battles with private landholders and the Department of Interior. But through a series of court settlements and astute reinvestments in real estate, joint energy ventures, and securities, the tribe has assembled a $1.45 billion energy conglomerate, making it one of the richest tribes in the nation. It is one of the very few tribes whose wealth doesn't hinge on gambling.

From where I write in southwestern Colorado, just down from the serene hilltop where my discovery of arrowheads several years ago spawned this book, I find it difficult to imagine the bloody horror played out over a century ago on a similarly pastoral setting. If the Battle of Milk Creek was one of the most decorated in U.S. military history, what must the Utes have suffered? And how had the Indians honored their heroes? I do not know. But a Ute told me their spirits live here, in a country no longer their own.

Ticket to Hollywood

Gary Reilly

I WOKE UP ON Wednesday morning feeling invigorated, I made another eggburger before setting out for Rocky Cab. I stood eating it and sipping my Coke and looking out the kitchen window at clouds moving over the city. Snow clouds. I had mixed feelings. We cabbies refer to snow as "white gold." The radios in our taxis start hopping when snow starts falling, because people hate to drive in the snow. I'm talking Colorado people. Don't ask me to explain that, although the influx of Californians during the past few years might. I myself hail from Wichita, Kansas, where the air is humid and the snow is wet. Denver has dry snow. I love science.

I thought about not driving that day because I hate driving when normal people are afraid to drive—it makes me feel like the wrong kind of outsider. But the odds were good that I would score a hundred bucks without even trying. It's a funny thing about a sure score. It makes you lethargic. The challenge disappears. I stood there chewing my eggburger and just staring out the window, feeling as if the money was already in my pocket and there was no reason to get a move on. It was the same feeling I had in college when I started writing my first novel. The doldrums appeared when I received my first rejection slip.

I closed my crow's nest and climbed down the fire escape, and already tiny flakes were tickling my face. I fired up my heap and headed for Rocky Cab. I had to turn on the windshield wipers before I got halfway there. This was going to be one of "those" snows, I could sense it. By the time I got to Rocky, the flakes had become big enough to recognize two of a kind.

The on-call room was packed with a few newbies as well as a lot of white-gold sourdoughs who would even go to work on a Saturday just to get in on the motherlode. When the radio is jumping and the old pros are working the asphalt, the newbies don't stand a chance. You don't just stroll into the Yukon and start picking up nuggets off the permafrost. You have to know your Jack London inside and out, and newbies don't know jack about snow driving. I felt sorry for them, just as I had felt sorry for myself back when I was a newbie.

I paid for my daily lease and picked up the key and trip sheet for 127 from Rollo, who was too busy to even eat donuts. When I got outside the big flakes were coming down steadily. A night driver had just brought 127 in, so the cab was warmed up for me. That's always pleasant on a day like this. It added to my lethargy. I checked the oil and water and looked for new dents on the body, which you always have to do or you get blamed for it—like everything else in life.

I drove to a 7-Eleven and gassed up and bought a Coke and Twinkie, then headed for downtown Denver listening to the radio, which was already jumping. I wanted to sit in front of a hotel while I ate brunch and see if I might score an airport run before diving into the gold fields. The line at the Brown Palace Hotel was short, so I barely had time to finish my Twinkie before a businessman came out wearing an overcoat and carrying a briefcase. "DIA," I said to myself. I was feeling both lethargic and smug. The man climbed into the backseat and said, "The history museum."

That burst my lethargic balloon. The Denver Museum of Natural History is on the east side of City Park. It's a $6 fare at best, maybe $7 with a tip. But I didn't mind so much. Money is money, and this trip would thrust me into the gold fields. I knew I would be jumping bells after I dropped him off. That's cabbie lingo for radio calls from headquarters. I pulled away from the hotel and circled around and got onto 17th Avenue and headed for Colorado Boulevard, which runs adjacent to City Park. I made small talk. The man said he was in charge of a new exhibit that was being brought in from Taiwan. Something to do with statues made of jade. I pretended to be interested, which I had been good at since first grade.

After he got out of my cab, I paused in front of the museum and filled out my trip sheet while listening for bells on that side of town. I didn't hear anything I liked. This is part of the smugness and lethargy and general cocksureness of driving on a day when half the city is desperate for cabs. I could have made a bundle just working the grocery stores, but that would have entailed loading my trunk with white plastic bags, standing in the snow, and then helping my fares carry the bags into houses. Need I say more?

Denver Museum of Natural History shown in 1908. Now known as the Denver Museum of Nature and Science, it has been expanded.

La Gente
Hispano History and Life in Colorado

Vincent C. de Baca, editor

THE HISTORY OF MIGRATORY farm work in the southwestern United States dates back to at least 1870 with the use of Chinese labor. At that time, an "open door" policy allowed the free flow of immigration into this country. In 1882, however, Congress passed the Chinese Exclusion Act, which prompted southwestern farmers to look to Mexico for inexpensive, temporary field hands who could be attracted across a virtually open border.

Political division, religious suppression, and a poor economy in Mexico resulted in cycles of Mexican immigration into the Southwestern United States after the Mexican Revolution in 1917. By the 1920s, Mexican nationals had begun immigrating into the United States in large numbers. World War I and the subsequent prosperity of the 1920s had created a shortage of labor north of the border, and American farmers and businessmen were pleased to have access to a large labor supply at such close proximity. Soon Mexican enclaves were found in cities offering employment throughout the United States, most notably in the five Southwestern states of California, Arizona, Texas, New Mexico, and Colorado.

In Colorado, Mexican migrant workers found employment in the railroad gangs and sugar beet fields. Although a restrictive immigration law was in place (the Immigration Act of 1917), it was loosely applied with regard to Mexican migration.

Early immigration laws, most notably the Alien Contract Labor Act of 1885, prohibited the contracting of temporary migratory workers from any country. However, a provision of exception in the Immigration Act of 1917 allowed for a massive influx of Mexican migrant workers. This was enhanced by the Immigration Act of 1924, which caused the exclusion of Asian immigrants and thus increased the demand for Mexican labor.

The legacy of the Mexican migratory worker in Colorado is largely tied to agriculture. By 1900, Colorado's soil had proven itself fertile for sugar beet farming, and the state soon led the nation in sugar manufacture. Large-scale sugar mills developed in the southeastern Colorado counties of Otero, Bent, and Prowers around the towns of Rocky Ford, La Junta, Lamar, Holly, and, of course, Sugar City. The area had seen a shortage of temporary labor since about 1900. Sugar beet farming was labor intensive, and factories in the Arkansas Valley constantly competed for sources of cheap field labor. Germans from Russia, Mexican immigrants, Japanese immigrants, and Native Americans were solicited to work in the fields. Mexican migrant workers, due to need, cost, and proximity, quickly filled the void. By the 1920s, four very profitable sugar beet mills in southeast Colorado were using primarily Mexican migratory workers as their source of labor. State legislative attempts to restrict Mexican immigration were successfully lobbied against by the large-scale growers, sugar companies, and industrial concerns.

Beet farmers and sugar factories encouraged migrations from Mexico in order to have a long-term supply of inexpensive labor. Local Anglo and Spanish citizens themselves encouraged it because it was work they were unwilling to do for the price. Thus, Mexican migrant workers had long been welcomed in the area until the severity of the Depression put some 12 million Americans out of work.

For a number of reasons, certainly low wages, the Mexican migrant worker was quickly preferred over the native Spanish speaker who lived in this area of Colorado's vast sugar beet fields. However, indigenous Spanish-speaking people would soon be called back into the Colorado fields when nativist policies forced Mexican migrants out during a 1936 repatriation.

Because of the seasonal nature and low pay of work in the beet fields, migrant workers often could not afford the cost of transport back to Mexico. They were thus forced to spend the off-season in Denver's slums and Pueblo's barrios. There they looked for low-paying work or went on relief for the winter. Historian Daniel Elazar wrote of Colorado migrants:

> Kept segregated and relegated to subcitizen status, it would be another generation before they (or their children) would begin to enter Colorado's political life. Their neighborhoods in Denver and their barrios located around Pueblo and the state's smaller cities became Colorado's equivalent of the black ghettos of the East.

Apparently, however, the sugar beet companies tried to keep their seasonal Mexican workers in the area. If not forced outright to stay in the area during the winter due to debt, they were certainly encouraged to stay. Often their final contract pay was withheld, making them virtual slaves in a foreign country. It is easy to see why the sugar beet companies preferred the "unspoiled Mexican," for they were able to treat them little better than cattle.

By the end of the 1930s, many thousands of Mexican immigrants considered America and Colorado their home. Many had borne children here, who automatically became U.S. citizens under the 14th Amendment. It is difficult today to estimate the number of Mexican immigrants who either crossed the border temporarily or stayed in the United States, as there was constant legal and illegal movement back and forth. It was a small matter to report oneself at a border station, and immigrants moved around the United States as they settled into different communities during the 1920s and 1930s. The U.S. Census Bureau also tended not to distinguish between generations-old Spanish American citizens and Mexican nationals, preferring to lump them together as one cultural group. This changed, however, with the 1930 census, which specified Mexican as a race unto itself.

Once here, the Mexican immigrant, due to his immigrant status, generally remained locked into low-paying, unskilled labor or farm work. But there was also a great deal of reluctance on the part of Mexican immigrants to become naturalized American citizens. Like other immigrants to the United States, many Mexican nationals believed they would eventually return to Mexico. Others did not become citizens because they felt they would not receive adequate justice at the hands of the Anglos as "lower-class" Mexican American citizens as they would as citizens of Mexico.

With the onset of the Great Depression, there began a "national call" to repatriate the roughly 400,000 illegal aliens in the country. As historian Abraham Hoffman states, "Repatriation means a return to one's homeland—more than a return—a sending back." In the 1940s, many went back because they *wanted* to go back; they had always intended to go back and may have been encouraged to do so by the improving Mexican economy. The thinly veiled border made it easy to go back and forth.

SECTION XII

Queen City of the Plains

On the Road

Jack Kerouac

THE BUS STATION was crowded to the doors. All kinds of people were waiting for buses or just standing around; there were a lot of Indians, who watched everything with their stony eyes. The girl disengaged herself from my talk and joined the sailor and the others. Slim was dozing on a bench. I sat down. The floors of bus stations were the same all over the country, always covered with butts and spit and they give a feeling of sadness that only bus stations have. For a moment, it was no different from being in Newark, except for the great hugeness outside that I loved so much. I rued the way I had broken up the purity of my entire trip, not saving every dime, and dawdling and not really making time, fooling around with this sullen girl and spending all my money. It made me sick. I hadn't slept in so long I got too tired to curse and fuss and went off to sleep; I curled up on the seat with my canvas bag for a pillow, and slept till eight o'clock in the morning among the dreamy murmurs and noises of the station and of hundreds of people passing.

I woke up with a big headache. Slim was gone—to Montana, I guess. I went outside. And there in the blue air I saw for the first time, far off, the great snowy tops of the Rocky Mountains. I took a deep breath. I had to get to Denver at once. First, I ate a breakfast, a modest one of toast and coffee and one egg, and then I cut out of town to the highway. The Wild West festival was still going on; there was a rodeo, and the whooping and jumping were about to start all over again. I left it behind me. I wanted to see my gang in Denver. I crossed a railroad overpass and reached a bunch of shacks where two highways forked off, both for Denver. I took the one nearest the mountains so I could look at them and pointed myself that way. I got a ride right off from a young fellow from Connecticut who was driving around the country in his jalopy, painting; he was the son of an editor in the East. He talked and talked; I was sick from drinking and from the altitude. At one point, I almost had to stick my head out the window. But by the time he let me off at Longmont, Colorado, I was feeling normal again and had even started telling him about the state of my own travels. He wished me luck.

It was beautiful in Longmont. Under a tremendous old tree was a bed of green lawn grass belonging to a gas station. I asked the attendant if I could sleep there, and he said sure; so I stretched out a wool shirt, laid my face flat on it, with an elbow out, and with one eye cocked at the snowy Rockies in the hot sun for just a moment. I fell asleep for two delicious hours, the only discomfort being an occasional Colorado ant. And here I am in Colorado! I kept thinking gleefully. Damn! Damn! Damn! I'm making it! And after a refreshing sleep filled with cobwebby dreams of my past life in the East, I got up, washed in the station men's room, and strode off, fit and slick as a fiddle, and got me a rich, thick milkshake at the roadhouse to put some freeze in my hot, tormented stomach.

Incidentally, a very beautiful Colorado gal shook me that cream; she was all smiles too; I was grateful; it made up for last night. I said to myself, Wow! What will *Denver* be like! I got on that hot road, and off I went in a brand-new car driven by a Denver businessman of about 35. He went 70. I tingled all over; I counted minutes and subtracted miles. Just ahead, over the rolling wheatfields all golden beneath the distant snows of Estes, I'd be seeing old Denver at last. I pictured myself in a Denver bar that night, with all the gang, and in their eyes I would be strange and ragged and like the Prophet who has walked across the land to bring the dark Word, and the only Word I had was, "Wow!" The man and I had a long, warm conversation about our respective schemes in life, and before I knew it we were going over the wholesale fruit markets outside Denver; there were smoke stacks, smoke, railyards, red-brick buildings, and the distant downtown graystone buildings, and here I was in Denver. He let me off at Larimer Street, I stumbled along with the most wicked grin of joy in the world, among the old bums and beat cowboys of Larimer Street.

Colorado

William MacLeod Raine

AS THEY CROSSED THE BRIDGE into Denver, the two men could look down Cherry Creek to the Platte. Hundreds of tents and covered wagons lined the banks of both streams. In the darkness, these could not be seen, but scores of campfires gleamed among the cottonwoods. The population was a continuously shifting one. Many immigrants arrived each day, and many left for the diggings at the gold camps. Another wave of travel beat back from the hills. It was made up of dissatisfied miners who had sold their tools and superfluous provisions and were heading back for "the States." The two men sauntered up F Street and along Larimer. They were in no hurry, and the life outside was as interesting as that inside the gambling halls and saloons, which offered the only amusement in the town.

The thoroughfares surged with humanity. On either side of the road were one-story frame buildings devoted to games of chance. Some of these resorts were more pretentious, notably the Criterion and Denver Hall.

Into the latter, Tom and his companion drifted. The dirt floor had been well sprinkled to keep down the dust from hundreds of moving feet. A long bar ran part way down one side of the room. This was lined with customers drinking and smoking. Hundreds of roughly dressed men moved to and fro, wandering from one gaming table to another. Others sat steadily in one place, intent on the game before them, whether it was faro, roulette, Mexican monte, or poker.

One group stood in front of a man on a box behind a raised table. The patter of his sing-song monologue came to Tom, and he recognized the voice before he caught sight of Mose Wilson's bearded face.

"Here y'are, gents. This ace of hearts is the winning card. Watch it. Keep yore eye on it as I shuffle. Here it is now—now here. I lay all three cards face down on the table. Which one is it? Point it out the first time, an' I lose, you win. Right here it is, see. Now watch again." He shuffled the three cards once more. "I take no bets from paupers, children, or cripples. The ace of hearts, gents. A square game. The hand is quicker than the eye. Tha's my proposition. The ace of hearts, gents. If you pick it first time you win. Who'll go me 20?"

A man shuffled forward. "Go you once," he growled.

Tom, on the outskirts of the group, stood on tiptoe. The man was Buck Comstock. He was, Tom guessed at once, a capper. Comstock slapped down a $20 gold piece, and the three-card-monte man covered it with another. The capper picked the ace, pocketed the money, and swaggered through the crowd boasting how easy it had been.

"My friend, you won. You're a stranger to me, but no hard feelings. Next time I'll win—maybe. Who else wants easy money?" asked Wilson.

He continued to deal the cards. One interested tenderfoot edged a little closer. The dealer marked him for his prey without ever letting his eyes rest on him. The patter ran on without ceasing.

Tom watched the tenderfoot and could almost read his thoughts. This game looks simple. The dealer has, evidently without noticing it, turned up slightly one corner of the ace. Now is the time to bet. The tenderfoot tosses out a gold piece. He points to the card with the raised corner, but alas! It is not the ace. Puzzled and chagrined, he retreats, aware that somehow he had been tricked and that the hand is quicker than the eye.

The "Real Denver" is Gone Forever

Gene Amole

Cowtown

THE HEADLINE ON William Gallo's Sunday *News* story about downtown architecture asked, 'Where is the real Denver?'

He talked to architects and critics about our downtown. They agreed that our skyscrapers ignore Denver's individuality. Almost identical structures can be found in Houston, San Francisco, New York, Chicago.

Absolutely true. We have traded our soul to the devil for the big time. Denver has been lusting after the big time since I can remember.

We apologized for being an "overgrown Cowtown" by proclaiming, "We are a mile closer to the sun," or, "We have the largest whatever between Kansas City and the West Coast."

But we were just kidding ourselves. We really wanted those cookie-cutter tall buildings, freeways, suburbs, and all the other superficial accouterments of the big time. We wanted to look like New York, San Francisco, and Chicago. Well, we got our big time, and the devil claimed our soul. Perhaps the most important question is, "What was the real Denver?"

We have always had imitative architecture. Our cherished D&F Tower is a copy of St. Mark's campanile in Venice. The old Windsor Hotel was supposed to look like Windsor Castle. And our post office is a poor replica of a Roman bathhouse.

If there is anything traditional about us, it is that we have coveted other architectural styles. In our pursuit of the big time, we never really made the effort to create an appropriate style for our climate, our terrain, our people.

Our lost "real Denver" had less to do with structures than it did with the consequences of making the big time. We had to give up our small time—our overgrown cowtown.

The Loop at 15th and Arapahoe is gone. It was the Denver Tramway Co. Terminal where the old trolleys turned around, and where, as Elwood and Max Brooks advertised, "working people can bank on a transfer at the Central Bank & Trust Co."

We lost an important part of downtown when the Home Public Market closed. Remember the rich smells of warm bread, pickled herring, and fresh ground coffee? The butchers walked on sawdust behind the counters. Produce gleamed like rows of jewels. There was clatter, loud talk, and cash registers jingling. It closed when the *Denver Post* moved there from its "bucket of blood" plant on Champa Street.

We were ashamed of gaudy old Curtis Street with its Empress, Isis, and Rialto theaters. But didn't those Coney Islands and fried onions smell great in Sam's No. 3?

Hardly anyone remembers Hop Alley. And not many will admit remembering the old Ace High bawdy house.

We gave up Keables' sandwich shops, the Tabor Grand, the Oxford Hotel coffee shop, Harry Bramer's, the Mozart Bar, Pell's Oyster House, McVittie's, the Blue Parrot Inn, the Golden Eagle, Boggio's, the Navarre, the Shirley Savoy, the Albany, and the Mizpah Arch.

That Denver is gone. Forever.

February 22, 1983.

Chinatown

Emil Habdank Dunikowski

WE DEPARTED MANITOU late at night and having been awakened after a short sleep by the warm rays of the sun, we left our train. We immediately found ourselves in the heart of downtown Denver, a fascinating young giant which has developed in the most amazing way. In 1859 the first "blockhouse" was built here; in 1870, the town still numbered only 4,700 inhabitants; in 1880, 35,628; and at present [1891], the population has exceeded 150,000.

Denver is the Queen [City] of the Great Plains, the Empress of the Rockies! We found ourselves on a flat upland. The mountains are far behind us—undoubtedly they have already disappeared. ... No ... they have not! For to the west one sees a magnificent picture unfolding before him! Resembling a great, jagged blue wall, the Front Range lies some 15 kilometers behind the city. From this mountain belt, our eyes can encompass a section at least 240 kilometers long. Numerous peaks, covered here and there with white patches of snow, shoot up high into the air; we can clearly make out Long's Peak … Gray's Peak … Mount Evans … Pike's Peak, and many others.

Satiated with the view of the mountains, we began to walk about the city. It is exceptionally beautiful. Expensive homes, wide streets, many shade trees and gardens, excellent water, marvelous air—one can easily envy the Denverites. Of all the larger American cities, Denver has the lowest mortality rate ... 10 per every 1,000 inhabitants. In view of this, we children of the Old World are indeed less fortunate in the mortality rate of our cities, which annually lose some 30-odd people per 1,000 inhabitants.

On all the more important [Denver] streets, we see electric trams. The illumination [i.e., street lights] are also electric—the same as in Detroit—that is, a whole wreath of lamps on a high steel pole. The homes, however tasteless, are magnificent and expensive. Above all, one is struck by the variety and beauty of the building materials, all of which are obtained from within Colorado and primarily in the vicinity of Denver itself. One of the most beautiful and most frequently used building materials, especially for large public edifices, is glossy riolitic tuff stippled black by biotite, which comes from the tertiary areas south of the city.

The most beautiful public buildings in Denver are the State Capitol—located at the highest point in the city, affording a magnificent view of the surrounding area—the County Courthouse, and the University. At every step, one can see that the city is very young—all the trees, primarily plane-trees and maples, obviously have been recently planted, since none of them is more than 30 years old. Everywhere one sees construction, the laying of pavement and of pipelines—in a word, a young giant is growing up before our eyes. Some 250,000 shade trees already have been planted so that [the reader] can imagine how beautiful it looks. The water here is extremely good, so it is therefore not surprising that the general health [of the population] is excellent. Several years ago, while exploring for a seam of coal near Denver, they even reached water which burst forth like an artesian well at a depth of 175 to 1,200 feet.

* * *

As soon as the electric lights came on in the city, we went with a policeman to the local Chinese quarter. After San Francisco, this is the largest Chinatown in the United States. The children of Heaven have set up things here just as in their own country and have managed to cleverly circumvent local municipal laws. Since the Chinese do not like wide streets, in the middle of the blocks belonging to them—that is, where buildings themselves should stand—they have arranged things in their own way, creating something resembling a miniature town within a larger city.

Narrow little streets, dark passageways, breakneck stairs, and hiding places in which an individual would get hopelessly lost without a guide—this, in essence, is the dwelling place of the Chinese. Our policeman leads the way, occasionally lighting wax matches en route, and we follow him with great interest. We visit the Chinese stores offering for sale thousands of the most varied kinds of items whose identity and usefulness are known only [to the Chinese]. Naturally, our "collectors" of curios buy whole piles [of them], with the policeman serving as an intermediary in the bargaining process.

From the stores we went to the Chinese restaurants and tea parlors. What an unpleasant smell, what strange dishes do the Sons of the Heavenly Kingdom eat with chopsticks—and so elegantly that they don't drop a single grain of rice! Our Chinese host invited us to a banquet at which we sampled some kind of dish made from worms' ganglion or trotters, and we had enough.

Nearby were alcoves with gaming tables. In front of the slant-eyed banker lay piles of Chinese coins in small denominations. Around him, gamblers played with such concentration and enthusiasm, which is hard to imagine unless seen for yourself.

Denver's Larimer Street

Thomas J. Noel

ON SEPTEMBER 14, 1958, a Mexican family arrived in Denver with their life savings of $500. Gonzalo G. Silva brought his wife and nine children. They liked the vacant one-story hall at 2010 Larimer. From 1920 to 1947, it had been the jewelry store of H.T. Osumi. Then, William Katchen and his son had operated a jewelry and clothing shop there.

"We thought that $500 would be plenty to open a restaurant," recalled Manuel Silva. "But Public Service wanted a $350 deposit, and the phone company wanted $35. And in this part of town it is hard to get credit. So we just sat here with no heat, light, or phone.

"Finally, Mariano Galindo of La Popular next door came over and asked us what was happening. Then he borrowed $300 from the St. Cajetan Credit Union and gave it to us. Tomas Molino of Molino Foods also loaned us money. So we opened the Monterey House #1 here and, within a year, paid Mariano and Tomas back."

The Silvas served only Mexican food and made nearly everything from scratch. Gonzalo Silva prospered and decided to retire to Mexico. His son, Manuel, took over the restaurant in 1974. "Mexican people from all over come down here," Manuel reports. "They come from Greeley, Fort Lupton, and Pueblo because this block has everything they need and everybody speaks Spanish—even the Jews and Italians.

"Mexican people also come because they can sell their chiles, peppers, onions, tomatoes, tamales, and tortillas to the little stores here. I buy from them. They bring in produce that is twice as good and half as cheap as Safeway." Manuel can be found cooking in back or cashiering in front of the century-old building six days a week. "I will stay here," Manuel promises, "where we got our start." "You'd be surprised," says Manuel, "but Larimer Street is one of the safest in Denver. Too many witnesses here. Some break-ins but no hold-up-hands much.

"I keep peace here. Jukebox cause fights, so I have no more jukebox. Once when I close a man tells me, 'hold up hands.' He stick gun in my face. But his hand shake so much I get nervous. So I tell him, 'Give me gun.' He did. I let him go. He came back eight days later for the gun.

"On Larimer, we have the craziest hold-up-hands. A guy make hold-up at Hunchie's Bar. Have everybody lie on floor. Then the guy emptying garbage comes in and bangs down a trash can. The noise frightened the robber and he dropped his gun. They grabbed him, beat the shit out of him and made him call the cops on himself.

"Another time at the bakery, two robbers see paddy wagon and two cops out front. But they think it is bakery truck and that the cops are delivery men. So they went to jail in the bread truck."

My Larimer Street: Past and Gone

Harold Woods

Thursday P.M. 4:25, Mr. Harold Woods:

DEAR FRIEND:

I just had returned from a five-cent cup of coffee at the U.S. Drug where Mamie sent me for a dog book Clover Leaf. If she don't start hitting a winner pretty soon, you'll have to see what you can do about her rent, as we'll all be sleeping in under the bridge. Well, I was in hopes you might drop around today. I had quite an experience the other A.M. with some good-looking square and what she asked me to do will not be permitted to be explained through Uncle Sam's mail—even though he did up the ante a penny; and besides, it might be opened by the wrong person should you decide to take the day off. I told her to talk to old Tom the Cashier, as for my part I'd stick to Cabbage after all there is a slight Variation unless the cabbage is left to rot in the Patch. I saw the galloping Swede (Smitty's old buddy) they both used to have the same gal. You must have seen her around, about 7 ft. tall. I went up to see Smitty once about four yrs. ago, and Swede was snoring on one side of the bed, and Smitty on the other big skinny June was in the middle clutching a big bottle full of "sweet Lucy," all knocked out with her dirty feet protruding a good 10 inches over the foot of the mattress. I couldn't wake none of them so I helped myself to June's Jug and made a quiet but hasty exit taking along the bottle as in my drinking days I sent Swede to make a run and he got his room numbers mixed and brought the wine in to his old lady and me ready to die and my last buck. So I didn't steal the jug; I just collected what I had coming. About an hour later, I was beyond any knowledge of what transpired of yeah I shook the Swede's pants down and found my 35 cents Change and a half buck and a dime. I left the dime and took the 4 bits as a gentleman's agreement as a precautionary measure for any future occasion I might have to be silly enough to trust the Swede on another errand of mercy.

June came pounding at my door. The Swede and Smitty were still asleep and she needed a drink. She had forgotten about having the Jug in bed and pulled out a buck and it was 5:30 A.M. and she said she'd give me a buck for the half bottle of wine I had on my dresser so I poured myself a stiff water glass full gulped it down coughed and sneezed and dam near heaved and said between burps, "What was it now You said June" I don't hear so good in the A.M. at such an early hour. She said I'll give you 6 bits now for the rest of your Jug. "No dice June I just paid two for it full from a bootlegger clown on the street I'll take a buck for the 3/5 that's left or you don't drink. She's crooked too I suppose rolled Smitty for the frog skin she had. Any way June's thirst for the grappo overpowered her peneuryism and, she reluctantly handed me my fee leaving me with the total sum of $1.60 $1.40 for 2 Jugs at .70 per Copy and a pkg. of Domino Cigarettes with the extra 20 cents 18 cents per pk. Stamps were 2 cents in the city then so that killed my purse and put me right back in my sad but daily expected financial status once more I was staying at Franks then and had but to ask Murdock or anyone for that matter and prove I had a jug and was welcome as the prodigal Son or did you hear about him. I heard it once. Well I went to murdocks room and Lo and behold what did I run into? 4 guys sleeping on the floor and full Jugs and half Jugs all over the floor and all passed out but Murdock who said, Hey Lion I pounded on Your door but you didn't answer You was in the John I guess. Sit down and help Yourself as You aren't drunk and I'm hungry and Will send You with a buck to the owl to get me a bowl of Oysters. I said "come up with the buck before I get my nose in any more of that panther P or the oysters may well have stayed in the sea.

So I got the oysters and made that Greek give me a recpt as I didn't think Murdock would believe the price 91 cents Boy he must have rolled every sheepherder on the floor. I told you once Mr. Woods that Im not a petty thief fur that stealing from each other seemed to be the only way You could be a member of that benevolent Society of Jack rollers. Even stoled my leather Jacket once. But wait I'm going past the horse in my sulky. First things first. While getting the oysters some guy approached me I asked him if I could be of any service as I had no hat nor coat on as usual and he said where can I get a jug for 2.00? Now there was 1 full gallon and seven and a half quarts in Murdocks room so I asked Murdock for a quart to take to my room. He was pleased With the oysters and always was my good friend since I always helped him up and down the stairs he said hell yes take one but don't go home yet as one of these guys got 320.00 in the office and a good old ex-con friend of mine. He will give me 50 and we'll run these other 3 bums out when they come too and have a hell of a party. A bird in the hand is worth two in the bush so I told Murdock I'll play it safe and take mine now Case the guy who bought it all came to and Changed his mind about his promise. Boy luck was sure with me Murdock copped out to beating the guy for $20.00. He'd have let one of the prostitutes take it any way and, Murdock needed it worse. He'd let any friend share his room and poor boy sandwiches. I hurried out with the bottle not to my room but back to the owl Cafe where the hay hand waited itching to give me the duce for the merchandise I had stuffed under my shirt. I sat down with him to complete the transaction in the booth and in walked two cops. I thought the guy fixed a plant for me, but everything so far was legal. The stamp was intact on the Jug, and no evidence of an illegal sale but it turned out they just went to the back booth for free Coffee black and believe it or not one of them pulled out a silver flask like a Cigarette Case and they made a couple Coffee Royals. I slid the Jug under the table and he handed me the 2.00 I shook hands and took off for Murdocks as I was getting dry all over again what with all the business transactions and running around. I opened Murdocks door and Woodsie I'm a sober man now I hate the stuff but Just as I entered the room I don't know what made me glance under Murdocks bed but there in plain sight was a five spot and I waited a while before Murdock spoke and when he did it was sweet music. Like I said I was the best friend he had up there who was like the 3 proverbial monkeys and him being a loser himself Went for me any way he says you stay here Leo and if the guy dont miss these 4, $5.00 bills I'll give you one. Wow! I had to pinch myself here was more money than I'd seen since I paid the Jap my rent. Well me and Murdock lowered the boom on that gallon Jug we took it down about 3 inches I guess and murdock decided that it being near 7 A.M. We would go down to Denvers oldest for a can of cold beer as the wine was hot He wasnt too drunk nor was I. He said throw my pants to me. My mind had to do double action before he got up and spied the 5 under the bed so I threw him his pants right over his face at the same time doing a double take with my free hand and sweeping up the five from its resting place. I now had 9.00 in my kick and prospects of 5.00 more if the chump Murdock had didn't get wise. Murdock woke up the 3 other bums and told them to grab a bottle and get lost as he was going out. Those fellows wanted to stay till the big money man woke up but Murdock could be tough when I was there and these guys were in no physical shape to argue so they took off. Murdock told them that he let them sleep there and his pal furnished the drinks and gave them each $1.00 for breakfast and now they had a Jug what more did they expect and to get lost quick. Now that I have no further desire to drink again and pray God it never returns, some of my experiences are enough to write a book like Jack London. Maybe I will some day. Its better for you to read all this so when it gets too dull you can discard it and not feel embarrassed as I can't see You like as if I told it to You and You'd get up and go. As soon as they went Murdock woke up the financier of the spree and told the guy the beer joint was open and they had plenty of wine. The guy never remembered having any money left so took a couple drinks from the gal. Jug and layed across the bed. All of a sudden he said gee I spent a lot I got to draw 40 or 50 from Frank. I'll be back. While he was gone Murdock true to his word gave me the 5 and another bottle there was 7 all together and the 1/2 gal. I took it to my room and didn't go back as I was afraid Murdock might roll him again when he passed out and someone might lay the blame on me. I had 14.00 a jug of wine and already 3 sheets in the wind so I let well enough alone I'll finish this when I see you. Woodsie I'd hate to live that life over I was only free from pain when I was drunk. But no more ever.

Mr. Woods:

I just came up from the floor. I didn't get hurt. (Thank God) Woodsie! I am all alone with my spells. This is something they can't do anything about, even the Mayo Clinic.

Daniel P. Webster The Boy who wrote the "Dictionary was an epileptic. He was well educated. I'm sorry Mr. Woods; I hate like hell to make you feel bad. I only hope you feel better. To heck with me. I'll get by one way or another.

Good nite now.

Downtown Denver in the 1920s

Forrest Hall Johnson

DOWNTOWN DENVER in the 1920s, and for a while before, was more or less a wide-open town. Almost every drug store had a slot machine, a punch board and a "26" dice game at the cigar counter. Many of the hotels from Larimer to Welton Street were of a dubious reputation, and Ladies of the Evening were pretty much tolerated by the authorities. Professional pool hustlers, cold-deck artists, and dice sharpies were plentiful, and prohibition being in effect, bootlegging was big business—a quart of bath rub gin, with a genuine counterfeit label, bringing $16.

The legitimate theater was in ascendancy in Denver until the opening of Harry Lubelski's Novelty at 1632 Curtis in 1903, which became Denver's first electrically lighted movie house. A Variety Show with two very popular black-face comedians, vaudeville, and short two-reel movies were offered here—with great success. After the Princess opened in 1909 showing the first six-reelers, more and more theaters were built on Curtis, and by World War I, vaudeville and movies had taken over.

In 1915, when on a visit to Denver, Thomas Edison reportedly said that Curtis was "the best-lighted street in the world," between 15th and 18th. At night, it was almost as bright as day—so bright in fact, that no city street lights were ever used.

Every theater lobby was a dazzling place, jammed with waiting patrons. Marquees were ablaze with traveling electric words and signs. Blinking and intermittent spot and floodlights were on every business establishment, and surplus World War I carbon arc anti-aircraft searchlights roamed the sky.

Going north, on the west side of Curtis, were the Tabor, America, Empress, Colonial, Palace, Plaza and Paris (later the Rivoli). The Rialto, Princess (later the Victory), Strand (later the State), the Beautiful Isis—with Franz Rath, that master improvisor, at the Wurlitzer organ—the Iris (later the Gem), and the Riant, were on the opposite side. I played silent picture organ at most of them. Only three are not torn down (1967).

In between the theaters were cotton candy, cherry cider, and root beer stands, self-photo booths, song-plugger offices, Chinese restaurants, freak side shows, pig-ear sandwich wagons, pool halls, pitch men, and taxi-dance halls with their bleached and painted dime-a-dance girls.

A group of them waited inside the entrance behind a velvet rope, and the customer picked the one he wanted. She collected a ticket from him for every two-minute dance and, at closing time, received 10 cents for every other ticket she had.

The WPA Guide to 1930s Colorado

Works Projects Administration

DENVER (5,280 ALT., 287,861 POP.), "Queen City of the Plains," the State's capital and largest community, radiates a wide influence throughout the Rocky Mountain region as a commercial, financial, and tourist center. Here, a mile above the sea, in 58 square miles of high plains at the junction of Cherry Creek and the South Platte, lives almost a third of all Coloradoans. Eastward, and to the north and south, stretch the tawny plains as far as the eye can see. Some 12 miles to the west abruptly rise the brown and green foothills of the Rockies; beyond them towers the snow-capped Front Range, visible on clear days from Pikes Peak on the south to Longs Peak on the north, a distance of 150 miles.

In the older section of the city, close to the creek and river, lies the wholesale district with rough brick-paved streets, faded brick buildings, and dingy rooming houses. The business and shopping district, its skyline dominated by a department store observation tower and a fifteen-story office building, is laid out at a 45-degree angle to the streets of the residential areas, no doubt because the founders wisely fitted it into the angle formed by the South Platte and Cherry Creek.

Many of the downtown thoroughfares have their distinguishing features. Larimer Street serves roughly as a dividing line between the older and newer business districts. Denver's Broadway, when the old Windsor Hotel was in its glory, is today a down-at-the-heels street of shabby brick and granite structures housing innumerable pawnshops, saloons, second-hand stores, upstairs hotels, and employment offices. Along its uneven sandstone sidewalks congregate cowmen, miners, and ranchers from the hills and prairies, and derelicts from the four points of the compass. Just off Sixteenth Street, its faded lettering still discernible high on the façade, stands the brick structure that housed the noted Delmonico's of the West, which often served banquets at $100 a plate, with beaver-tail soup as the specialty.

Northeastward along the street live Orientals, Spanish-Americans, and Negroes; jogging southwestward across Cherry Creek, Larimer Street looks down from a broad viaduct upon a maze of railroad sidings, junk yards, and the Platte before merging with West Colfax.

Along Sixteenth Street stand the large department and chain stores, smart shops, and larger motion picture houses. For a stretch of two blocks, Curtis Street until recently blazed as the local Rialto and the most brightly lighted thoroughfare in the West, but has declined to a midway of small picture theaters, shooting galleries, penny arcades, soft drink and sandwich shops. Seventeenth Street, known as the Wall Street of the West, runs a short course from Union Station to Broadway. Here, between Curtis Street and Broadway, are the large banks and brokerage firms of the "17th Street Crowd," many of whom are descended from pioneers. Along the street also are travel bureaus, bus stations, railroad ticket offices, headquarters of sightseeing companies, and a plethora of curio shops. Broadway, the principal north-south thoroughfare and the route of two U.S. highways, extends southward from lofty hotels and gleaming cocktail lounges to split the broad lawns of the Capitol and the Civic Center and become neon-lighted Automobile Row.

East of the Civic Center, in the old Capitol Hill residential section, ornate sandstone dwellings have long since been abandoned by their wealthy builders and converted into rooming and boarding houses. Their "mounting blocks" along the curbing and their cast-iron curb hitching posts in the form of jockeys have gone the way of their stables. Many of the houses have been torn down to be replaced by apartment buildings and small hotels. The better residential sections today lie in the Cherry Hills and Country Club districts and east of City Park.

North of Capitol Hill live the majority of the city's 7,000 Negroes, employed for the most part as laborers and domestic servants. The settlement has two weekly papers, 17 churches, and a motion picture theater. Nearby is the Spanish-American settlement, with its small stores, restaurants serving native dishes, recreational centers, newspapers, and the Teatro Mexicala, which presents Mexican-made films. Residents here hold to their Latin characteristics and colorful fiestas. Spanish is the common tongue, and most shop window signs are in that language. Many of the 15,000 inhabitants of this area leave the city during summer to work in the beet fields.

Jewish people early settled along West Colfax Avenue west of the Platte. Their kosher restaurants, poultry stores, and shops line the streets in this section, and they have their own newspapers and motion picture houses. The Jews have contributed much to the development of Denver; through their efforts the first large, free, non-sectarian tubercular hospital in the United States was established here in 1899.

The highlands north across the Platte from the business district have a large Italian population, which has retained many Old World customs, including gay feast days and the use of community ovens for the weekly baking of bread. The small well-scrubbed houses of other groups—Poles, German-Russians, and Austrians—cluster around Globeville in extreme north-central Denver, where a smelter, railroad yards, stock yards, packing plants, and pipe and clay manufactories provide employment for the majority of the residents. Like the Spanish-Americans, many of these families migrate to the beet fields in summer. The Globeville district has eight churches but no theater.

The State's transportation system pivots upon Denver. Seven major railroad lines have their terminals here; more than 60 passenger trains enter and leave Union Station daily during summer; it has been estimated that 4,000,000 travelers pass through the station annually, while an average of thirty interstate buses roll in and out of the many terminals every twenty-four hours. Four main highways converge here, and the majority of tourists visiting the State pass through and usually remain a few days before scattering to the many mountain resorts.

Denver's greatest asset is its summer climate and its proximity to beautiful mountain playgrounds. With country-wide motor travel there came into existence a large number of small hotels, furnished cottages and apartments, auto camps, sightseeing companies with fleets of buses. This commerce from June through August constitutes one of the city's chief sources of revenue. During these months, the streets are thronged with cars from every State in the Union; visitors in gay sport attire, in khaki, in overalls, throng the shopping centers and hotels, and tax the parking lots in the heart of the city. Restaurants hang out signs to welcome tourists, with the invitation: "Come in as you are." Booklets, maps, and racks of picture postcards are everywhere displayed. Shop windows are filled with Indian silver jewelry, beads and blankets, ore specimens, playtime clothes, and hunting, fishing, and camping equipment. Newcomers from the East exclaim over silver dollars given them in change for paper bills and usually carry away several newly minted "cart wheels" as souvenirs. But vacationing and outings are not alone for tourists. With dozens of mountain resorts, lakes, trout streams, and campgrounds within a few hours' drive, Denverites pour out of the city on every summer weekend and holiday.

Denver's 40 municipal parks contain almost 2,000 acres; and the city, one of the first in the United States to establish a chain of mountain parks, has 25 natural playgrounds, many with camping facilities; these embrace more than 121,000 acres scattered through the Front Range and adjoining mountains, all easily accessible by improved highways.

The character of the city has been influenced by the establishment of more federal government offices here than in any city but Washington, D.C. Denver is proud of being known as "the western Capital." Four large federal buildings house the activities of more than 64 federal units; others, chiefly of an emergency nature, are quartered in downtown office buildings. Among the more important are the national office of the Supervisor of Surveys; the regional offices of the Forest Service; the Bureau of Public Roads; the Farm Security Administration; the Veterans Bureau; and the field offices of the Bureau of Reclamation. Denver has one of three U.S. coinage mints, and nearby is an Army post, an Army hospital, and an air corps technical school.

With its dry air and its sunshine, Denver continues to attract health-seekers although in diminishing numbers, and some health institutions have been closed since the World War. The city has nine large hospitals, two of which are tax-supported. Several large sanatoriums, specializing in the treatment of respiratory diseases, have attained prominence for their laboratory experiments and clinical care—among others, the $4 million Fitzsimons General Hospital established by the Federal Government in 1918.

The first settlers did not build for permanency, as few expected to remain. Their houses, stores, and offices were flimsy structures, and few erected before 1870 still stand. The city's architecture records the stages of its growth. The weathered stone office buildings, churches, and clubs still standing in the business district date from the 1880s, as do the brick and sandstone houses in the once-fashionable residential sections. Massive government structures of granite and marble, neo-classic memorials, the increasing use of tile and glass brick in the business area, and the Romanesque design of public school buildings mark the trend since the World War. The better new houses, usually of brick or stucco, are in Georgian Colonial, Tudor, and variations of Mediterranean design.

Since 1886, fire ordinances have restricted Denver buildings to masonry construction and moderate height, and constant rebuilding imparts a new, bright aspect to the city. Wide, straight, shaded streets, many parks, and rows of trim brick houses with well-tended lawns and flower gardens create a cool and spacious pattern. The thousands of oaks, maples, elms, and poplars that border residential streets and shade the parks, and all of the lilacs, snowballs, roses, bridal-wreath, and shrubbery that ornament front lawns represent an incalculable amount of patient care and labor, for the city was built on desolate hills and bluffs, with only a scattering of cottonwoods and willows along the watercourses. Denver has changed vastly since Isabella Bird, English journalist, recorded her impression of it in 1872: "I looked down where the great braggart city lay spread out, brown and treeless, upon a brown and treeless plain which seemed to nourish nothing but wormwood and Spanish bayonet. ... I saw a great sandstorm which in a few minutes covered the city, blotting it out of sight with a dense brown cloud."

Water is and always has been a precious commodity here. The supply from the 11 great mountain reservoirs, some more than 100 miles distant, depends wholly upon snowfall; the heavier the snow on the ranges, the greater is Denver's rejoicing. Novel to many is the sight of householders lovingly sprinkling their lawns and shrubbery both mornings and evenings. No newspaper reports are scanned more attentively than the edicts of the Denver Water Board governing the hours of irrigation. Residents pay a flat rate based upon the number of outlets on their property; automobile owners pay an additional 50 cents quarterly.

No one man or group of men was solely responsible for the founding and development of Denver, which, in a sense, just "growed" like Topsy. It was not the first white settlement in Colorado. The site was and still is well away from the main overland routes of commerce. Other towns were nearer the gold and silver strikes or were in more prosperous agricultural districts. Yet, in spite of this, Denver has thrived from the start. One after another, boom towns challenged its supremacy in the Territory and then in the State; one after another, they were outdistanced; Colorado City, Silver Cliff, and Golden were serious rivals in the race to become the State capital, but eventually Denver triumphed.

The Lillies of the Field

William E. Barrett

THE CITY WAS TRAFFIC-CHOKED and noisy, and its lights were bright. The heat of summer rested on it like a cloud without rain, but a man could wet his throat with cold beer in the daytime and mingle with his own kind at night, eating and drinking whatever he found. He could listen to loud, rhythmic sound from juke boxes and dance with women and laugh at jokes. He could look into the eyes of women and see himself there, feeling pride in his manhood. He could stand big in his body with gray fog in his mind and hear his own blood running in his veins. He could go to the Baptist church on Sunday and sing hymns that his mother and his father sang before he was born, weeping a little because he had been a sinner all week. He could leave the church with all the sin washed out of him, feeling clean.

Homer Smith loved all of it, the standing tall and the falling down. Most of all, he liked the speech of men and women like himself, and the humor of them. A man heard no funny stories from people of another language who could not speak English well, and he could tell no funny stories. Humor belonged to the language that a man knew. He liked companionship and his room in the boardinghouse, and the bathroom down the hall where he could bathe in a tub instead of showering himself from a bucket. He liked the hard feel of pavement under his feet, the odor of cooking food that floated out of strange windows and doorways, the children who were in constant motion around him. He liked the sirens of police, fire, and hospital vehicles, the bright exteriors of taverns and the twilight dimness within. This was the city.

The nuns and a town named Piedras and the Livingston Construction Company belonged to a hazy dream, as unreal as incidents in the life of another man. He never sat down deliberately to think about them, and such stray memories as floated in and out of his mind did not disturb him. His life in the Army was gone, too, to be recalled only through conscious effort and not worth that. He lived in what he had, and with what he had, finding life good.

His money ran low in ten days, and he went to work for a wrecking company. His first job was with a crew that was wrecking a carbarn no longer used by the tramway company. It was heavy, dirty, dangerous work, with much steel to handle and grime over everything. The next job, by comparison, was easy. A half-block of houses had to come down to create a blank which could be converted into a parking lot. They were small and old, low-rent houses, known in the South as row houses but in the West as terraces; houses all alike, built together wall to wall. Everything that could be stripped by hand was stripped, then a crane, with a big metal ball, knocked the walls down. The job took three days.

On the third day, Homer was sorting through the salvage, stacking the theoretically usable doors, window frames, and fixtures. There were sinks, basins, eight bathtubs. He piled the bathtubs, then stood looking at them, hearing in his mind a high, clear call as compelling as a coyote's cry to the moon.

"Those girls need a bathtub," he said.

It was the first time he had consciously thought about the nuns, and they were suddenly alive in his mind. He had seen them hauling buckets of water from the well in the evening, many buckets, and he had seen how crude everything was about the house. Gus Ritter, that old German farmer, had been a tight-fisted man. He didn't improve a place except where it paid him.

The foreman was a big man, almost as big as Homer was. Homer sought him out. "How's to buy one of those tubs?" he said.

"Sure enough? You want your own personal tub, boy?"

"How much?"

"You could steal it and nobody would care. That kind is no good. You got some way to haul it?"

"Yes."

"Okay. Give me two bucks to keep it honest."

Homer gave him the two dollars. He saw the bills go into the foreman's pocket, and he knew that the company would never see those bills. That didn't matter. He'd bought what he wanted at the price asked. The bathtubs were high and narrow, standing on dragon feet. He picked the best one of them. It wouldn't go into the station wagon, so he upended it on the top, the feet pointing skyward, lashing it in place with rope. The bathroom windows had been removed intact, small windows of red, yellow, and green glass in diamond pattern. He bought two of them from the foreman for a dollar each and, with the purchase, a vision returned, haunting him.

He drew his pay at the end of the day and headed for the hills.

It was afternoon on Friday when he drove into familiar territory. He stayed on the highway when it looped around North Fork. The crops were prospering under a bright sun: potatoes, wheat, barley, lettuce, cauliflower. The hazy blue mountains were on his right. Within a few miles, the fields on his left became bleak, sage, and greasewood, sprinkled with a few indomitable flowers of blue, yellow, and pink. A hawk floated low, gliding on motionless wings, and a rabbit scurried across the road.

Homer drove over a small bridge, and the stream below it was a thin trickle. He turned to his right on a rutted road, and the nuns were in the field, working on their variegated crop, fighting for their growing plants against weeds and voracious insects and the parched dryness of the soil. It was good to see them again, but he did not slow down nor look in their direction. He was not certain of his reception, and he was willing to defer it. He parked in his accustomed spot and sat looking at his unfinished church.

Nobody had disturbed it, and no one had brought bricks with which to complete it. It had a desolate look; one wall built as high as a man's shoulder, the others low; the chimney pointing upward like the skeleton finger of a giant. There was an untidy scattering of rubble on the ground. Homer got the scoop shovel from the barn toolroom and started shoveling. He cleared the area and dug a hole with his spade into which he tumbled the debris.

The bell rang, and he straightened. Old Mother never rang the bell for the nuns because they knew when to come for meals. That bell was for him. He laid the spade aside, carried his bucket to the well, washed his hands, and walked into the house. They were waiting for him, standing in their places at the table, just as if he had never been away. He bowed his head while they prayed. When he looked up after the "Amen," they were all looking at him happily. Nobody said anything, but they were glad that he was home. A man felt a thing like that. Nobody had to say anything.

There was an omelet and coarse bread, but there were vegetables, too, fresh vegetables. The farm was starting to pay off.

They resumed the English lessons after supper, and Homer's ear was sharper because he had been away. They were doing better with the language, but he could hear the soft echo of South Carolina coming back to him when they spoke.

Better than a phonograph accent, he thought. Used to be you could hear the turntable going around when they spoke anything in English.

He did not unveil the bathtub until after breakfast the next day. He drove the station wagon close to the house and eased the tub down from the top. He called Old Mother out to see it. Sisters Gertrud and Albertine came with her. He made an awkward gesture toward the tub, not naming it. After all, these were girls who built a high fence around the privy.

"A present," he said.

He was facing Mother Maria Marthe. Her eyes squinted as though she found the sun too bright. "Das ist gut, Schmidt," she said, "Das ist gut."

She said something in German to the two nuns and went hurriedly into the house. Homer did not have to explain to her that he needed a place in which to install the tub. When she returned, she led him to a pantry off the kitchen. This was the deepest penetration that he had made into the nuns' quarters. He had not even known that the pantry existed.

"Here," she said.

It was a small room, but that was her problem. He hauled the tub in and set it on its feet. He had taken some pipe as a necessary accessory to the tub, and he had bought a secondhand blowtorch in the city. He cut a hole in the floor where it met the wall and angled the pipe through it, attaching it to the drain pipe of the tub and soldering it in place. He put the rubber plug in the drain, and the tub was in business. He dug a trench outside the house to run the water off. They would still have to haul water because he couldn't give them a pump and a plumbing job, but this was something. He felt good about it.

Raise the Titanic!

Clive Cussler

UNITED'S EARLY FLIGHT touched down at Denver's Stapleton Airfield at eight in the morning. Mel Donner passed quickly through the baggage claim and settled behind the wheel of an Avis Plymouth for the 15-minute drive to 400 West Colfax Avenue and the *Rocky Mountain News*. As he followed the west-bound traffic, his gaze alternated between the windshield and a street map stretched open beside him on the front seat.

He had never been in Denver before, and he was mildly surprised to see a pall of smog hanging over the city. He expected to be confronted with the dirty brown and gray cloud over places like Los Angeles and New York, but Denver had always conjured up visions in his mind of a city cleansed by crystal clean air, nestled under the protective shadow of Purple Mountain Majesties. Even these were a disappointment; Denver sat naked on the edge of the great plains, at least 25 miles from the nearest foothills.

He parked the car and found his way to the newspaper's library. The girl behind the counter peered back at him through tear-shaped glasses and smiled an uneven-toothed, friendly smile.

"Can I help you?"

"Do you have an issue of your paper dated November 17, 1911?"

"Oh my, that does go back." She twisted her lips. "I can give you a photocopy, but the original issues are at the State Historical Society."

"I only need to see page three."

"If you care to wait, it'll take about 15 minutes to track down the film of November 17, 1911, and run the page you want through the copy machine."

"Thank you. By the way, would you happen to have a business directory for Colorado?"

"We certainly do." She reached under the counter and laid a booklet on the smudged plastic top.

Donner sat down to study the directory as the girl disappeared to search out his request. There was no listing of a Guthrie and Sons Foundry in Pueblo. He thumbed to the Ts. Nothing there either for the Thor Forge and Ironworks of Denver. It was almost too much to expect, he reasoned, for two firms still to be in business after nearly eight decades.

The 15 minutes came and went, and the girl hadn't returned, so he idly leafed through the directory to pass the time. With the exception of Kodak, Martin Marietta, and Gates Rubber, there were very few companies he'd heard of. Then suddenly he stiffened. Under the J listings, his eyes picked out a "Jensen and Thor

Metal Fabricators" in Denver. He tore out the page, stuffed it in his pocket, and tossed the booklet back on the counter.

"Here you are, sir," the girl said. "That'll be 50 cents."

Donner paid and quickly scanned the headline in the upper-right corner of the old newsprint's reproduction. The article covered a mine disaster.

"Is it what you were looking for?" the girl asked.

"It will have to do," he said as he walked away.

Desperado

Grace Lichtenstein

> I should hate even to spend a week there. The sight of those glories [the mountains] so near and yet out of reach would make me nearly crazy.
>
> —Isabella Bird,
> writing of Denver, in
> *A Lady's Life in the Rocky Mountains*

A YEAR AFTER MY ARRIVAL in Colorado, during an interview, I asked Henry John Deutschendorf, also known as John Denver, why he had ever named himself after such a boring city. "Why, because I liked the mountains," he replied innocently.

Ah, how myths grow. As it is, John Denver (both his name and his music) must be held a tiny bit responsible for Denver—the-city's currently inflated reputation.

Not that there is anything terribly wrong with Denver. It compares favorably with many places. Omaha, for instance. But there is a popular image of Denver—of Colorado as a whole—as a paradise of towering peaks and stoned freaks. Outsiders flock there prepared to find blond folk-singers in flower-embroidered shirts greeting their Greyhound bus, eagles soaring over Colfax Avenue, and streets paved with wildflowers.

Blues for the Buffalo

Manuel Ramos

"USE IT OR LOSE IT, Luis."

Not exactly young Dr. Kildare, but I got the idea. The good Doctor Webster had prescribed long walks, every day, if my knee was to have any future.

I worked out a regimen of physical exertion that Webster approved of, even though he was doubtful that I would keep with it. I'd start out from my office in midmorning and make my way through the different Northside neighborhoods that surrounded the business intersection of 38th Avenue and Federal Boulevard. Sometimes I'd make it back before noon, and sometimes I kept at it until I had to eat. On those energetic days, I'd grab a throat-scorching burrito from Chubby's at the distant east end of 38th or something kinder and gentler from the Taqueria Patzcuaro on 32nd, near my own digs.

I grew up on 38th, a straight shot of bruised houses hunkered against the traffic. It was a too-busy street that stretched across the heart of the Chicano community in Denver's northwest quadrant. Buildings that changed fronts as often as the calendar changed months struggled valiantly to add to the woeful tax base of my part of the city. Homes with small patches of lawn shared the avenue with fast-food joints, liquor stores, gas stations, and the imaginative hopes of eager, small-time entrepreneurs—the backbone of the U.S. economy—as my high-school social studies teacher once asserted.

If I wanted to, I could walk the several miles of 38th from Sheridan to Lipan and buy just about anything I might ever need: Italian sausage and pastries; a rebuilt carburetor for my gasping Bonneville; rebuilt boots from a *zapatero* from Zacatecas; a ride on a rollercoaster; a Big Mac or a Whopper or the Colonel's Extra Crispy; a miniskirt from Ropa Guapa for that someone special; life insurance; or porno paperbacks in Spanish or English. The enterprising consumer could even shop around for the best deal on legal advice from a cluster of Chicano attorneys whose offices dotted 38th with signs proudly displaying the Spanish surnames and the useful information that, *Sí, se habla Español.*

There were a few drawbacks to using one of the city's main arteries as my exercise path. The avenue was noisy, and the pollution could lay a stubborn gray film of grit and grime on my all-season, never-need-pressing sport coats. Some of the young men who cruised its lanes were just obnoxious enough to keep me away. When a smartass pair of low-riding homeboys in a pretty, tricked-up black-and-orange minitruck with diminutive wheels sprayed me with what I hoped was water from a double-barreled water cannon, I gave up on using 38th as my personal training center. I wandered the other streets of the Northside.

The 70-year-old elms and the 50-year-old houses eased me into the comfort zone that meant home. Often, the scenes were familiar and repetitive. I'd watch a pair of sweethearts from somewhere in Mexico where people dressed in cowboy hats and tight jeans, hugging and kissing while they washed the family station wagon; children chasing each other through alleys, laughing and crying until they collapsed in a cluttered yard; and a friendly but mangy and thirsty black Chow who roamed the streets in search of a handout.

And then there were days when everything was different.

I had been back in Denver from my vacation for about a week. My walk had taken me past a pair of young girls in shorts and halter tops, smoking marijuana in what was supposed to be their front yard. They reminded me of many others, from years before, some of whom still lived in the area. These girls could have been their daughters. The hard-looking underage beauties swayed to loud Kid Frost and A Lighter Shade of Brown instead of James and Bobby Purify or El Chicano, but the idea was the same as when I had sat around a picnic table on stale summer afternoons with Gato, Frankie, and Chopper, chugging cheap red wine, getting a nasty headache, and having a good time. I played my role and did not ask the girls for a toke. Summer in the city, yes, oh yes.

A few minutes away, I found the grand opening of the latest gift shop along West 32nd Avenue, east of the restaurants, closer to the bars and the really ugly apartment houses.

I strolled into an open doorway with a sign that said GIFTS—PARTY ITEMS—GROCERIES. A middle-aged man with prison tattoos stood behind a counter covered with balloons, cheap novelties, and a box of last year's baseball cards. Along the back wall a shelf swayed under new stock: cellophane bags of chile powder, cans of hominy, bags of beans, and other basics of a midweek supper.

"Come in, come in. What can I do for you?" I assumed he spoke in English in deference to my tie and sweat-stained white shirt.

"I could use something to drink."

He almost ran to an old soda pop machine that chugged in the corner. He lifted the bent cover and extracted a wet, dripping can. I accepted it and handed him a dollar. I waved off his reluctant tender of change.

He said, "Let me introduce myself. Abel Tapia. This is my place. Tell your friends."

"Sure, Tapia. Good luck."

Tapia turned his attention to another man who had entered his store behind me. I had seen him earlier, up the street near the party girls, where I had thought he paid too much attention to my limp.

My first good look at him gave me a smiling, thin Chicano dressed in a very weary tan linen suit over a black tee shirt. Bare ankles showed beneath the cuffs of his pants, but the shoes were excellent—expensive-looking loafers with tassels and dingle-balls. They looked soft enough to take a nap in.

He walked straight to me and offered his hand.

"Mr. Montez? I've been looking for you. I went to your house, but it was empty. I wandered around until I saw you walking. I, uh, I followed you—hope you don't mind. I wasn't sure, you know."

I was abruptly interrupted by a pair of guys in ski masks.

"Everyone on the floor! *Now*, motherfuckers! We'll blow you assholes away! On the fucking floor!"

One was much taller than the other, and they each carried semiautomatic handguns, but that was all I saw before the shorter one ran up to me and raised his gun to knock me to the floor, since I was a bit slow in doing what he had demanded. I ducked, instinctively, and pushed myself into his hips. From between his legs, I watched Valdez slam the edge of his hand into the other guy's neck. Tall Bozo swirled and careened into the bags of chile and cans of hominy, and he was out. My guy was screaming and hollering, swinging his gun hand, but I had rolled out of the way. He ended on his knees, aiming his gun at the cowering store owner. Valdez jumped the holdup man from behind. His hands and legs moved quicker than I could put it together, but it meant that Short Bozo had been smashed a dozen or so times with hammer blows on all parts of his body. Short Bozo groaned, twisted into a ball, and collapsed on top of his buddy.

The sudden silence in the store did not last long. We were surrounded by a mad rush of excited neighborhood kids who had seen the aborted stickup from the street. They stood around us, glaring at the inert robbers and, in a frantic mix of Spanish and English, noisily admired the Chicano PI with the fists of stone and the wrinkled clothes. Another Northside legend.

The Colorado State Capitol
History, Politics, Preservation

Derek R. Everett

The Heart of Colorado

GEOGRAPHICALLY, THERE IS NO sensible reason for the state of Colorado to exist. Four arbitrary lines drawn by national politicians hundreds of miles away bound together environments with little in common. Plains of sandhills and grasslands, vast plateaus dotted with sagebrush, shallow rivers that swell with spring runoff, shadowy chasms, towering snowcapped mountains, isolated basins, all of which endure violent weather, from relentless winds to blinding snowstorms to searing heat to freezing cold—these elements and more make up Colorado. Aridity affects practically all parts of the state, as well as much of the western United States, but the simple rectangle that demarcates Colorado's boundaries affords practically nothing else capable of bringing this disparate region into a single political entity.

Many states in the Union suffer the same difficulty as Colorado, constricted by indiscreet boundaries that offer perhaps the most obvious modern legacy of European colonial policies. Shortly after the Revolution the federal republic adopted similar measures as a relatively straightforward way to manage newly acquired lands in the West. In Colorado's case, sectional U.S. politics in the 1860s inspired much debate over drawing these four simple divisions, but eventually compromise resulted in a territory and later a state that lacked a common cultural or physical landscape. Settlers from the United States at the base of the mountains and in mining camps, Hispanics along the southern border, American Indians to the east and west, and many other ethnicities merged, however unwillingly, into this federally imposed community. As the inhabitants of this new region gathered together into a political society, they needed something to unify them as a people, a symbol that transcended the hodgepodge of geography and cultures. In the decades that followed, they came together to erect and utilize a physical representation of their collective identity, the Colorado State Capitol.

Crowning the summit of Brown's Bluff with granite and gold, the capitol symbolizes the political community created by all the citizens of the Centennial State. It provides a stage for the dramas of a society, celebrations and protests alike, a great gray temple of popular sovereignty surveying the capital city. By housing the democratically elected representative government, the statehouse brings together the needs and interests of every Coloradoan, from Four Corners to Julesburg, from Brown's Park to the Cimarron River. Although the capitol stands in the state's largest city and events in Denver by necessity impact the structure most directly, it belongs to every citizen equally as the seat of civil authority. The governor does not dominate the building by holding that office, nor does a legislator simply by serving in the General Assembly. All Coloradoans own the capitol by virtue of its purpose and its history. As he gazed up at the dome in 1950, *Denver Post* reporter Bert Hanna glowingly remarked: "You look at this fine old building and you think of all the tremendous work and pride that went into it. It is the heart of Colorado." The Capitol pulses in accordance with the interests of the people, and its condition reflects the ways they interpret the needs of their political community. The Statehouse's history is Colorado's history, changing with the times to meet contemporary needs while always hearkening back to the vibrant past of the state. Nothing else better exemplifies this region made up of disparate landscapes and peoples.

Guide to Denver Architecture

Mary Voelz Chandler

Study a city's architecture and you learn about its people. About its growth and progress; its challenges and travails; foibles and dreams.

Denver skyline around midnight from I-25 and Speer Blvd. Photo by Matt Wright, 2016.

Armistice Day

Nick Arvin

PEACE HAS COME, and in the Manhattan on Larimer Street, where the menu offers steak for 35 cents, a chaotic, exuberant noise rises from the tables. Over the last week, the Spanish Flu epidemic has ebbed, and today came word of a signed armistice—soon the boys in France will be coming home! Few still bother to wear the gauze masks that the city mandated to combat the influenza, but a pair seated at a table near the front door wear theirs—white cloths tied back over the ears, covering nose and mouth.

"Someday you'll kill me," the big one says to the little one.

"Sure I will."

"That's what sons do to their fathers."

The boy looks about 10 years old. His father has a deep crease fixed into his forehead, as if his mouth, frustrated by the mask, migrated upward. The boy has small, dark eyes, and he is unlikeable. His father is also unlikeable, however, which works out, in a sense. If only one or the other had been unlikeable, they would be at cross-purposes, but as it is they project a peculiar energy together and seem, if unlikeable, also singular.

They cut pieces of steak, lift their masks to put the food into their mouths, let the masks down again to chew.

Their unlikeability has already impressed those at the tables around them. The two talk loudly while watching the door and the celebrating crowds that wander outside. They have a small round table but sit nearly side–by side. The father, eating left-handed, jostles his son, right-handed.

"What're you going to kill me for?"

"For picking your nose and a funny look," the boy says. He lifts his chin to speak in a curious, mock-theatrical style.

"You have a very disrespectful manner."

"If there's an apple on the ground, chances are the tree's nearby."

Men, arm—in arm, pass the door singing. A paperboy casts his voice into an unnerving register, calling the headline, "THE WAR IS OVER."

"You are assuming that you are, in fact, my son."

"I'm hoping I ain't."

"I indulge, but you may provoke me only so far."

"Your patience is legendary."

"You are a little cur."

At the nearest table sit two ladies and two men, all well-dressed. One of the men, particularly wide in shoulders and chest, with a scar across his nose, glances over repeatedly.

"A son of a bitch, then," the boy says.

"I'll put you over my knee right here," the father says.

The boy lifts his mask and places a piece of steak in his mouth.

The waitress comes and looks at them and goes away.

"You should tell her that we can't pay," the boy says.

"I can pay."

The father and son look at each other. The father reaches into his jacket, draws out a wallet, opens it, peers inside.

He curses; the table goes over and crashes as he falls on the boy, knocking over both their chairs; the boy screams. All around the restaurant people stand to look. The father punches his son in the chest.

The man with the scarred nose gets there first and lifts away the father; the boy, still screaming inarticulately, slips out; the father scrambles and writhes, bellowing guttural syllables, while the man with the scar tries to pin him. The boy presses close, livid, and shouts insults.

Suddenly the boy backs away. A half second later the man with the scar stands straight up to feel the pocket of his pants. "You!" He turns to follow the boy, but the boy is gone. The man peers out the door. His wallet has been taken, and when he turns back, the father—the accomplice—has also vanished. The diners begin to chatter again among themselves. The man looks out once more at the passing happy crowds.

The pickpockets, 1818. Legaat van de heer S. Emmering, Amsterdam

Denver in Slices

Louisa Ward Arps

Preface

> "Goldrick has got home and in Sunday's TIMES promises his readers 'Denver in Slices' for a week or two.'"
>
> *Rocky Mountain News,* January 23, 1867

SINCE THE AUTHOR of this book has borrowed practically everything else in it from earlier writers—only the inevitable mistakes are hers!—it seems fitting to borrow the title. *Denver in Slices* is appropriate to the present book, which is not a history of Denver—just a slice here and a slice there with enough of the "Whole Loaf" to indicate the position of the slices.

The fastidious Irishman, Owen J. Goldrick, who thought up the title in 1867, was Denver's first school teacher. After two years of nearly starving on the proceeds of his private school, he superintended the organization of a public school system in 1861, then turned to journalism for a living. At his death in 1882, he was editing the *Rocky Mountain Herald.* The only reason the present author has presumed to borrow a title from this professional writer, this traveler, this man with a classical education from Dublin University who talked Latin to his oxen, and whose flowery style was saved by an Irish wit, is that, like her, he enjoyed writing in Denver. Perhaps, from whatever corner of the Hereafter he enlivens, Goldrick joins the author in hoping that the reader, too, will have fun with *Denver in Slices.*

Hell's Belles
Denver's Brides of the Multitudes

Clark Secrest

Jennie Rogers and Mattie Silks: Queens of the Denver Row

MATTIE'S AND JENNIE'S LADIES were of the highest class within the profession as it existed between St. Louis and San Francisco. In Jennie's houses, writes historian Caroline Bancroft, each room had an enamel or brass bed, a dresser, commode, slop jar, rocking chair, straight-back chair, a rug, lamp, lace curtains, and some even had a writing desk. Mattie's and Jennie's employees were possessed of the prettiest of faces, the tiniest of waists, the creamiest of bosoms, the daintiest of giggles, the best of conversational skills, the most imaginative of techniques, the perkiest of personalities (their sparkling eyes owing to the use of belladonna and its dilation of the pupils), and the best of acting abilities (leading the customer to believe that she really cared). As importantly, none of them is ever recorded to have stolen from a client.

Mattie and Jennie called their places "young ladies' boarding houses." This was an apt description, since the girls were required to pay for their room and board, ranging upwards from five dollars a week; and further, they were obliged to split some 50 percent of their earnings with the madams. The boarders were required to dress attractively and were encouraged to charge clothing to the madams' accounts at the local stores. This could keep the girls constantly in debt, affording the madams other means of keeping them in line. Kickbacks from the dressmakers to the madams were common.

In Denver as elsewhere, the denizens of the parlor houses had to be of the highest class, beautiful, and—ideally—of some cultural or educational accomplishment.

> A visit to a perfectly managed parlor house was much like a visit to a private home, and the prostitutes in residence resembled, in decorum and dress, the daughters of the house. Some asserted that the only difference was that the prostitute was more attractive, more intelligent, and more accomplished than the young society lady.

The guest was conducted into the velveted parlor by the madam, and there he might encounter business acquaintances chatting with attractive women. Following a glass of brandy, the patron was conducted to a fine room for whatever activities were of his pleasure. The madam collected the fee in advance, which was considered better manners than having the girl do it. The madam of a sophisticated house infrequently or never practiced prostitution herself, as this would put her in direct competition with her boarding girls. There is no direct evidence, such as an arrest record or even a newspaper account, that Mattie Silks or Jennie Rogers was a prostitute. If either was, however, it very likely would have preceded her arrival in Denver.

None of the foregoing rules of propriety and good manners applied to the seamier houses or cribs, where there was no madam, where the girl accepted her own payment, and the quantity of customers took precedence over the quality of the service. In 1913, onetime reporter Forbes Parkhill recalled the Market Street cribs of some 25 years earlier:

> [They were] just wide enough for a door and a single window. Each contained two rooms: a parlor and a boudoir. At that time they rented for from $15 to $25 a week, payable daily. In the white section the cribs were known as 'dollar houses,' but in the 'black belt' beyond 21st [on Market], they were 'two-bit houses.' Prices in the parlor houses ranged from $5 up. No matter how many partook, a round of beer, served in containers only slightly larger than a shot glass, was always $1. At this time, a nickel would buy a schooner of beer on Larimer street so large it almost took hands to lift it.

In Colorado, one of Laura Evens's girls, LaVerne, offered insight as to the manners expected of a lady in a proper house of Market Street. Very probably dating to the 20th century, it is the only statement discovered during this study which is attributed to a Market Street woman:

> "Miss Laura never wanted us girls to talk loud, and we were always wearing low-neck, knee-length dresses and black silk stockings and were always taught to watch our language. We parlor house girls never used four-letter words. Miss Laura would tell us never to come in the parlor with a gingham dress on—that's what a man sees all day at home. Under our evening clothes, we first-class girls always wore panties and a bra. This was because—after we were inside our room with a man—if the girl took off her dress and had nothing under it, the shock would probably kill him. I don't mean it might *really* kill him, but it might be too much for him all at once.
>
> We'd take our evening gowns right off as soon as we could. We didn't want them to get messed up or torn or anything, for

sometimes a man, first of all, would try to start taking off our gowns himself, and we'd have to beat him to it, for he really didn't know the right way to take off a gown usually, and the more excited he'd get whenever he tried, the clumsier he'd get. There was no telling what might happen to our dresses if we didn't take them off by ourselves as soon as we could.

We girls took our own panties off, too, for they might get torn if a man took them off. Most men usually got a kick out of seeing us girls take our panties off. That is, unless the man was too busy taking his own pants off. And it had this advantage, besides—the more steamed up and excited the man got while watching us take our panties off, that would usually save us girls from just that much more work later.

Mattie Silks, also known as Queen of the Tnderloin, was one of the most successful madams of the 19th century American West.

Murder at the Brown Palace

Dick Kreck

Isabel Springer: "The Butterfly"

"ONE BY ONE, THE PETALS FELL from the blooms of the primrose path to bring her, at last, into the tangle of thorns which snarled themselves at the end—which enmeshed her, tore at her with their poison-tipped lances, which dragged her downward, downward to the mire."

Courtney Ryley Cooper's flowery obituary on page one of *The Denver Post* on April 20, 1917, wrote an unglamorous finish to a decidedly glamorous woman. When she died in a New York City hospital charity ward, Isabel Patterson Springer was alone except for an actress friend.

In her lifetime, she rose to the top of Denver society, blessed with not one but three homes and showered with adulation. As the bride of John W. Springer, one of the city's most respected businessmen, she lived among the luxuries of the Brown Palace Hotel and the city's attractions, particularly the theater, which she attended frequently. She and her wealthy husband traveled widely, wintering in Pasadena, California, and visiting New York City often.

Isabel was a woman of charm and exceptional beauty, with large dark eyes and a soft, almost cherubic, countenance. She had a bountiful bosom and narrow waist of the type popular with turn-of-the-century women and their admirers. She preferred to wear her ample brown hair in the swept-up Gibson Girl style. Her dark eyebrows emphasized her piercing brown eyes. Her nose was more prominent than she might have liked, but it gave her face strength. She was born in 1880 to James and Amelia Evarts Patterson, either in Arkansas or in Michigan, both of which she claimed at various times. As a child, she moved to St. Louis with her family and grew up in comfortable surroundings. Her family was among the city's social set.

In 1900, when she was only 20 years old, she married John E. Falck, a traveling shoe salesman. The couple moved to Memphis, Tennessee, but the marriage was unhappy almost from the beginning. Falck drank heavily and frequently pummeled her with abusive language and his fists. She was young, vibrant, and accustomed to the gay party life she had in St. Louis. Her husband was frequently away from home, peddling footwear on the road in Missouri, Arkansas, and the Indian Territory. By June 1906, the two were separated.

Isabel moved back to St. Louis and took up residence in the Jefferson Hotel, center of the city's social scene. She was much in evidence among the gay set, earning the sobriquet "The Butterfly" because of her fondness for attention and diversion. She and the wife of a wealthy St. Louisan were often observed cruising the city in the friend's eighty-horsepower touring car, "perhaps the finest then in St. Louis."

As a woman of leisure, she enjoyed ample time to read romantic fiction that created an ideal of the softly genteel but indomitable female, and magazines that gave practical how-to instructions for achieving the ideal. Articles preached decorum and cautioned against dangerous new ideas. They were warnings she chose to ignore.

It was at the Jefferson Hotel that she met Springer and began her rise to the upper reaches of society. He was on his way to Kentucky to buy trotting horses when the two met. They hit it off immediately; and before summer's end in 1906, she was visiting him in Denver and was seen frequently on the city's streets, riding beside Springer in one of his finest coaches.

By that December, Isabel was in divorce court in St. Louis, seeking to end her marriage to Falck. She described Falck's abusive behavior, although she was unable to supply exact dates and places. Nevertheless, the judge, noting that her husband did not contest the divorce, made it official on December 23, leaving her free to pursue life with Springer. The two were married at the Jefferson on April 27, 1907, and left immediately for their new home in Denver.

* * *

Isabel Springer arrived in a city that was shedding frontier dust and hardships.

A post card of Denver's Brown Palace Hotel circa 1900.

In the first decade of the 20th century, Denver boasted 14 parks covering 1,200 acres. There were 200 miles of street railways, 60 hotels, 12 theaters, and 65 grade schools with more than 30,000 pupils, and 100 trains a day passed through the massive Denver Union Depot. There was a newly built U.S. Mint and a beautiful new public library. The city's streets, some paved, were swarming with an estimated 2,000 of the newest playthings of the rich, the automobile, a sure sign of sophistication and wealth. For these motorists, Mayor Robert W. Speer had begun constructing an elaborate system of parkways. It wasn't St. Louis, but it wasn't the wild frontier either.

No sooner did Isabel arrive in the Queen City than newspaper society chroniclers were gushing over her. "We always thought John W. was pretty fair looking, but his wife is a stunning beauty, and it is safe to prophesy that the Springer home is going to be a social center," *Denver Post* columnist Eselyn Brown reported:

> Yesterday's bright sunshine brought forth a fine parade of automobiles and harness vehicles. Who failed to see the grand and shiny dogcart which traveled up and down 16th Street just when the crowd was thickest? It looked as good as candied cherries and the color tallied exactly, too. The man who handled the reins wore an air of "see the conquering hero comes," and the lady at his side was a sight to behold. Just as you are asking yourself, "Whence comes all this grandeur?" the handsome man in a perfect fashion-plate outfit of the new leather-brown shade clothes turns his radiant face toward you, and behold—it is John W. Springer. So the stunning lady at his side is the new Mrs. Springer? Well, she certainly is as queenly and beautiful as a three-sheet poster of Lillian Russell.

Isabel's life in Denver was idyllic. In addition to her castle-like home on Springer's ranch, she was mistress of the couple's two-story mansion at 930 Washington Street. She fit smoothly into the city's party circuit.

Winter Counts

David Heska Wanbli Weiden

AS PROMISED, CASA BONITA was a weird blend of amusement park and Mexican food joint. The place was huge, with a giant pink bell tower standing in the middle of a parking lot. Inside, we were amazed to discover a 30-foot-high waterfall and pool, cliff divers, strolling mariachi bands, puppet shows, and even a pirate cave. The hostess took pity on us and seated us away from the families with shrieking children. We were led up a series of stairs to a table near the top of the waterfall. The table was surrounded by fake palm trees and tiki torches, giving us some privacy and a close view of the divers. They appeared to be college kids, dressed up as bandits, pirates, and, yup, Indians. The divers would shout out the lines of their skits, which all seemed to revolve around good guys being chased by villains, before diving into the pool below. I was relieved to see that the bad guy was not a faux Indian but a person dressed up in a gorilla suit. After the divers made their jumps, the kids below us screamed their appreciation, and it was easy to get in the spirit of the place.

Our food came, and it was pretty far from the street tacos I'd had at Taco Mex. This was gringo fare masquerading as Mexican food, like a white man wearing a sombrero. Bland tacos, tasteless enchiladas, and mild refried beans. Three Coronas for Marie; a Coke for me. I'll admit that the desserts were pretty good. At first, I thought they'd brought us frybread, which surprised me, but the waiter told me these were sopapillas or "little pillows" in English. Sweet fried dough, topped with powdered sugar, and dipped in honey. They were lighter than Indian frybread—and, it pained me to admit, much better.

After our plates were cleared, we strolled around the place. We visited the run-down arcade, where we played Skee-Ball and ancient video games. Then we wandered through Black Bart's Pirate Cave, a sort of haunted house with battered skeletons, treasure chests, and weathered old skulls, trying not to step in the random pools of liquid left by overenthusiastic children.

"What do you think of this place?" I asked.

"I love it." Her eyes gleamed like the polished gems we'd held in the gift shop. "If I had a child, I'd take her here every week."

I wondered what it would be like to have a child with Marie. Her smarts; my toughness. A little son. Maybe a daughter? I looked over at Marie and wondered if she was thinking the same thing I was. The music drifted through the fake palm trees, and it was easy to imagine that we were really in Mexico at some beach resort.

I turned to Marie. She moved closer, waiting for me. I started to embrace her, but I hesitated. I'd dreamed of this; but in an instant, I also remembered the pain and depression I'd felt when she left me. The heartbreak had been so overwhelming; I wasn't sure I'd ever recover. For months, I visited that grief every evening. I'd buy a 12-pack of beer and play some gloomy songs. It was strange because, after a while, I'd started to look forward to those late-night sadness sessions—just my music, my beer, and my grief. It had become a part of my life. My new routine. The nightlands.

I'd finally gotten past that sorrow—and the booze—and carved out a good space for Nathan and myself. Things weren't perfect, but I was content with the life we had. What would happen if I started things up again with Marie? I didn't want the complications and the problems, not when I'd finally gotten some steadiness back in my life. It had been tough to get over Marie, but I'd made it through.

But then I smelled Marie's perfume. Not just her perfume, but the scent of Marie herself.

It hit me right in the chest, and it seemed that I sensed it with every cell in my body. It was overwhelming, the aroma of her, and I felt desire travel throughout my body. My resolve slipping, I tried to tell myself this was a mistake, that I should leave things as they stood. But that scent …

I dove off the cliff.

A view of the waterfall and diving area at Casa Bonita Restaurant in Lakewood, Colorado. Casa Bonita was designated a historic landmark of the city in 2015. Photo by Kevin Payravi.

Permissions

Every attempt has been made to secure permission for reprinting of material in *The Colorado Book*, second edition. Enquiries may be addressed to Fulcrum Publishing, Lakewood, Colorado.

Authors

"'The Real Denver' Is Gone Forever" by Gene Amole. Reprinted with permission of the *Rocky Mountain News.*

Killing for Coal: America's Deadliest Labor War by Thomas G. Andrews, Cambridge, Mass.: Harvard University Press, Copyright © 2008 by the President and Fellows of Harvard College. Used by permission. All rights reserved.

From *The Coloradans* by Robert Athearn © 1976 University of New Mexico Press. With permission of the University of New Mexico Press.

Reprinted from *Tomboy Bride* by Harriet Fish Backus. Copyright © 1969 by Harriet Fish Backus. Reprinted by permission of Pruett Publishing Company.

Reprinted from *Silver Queen: The Fabulous Story of Baby Doe Tabor* by Caroline Bancroft. Copyright © 1950 by Caroline Bancroft. Reprinted by permission of Johnson Books.

Reprinted from *The Light Shines from the West: A Western Perspective on the Growth of America* by Robert C. Baron. Copyright © 2018 by Robert C. Baron. Reprinted by permission of Fulcrum Publishing.

Reprinted from *Thomas Hornsby Ferril and the American West* edited by Robert C. Baron, Stephen J. Leonard and Thomas J. Noel. Copyright © 1996 by Thomas Hornby Ferril Literary Trust. Used by permission of Anne Ferril Folsom.

Reprinted from *The Lilies of the Field* by William E. Barrett. Copyright© 1962 by William E. Barrett. Copyright© renewed 1990 by William E. Barrett, Jr. Reprinted by permission of Harold Ober Associates, Incorporated.

Reprinted from *Valley of the Dunes: Great Sand Dunes National Park and Preserve* by Audrey Benedict (Author), and Wendy Shattil (Photographer) and Bob Rozinski (Photographer). Copyright © 2005 by Audrey DeLella Benedict

(Text) and Bob Rozinski (Photos) and Wendy Shattil (Photos). Reprinted by permission of Fulcrum Publishing.

Reprinted from *A Lady's Life in the Rocky Mountains* by Isabella L. Bird. New edition. Copyright © 1960 by the University of Oklahoma Press. Reprinted by permission of publisher.

Reprinted from *High, Wide and Lonesome* by Hal Borland. Reprinted by permission of author.

Reprinted from *Strip Search* by Rex Burns. Copyright© 1984 by Rex Raoul Stephen Sehler Burns. Used by permission of Viking Penguin, a division of Penguin Books USA, Inc.

Reprinted from *The Updated Colorado Guide: Landscapes, Cityscapes, Escapes* by Bruce Caughey and Dean Winstanley. Copyright © 1989 by Bruce Caughey and Dean Winstanley. Reprinted by permission of Fulcrum Publishing.

Reprinted from *Guide to Denver Architecture* by Mary Voetz Chandler. Copyright © 2013 by Mary Voetz Chandler. Used by permission of Fulcrum Publishing.

Reprinted from *Harvey* by Mary Chase. Copyright© 1943 by Mary Chase (Under the title *The White Rabbit);* Copyright © renewed 1970 by Mary C. Chase. Copyright © 1944 by Mary Chase (under the title *Harvey);* Copyright© renewed 1971, by Mary Chase. *Caution: Harvey,* being duly copyrighted, is subject to a royalty. The amateur performance rights in this play are controlled exclusively by the Dramatists Play Service, Inc., 440 Park Avenue South, New York, New York 10016. No amateur production of the play may be given without obtaining in advance the written permission of the Dramatists Play Service, Inc., and paying the requisite fee. All inquiries regarding all other rights should be addressed to Robert A. Freedman Dramatic Agency, Inc., 1501 Broadway, Suite 2310, New York, New York 10036.

Reprinted from *Chief Left Hand: Southern Arapaho* by Margaret Cole. Copyright © 1981 by University of Oklahoma Press. Used by permission of University of Oklahoma Press.

Excerpt from *Raise the Titanic* by Clive Cussler, copyright © 1976 by Clive Cussler. Used by permission of Viking Books, an imprint of Penguin Publishing Group, a division of Penguin Random House LLC. All rights reserved.

Reprinted from *The Last Midwife* by Sandra Dallas. Copyright © 2015 by Sandra Dallas. Reprinted by permission of Sandra Dallas.

Reprinted from *Amidst the Gold Dust: Women Who forged the West* by Julie Danneberg. Copyright © 2001 by Juli Danneberg. Used by permission of Fulcrum Publishing.

Reprinted from *Dying for Chocolate* by Diane Mott Davidson. Copyright © 1991 by Diane Mott Davidson. Used by permission of Diane Mott Davidson.

Reprinted from *La Gente: Hispano History and Life in Colorado* edited by Vincent DeBaca. Copyright © 1999 Colorado Historical Society. Used by permission of History Colorado.

Reprinted from *"The Utes Must Go!": American Expansion and the Removal of a People* by Peter R. Decker. Copyright © 2004 by Peter R. Decker. Used by permission of Fulcrum Publishing.

Reprinted from *God is Red: A Native View of Religion,* by Vine Deloria, Jr. Copyright © 1993 by Vine Deloria, Jr. Used by permission of Fulcrum Publishing.

Reprinted from *Dizzying Heights* by Bruce Ducker. Copyright © 2008 by Bruce Ducker. Used by permission of Fulcrum Publishing.

Reprinted from" Across the Rocky Mountains in Colorado" by Emil Habdank Dunikowski ln *Essays and Monographs in Colorado History*, 5 (1987). Translated by Stanley Cuba. Reprinted by permission of Colorado Historical Society.

Reprinted from *Denver* by John Dunning (Times Books, 1980). Copyright© 1980 by John Dunning. Reprinted by permission of Harold Ober Associates Incorporated.

Reprinted from *Minerals of Colorado* by Edwin B. Eckel ; updated & rev. by Robert R. Cobban, Donley S. Collins, Eugene E. Foord, Daniel E, Kile, Peter J. Modreski, and Jack A. Murphy. Copyright © 1997 by Friends of Mineralogy. Reprinted by permission of Fulcrum Publishing.

Reprinted from *The Life of an Ordinary Woman* by Anne Ellis. Copyright © 1929 by Anne Ellis. Copyright © renewed 1957 by Neita Carey and Earl E. Ellis. Reprinted by permission of Houghton Mifflin Company. All rights reserved.

Used with permission of University Press of Colorado, from *The Colorado State Capitol: History, Politics, Preservation* by Derek Everett, 2005; permission conveyed through Copyright Clearance Center, Inc.

Reprinted from *Wait Until Spring, Bandini* by John Fante. Published by Stackpole Books, 1938. Reprinted by permission of publisher.

Reprinted from *Emily: The Diary of a Hard-Worked Woman* by Emily French, edited by Janet Lecompte, by permission of the University of Nebraska Press. Copyright © 1987 by the University of Nebraska Press.

Reprinted from *Wah-To-Yah and the Taos Trail* by Lewis H. Garrard. New edition copyright© 1955 by the University of Oklahoma Press. Reprinted by permission of publisher.

Reprinted from *Founder's Praise* by Joanne Greenberg. Copyright© 1976 by Joanne Greenberg. Reprinted by permission of Joanne Greenberg.

Reprinted from *First of State* by Robert Greer, 2010. Rights reverted to the author. Used by permission of Robert Greer.

Reprinted from *The Woolly West* by Andy Gulliford by permission of Texas A&M University Press.

Reprinted from *Inside U.S.A.* by John Gunther. Copyright© 1946, 1947 by John Gunther. Copyright © renewed 1947 by The Cunis Publishing Company. Reprinted by permission of Harper Collins Publishers.

Reprinted from *Colorado without Mountains* by Harold Hamil. Copyright© 1976 by Harold Hamil. Published by The Lowell Press, Inc., 115 East 31st Street, Kansas City, Missouri 64108. Reprinted by permission of publisher.

Reprinted from *Children of the Storm: The True Story of the Pleasant Hill School Tragedy* by Ariana Harner and Clark Secrest. Copyright © 2001 by Ariana Harner and Clark Secrest. Used by permission of Fulcrum Publishing.

Reprinted from *Durango* by Gary Hart. Copyright © 2012 by Gary Hart. Used by permission of Fulcrum Publishing.

Reprinted from *Amache: The Story of Japanese Internment in Colorado During World War II* by Robert Harvey. Copyright © 2003 by Robert Harvey. Used by permission of Robert Harvey.

Reprinted from *A Bloomer Girl on Pikes Peak, 1858by* Julia Archibald Holmes. Edited by Agnes Wright Spring. Reprinted by permission of Western History Department, Denver Public Library.

Used with permission of University Press of Colorado, from *Colorado's Japanese Americans: From 1996 to the Present* by Bill Hosokawa, 2005; permission conveyed through Copyright Clearance Center, Inc.

Reprinted from *Life of George Bent: Written from His Letters,* by George E. Hyde. Copyright© 1968 by the University of Oklahoma Press. Reprinted by permission of publisher.

Excerpt from *On the Road* by Jack Kerouac. Copyright© 1955, 1957 by John Sampas, Literary Representative, the Estate of Stella Sampas Kerouac; John Lash, Executor of the Estate of Jan Kerouac; Nancy Bump; and Anthony M. Sampas. Used by permission of Viking Books, an imprint of Penguin Publishing Group, a division of Penguin Random House LLC. All rights reserved.

Excerpt from *Blood Betrayal* by Ausma Zehanat Khan. Copyright © 2023 by Ausma Zehanat Khan. Reprinted by permission of St. Martin's Publishing Group. All Rights Reserved.

Reprinted from *The Shining* by Stephen King. Copyright © 1977 by Stephen King. Used by permission of Doubleday, a division of Bantam Doubleday Dell Publishing Group, Inc.

Reprinted from *Going to Meet a Man* by William M. King. Reprinted with permission of the University Press of Colorado.

Reprinted from *Murder at the Brown Palace: A True Story of Seduction and Betrayal* by Dick Kreck. Copyright © 2003 by Dick Kreck. Used by permission of Fulcrum Publishing.

Reprinted from *Second Banana* by Dottie Lamm. Copyright© 1983 by Dottie Lamm. Reprinted by permission of Johnson Books.

Reprinted from *The Governor's Chessboard: A Lifetime of Public Policy* by Richard Lamm. Copyright © 2019 by Richard Lamm. Used by permission of Fulcrum Publishing.

Reprinted from *The Cowboy: Reflections of a Western Writer* by Louis L'Amour. Used by permission of History Colorado.

Reprinted from *Cripple Creek Days* by Mabel Barbee Lee. Copyright© 1958 by Mabel Barbee Lee. Used by permission of Doubleday, a division of Bantam Doubleday Dell Publishing Group, Inc.

Reprinted from *Desperado* by Grace Lichtenstein. Copyright© 1977 by Grace Lichtenstein. Used by permission of Doubleday, a division of Bantam Doubleday Dell Publishing Group, Inc.

Reprinted from *A Ditch in Time* by Patricia Nelson Limerick and Jason L. Hanson. Copyright © 2012 by Patricia Nelson Limerick and Jason L. Hanson. Used by permission of Fulcrum Publishing.

Reprinted from *Down the Santa Fe Trail and into Mexico: The Diary of Susan Shelby Magoffin, 1846-1847.* Edited by Stella M. Drumm. Published by Yale University Press. Copyright© 1926 Yale University Press. Reprinted by permission of publisher.

Reprinted from *The Color Orange: A Superbowl Season with the Denver Broncos* by Russell Martin. Copyright © 1987 Russell Martin. Reprinted with the permission of the author.

"Wolf Creek Pass" by C. W. McCall. Lyrics reprinted by permission of C. W. McCall.

"A Hit at the Times" by A. O. McGrew. In *Poems of the Old West.* Reprinted by permission of Ayer Company Publishers, P.O. Box 958, Salem, New Hampshire 03079.

"Colorado Owns a Chunk of Glenn Miller" by Frances Melrose. Reprinted with the permission of the *Rocky Mountain News.*

Excerpt from *Centennial* by James A. Michener. Copyright© 1974 by James Michener. Used by permission of Random House, an imprint and division of Penguin Random House LLC. All rights reserved.

Reprinted from *Blood on the Tracks* by Barbara Nickless. Copyright © 2016 by Barbara Nickless. Used by permission of Barbara Nickless.

Reprinted from *Colorado: A Liquid History and Tavern Guide to the Highest State* by Thomas Noel. Copyright © 1999 by Thomas Noel. Used by permission of Fulcrum Publishing.

Reprinted from *Backroads of Colorado* by Boyd and Barbara Norton. Copyright © 1978 by Rand McNally & Company. Used by permission of Boyd Norton and Barbara Norton.

Reprinted from *Marmalade and Whiskey: British Remittance Men in the West* by Lee Olson. Copyright © 1993 by Lee Olson. Used by permission of Fulcrum Publishing.

Chapter 2, Pages 9-12, 14/2,326 words requested from *Blues for the Buffalo* by Manuel Ramos is being reprinted with permission from the publisher (1997 Arte Publico Press – University of Houston).

Some content taken from *All That is Secret* by Patricia Raybon. Copyright © 2021. Used by permission of Tyndale House Publishers. All rights reserved.

Reprinted from *Ticket to Hollywood* by Gary Reilly, 2011. Permission granted by Mark Stevens, Running Meter Press.

Used with permission of University Press of Colorado, from *Pleas and Petition: Hispano Culture and Legislative Conflict in Territorial Colorado* by Virginia Sanchez, 2021; permission conveyed through Copyright Clearance Center, Inc.

Reprinted from *Mollie: The Journal of Mollie Dorsey Sanford in Nebraska and Colorado Territories* by Mollie Dorsey Sanford. Copyright© 1959 by the University of Nebraska Press. [Rights: Norwest Bank, Denver.] Reprinted by permission of Norwest Bank.

Reprinted from *Champion of the American Family* by Patricia Schroeder (New York: Random House, 1989). Copyright © 1989 by Patricia Schroeder. Reprinted by permission of the author.

Reprinted from *Hell's Belles: Denver's Brides of the Multitudes* by Clark Secrest. Original Edition 1996. Used by permission of Clark Secrest.

Reprinted from *The Rocky Mountain West in 1867* by Louis L. Simonin, translated and annotated by Wilson O. Clough, by permission of University of Nebraska Press. Copyright© 1966 by University of Nebraska Press.

Used with permission of University Press of Colorado, from *Horace Tabor: His Life and the Legend* by Duane A. Smith, 1989; permission conveyed through Copyright Clearance Center, Inc.

Used with permission of University Press of Colorado from *The Trail of Gold and Silver: Mining in Colorado* by Duane A. Smith, 2009; permission conveyed through Copyright Clearance Center.

Reprinted from *The Life and Legend of Gene Fowler* by H. Allen Smith. Copyright© 1977 by Nelle Smith. Reprinted by permission of Harold Matson Company, Inc.

Reprinted from *Newport in the Rockies: The Life and Good Times of Colorado Springs,* by Marshall Sprague. Revised for the 1990s (revised 2d edition,

1987; reprinted 1990). Reprinted with permission of Ohio University Press/Swallow Press, Athens, Ohio.

Reprinted from *Daze on the Plains* by Pat Staten. Copyright © 1992 by Pat Staten. Used by permission of Fulcrum Publishing.

Reprinted from *Second Hoeing* by Hope Williams Sykes, by permission of University of Nebraska Press. Copyright © 1935, 1962 by Hope Williams Sykes.

Reprinted from *Fire Line: The Summer Battles of the West* by Michael Thoele. Copyright © 1995 by Michael Thoele. Used by permission of Fulcrum Publishing.

Reprinted from *A Tenderfoot in Colorado* by Richard Baxter Townshend. New edition copyright © 1958 by the University of Oklahoma Press. Reprinted by permission of publisher.

Reprinted from *The Colorado* by Frank Waters. (Ohio University Press/ Swallow Press, 1985, reprinted 1991.) Reprinted with permission of Ohio University Press/Swallow Press, Athens, Ohio.

Used with permission of University of Washington Press from *Asians in Colorado* by William Wei, 2016; permission conveyed through Copyright Clearance Center, Inc.

Reprinted from *Winter Counts* by David Heska Wanbli Weiden. Copyright © 2020 by David L. Weiden. Used by permission of David Weiden.

Contested Plains: Indians, Goldseekers, and the Rush to Colorado by Elliot West, published by the University Press of Kansas ©1998. Used by permission of the publisher.

Reprinted from *Butcher's Crossing* by John Williams. Copyright© 1988 by John Williams. Reprinted by permission of the University of Arkansas Press.

Reprinted from *Stampede to Timberline* by Muriel Sibell Wolle. (Ohio University Press/Swallow Press, 1974, reprinted 1991.) Reprinted with permission of Ohio University Press/Swallow Press, Athens, Ohio.

Reprinted from *Beyond the Aspen Grove* by Ann Zwinger. Copyright© 1970, 1981 by Ann Zwinger. Reprinted by permission of Colorado College Special Collections.

Photos and graphics

Many of these images were found through WikimediaCommons.com

Pg 5—Photographic portrait of American writer Robert Frost (1874-1963) sitting at a desk. From *Tendencies in Modern American Poetry*, by Amy Lowell, 1917. Public Domain.

Pg 7—Autumn cottonwood trees near the Lamar River, Wyoming. Photo taken by the National Park Service, 2021. Public Domain.

Pg 8—The Colorado River near Horseshoe Bend, Arizona. Photo by Luca Galuzzi, 2007, https://commons.wikimedia.org/wiki/User:Lucag; http://www.galuzzi.it, Creative Commons 2.0.

Pg 16—Autumn aspen trees in Idaho Falls District, Idaho. Photo by the Bureau of Land Management, Public Domain.

Pg 21—A rough and tumble with a grizzly by H. Bullock Webster, circa 1875. http://digitalcollections.library.ubc.ca/cdm/singleitem/collection/bullock/id/132. Public Domain.

Pg 23—Albert Bierstadt was commissioned by the Earl of Dunraven to make a painting of the Estes Park and Longs Peak area, Colorado, in 1876 for $15,000. The painting is now on display at the Denver Art Museum (on loan from the Denver Public Library). Public Domain.

Pg 28—Bent's Old Fort, National Historic Site. Photo by Sally Pearce, Colorado Department of Transportation; cleaned up and color-corrected by Howcheng. Public Domain.

Pg 31—An 1869 oil painting by Albert Bierstadt of emigrants on their way to Oregon. Thought to be inspired by a fifty-wagon train of German emigrants who crossed Bierstadt's path during his 1863 expedition. Public Domain.

Pg 36—"We have it rich." Washing and panning gold, Rockerville area, South Dakota. Old timers, Spriggs, Lamb and Dillon at work. Photo from the John C. H. Grabill Collection, Library of Congress, Reproduction number: LC-DIG-ppmsc-02669. Public Domain.

Pg 40—Tornado on the ground, near Scottsbluff, Nebraska. Department of Agriculture. Weather Bureau. Central Regional Weather Bureau Office. June 27, 1955. Public Domain.

Pg 45—Pikes Peak from near Colorado City. El Paso County, Colorado. 1870. (Stereoscopic view). Photo by U.S. Geological Survey (https://www.flickr.com/people/usgeologicalsurvey/). Public Domain.

Pg 54—American Bison, Pelck's Scenic and Art Studio, May 1, 1906. From the Library of Congress. Public Domain.

Pg 57—Prairie Dogs from Theodore Roosevelt Park, North Dakota. Photo by Amaury Laporte, 2022. https://www.flickr.com/photos/8283439@N04/52482332609/. Creative Commons 2.0.

Pg 61—William Henry Jackson, pioneer photographer, circa 1939. Photo from the United States Geological Survey. Public Domain.

Pg 65—Maps of: Colorado Springs, January 1874; Colorado City and Manitou 1871, El Paso County, Colorado. From the Denver Public Library. Public Domain.

Pg 69—Enos Mills, Father of Rocky Mountain National Park, Colorado, at the door of the cabin he built as a teen (late 1880s) on Longs Peak. Public Domain.

Pg 71—Isabella L. Bird from her 1891 book Journeys in Persia and Kurdistan. Public Domain.

Pg 75—The plateau as seen when descending the mountain side of Kenosha Pass, Colorado. From the book Birds of the Rockies, 1902. Public Domain.

Pg 85—Mountain-sunset view from Telluride, once a mining boomtown and now a popular skiing destination in Colorado. Photo by Carol M. Highsmith. Public Domain.

Pg 87—Aspen catkins, 2019, by Wolfman. https://commons.wikimedia.org/wiki/User:Wolfmann. Creative Commons Share Alike 4.0.

Pg 138—Shropshire Sheep in Colorado. From the book *Sheep Farming in America* by Joseph E. Wing. Public Domain.

Pg 145—A Restaurant in the French Quarter, color engraving, 1889. From the January 26, 1889 issue of *Harper's Weekly*. Illustration by W.A. Rodger. Public Domain.

Pg 148—Henry Sandham's 1883 illustration showing sluce box mining of placer gold in California. Titled "The Cradle," from the Library of Congress Prints division. Public Domain.

Pg 195—Mule deer in Yellowstone National Park, 2021. Photo by Lucas Golden, https://commons.wikimedia.org/wiki/User:LAG6470. Creative Commons 4.0.

Pg 205—The Summit, Pikes Peak, Colo. Detroit Publishing Company postcards. Public Domain.

Pg 210—William N. Jennings, Lightning Photograph, 1885. Glass lantern slide. The Franklin Institute, Philadelphia. Public Domain.

Pg 217—Oscar Wilde by Napoleon Sarony, 1882. Public Domain.

Pg 223—Color photochrome postcard depicting an aerial view of Denver Mile High Stadium circa 1984. Public Domain.

Pg 235—Tuberculosis patients lie in beds on the porch of a building at the Jewish Consumptive Relief Society (J.C.R.S.) sanatorium, 1600 Pierce Street, Lakewood, Colorado. Nurses attend to some patients. Public Domain.

Pg 239—Illustration by Arnold Goodwin for an article on "Child Labor and the Home," 1912. In *The Masses*. Public Domain.

Pg 247—Painting of the Battle of Washita (River)—Sand Creek Massacre by Frederic Remington, circa 1890. Public Domain.

Pg 253—Portrait of Eleanor Greatorex, c.1874, albumen print, Department of Image Collections, National Gallery of Art Library, Washington, DC. Public Domain.

Pg 257—*Cinque persone* (five people in a coffee shop, in Italy) by Carlo Cainelli. 1920 drypoint print. Public Domain.

Pg 262—Granada Relocation Center, Amache, Colorado. December 1942. Photo by Tom Parker. Public Domain.

Pg 265—*At the Sand Creek Massacre* by Cheyenne eyewitness and artist Howling Wolf, circa 1875. Public Domain.

Pg 266—A service is held outside for victims of the Ludlow Massacre in Colorado, 1914. Public Domain.

Pg 281—A flophouse style room by Bobjob, 2009. Public Domain.

Pg 306—*The Pacific Tourist* by Henry T. Williams. His illustrated trans-continental guide of travel, from the Atlantic to the Pacific Ocean, 1877. Public Domain.

Pg 311—Colorado Governor Ralph Carr, 1940. From the Library of Congress collection. Public Domain.

Pg 313—Studio portrait of Plains Indian, circa 1860. Photographer unknown. Gilman Collection, Museum Purchase, 2005. Public Domain.

Pg 319—Cowboy riding his horse in an empty field. Photo by simpleinsomnia (https://www.flickr.com/photos/simpleinsomnia/14630326308/). (https://www.flickr.com/people/95329455@N02). Creative Commons 2.0.

Pg 320—The Ghost Dance of the Sioux Indians in North America. Gravur artwork. Originally published by *The Illustrated London News*, January 3, 1891. Public Domain.

Pg 323—Colorado Museum of Natural History, 1908. Photo courtesy of the Bailey Archive, Denver Museum of Nature and Science. Public Domain.

Pg 352—Denver skyline around midnight from I-25 and Speer Blvd. Photo by Matt Wright taken on July 14, 2006. https://en.wikipedia.org/wiki/User:MattWright. Creative Commons Share Alike 2.5.

Pg 354—Man wordt bestolen voor een prenthandel. Dandy Pickpockets diving. Prentmaker: Isaac Cruikshank, 1818. Legaat van de heer S. Emmering, Amsterdam. Public Domain.

Pg 358—Mattie Silkes, Colorado State Archives. Public Domain.

Pg 360—A post card showing the Brown Palace Hotel, Denver, Colorado, circa 1900. Public Domain.

Pg 363—Casa Bonita waterfall and dining area, Lakewood, Colorado. Photo by Kevin Payravi, 2024. https://commons.wikimedia.org/wiki/User:Kevin_Payravi. Creative Commons Share Alike 4.0.

Index of Authors